THE
TRANSITIONAL
ELEMENTARY
SCHOOL
AND
ITS
CURRICULUM

BROWN

EDUCATION SERIES

Edited by

Lowry W. Harding, Ph.D.
The Ohio State University
Columbus, Ohio

THE
TRANSITIONAL
ELEMENTARY
SCHOOL
AND
ITS
CURRICULUM

OSCAR T. JARVIS
Assistant Professor of Education

LUTIAN R. WOOTTON
Associate Professor of Education

University of Georgia

WM. C. BROWN COMPANY PUBLISHERS
135 SOUTH LOCUST STREET • DUBUQUE, IOWA 52003

Manufactured by WM. C. BROWN CO. INC., Dubuque, Iowa
Printed in U. S. A.

Preface

THE TRANSITIONAL ELEMENTARY SCHOOL AND ITS CUR-
RICULUM sets forth the practical understandings, appreciations, and skills
which are requisite for effective teaching in the elementary school. The
ideas presented depict the various facets of the child-oriented curriculum
which are basic to the professional endeavors of the teacher and administrator in the elementary school. The book has been divided into three sections: (1) elementary education in transition, (2) children and the learning
environment, and (3) the teacher and the learning environment.

Section one places the contemporary elementary school in its historical
perspective. It presents the efforts of schools in America to provide an
appropriate program of instruction for each period from Colonial times
to the present. The developmental stages of the elementary school, various
organizational patterns which have been utilized, and numerous innovations in curriculum design are analyzed.

The second section focuses on aspects of a desirable learning environment for elementary school children. Major emphasis is centered on the
importance of understanding the child. Grouping practices and procedures
are analyzed as they relate to the establishment of an effective learning
environment. Practical suggestions for creating a stimulating classroom
environment are treated. Evaluating, recording, and reporting pupil progress are presented as a vital aspect of helping the individual child adjust
successfully to the learning environment.

Section three shows how the elementary teacher, equipped with a
knowledge of the elementary school's function in our society and an understanding of children, uses this information for effective teaching. It sets
forth the premise that the problem solving approach is fundamentally applicable to learning in every subject matter area of the elementary school

curriculum. Major emphasis is given to utilizing unit teaching wherein the content of the various disciplines becomes significant as it is integrated and related to the needs of the student in the problem solving approach to learning. Such an approach also shows how skills, which are essential to learning, are learned best through the unit of work. Various types of instructional media are set forth as instruments for learning which the teacher utilizes in problem solving procedure.

Fundamental to the education of the learner is the well prepared, professional teacher who is creative and possesses the ability to adjust the learning experiences to the individual in a manner which motivates his desire to learn. This text therefore concludes with an evaluative exposition of qualities of the teacher which contribute to successful instruction in an everchanging, effective elementary school curriculum.

This text will have served its purpose if the reader acquires a deeper understanding of the function of the elementary school in our society, an increased knowledge of the children it educates, and a revised philosophy of good teaching technique. Just as every facet of elementary education can be classified as being transitional in nature, so must the teacher's concept of his professional responsibilities be ever-changing.

Contents

PART ONE
Elementary Education In Transition

PART TWO
Children and the Learning Environment

PART THREE
The Teacher and the Learning Environment

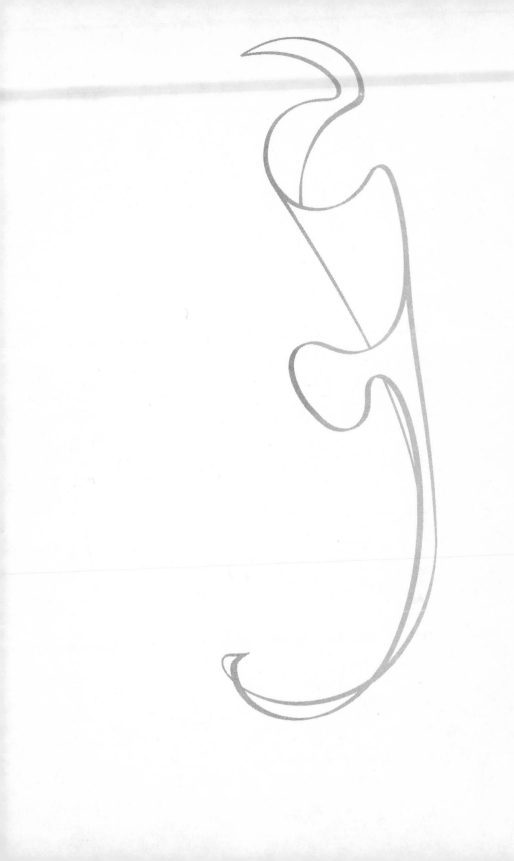

Our schools have kept us free . . . .
For a century and a half American
schools have served and strengthened
the commonwealth. They provided a
citizenry as enlightened as any on
earth. They justified and vindicated
democracy's promise. If society clearly
defines the new duties it wishes our
schools to fulfill and if it steadfastly
supports them not only with money but
also with faith, they will surely justify
that faith in the future as they have in
the past. HENRY STEELE COMMAGER.

Part One
Elementary Education
in Transition

The contemporary elementary school plant accommodates appropriate learning experiences for children.

Chapter 1

Development of the Elementary School and Its Curriculum

Any person who is truly desirous of learning about and understanding the elementary school and its curriculum must view it in its entire social and cultural perspective. In so doing, he will recognize that our American schools have a peculiar origin and unique heritage. The development of our public elementary school system in the United States from its inception, as an instrument for teaching religion, to our present comprehensive contemporary program presents a picture of gradual growth and change. The struggles of the American people to educate their children for the future is a heritage deserving the attention and understanding of every person interested in the profession of teaching.

The origin of the earliest schools in America can easily be traced to the Protestant Revolutions in Europe. These revolutions were precipitated by reformers who were insistent that a knowledge of the Gospel was necessary in order to acquire personal salvation. If one was to possess such a knowledge of the Scriptures, it logically followed that he must have facility in reading in order to understand the Commandments of God which were recorded in the gospel. Since the reformers of the reformation era could not live, worship, and educate their children as they desired, many of them left the old homelands of Europe and migrated to the American wilderness where they established a civil government based on the precepts of their convictions. Here they set up a system of religious training, which was based on European ideas, for their children. Thus the origin of American education can be linked to a European background.

The heritage of our American schools can be traced to three main sources: (1) the Greeks, (2) the Romans, and (3) the Christians. From the Greeks we inherited our ideals of personal and political freedom as well as a knowledge of and an appreciation for literature, art, and philosophy. We are indebted to the Romans for our inheritance of an understanding of law, government, and the practical arts. Out of the Christian movement we acquired most of our current civilization ideals. The Christians synthesized Greecian cultural ideas and the Roman system of law and government and gave to all subsequent generations a foundation upon which a way of life could be developed that would respect the individual and group rights of all mankind.

EARLIEST EDUCATION IN COLONIAL AMERICA

When our Colonial forefathers settled in the wilderness along the New England coast in small religious groups, they established a combined civil and religious form of government which was to become known as a New England town. The manner in which education was first provided in these small towns has been described well by Cubberley:

> At first home instruction and the old established type of apprenticeship training were depended upon to furnish the necessary ability to read and to participate in the home and church religious services, the great religious purpose which had brought the colonists to America being the motive which was to insure such instruction. . . . Clergymen also, in many instances, undertook, in addition to their regular duties, the instruction of a few boys in classical learnings, acting either as a tutor for them or receiving them into their families as boarding pupils. The next step was the organization of town free schools.[1]

Earliest education in Colonial America, therefore, was centered around two voluntary types of programs. These programs may be described as: (1) private instruction in reading and religion which was carried on either in the home or taught by the master of apprentices, and (2) Latin grammar schools, provided in the largest New England towns, which prepared boys for entrance into either the English college, of which Harvard was the first to be endowed in 1636, followed in 1701 by Yale where ministers were prepared for the churches, or the colony college where nonministerial students continued their scholarly pursuits.[2]

---

[1]Ellwood P. Cubberly, *Public Education in the United States* (New York: Houghton Mifflin Company, 1934), pp. 15-16.
[2]*Ibid.*, p. 16.

THE BEGINNING OF COMPULSORY EDUCATION

It soon became apparent to the colonists that these voluntary efforts to promote general education on the part of the people and the towns would not suffice to propagate their puritanical religious beliefs because of the extremely hard pioneering conditions which were existent in the New England wilderness. As a result of these almost insufferable conditions, education was being neglected in the homes as well as by the masters of apprentices. To rectify this situation and insure general education for the colonists' children, the Colonial legislature of Massachusetts acted in 1642 by ordering that all children be taught to read, thereby compelling the masters of apprentices and parents to fulfill their teaching obligations. This action was known as the Massachusetts Law of 1642. Provisions of the law:

> . . . . directed the officials of each town to ascertain, from time to time, if parents and masters were attending to their educational duties; if all children were being trained "in learning and labor and other employments profitable to the Commonwealth"; and if the children were being taught "to read and understand the principles of religion and the capital laws of the country." The officers were empowered to impose fines on those who failed to give proper instruction. . . and the courts were insistent that the towns be compelled to obey the law.[3]

The Massachusetts Law of 1642 established a precedent among English-speaking people which has endured until present times. This was the first legislation on the part of a state which decreed that all children, boys and girls, would be taught to read. The importance of its contributions can be judged only as one views educational history in retrospect.

It was not long, however, before it was discovered by the colonists that the Law of 1642 was no real panacea for all of the ills confronting education of the day. The principal weaknesses in the law were that it did not provide for the establishment of schools, nor did it make provision for employing teachers. Basically, it only made the teaching of reading compulsory but left the actual responsibility for instruction with the home or with the master of apprentices. Realizing the shortsightedness of the Law of 1642, the Massachusetts legislature moved to rectify the situation five years later by passing what has become known as the famous Old Deluder Satan Act, or the Massachusetts Law of 1647. This law ordered:

> 1. That every town having 50 householders should at once appoint a teacher of reading and writing, and provide for his wages in such manner as the town might determine; and

---

[3]*Ibid.*, p. 17.

2. That every town having 100 householders must provide a (Latin) grammar school to fit youths for the university, under a penalty of £5 for failure to do so.[4]

The passing of the 1647 law marked another milestone in the progress of American education. By statute all New England towns were required to provide an elementary school system and the larger towns were required to establish and maintain a secondary school in addition. Failure to abide by this statute would result in assessment of a fine by the state. Together the Massachusetts Laws of 1642 and 1647, in addition to the Laws of 1634 and 1638, which provided for the levying of equalized compulsory taxation of property to meet all town expenditures, created the foundation upon which the American public school systems have been constructed. The significant action taken by this early day Colonial legislature has been well stated by the Massachusetts public school historian Martin, as cited by Cubberley:

> It is important to note here that the idea underlying all this legislation was neither paternalistic nor socialistic. The child is to be educated, not to advance his personal interests, but because the State will suffer if he is not educated. The State does not provide schools to relieve the parent, nor because it can educate better than the parent can, but because it can thereby better enforce the obligation which it imposes.[5]

All of the other New England colonies which were founded on the basis of religious freedom except Rhode Island soon adopted similar legislation based on the precedent which had been established in Massachusetts; that is, compulsory education with salaried teachers provided at public expense. It is true that there were different provisions made for education in the parochial schools of the middle colonies and in the pauper schools of the deep south, but these plans were short lived and the compulsory-maintenance program which evolved in the New England colonies became the established framework of school management and support in the United States.

TRANSITIONAL METHODS OF ELEMENTARY SCHOOL ORGANIZATION

Contrary to common belief the graded elementary school as we know it today did not have its origin in the early New England colony schools.

---

[4]*Ibid.*, p. 18.
[5]*Ibid.*, p. 19.

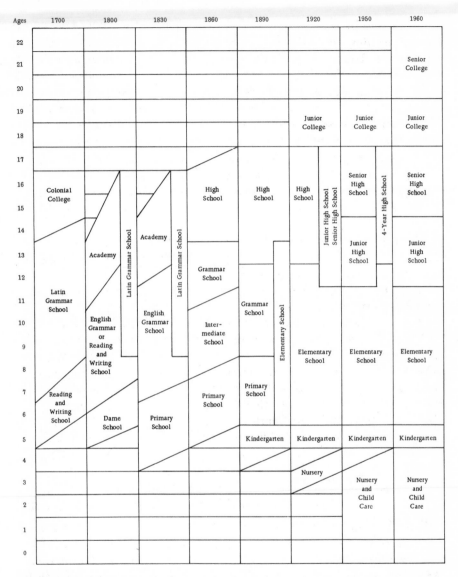

Figure 1. *Evolution of the Essential Features of the American Public School System.* Roscoe V. Cramer and Otto E. Domian, *Administration and Supervision in the Elementary School,* (New York: Harper & Brothers, 1960), p. 56; as adapted from E. P. Cubberley, *Public Education in the United States,* (Boston: Houghton Mifflin Company, 1934) p. 140. Reprinted by permission of Harper & Row, Publishers, Inc. and Houghton Mifflin Company.

7

In fact, it did not have its inception until 1848 in the Quincy Grammar School of Boston, Massachusetts. This was 206 years after the Massachusetts Law of 1642 which made the teaching of reading compulsory in Colonial Massachusetts. Prior to the graded elementary organizational plan of the public school there were many antecedents, as can be seen in Figure 1.

The earliest elementary schools were very simple in organizational structure and were conducted in extremely crude surroundings. These conditions have been described well by Bunker's statement that:

> Much of the elementary instruction which was provided in that day was given in vacant carpenters' shops, in spare rooms in old dwellings, in unoccupied barns, in basement rooms, and in such other places as chance presented.[6]

In compliance with the Massachusetts Law of 1647, parents of the smaller towns either taught their children at home or clubbed together and employed a teacher to give instruction in reading and writing. In the larger towns, usually those having 100 householders or more, elementary schools were established and teachers hired at public expense. One of the earliest town schools established at Dedham, Massachusetts in 1648 can be seen in Figure 2.

Figure 2. Town School at Dedham, Massachusetts, built in 1648. Adapted from E. P. Cubberley, *Public Education in the United States*, p. 17. Reproduced by permission of, and arrangement with, Houghton Mifflin Company, 1934.

THE DAME SCHOOL

The first type of organized school system provided for by the colonist was the dame school. These schools were usually conducted by a young woman "who in her youth, had obtained the rudiments of an education, and who now desired to earn a pittance for herself by imparting to the children of her neighborhood her small store of learning."[7]

The instruction offered in the dame school generally consisted of learning to read, spell, occasionally to write, and lessons in the catechism. These schools were most prominent in New England between the years 1650 and 1800. Generally, the enrollment of the dame school, as shown in Figure 3,

[6]F. F. Bunker, *Reorganization of the Public School System* (Washington, D. C.: U. S. Bureau of Education Bulletin No. 8, 1916), p. 2.
[7]Cubberley, *op. cit.*, p. 27.

"did not exceed thirty pupils consisting of boys aged four to seven and girls of all ages from four years upward."[8]

Figure 3. A Dame School. E. P. Cubberley, *Public Education in the United States*, 1934, p. 28. Reproduced by permission of, and arrangement with, Houghton Mifflin Company.

THE THREE R'S SCHOOL

Another innovation in elementary school organization for instruction of this era was the very short lived writing school "in which writing, reckoning, and the simplest elements of merchants' accounts were taught."[9] This plan never did attain common acceptance in New England because of the urgency of the times in which parents clamored for better education for their children. As a result of the exigencies of the new sparsely settled frontier, the second most widely accepted organizational pattern was adopted by combining the dame school and the writing school to form the Three R's school in which reading, 'riting, and 'rithmetic were taught. Hence, the historical background of the Three R's was established — the foundation from which our elementary schools have evolved.

---

[8]Henry J. Otto, *Elementary-School Organization and Administration* (third edition; Appleton-Century-Crofts, 1954), p. 8. Reprinted by permission of Appleton-Century-Crofts.
[9]Cubberly, *op. cit.*, p. 29.

THE LATIN GRAMMAR SCHOOL

The third type of school established by the New Englanders was the traditional Latin grammar school in which classical learnings in Latin and Greek were taught. The Latin grammar school was very prominent in New England from about 1650 to 1800. Children entering this school for study were boys about seven or eight years of age who had learned to read and write in the dame school and who were headed toward higher education in the Colonial or English type college. Generally the students had acquired much proficiency in Latin and Greek by the age of fifteen and were deemed acceptable scholars for pursuing deeper studies in the curriculum of the college. The era of the Latin grammar school was destined to be of short duration, however, because the commercial interests of the new country insisted on a curriculum which was based on "more practical studies, such as merchants' accounts, navigation, surveying, and the higher mathematics."[10]

THE ENGLISH GRAMMAR SCHOOL

The Latin grammar school yielded to the public pressures which insisted on a more practical and less classical type curriculum, resulting in the eventual evolution of the English grammar school. To be admitted to the English grammar school of the 1800's a student was required to have some knowledge of reading and arithmetic. Prior to 1800 the students had acquired this knowledge from their studies in the dame schools of New England. About this time, however, there was an increasing demand on the part of the public for universal education and the dame schools simply could not take care of the increasing number of students in the rapidly growing Colonial towns.[11]

THE PRIMARY SCHOOL

To fulfill the educational needs of an expanding New England population, which the dame schools could no longer meet, and give credence to the idea of universal education, the city of Boston moved steadfastly in 1818 to create 20 primary schools within the confines of its school system, thereby insuring instruction in the rudiments of reading, writing, and arithmetic to their constituents' children. Other New England states were soon to follow the precedent set by Boston in establishing primary schools and equip students for admission into the English grammar school. The growth

---

[10]*Ibid.*, p. 31.
[11]Otto, *op. cit.*, p. 10.

of the primary schools was unprecedented. In Boston alone there were 193 such schools by 1855. Their popularity can be explained in part by the fact that they were thought of as community institutions since there were numerous buildings placed close to the pupils' homes. Each one of these buildings was a one-teacher school equipped to handle 30 to 40 pupils in the age range of from four to seven or eight.[12]

THE LANCASTRIAN SCHOOL

The Lancastrian or monotorial method was another organizational plan for offering instruction to the primary school age children of this era. This organizational pattern was very popular from about 1815 to 1830, but by 1840 it had generally passed out of the picture, except in New York City where it was to continue in partial use until 1853. Figure 4 depicts a mono-

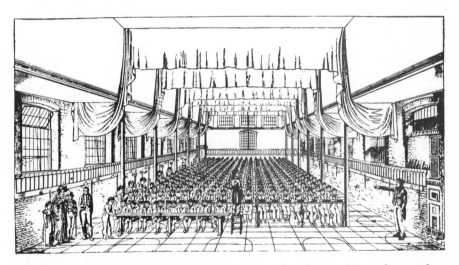

Figure 4. A Lancastrian school in operation. This shows 365 pupils seated, monitors standing at the left, and "stations" around the walls. Adapted from E. P. Cubberley, *Public Education in the United States*, p. 130. Reproduced by permission of and arrangement with, Houghton Mifflin Company, 1934.

torial school of the time with 365 pupils in attendance. Cubberley has described this plan well in stating that:

The essential features of the Lancastrian plan were the collection of a large number of pupils in one room, from 200 to 1000 being possible. . .

12*Ibid*, p. 10.

The pupils were sorted and seated in rows, and to each row was assigned a clever boy who was known as a monitor, and who was the key to the entire system. A common number for each monitor to instruct and look after was ten. The teacher first taught these monitors a lesson from a printed card, and then the monitors, "youthful corporals of the teacher's regiment," took their rows to "stations" about the wall and proceeded to teach the other boys what they had just learned.[13]

Instruction under the Lancastrian system at first involved the teaching of reading and the catechism. Eventually the curriculum was enlarged to include writing, arithmetic, and spelling. The abandonment of the Lancastrian plan was due to its rigidly structured program which was not well adapted to the mental or cultural needs of children.

THE GRADED ELEMENTARY SCHOOL

The first graded elementary school, founded in 1848 at Quincy Grammar School of Boston by J. D. Philbrick, did not closely resemble our contemporary graded elementary school. There were at least four steps in the evolution of the graded elementary school plan before it began to approximate the program that we are familiar with today. First, there was the horizontal division of the elementary program into two or more grades. The most commonly utilized method was one grade for the primary and one for the grammar school. A variation consisted of three grades; primary, intermediate, and grammar. The second phase in evolving the graded elementary school was housing these broad grade-units within the same building. The names of these broad grade-units are in common usage even today. The third step was the classification of pupils into one of the grade-units and the fourth action was to change the type of building construction which would provide several small classrooms. Within each classroom all of the subjects were taught by one teacher to the pupils who had been assigned to her.[14] The first graded elementary school established by Philbrick in Boston can be seen in Figure 5.

CONTEMPORARY ORGANIZATIONAL PATTERNS

By the early twentieth century the elementary school organizational plan had evolved into a program of grades one through eight with the four year high school added at the top. In the more metropolitan districts it was not uncommon to find the preschool class, designated as the kindergarten. Today in the mid-twentieth century our public school educational program

---

[13]Cubberley, *op. cit.*, pp. 131-2.
[14]Otto, *op. cit.*, pp. 11-12.

Figure 5.   Quincy Grammar School, Boston, 1848. From C. L. Spain, *The Platoon School* (New York, The Macmillan Co. © 1924), p. 123. Reprinted by permission of the publisher.

organization can be seen in such variations as the 6-3-3, 8-4, or the 6-2-4 plans.[15] The contemporary organizational pattern, therefore, has more or less crystalized into the grade-units of kindergarten, primary, intermediate, junior high, and senior high school.

EVOLUTION OF THE ELEMENTARY SCHOOL CURRICULUM

Our Colonial forefathers established compulsory education financed at public expense with the passage of the Massachusetts Laws of 1642 and 1647 in order that their children, as well as subsequent generations, would be guaranteed the opportunity and privilege of learning to read. Thus, reading became the first dominant subject of the elementary school curriculum. Although writing was included in the Law of 1647, it actually received minor emphasis. Gradually arithmetic was added to the curriculum and by 1775 the schools were teaching what was to become known as the Three R's: reading, 'riting, and 'rithmetic. Of course the catechism was included in the curriculum of the schools of this era in order that the colonists could propagate their religious teachings. Spelling was the next curricular offering

---

[15]R. Freeman Butts and Lawrence A. Cremin, *A History of Education in American Culture* (New York: Henry Holt and Company, Inc., 1953), pp. 585-6.

to be added between 1775 and 1800. The curriculum of the elementary school of the Colonial period by the year 1800 therefore consisted of reading, writing, arithmetic, catechisms, and spelling.

1775	1825	1850	1875	1900
READING	READING Declamation SPELLING* Writing	READING DECLAMATION SPELLING WRITING	READING Literary Selections SPELLING	READING LITERATURE* Spelling Writing*
Spelling Writing Catechism Bible Arithmetic	Good Behavior Manners and Morals ARITHMETIC*	Manners Conduct MENTAL ARITH. * CIPHERING	PENMANSHIP* Conduct	. . . .
			PRIMARY ARITH. ADVANCED ARITH.	ARITHMETIC
	Bookkeeping GRAMMAR Geography	Bookkeeping Elem. Lang. GRAMMAR Geography History U.S.	. . . . Oral Lang. * GRAMMAR Home Geog. TEXT GEOG. U.S. HISTORY Constitution	. . . . ORAL LANG. Grammar Home Geog. TEXT GEOG. * History Stories* TEXT HIS. *
		Object Lessons	Obj. Lessons* Elem. Science* Drawing* Music* Phy. Exercises	Nature Study* Elem. Sci. * Drawing* Music* Play Phy. Train. *
	Sewing and Knitting	. . . .	. . . .	Sewing Cooking Manual Training

CAPITALS = Most important subjects.
  Roman = Least important subjects.
        * = New methods of teaching now employed.
Underlined = Subjects of medium importance.

Figure 6. The evolution of the elementary-school curriculum, and of methods of teaching. Adapted from E. P. Cubberley, *Public Education in the United States,* p. 473. Reproduced by permission of, and arrangement with, Houghton Mifflin Company, 1934.

The evolution of the elementary school curriculum from 1775 to 1900, as set forth in Figure 6, reveals the fact that by 1900 the essential subjects were considered to be reading, literature, arithmetic, oral language, geography, and history. By this time there were at least twenty subject matter offerings known to the elementary school curriculum.

The Three R's consumed 91.7 per cent of the total daily instructional time of the Colonial elementary school curriculum in 1826 as is shown in Table 1. By 1935, however, the amount of daily instructional time given over to the Three R's had decreased to 51.3 per cent. This trend shows that while the Three R's were receiving 40.4 per cent less time daily in 1935 as compared with 1826, the content subjects of history, geography, and

TABLE 1

Time allotment in the elementary subjects from 1826 to 1935.

Dates	Three R's	Content Subjects	Special Activities
1826	91.7%	0.0%	8.3%
1856	70.1%	15.7%	14.2%
1866	63.0%	12.5%	25.5%
1904	61.8%	12.3%	25.9%
1926	51.7%	11.8%	36.5%
1935	51.3%	14.5%	34.2%

Figures are per cent of total school time. Three R's consists of reading, 'riting, and 'rithmetic; content subjects include such subjects as history, geography and science; special activities consist of music, drawing, and opening exercises, and other content not readily classified under the Three R's or content subjects.

B. Othanel Smith, William O. Stanley, and Harlan Shores, *Fundamentals of Curriculum Development.* (Second edition; New York: World Book Company, 1957), p. 198. Reprinted by permission of Harcourt, Brace & World, Inc.

science were being increased to 14.5 per cent. Special activities, which consisted of music, drawing, recess, and opening exercises were also being increased to an average of 34.2 per cent of daily instructional time.

This percentage loss to the Three R's, however, was only relative, because the length of the school year was being increased to such an extent that actually more time was now being given to instruction in reading, writing, and arithmetic. Whereas, in 1826 the total annual hours of instruction in the Three R's was 934 hours utilizing 91.7 per cent of the instructional day, they had increased to 3,565 hours of annual instruction by 1926 using only 51.3 per cent of the instructional day as Table 2 depicts.

Ayer made a study of forty-nine metropolitan school districts in 1925 to determine the amount of annual time devoted to the various curricular offerings of the elementary school for the year 1924. He computed the mean annual time spent on each subject, ranked them on the basis of the largest to the smallest allocations, and compared them with similar allotments of years 1888, 1904, and 1914. It was found that reading, arithmetic, and language ranked 1, 2, 3 in annual instructional time for all the years between 1888 and 1924, as can be seen in Table 3. By 1924 the five subjects

TABLE 2

Effects of increase in total time allowed for schooling upon amount of time given to the Three R's.

Dates	Average No. of Days of Schooling	Average No. of Hours Per School Day, Elementary Grades	Total No. of Hours of Schooling	Per Cent of Time Given to Three R's	Average No. of Hours Instruction in Three R's
1826	163	6. 25	1, 019	91. 7	934
1866	523	5. 22	2, 730	62. 0	1, 693
1926	1, 360	5. 07	6, 895	51. 7	3, 565

Carleton H. Mann "How Schools Use their Time" *Teachers College Contribution to Education No. 333*, 1928, p. 50. Reproduced by permission of Bureau of Publications, Teachers College, Columbia University, New York.

of the elementary curriculum receiving the most time allocation were reading, arithmetic, language, physical training, and geography.

THE CONTEMPORARY ELEMENTARY SCHOOL CURRICULUM

Currently the elementary school curriculum has evolved into a pattern of subjects designated as language arts, social studies, health and physical education, arts and crafts, science, arithmetic, reading, and music for most schools. In the language arts block of courses one would find such subjects as spelling, handwriting, grammar, composition, and oral composition. Although in actuality reading is a part of the language arts, it has maintained its separate identity because of the great importance attached to its mastery. Within the social studies the courses of geography, history and civics are included. Arts and crafts include studies in the disciplines of home arts, fine arts, and manual arts.[16] Included in the health and physical education area would be found formalized instruction in health per se and organized physical training.

The elementary curriculum of today's school may be said to include all the experiences of the child which come under the supervision of the school. Or to put it another way, it is the strategy whereby the school attempts to meet the goals of education.[17] Thus we see a complete revolution

[16]George A. Beauchamp, *Planning the Elementary School Curriculum* (New York: Allyn and Bacon, Inc., 1956) pp. 71-72.

[17]J. Murray Lee and Doris May Lee, *The Child and His Curriculum* (New York: Appleton-Century-Crofts, Inc., 1960), p. 148.

TABLE 3

The amounts of time allotted to the elementary subjects and their comparative ranks for the years 1888, 1904, 1914, and 1924.

SUBJECTS	1888		1904		1914		1924	
	Min.	Rank	Min.	Rank	Min.	Rank	Min.	Rank
Reading	2,332	1	2,250	1	2,032	1	2,003	1
Arithmetic	1,671	2	1,790	2	1,521	2	1,451	2
Language	1,212	3	1,488	3	1,316	3	1,417	3
Physical Training	373	10	353	12	489	11	873	4
Geography	598	8	763	4	735	4	760	5
Recess	800	6	700	5	701	6	752	6
History–Civics	303	11	456	10	558	8	739	7
Drawing	696	7	663	6	609	7	661	8
Spelling	832	5	497	9	704	5	598	9
Music	403	9	536	7	556	9	591	10
Penmanship	902	4	502	8	550	10	567	11
Industrial Arts	0	15	246	15	451	12	410	12
Miscellaneous	300	12	345	14	345	15	381	13
Opening Exercise	24	14	329	13	375	14	377	14
Science·	290	13	424	11	406	13	354	15
Totals	10,736		11,341		11,348		11,934	

Fred C. Ayer *Fundamentals of Instructional Supervision*, (New York: Harper and Brothers, 1954), p. 403. Reprinted by permission of Harper & Row, Publishers, Inc.

of the function of the curriculum from teaching the Three R's in a purely academic manner in the early school to guiding the child in acquiring a broad array of knowledge and skills which assist him in becoming a self-supporting and contributing member of the society in which he lives.

SUMMARY

This chapter has traced the origin and heritage of our modern day elementary schools through a brief synopsis of earliest school legislation, organizational patterns, and curriculum changes. These factors viewed in their proper historical perspective should enable the student of education to understand the elementary school as it exists today. It is anticipated that an understanding of these facts will endow him with an appreciation for what has gone before and serve as a knowledgeable basis upon which steps for improvement can be made in the future.

Earliest school legislation in the New England colonies fixed the responsibility for education as a function of the state. Since this precedence was established by Massachusetts in 1642, all of the states in the nation have passed legislation which has provided for free, tax-supported public schools with compulsory attendance laws. This function of the state does not impede the operation of private and parochial educational institutions, thereby affirming our belief in political and religious freedom.

The elementary school has seen the genesis and exodus of many organizational plans for instruction. Some of the foremost organizational plans investigated were the dame school, the primary school, the Lancastrian or monotorial system, and the graded elementary school. Each pattern was unique and served as a vehicle for meeting the educational demands of the time. The graded elementary school has been with us since 1848. It too is unique and has served education well. It should not be viewed as being sacred, however, since by common agreement it is not recognized to be a complete panacea for the transitional needs of education in the Space Age.

The curriculum of the elementary school has likewise seen many innovations. The Three R's curriculum of our pioneer forefathers has given way to the addition of many content or special-activities subjects. The elementary school curriculum became so cumbersome by the mid-twentieth century that consolidation of courses and streamlining of programs were necessary. Currently the curriculum usually consists of a combination of the language arts, social studies, arithmetic, arts and crafts, health and physical education, music, reading, and science. A conscious effort is being made by educators to interrelate the various content and skills of each subject area in order to provide the learner with an integrated educational program.

QUESTIONS FOR DISCUSSION

1. What was the relationship between the development of free public schools and the Pilgrims' conviction that a personal knowledge of the Gospels was necessary to salvation?
2. Was the reasoning behind compulsory schooling consistent with the philosophy of individual freedom which impelled the early settlers to migrate to the New World? Explain.
3. It has been said that the Dame School was an "education monstrosity" as well as an economic necessity. Is this a justifiable statement? Why or why not?

4. How do you account for the fact that reading has continually received less time daily since the early 1800's but has actually had more annual teaching time devoted to it over this same period of years?
5. It has often been said that the public school is the handmaiden of society. Can you cite information which supports this statement? Analyze the evolution of the elementary curriculum accordingly.

TOPICS FOR RESEARCH

1. Determine the amounts and types of education available to the early colonists prior to their migration to the New World.
2. Make an analytical study of the apparent relationship between economic conditions in the colonies at various times and the amount and type of education provided for children.
3. Outline the reasons for the rapid rise and rapid decline of the Lancastrian School.

BIBLIOGRAPHY

AYER, FRED C., *Fundamentals of Instructional Supervision*. New York: Harper and Brothers Publishers, 1954.

BEAUCHAMP, GEORGE A., *Planning the Elementary School Curriculum*. New York: Allyn and Bacon, Inc., 1956.

BUNKER, F. F., *Reorganization of the Public School System*. Washington: U. S. Bureau of Education Bulletin No. 8, 1916.

BUTTS, R. FREEMAN, AND LAWRENCE A. CREMIN, *A History of Education in American Culture*. New York: Henry Holt & Company, Inc., 1953.

CRAMER, ROSCOE V., AND OTTO E. DOMIAN, *Administration and Supervision in the Elementary School*. New York: Harper and Brothers, 1960.

CUBBERLEY, ELLWOOD P., *Public Education in the United States*. Boston: Houghton Mifflin Company, 1934.

GOOD, H. G., *A History of Western Education*. New York: The Macmillan Company, 1947.

KNIGHT, EDGAR W., *Public Education in the South*. New York: Ginn & Company, 1922.

LEE, J. MURRAY, AND DORIS MAY LEE, *The Child and His Curriculum*. New York: Appleton-Century-Crofts, Inc., 1960.

MANN, CARLETON HUNTER, *How Schools Use Their Time*. Contribution to Education, No. 333, New York: Teachers College, Columbia University, 1928

OTTO, HENRY J., *Elementary School Organization and Administration*. Third edition, New York: Appleton-Century-Crofts, Inc., 1954.

REISNER, EDWARD H., *The Evolution of the Common School*. New York: The Macmillan Company, 1930.

SMITH, B. OTHANEL, WILLIAM O. STANLEY, AND J. HARLAN SHORES, *Fundamentals of Curriculum Development*. Second edition, New York: World Book Company, 1957.

SPAIN, C. L., *The Platoon School*. New York: The Macmillan Company, 1924.

The teacher and students organize cooperatively the day's schedule of activities.

2

Organization of the Elementary School to Enhance Its Curriculum

There is a close relationship in the elementary school between the plan of organization and the curriculum. If one is to devise an organizational pattern through which the curriculum content can be adjusted to the levels of individual differences among pupils and meet the needs of the slow, fast, and average learners, then a plan of organization with flexible features must be created. Such a plan should be sufficiently flexible to insure proper grouping of students for instruction on a continuous progress basis. There are many problems related to an organizational pattern which is compatible with this curriculum theory such as regulating pupil progress and differentiated instruction. The subsequent pages of this chapter therefore attempt to point out the factors in organization which influence curriculum development.

BASIC ORGANIZATIONAL FACTORS

Most educators are agreed that the elementary school should be organized in such a manner that the type of experiences desired for the pupils should dictate the organizational pattern. This premise, however, regrettably receives only lip service in most instances. Instead of the educational experience of the students determining the organizational pattern, the pattern itself has traditionally determined what experiences the students will have. This is a paradox; as profesional educators we know what is considered best concerning organization for learning experiences, but we have become too dominated by tradition to break out of our lethargy. The source of the problem inciting this dilemma is the graded elementary school plan of organization. This plan does little more than provide a convenient vehicle for sectioning or classifying children for instruction primarily on the basis of chronological age or preconceived academic standards. Since this plan was devised by Philbrick at Quincy Grammar School in Boston in 1848, it has become the most widely accepted plan for organization of instruction in the United States today. One cannot travel anywhere in this nation but that he does not find the graded organizational plan prevailing.

Why has it become so popular and so universally accepted? Does it do something for the instructional program which no other system of organization can do? Does it insure better mental health among its students? Will it guarantee maximum pupil achievement? The answer to these and related questions is that it has obtained universal acceptance primarily on the basis of its simplicity of organizational design, not on the basis that pupil outcomes are superior to those of other plans.

So firmly entrenched has the graded elementary school plan become that we now think of a given body of content within such course offerings as social studies, reading, arithmetic, or science as being "second grade" or "fifth grade" work. As one realizes this he sees all too clearly that the graded plan of organization dictates what educational experiences the children of the various grades will have. Remembering that the graded school is predicated on classifying pupils on the basis of chronological age or preconceived academic standards, it seems almost unbelievable that this organizational pattern would continue to flourish and grow when it largely denies such concepts as readiness or individual and trait differences among and within the students.

ORGANIZATIONAL PATTERNS ATTEMPTING TO INDIVIDUALIZE INSTRUCTION

Individual and trait differences, which are discussed in greater detail in a subsequent chapter of this text, are very pronounced at any grade level. Any experienced teacher knows that at the first grade level achievement differences among six-year-olds will vary as much as four years. At the fourth grade level they may have widened to five or six years and by the sixth grade level the differences in achievement may vary as much as seven years or more. Aroused by an awareness of this unique situation forward thinking educators[1] attempted in the past to break the lock-step organiza-

---

[1]Educators identified with various organizational patterns which attempted to break the rigid lock-step approach of the graded elementary school are: Wirt, Platoon School; Burk, Washburne, and McDade, Winnetka and McDade Plan; Parkhurst, Dalton Plan; Goodlad and Anderson, Nongraded Plan; and Stoddard, Dual Progress Plan.

tional pattern of the graded elementary school plan to provide more adequately for these individual and trait differences. They sought to let the desired educational experience dictate the organizational pattern.

Some of the earliest plans devised to individualize instruction were the "Platoon School," the "Winnetka and McDade" plans, and the "Dalton Plan." These plans flourished briefly in isolated regions of the nation from about 1900 to 1930, and then gradually faded out of the educational picture as a proposed panacea to escape the rigidity of the graded elementary school and meet individual differences more completely. Although these organizational plans were short lived, they did stir sentiment among educators to find a more suitable method than the graded elementary school plan for developing the innate abilities of the individual student.

THE PLATOON SCHOOL

One of the first movements in the twentieth century toward instruction geared to meet individual needs was instituted by Superintendent William A. Wirt of the Bluffton, Indiana, Public Schools. In 1900 he established the "work-study-play" type curriculum which emphasized social living rather than isolated subject matter per se. This plan was known as the "Platoon School."

In the platoon schools contemporary learnings significant to the pupil were stressed rather than deferred learnings which would be needed in adult life. Proportional time was given over to the child life problems of work, study, and play. This organizational pattern provided for the full utilization of the school plant itself in that the auditorium, gym, library, art, and music room were under full schedule. The platoon school has been described by Otto:

> . . . as a plan of organization which provides for the division of the pupils of the school into two groups, called platoons, and which provides a schedule of classes arranged so that one platoon is studying the fundamental subjects in home rooms while the other platoon is engaged with activity subjects in special rooms.[2]

The fundamental subjects consisting of reading, arithmetic, writing, spelling, language, history, and geography were taught for almost a half day in the homeroom. Instruction in these subjects was given by the homeroom teacher who reputedly was able to adjust the materials to the educational needs of the children because of his constant association with them. Because of the homeroom aspect, the teacher was in a better posi-

---

[2]Henry J. Otto, *Elementary-School Organization and Administration* (third edition; New York: Appleton-Century-Crofts, 1954), p. 137. Reprinted by permission of Appleton-Century-Crofts.

tion to correlate the learnings in the fundamental subjects as the children worked through the materials.

The special activities were music, physical education, library, nature study, home economics, auditorium, and art. They were handled on a more or less departmentalized arrangement in which special teachers for each subject gave the instruction in rooms particularly adapted for teaching in these areas.[3] There was practically no correlation between these activities and the fundamental subjects.

Critics of the platoon plan of organization held that there was a minimal amount of transfer of learning taking place in the special activities segment of the curriculum. They also contended that too much time was being spent on the special activities and not enough time on the fundamental subjects. Spain and Courtis, as cited by Otto, pointed out, however, that just as much time was being spent on the fundamental subjects in the platoon schools as in the nonplatoon schools and that there was no difference in pupil achievement resultant from the different organizational plans.[4]

THE WINNETKA AND McDADE PLANS

Another attempt to break the rigid lock-step approach of organization was devised by Frederic L. Burk in 1913 at the San Francisco State Teachers College's training school. Burk's ideas concerning a plan of individualized instruction were not to reach fruition until the 1920's when Superintendent Carleton W. Washburne of Winnetka, Illinois, and Assistant Superintendent James E. McDade of the Chicago Public Schools adopted his philosophy and organized their elementary schools accordingly.[5] Burk's ideas found expression in what came to be known as the "Winnetka Plan" and the "McDade Plan."

In these plans a genuine effort was made to develop an instructional program flexible enough that there could be provision for individual differences. The curriculum was divided into segments. One portion was concerned with "common essentials" made up of learnings in arithmetic, reading, and spelling. The other segment was thought of as the "group and creative activities" in which pupils were engaged in learnings in music, art, literature, physical education, and handicrafts.[6] Concerning these two segments of the curriculum Washburne has stated:

---

[3]*Ibid.*, p. 138.
[4]*Ibid.*, p. 140.
[5]*Ibid.*, pp. 141-2.
[6]C, W. Washburne, "Burk's Individual System as Developed at Winnetka," *Twenty-Fourth Yearbook of the National Society for the Study of Education*, Part II (Bloomington, Illinois: Public Schools Publishing Company, 1925), pp. 79-82.

Those subjects which we want each child to master must be "individualized" — there is no other effective way of getting widely differing children to attain a common standard. But those subjects in which children may legitimately differ, or where we want to capitalize on their differences, may be socialized — we classify these as "group and creative activities."[7]

In order to provide for these two main divisions of the curriculum as found in the Winnetka or McDade plans, one-half of the morning and afternoon sessions were given over to individual work in the "common essentials," while the other half day of these periods was dedicated to "group and creative studies.[8] In describing the curriculum and how it works Washburne has further stated that:

Every child needs to know certain elements of arithmetic, needs to be able to read with a certain speed and comprehension, needs to spell certain common words, needs to know something about those persons, places, and events to which reference is constantly made. Since every child needs these things, and since every child differs from others in his ability to grasp them, the time and amount of practice to fit each child's needs must be varied. Under the old regime, in the effort to give different children the same subject matter in the same length of time, the quality of the children's work, the degree of their mastery, varied from poor to excellent, as attested by their report cards. But under the Winnetka technique of individual education, instead of quality varying, time varies: a child may take as much time as he needs to master a unit of work, but master it he must. The common essentials, by definition, are those knowledges and skills needed by everyone; to allow many children, therefore, to pass through school with hazy and inadequate grasp of them, as one must under the class lock-step scheme, is to fail in one of the functions of the school.

The part of the curriculum which should provide self-expression and group activities is quite another matter. Here there is no common skill or knowledge to be mastered. Here each child may legitimately differ from his neighbor in what he gets from school. It is the school's job to provide opportunities for his special interests and abilities to develop. In this field, education recognizes the importance to evolution of the law of variation, and therefore takes full advantage of children's differences. The children must learn how to contribute their special abilities to the undertakings of the group.[9]

---

[7]C. W. Washburne, *Adjusting the School to the Child* (New York: World Book Company, 1932), p. 2.

[8]C. W. Washburne, "Burk's Individual System as Developed at Winnetka," *Twenty-Fourth Yearbook of the National Society for the Study of Education,* Part II (Bloomington, Illinois: Public Schools Publishing Company, 1925), p. 80. Reprinted by permission of Bobbs Merrill Company, Inc.

[9]*Ibid.,* pp. 79-80.

"By providing flexibility of time for the mastery of common essentials and by providing opportunity for children to exercise and use their different interests and abilities,"[10] the Winnetka and McDade plans enabled the desired educational experiences of elementary children to dictate the organizational pattern of the school. Thus, a real break in the lock-step approach of the graded elementary school was effected in these two plans.

THE DALTON PLAN

Helen Parkhurst is credited with developing the Dalton laboratory plan in 1919 in which another method of elementary school organization was devised which was based on the philosophy of meeting the individual needs of the pupils more effectively than the conventional graded elementary school plan. This plan was first adopted by the Dalton, Massachusetts schools in 1920, thus its name the "Dalton Plan." The philosophy of this plan was based upon three premises: (1) freedom for the pupil to engage in uninterrupted work in which he could pursue his interests, thereby fully developing his powers of concentration, (2) cooperation and interaction of group life, or community living, and (3) the proportion of effort to attainment, or budgeting time.[11]

A typical Dalton plan included a curriculum composed of five disciplines: English, history, geography, mathematics, and science. The manner in which a student pursued his studies in these courses was to enter into a "contract" for a month of unit work in each discipline with his teachers. In so doing, he would have five contracts to complete within twenty school days or one calendar month. Within each contract there were usually twenty separate lessons called "units." It is easy to see, therefore, that if the average student had five contracts to complete in twenty school days with twenty units in each he had contracted a work load of 100 units to be completed in this length of time.

As the student proceeded to complete his contracts he moved from one teaching station to another as he desired. Each one of these teaching stations, which was called a laboratory, was presided over by a teacher who was a specialist in his subject matter field. Further, each teaching laboratory contained the very latest materials and equipment. During the morning hours from 9:30 to noon, the pupils from different grade levels, that is grade four and above, were free to choose the laboratory wherein they would work for that time. After each child selected a laboratory for a given day in the areas of English, history, geography, mathematics, or

---

[10]*Ibid.*, p. 82.
[11]Helen Parkhurst, "The Dalton Laboratory Plan" *Twenty-Fourth Yearbook of the National Society for the Study of Education,* Part II (Bloomington, Illinois: Public Schools Publishing Company, 1925), p. 84.

science all would congregate at this teaching station to pursue their contracts individually. Although it was not uncommon to find similar age groups working together in each of these laboratories, many different aged children worked together, thereby duplicating community life outside of the school. The teacher's role was mainly one of individualized instruction or group guidance. It must be pointed out, however, that the Dalton plan was not recommended for children below grade four since it was held that they had not matured enough to plan and utilize their time for individual study effectively.

To insure that the pupils delved sufficiently into all five of the disciplines (English, history, geography, mathematics, and science) and did not concentrate on their favorite course or courses, they were required to maintain an even front at the close of the contract period in all of the subject matter areas. In addition they could not enter into another contract in any of the areas until all of the previously agreed-upon contracts had been satisfactorily completed.

Provisions for individual differences of the bright, average, and slow students were included in the Dalton Plan. Any student completing his contracts satisfactorily in advance of the agreed-upon twenty school day period could enter into the next sequence of contracts. The slower students who could not complete their contracts in the regulation twenty school day periods could have extended time to finish their work acceptably.[12]

Under the Dalton Plan the nonacademic subjects consumed the remainder of the school day, which was normally the afternoon periods. These were thought of as the "physical, social, and emotional subjects such as physical training, literature, excursions, nature study, and lantern lectures."[13] In these nonacademic pursuits the children were classified for work on the basis of chronological age.

In theory the Dalton Plan seems quite feasible. In practicality one must answer the question of whether or not intermediate grade children have sufficient maturity to budget their time wisely and plan their own work schedules. It can be said with surety that this plan was conceived on fundamental logic that would effectively provide for individual differences among public school students.

THE DEPARTMENTALIZED PLAN

The graded elementary school plan of organization for instruction lends itself well to departmentalized teaching. Ordinarily this type of or-

---

12*Ibid.*, pp. 83-92.
13Otto, *op. cit.*, p. 146.

ganizational plan is not utilized below the intermediate grades, with grade four normally being the lowest grade wherein departmental work is deemed advisable.

Departmentalization may be thought of as a plan of organization in which the various courses of the elementary curriculum are taught by teachers who are considered to be subject matter specialists. These teachers have had extensive training in their professional preparation in a given subject and are therefore considered specialists in their area. Generally they are stationed in a classroom which is equipped specifically for the teaching of their specialty, as in the areas of science, music, mathematics, or foreign language. The pupils come to the subject matter specialists' rooms for predetermined time periods of formalized instruction. Normally these rooms are equipped to handle up to forty-five students, with about thirty the desirable number. It is not uncommon for the departmental teacher to work with as many as 150 students daily since he may have thirty pupils in as many as five separate sections.

In a typical departmentalized intermediate elementary grade organizational pattern one would likely find subject matter specialists for the language arts, social studies, mathematics, science, music, art, and physical education. As a general rule there would be longer class periods for the language arts in which reading, writing, language, and spelling are taught, and in the social studies where learning in history, geography, and civics is pursued, than for the other curricular offerings.

There are both advantages and disadvantages to the departmentalized plan of organization for instruction in the intermediate elementary school grades. There are at least three real advantages of the plan. First, the teachers are subject matter specialists. There is nothing which will improve a teacher's self-perception and self-confidence more than the feeling of security which comes with knowing one's subject matter thoroughly. Second, outstanding sequential development of subject matter within a given content area can be effected through the departmentalized plan. As an example, consider the mathematics teacher who instructs fourth, fifth, and sixth graders. He is in the unique position of being able to take a group of pupils at the beginning of the fourth grade and build one concept upon another until they have completed the sixth grade and are ready for entrance into junior high school. Third, the departmental teacher, a subject matter specialist, has the opportunity to select and continually use teaching aids and materials appropriate to his instructional area effectively.

Disadvantages of the departmentalized organizational pattern are many. Foremost among them is the element of time. When the departmentalized plan is put into action with bells ringing at forty-five minute intervals to signal the end of class periods, one can readily see that an inflexible frozen schedule has ensued. A by-product of this inflexible schedule can be seen within the individual classroom. There the "teach-able moment" might have just been established with a group of children on a given topic only to be disturbed and perhaps lost forever by the clanging of the bell, indicating to the pupils that they are to stop what they are doing, put their materials away, and move to their next regularly scheduled class. A second disadvantage is that the departmentalized teacher may work with as many as 150 students in five sections of classes, and therefore cannot be expected to become acquainted with the educa-tional status of each child sufficiently to adjust his instruction to individual pupil needs adequately. A third and perhaps the greatest objection to departmentalized teaching is that correlation of learning experiences with other content areas is minimized through the subjects-in-isolation ap-proach.

The completely departmentalized organizational pattern of the inter-mediate grades is used only infrequently. As an example, in a 1962 survey of sixty-four Texas Gulf Coast elementary schools it was found that de-partmentalization was being practiced to some extent in grades four, five, and six in only 17 per cent of the schools.[14] Dean reported in a 1960 national survey that the incidence of departmentalization in grades 1 through 6 was only about 1 per cent.[15] However, with the increased in-terest in and emphasis on science and mathematics by the government and the public since the launching of the Russian Sputnik in 1957, as evi-denced by the passage of the National Defense Education Act of 1958, more schools may move toward the departmentalized system in order to utilize teacher-subject-matter strengths more effectively in these areas.

THE SELF-CONTAINED CLASSROOM PLAN

There are at least two self-contained classroom plans of organization in vogue in the modern graded elementary school. They are the completely self-contained and the partially self-contained methods.

In the completely self-contained classroom one would find a classroom teacher who works with approximately thirty students who have been

---

[14]Oscar T. Jarvis, *Time Allotments and Pupil Achievement in the Intermediate Ele-mentary Grades* (University of Houston: Bureau of Education Research and Services, Research Study No. 8 November, 1962), p. 32.

[15]Stuart E. Dean, *Elementary School Administration and Organization* (Washington: U. S. Department of Health, Education and Welfare, Office of Education, 1960), pp. 30-31.

assigned to him for the entire school year. In this arrangement the class-room teacher provides instruction in all of the subjects of the elementary school curriculum to his assigned pupils. In so doing, he would be charged with the responsibility for directing pupil study in the language arts (reading, language, spelling, and writing), social studies (history, geography, and civics), arithmetic, science, physical education, health, music, art, and handicrafts.

The method of pupil assignment to the completely self-contained class-room is usually an arbitrary one. Although many schools have a policy of making these room assignments on the basis of ability or homogenous grouping, it is done essentially on the basis of chronological age. As a result, the range of individual and trait differences within the completely self-contained classroom is very evident. In order to cope with this situation effectively, the classroom teacher normally has two or three intraclass groupings designed to narrow the range of individual differences and thereby better enable him to adapt instruction to the level of the children working in each group.

The completely self-contained classroom has many unique advantages. It will suffice to mention four of the most outstanding. First, the self-contained classroom enables the teacher to integrate the materials of the various course offerings, thereby facilitating pupil transfer of learnings. Second, because the teacher works with the same students continuously throughout the school year, he gets to know his pupils' strengths and weaknesses well and consequently is in a good position to adapt instruction to meet their individual needs. Third, there are no school bells to ring and disturb learning taking place in the completely self-contained class-room because the schedule is quite flexible. The teacher, having established a "teachable moment" in any given subject, can see it through uninterrupted. A fourth advantage is that through social living experiences taking place among the students assigned to the completely self-contained classroom, democratic principles and concepts are fostered through group studying, working, sharing, and playing.

The completely self-contained classroom is not without its disadvantages, however. They too are numerous. Only the most outstanding will be enumerated here. Perhaps the greatest weakness is that one cannot expect a teacher to be equally proficient in all of the courses comprising the elementary school curriculum. Consequently, this organizational pattern would place an unusual expectation and strain on any teacher. A second problem is that should a weak teacher be employed for the completely self-contained classroom, the pupils would suffer the consequences of poor instruction because they would not have the opportunity of tute-

lage under any other instructor during the school year. A third major disadvantage is that teachers have a tendency to stress curricular areas
wherein they have particular competency or interest and, therefore, there
is the possibility that certain segments of the curriculum would be slighted.

The completely self-contained classroom plan of organization is widely
used. In his 1960 national survey, Dean found that 77 per cent of 4,307
schools surveyed had one teacher per classroom in grades 1 through 6.[16]

The partially self-contained plan, on the other hand, has been utilized
infrequently by elementary schools in the United States. Dean's study also
revealed that only about 10 per cent of the school's surveyed used this
organizational pattern for instruction.[17]

One may define the partially self-contained classroom as an organization in which the fundamental subjects are taught by the teacher to his
pupils, with the creative activities subjects being taught to the same children by a departmental teacher who is a specialist in his field. The fundamental subjects usually would be comprised of the language arts, social
studies, arithmetic, and science. The creative activities are normally composed of music, art, and physical education.

The room assignments of the children are made in basically the same
manner in the partially self-contained classroom as described in the completely self-contained classroom. The primary difference is that the children of the partially self-contained classroom move from their classroom
periodically to the departmental teachers' rooms for study in music, art,
and physical education. It therefore is easy to see that the schedule of the
partially self-contained classroom is more rigid than that of the completely
self-contained since every classroom teacher's program from grades 1
through 6 must be subservient to his pupils' designated period of studies
with the departmental teachers. Hence, by the very nature of its structure
there are frequent interruptions in the school day of the partially self-
contained organizational scheme.

In analyzing the strengths and weaknesses of the partially self-contained classroom plan of organization, it may be said that it has at least
three strong points. They are: (1) the classroom teacher is afforded the
opportunity of integrating the learnings in the fundamental subjects, (2)
because there are special teachers for the creative activities, the classroom
teacher has released time to plan his work while his pupils are engaged in
departmental work, and (3) since the classroom teacher works with the
same pupils for the bulk of the school day he is better able to understand

---

[16]*Ibid.*, pp. 30-31.
[17]*Ibid.*, pp. 30-31.

his students and make provision for adapting instruction to meet their individual needs.

The biggest weakness in the partially self-contained classroom organizational plan is the frequent interruption of the daily class schedule precipitated by the pupils' scheduled work with the departmental teachers. If the lunch and library periods were added to the music, art, and physical education classes, it could readily be seen that the school schedule becomes rigid and that frequent interruptions ensue which may disturb many "teachable moment" situations.

Another variation of the partially self-contained classroom organizational pattern can be effected through resource personnel working with the classroom teacher. In this scheme of organization, the classroom teacher is primarily responsible for teaching all of the subjects of the curriculum to the children. However, he is assisted by resource people who are commonly thought of as consultants. These resource people are usually specialists in such areas as reading, music, art, and physical education. Normally, they do not take over the classroom and teach, but through their consultatory roles they plan with the teacher the materials to be covered and the work to be done. In so doing, they are free to move about the building working with different teachers as much or as little as occasions demand.

THE NONGRADED PLAN

Theoretically the nongraded school, like most of the previously discussed organizational plans, is designed to implement an educational philosophy of continuous pupil progress and is easily recognized as a departure from the lock-step graded elementary approach. The plan was first introduced at Western Springs, Illinois, in 1934, but has since been discontinued there. Apparently the oldest nongraded plan now in existence was established in Milwaukee in 1942.[18] Since the late 1940's the nongraded movement has been closely associated with the work and experimentation of John I. Goodlad and Robert H. Anderson. They have stated their philosophy underlying this organizational pattern thusly:

> The nongraded school is designed to implement a theory of continuous pupil progress: since the differences among children are great and since these differences cannot be substantially modified, school structure must facilitate the continuous educational progress of each pupil. Some pupils, therefore, will require a longer period of time than others for achieving certain learnings and attaining certain developmental levels.[19]

---

[18]John I. Goodlad, "Classroom Organization," *Encyclopedia of Educational Research.* Chester W. Harris (ed.) (New York: The Macmillan Company, 1960), p. 222.
[19]John I. Goodlad and Robert H. Anderson, *The Nongraded Elementary School* (New York: Harcourt, Brace & World, Inc.), p. 52.

Essentially the nongraded approach is designed for the primary school. To illustrate its operation one may analyze the program of Milwaukee Public Schools, as cited by Goodlad and Anderson.[20] In their program, Milwaukee has the nongraded primary set up on a semester system basis. That is, the child entering the nongraded primary upon completion of the kindergarten is assigned not to a grade but to a class simply designated as "Primary School — Miss (Jones)." In this first semester of primary school above the kindergarten the child is labeled Pl. During his second semester he is labeled P2 and the labeling process is continued in this manner until he is ready for promotion out of the primary at the conclusion of P6 into the fourth grade. According to Goodlad and Anderson, in Milwaukee's program:

> Very bright and mature children may be ready to enter fourth grade following P5, or fifth semester. Slower learners have their program stretched out so that they may go through a P7, seventh semester, or P8, eighth semester, classification before entering fourth grade. The question of social and learning groupings is studied by the principal and the teaching staff in planning conferences at the close of each semester, in order that desirable changes in group assignments can be made. A given class could conceivably include children with classifications ranging from P3 to P7, for example although an attempt is made to organize groups so that a child is not more than one year older or one year younger than his classmates.
>
> Milwaukee keeps a special record on reading progress and social development for each child. . . On the same record is entered information about the child's progress in other areas, such as spelling and arithmetic. Whenever a child's progress is considered equal to that of which he is capable, it is indicated that his work is satisfactory. Conferences are arranged for parents with teachers as the situation dictates.[21]

Some of the advantages of the nongraded primary claimed by the Milwaukee schools as outlined by Goodlad and Anderson are:

> (1) . . . greater sensitivity of teachers to the needs and interests of children as they work with them over larger periods of time; (2) happier and more interested children because the fear of annual or semi-annual nonpromotion is eliminated; (3) the competition of children with their own records rather than their vying against each other; (4) more interested parents.[22]

Much has been written about the nongraded plan of organization. In the school year 1957-58 there were approximately 50 communities in the

[20]*Ibid.*, pp. 69-71.
[21]*Ibid.*, p. 70.
[22]*Ibid.*, p. 71.

United States which had adopted this organizational pattern for their primary schools. In the 1963-64 school year, there were 66 school systems within the state of Georgia alone which had initiated nongraded projects under the auspices of the State Department of Education.[23]

THE TEACHING TEAM PLAN

One of the more recent innovations in elementary school organizational patterns is the team teaching plan. In this plan there is usually a "team leader" who is a well-qualified and experienced teacher whose chief duties consist of teaching and coordinating the team's efforts. There are one or more "team teachers" who are members of the teaching team. These "team teachers" are all qualified, licensed people usually hand-picked on the basis of personality and cooperativeness. A teaching team may have a "master teacher" who in addition to a being qualified, licensed, and experienced teacher is usually a subject-matter specialist and skilled instructor. Occasionally a "community resource person" is brought in by the team to lead pupil learnings in his special area of competence.[24]

The word "team" as applied to the organization of pupils within the school for learning experiences has been well defined by Brownell and Taylor:

> In essence, a team is an instructional unit within a school. This unit is a combination of (1) a distinct student group, (2) a small faculty group responsible for teaching the student group, and (3) certain persons who assist the teachers and students.[25]

The team teaching method is a very adaptable plan of grouping children for instruction. Various continuum models of organization for team teaching in a hypothetical elementary school containing grades 1 through 6 with an enrollment of 600 children are presented in Figure 7.[26]

There are at least three basic premises underlying the team teaching philosophy. First, some materials in the elementary curriculum may just as well be taught to 50, 90, or 150 pupils at one time in a general assembly setting by one teacher as contrasted with the traditional practice of several teachers' giving the same instruction in their individual classrooms, where approximately 30 students are assigned. Second, once the general concept

---

[23]*Ibid.*, p. 55; Lutian R. Wootton, Lester D. Stephens, Prentice L. Gott, Hal W. Clements, *The Nongraded School Program.* Georgia ASCD, March, 1965.
[24]John A. Brownell and Harris A. Taylor, "Theoretical Perspectives for Teaching Teams," *Phi Delta Kappan* Volume XLIII, Number 4, (January, 1962), p. 151.
[25]*Ibid.*, p. 151.
[26]*Ibid.*, pp. 152-3.

MODEL I

At one end of the continuum, a team consists of all classes of a particular grade level. Such a team can be formed for each grade. In a very large school, more than one team per grade could be organized.

grades	1	2	3	4	5	6
classes			**team**			

MODEL II

At the other extreme, a team comprises one class from all grade levels. As many teams can be formed as there are vertical arrangements of classes.

grades	1	2	3	4	5	6
classes						
		team				

MODEL III

In a middle position, a team contains classes from two grade levels. In a six-grade school, more than one team per pair of grades could be organized.

grades	1	2	3	4	5	6
classes						
					team	

MODEL Ic

At one extreme, a team consists of one content area and pupils from one grade level. As many teams can be formed as there are major content areas in the curriculum.

grades	6					
classes	A	B	C	D	E	
lang. arts	**team**					
science	**team**					

MODEL IIc

In a middle position, a team comprises one content area and pupils from two or three grade levels. A team can be formed for each major subject area.

grades	1	2	3	4	5	6
science					**team**	
lang. arts		**team**				

MODEL IIIc

At the other extreme, a team comprises one content area and pupils from all grade levels. As many teams can be formed as there are similar content areas at all grade levels.

grades	1	2	3	4	5	6
lang. arts	**team**					
social stud.	**team**					
mathematics	**team**					

Figure 7. Various models of team teaching organizational patterns for instruction. Adapted from John A. Brownell and Harris T. Taylor "Theoretical Perspectives for Teaching Teams," *Phi Delta Kappan.* Volume XLIII, Number 4, January, 1962, p. 151, and reproduced with their permission.

on a given topic has been presented to the pupils in the large general assembly, the children can break out into smaller groups ranging from 2 or 3 students up to 50 or more on the basis of needs for drill and mastery or for extended learnings. The size and student constituents of each group may change from day to day depending upon pupil needs. A third postulate of the team teaching approach is that within every teaching team the particular strengths of each teacher are fully utilized since he will be in charge of instruction in the area of his professional specialization.

The function and operation of an elementary school teaching team has been described well by Brownell and Taylor:

> The faculty teams consist of several teachers, each with certain talents and training. Each team meets regularly to exchange ideas, to develop common policies and purposes, and to share information regarding pupils on their teams. By having each teacher assume responsibility for specialization in subject matter and in supporting activities such as remedial instruction, the faculty teams become self-sufficient units. By specializing, each team teacher can assist the other team members in planning curricula, in developing appropriate instructional techniques, and in meeting demands for increasingly specialized knowledge. When the faculty team deploys pupils into small and large groups for instructional periods, the specialists handle these groups as planned in team meetings. In schools organized into self-contained classrooms, exchange teaching (in which a team teacher takes the class of a colleague or perhaps several classes in a large group situation), brings to bear the specialization of one teacher upon all team pupils. Because team teachers meet regularly, they work not only on organization of material and high quality instruction, but also on problems confronting individual pupils, such as poor reading skills, low motivation, poor study habits, unwholesome behavior. Such interchange among team members will help to establish a professional faculty spirit and will deepen the regard for individual teacher talent. Inevitably, more responsibility for curriculum development will be in the hands of qualified classroom teachers.[27]

The team teaching plan of organization for instruction in the elementary school is unique. It is a plan in which there can be maximum utilization of each teacher's academic strengths. It also is a vehicle which will allow the flexible grouping of children on the basis of need and facilitate continuous academic growth for the slow, average, and bright student. The major disadvantage of the team teaching plan is that existing elementary school buildings are not designed properly for maximum use of the teaching team theory. Perhaps as new buildings are constructed for this purpose with removable partitions and flexible designs, this problem will be overcome.

---

[27]*Ibid.*, p. 153.

A second problem is the large annual turnover among elementary teachers. When a team is formulated and loses one or more of its members in subsequent years the loss is difficult to overcome. A suitable teacher replacement may be employed, but the orientation period would likely be more difficult than in the self-contained classroom. A third problem of no less magnitude is that of finding teachers who have the personality traits and cooperative spirit necessary to become a contributing team member. Team teachers must work very closely with one another, coordinating their efforts and correlating their materials. As a result, they must be able to share their ideas and talents and to evaluate their effectiveness professionally if the team is to become a truly adequate, functioning organism.

Team teaching is a relatively new concept in organization for instruction in the elementary school. It is worthy of profound consideration by the professional educator because of the soundness of the theory upon which it is based.

THE DUAL PROGRESS PLAN

"Life adjustment through learning" was the theory upon which the dual progress plan was recently conceived by Dean George D. Stoddard at New York University and instituted on an experimental basis in some of the public schools of Long Beach, New York, and Ossining, New York. This program was specifically designed to adjust teaching to the level of the slow, average, and fast learner. In theory it would "put an end to the concept of average ability for a class, calling for average performance under average teaching effectiveness."[28] If the theory were to be practiced effectively instruction would of necessity be geared to the needs of all learners.

The functional organization of the dual progress plan is very simple. A professional person known as a "home teacher" is responsible for two rooms. He spends a half-day in each room which may be considered a homeroom for two given groups of children. His duties consist of registration and counseling in addition to teaching reading and social studies. For the other half-day that the children are not working with the "home teacher" they are assigned to teaching specialists in mathematics, science, music, arts and crafts, recreation and health, and foreign language beginning in grade five on an optional basis. The special teachers in each subject offer instruction on a longitudinal basis for grades 1 through 6. A given student thus may be assigned to a "home teacher" on a grade level basis for instruction in

---

[28]George D. Stoddard, *The Dual Progress Plan* (New York: Harper & Brothers, 1961), p. 4.

reading and social studies, but his work in such areas as mathematics or science may range from grade 1 up through grade 6. In situations where there is a combined school throughout twelve grades his work may even go above grade 6 in these areas, depending on his aptitude and proficiency.[29]

The "home teacher" makes it his responsibility to know the individual students in his two rooms. He becomes acquainted with their environmental backgrounds and therefore is able to correlate this knowledge with learnings in the social studies or pass on helpful information concerning the pupils to the special teachers. The work of the special teachers in turn is offered as "(1) basic education for all, and (2) as an opportunity for the gifted."[30]

The dual progress plan in theory escapes the artificial segmentation of the layer-cake graded system by allowing the pupils to proceed at their own rate of growth in the special subjects. It is a plan of simple framework devised to meet the range of individual differences on a continuum of sequential learning experiences which merits serious consideration by professional and lay educators.

FACTORS AFFECTING ORGANIZATIONAL PRACTICE

In this chapter we have discussed the principles of elementary school organization in relation to many different types of organizational patterns as they affect curriculum development. Doubtless the self-contained and departmental systems of organization are more in keeping with the graded elementary school than other methods discussed. Other organizational patterns including platoon, Winnetka and McDade, Dalton, nongraded, team teaching, and dual progress plans were attempts to break down the rigid lock-step plan of the graded elementary school. Proponents of these more flexible programs, which reputedly are designed to more nearly meet the individual differences of the pupils, are in firm agreement with Goodlad's statement that:

> Graded structure suggests a relatively common sequence of learning tasks but lacks the virtue of facilitating continuous progress for learners of widely varying abilities. It is this lack, above others, that has motivated a century of attempts to modify the grade system. Subsequent experimentation with accompanying research must maintain perspective regarding the three central problems of learner variability, curriculum commonality, and administrative expediency.[31]

---

[29]*Ibid.*, pp. 2-3.
[30]*Ibid.*, p. 3.
[31]John I. Goodlad, "Classroom Organization," *Encyclopedia of Educational Research,* *op. cit.*, p. 223.

Perhaps in essence it is not the organizational/plan that insures that individual pupil needs will be met more effectively. The answer to this question may not lie in the plan but rather in the faith that the teachers have in it and their dedication to it. There is research evidence from the field of industry and technology which would indicate that this may be so.

The now famous Hawthorne experiments, which were conducted at Western Electric Company in 1924 by the Massachusetts Institute of Technology under the sponsorship of the National Research Council and the Illuminating Engineering Society, attempted to ascertain the relationship between illumination and factory production. The results of this and related investigations have since become known as the "Hawthorne effect."

Three separate series of experiments were conducted. In the first the investigators set up conditions in the factory in which three sections had different amounts of illumination. In the second there were two identical groups of employees set up in different sections of the plant with but one differing controlled variable — illumination. For the third experiment the investigators decreased illumination on the subjects rather than increasing it as in the first two studies. In all three investigations the results were the same for the experimental and the control groups; production was increased regardless of the degree of illumination.[32] The subjects participating in the investigation simply worked harder at their jobs whether they were members of the experimental or control groups.

By inference the "Hawthorne effect" has much to say to us about the type of organizational pattern which we adopt with the belief that it will more nearly meet the vast range of individual differences among students. In essence it says that teachers and students who identify themselves with any given program and approach their duties and obligations with enthusiasm, interest, and dedication will in the end achieve improved productivity. In short, it likely is not the plan which insures improved results but rather teacher and pupil identification with the uniqueness of that program and their willingness to make it work.

THE ELEMENTARY PRINCIPAL AS ADMINISTRATOR AND SUPERVISOR

The organizational pattern utilized in any given school is no better or no worse than its administrative leader — the principal. It is he who shoulders the major responsibility for implementing the scheme of organization which will insure a curriculum that is adjustable to and appropriate

---

[32]Desmond L. Cook, "The Hawthorne Effect in Educational Research," *Phi Delta Kappan.* Volume XLIV, Number 3, (December, 1962), pp. 116-8.

for the varying range of student needs and abilities in his community. In order to achieve a flexible curriculum which is sensitive to student needs, the principal needs to be released from as many teaching situations as possible, as well as from the minutia of administration, in order that he can concentrate efforts on supervisory endeavors which up-grade the instructional program.

AN OVERVIEW OF THE PRINCIPALSHIP

Basically there are two types of principals currently working in the modern elementary school — the teaching and the supervising principal. The teaching principal is one who spends one-half or more of the school day in instructional duties with the pupils. Consequently, the amount of time he has to give to administration and supervision is contingent upon the time given his teaching load. The supervising principal, on the other hand, is a professional person who spends less than one-half of his time teaching with the balance given to administering the affairs of the school and supervising its instructional program. Generally this principal gives the major part or all of his time to supervisory and administrative duties.[33]

It has now become custom in the United States to have a supervising principal in buildings where at least 12 teachers are assigned. The enrollment for the average 12 teacher school would be approximately 300 students. Current practice also makes it possible to have supervising principals in buildings with less than 12 teachers by assigning one full-time principal to two school buildings. In such instances the principal would share his services between the two buildings, usually on a daily basis.[34]

The trend away from teaching to supervising principals has been rather phenomenal in recent years, as Table 4 shows. In the ten year period from 1932-33 to 1942-43 the ratio of teaching principals to supervising principals remained fairly constant. However, the decade of 1942-43 to 1952-53 marked a period of the exodus of the teaching principal and the emergence of the supervising principal.

This marked shift to the supervising principal can be explained in two ways. First, the United States was going through a population explosion and as the school buildings began bulging at the seams it became evident that more time was needed by building principals for administration and supervision. As new schools were constructed the attendance areas were

---

[33]"The Elementary-School Principalship — Today and Tomorrow," *Twenty-Seventh Yearbook.* (Washington: The National Elementary Principal, National Education Association, September, 1948), p. 151.

[34]Roscoe V. Cramer and Otto E. Domian, *Administration and Supervision in the Elementary School* (New York: Harper & Brothers, 1960), p. 366.

TABLE 4

The number of teaching and supervising elementary school principals in the urban cities of the United States.

Year	Teaching Principals	Supervising Principals	Total Number of Urban Principals
1932–1933	7,682	7,449	15,131
1942–1943	7,040	8,542	15,582
1952–1953	4,923	14,651	19,574

Adapted from Roscoe V. Cramer and Otto E. Domian, *Administration and Supervision in the Elementary School.* (New York: Harper and Brothers, 1960), p. 366. Reprinted by permission of Harper & Row, Publishers, Inc.

made larger and the buildings were built large enough to house sufficient teachers to make the employment of a supervising principal possible. Second, a move toward excellence in teaching in the elementary school began to emerge and educators began to recognize the supervising principal as the most likely person to lead this movement. Yauch has well stated this point:

> One individual in the educational hierarchy is so situated that he can make immediate and profitable contribution to the improvement of school practices — the school principal. Regardless of the quality and character of the teachers he gets from the teacher education institutions, regardless of attitudes and predispositions of the community, and even regardless of the status and attitudes of present faculty members, he can begin at once to provide teachers with vital experiences that will progressively increase their ability to guide lives of boys and girls toward more effective democratic living.[35]

THE PRINCIPAL'S WORK

The work of the elementary school principal is extremely varied. He may be thought of as a liason person among the pupils, the teachers, the central office staff, and the community. It is his responsibility to help each of these groups become a functioning organism and in so doing create a school learning environment which is conducive to pupil growth and achievement in the academics as well as in wholesome social living. This is an almost monumental task. In order to accomplish this the principal must be an expert in his profession and a master at human relations. The

---

[35]Wilbur A. Yauch, *Improving Human Relations in Elementary Schools* (New York: Harper & Brothers, 1949), p. 10.

people with whom he works to establish a good learning environment in his school are shown in the graph of Figure 8.

It is interesting to note how the average full-time supervising principal spends his day. According to the *Twenty-Seventh Yearbook* of the NEA, the average principal spends 29.3 per cent of his time in administration; 24.1 per cent in supervision; 14.8 per cent working with pupil personnel; 15.1 per cent performing clerical duties, 2.3 per cent teaching; 9.3 per cent working in the community, and 5.1 per cent of his time in miscellaneous endeavors.[36] The study reveals, however, that the principals thought that ideally they should spend 37.3 rather than 24.1 per cent of their time in supervision and reduce their clerical duties from 15.1 to 3.5 per cent.[37] If the principal is to be freed of the minutia of clerical responsibilities so he can perform his job of instructional supervision, then sufficient clerical assistance must be provided him.

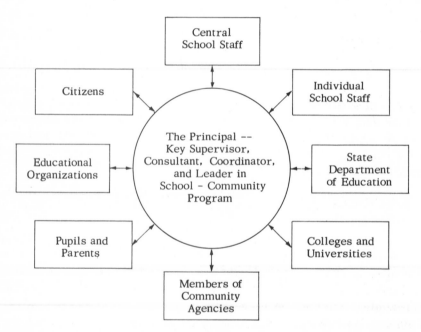

Figure 8. Human relations of a modern elementary principal. Adapted from Roscoe V. Cramer and Otto E. Domian, *Administration and Supervision in the Elementary School,* (New York: Harper and Brothers, 1960) p. 377. Reprinted by permission of Harper and Row, Publishers, Inc.

---

[36]"The Elementary-School-Principal — Today and Tomorrow," *Twenty-Seventh Yearbook, op. cit.,* p. 87.
[37]*Ibid.,* p. 90.

The principal and his building faculty have become the key to success in developing a curriculum suited to the needs of their children. In former years the responsibility for curriculum planning was thought to rest more or less with the central administrative staff and their corps of supervisors and consultants. Recent philosophy holds, however, that the elementary principal is the most feasible curriculum consultant and supervisor in the classroom, school, and community. Because of his proximity to pupil needs, the teachers, and the neighborhood he is in the unique position of being able to develop the curriculum upon the basis of student needs and coordinate its administration. Cramer and Domian summarize the principal's role in this effort well in stating that: "There can be no change of curriculum unless there is a change in people — teachers, children, and parents — in each elementary school. The local school unit becomes the most feasible place to make curriculum improvement."[38]

UTILIZING SPECIAL SERVICE PERSONNEL

In his new-found role as curriculum planner and developer, the principal brings to bear all of the teacher resources at his disposal and then has access to help from special service personnel from the central office staff as well as consultants from teacher education institutions and the state department of education. From these sources he receives valuable assistance in curriculum work. As he coordinates the work of these professional people to create a program that will develop to a maximum the innate capacities of the children, he must be an effective educational leader and a shrewd human relations tactician.

CURRICULUM ASSISTANCE FROM THE CENTRAL ADMINISTRATIVE OFFICE

As the principal and the teachers work for curriculum improvement and development in their instructional program, they may call upon many special service personnel to assist them. These personnel may come from the local central administrative office, resource persons assigned to their own building, the state department of education, or teacher education institutions. The function of each of these personnel is different, but the purposes are the same — improvement of the elementary curriculum.

THE CURRICULUM DIRECTOR

The person charged with the direct responsibility for curriculum development within a given school system is usually known as the director of

---

[38]Cramer and Domian, *op. cit.*, p. 382.

curriculum. Other names given to this office are: assistant superintendent of schools in charge of instruction, director of instruction, director of elementary education, and curriculum coordinator. In smaller school systems a person known as the general elementary supervisor may be employed for the purpose of developing the curriculum. Regardless of the name given to the office, its responsibilities and duties remain basically the same. The curriculum director works with the various building principals and their faculties under the direction of the superintendent of schools and the board of education to devise a curriculum in keeping with the needs of the children,. community, and contemporary society.[39]

Sharp identified five major areas of activities of the curriculum director. In descending order on the basis of time spent on each, he listed them as follows:

1. Curriculum improvement activities.
2. Activities to *facilitate* the curriculum improvement program.
3. Personal-professional growth.
4. Preparation and provision of resources.
5. Community relations.[40]

SPECIAL SUPERVISORS

In the performance of these duties the curriculum director therefore will have many coordinative and administrative responsibilities. To assist in this work, some school systems provide a staff of special subject supervisors in such curricular areas as art, library, music, physical education and health, reading, science, and speech. The extent to which curriculum directors have these specialists at their disposal nationally can be seen in a 1959 survey conducted by the United States Office of Education in cities with 2,500 or more inhabitants as shown in Table 5. The results of this survey pointed out quite clearly that the most commonly available specialist was in the area of music. The least available specialist was found to be in the science curriculum area.

The duties of the special subject teachers or supervisors are many and varied. Generally, they work under the direction of the curriculum director in cooperation with the building principal to upgrade the instructional program of the school. Gwynn has identified their major duties as:

---

[39]Aubrey Haan, *Elementary School Curriculum: Theory and Research* (Boston: Allyn and Bacon, Inc., 1961), p. 347.

[40]George M. Sharp, "Curriculum Coordinators Study Their Jobs," *Educational Leadership,* Volume XII, No. 8, May, 1955, p. 465.

TABLE 5

Special subject assistance in urban places with populations above 2,500 by U. S. totals and percentages.

Program	Per Cent with Specialists Available	Per Cent without Specialists Available
Music	89. 3	10. 7
Physical Education and Health	52. 4	47. 6
Art	51. 5	48. 5
Speech	39. 1	60. 9
Library	32. 7	67. 3
Reading	22. 8	77. 2
Science	8. 0	92. 0

Adapted from Stuart E. Dean, *Elementary School Administration.* (Washington, D. C.: U. S. Department of Health, Education, and Welfare, Office of Education, 1960), p. 76. Reprinted by permission of U. S. Department of Health, Education, and Welfare, Office of Education.

1. To aid the teacher and the principal in understanding children better.
2. To help the teacher to develop and improve individually and as a co-operating member of the school staff.
3. To assist school personnel in making more interesting and effective use of materials of instruction.
4. To help the teacher to improve his methods of teaching.
5. To make the specialized personnel in the school system of maximum assistance to the teacher.
6. To assist the teacher in making the best possible appraisal of the student.
7. To stimulate the teacher to evaluate his own planning, work, and progress.
8. To help the teacher achieve poise and a sense of security in his work and in the community.
9. To stimulate faculty groups to plan curriculum improvements and carry them out co-operatively, and to assume a major responsibility in co-ordinating this work and in improving teacher education in service.
10. To acquaint the school administration, the teachers, the students, and the public with the work and progress of the school.[41]

[41]Minor J. Gwynn, *Theory and Practice of Supervision* (New York: Dodd, Mead & Company, © 1961), pp. 27-32. Reprinted by permission of Dodd, Mead & Company, Inc.

As supervisors perform the functions enumerated by Gwynn, they should be careful to use procedures acceptable to the principal and his staff. In the past, too many teachers have thought of a "supervisor" as being a "snoopervisor," which resulted in poor relationships. Currently, however, supervisors are being thought of more in terms of being consultants. This new concept of the supervisor's role affects the manner in which he works but does not change the end result of his efforts. Shuster and Wetzler have well stated this modern concept of supervision in the following illustration:

> . . . one principal of a large elementary school planned with his faculty how they would make optimum use of their music consultant. The curriculum director and two elementary supervisors were invited to this planning session. In previous years this particular school had had a music teacher who taught the music in the traditional "pigeon hole" fashion, spending thirty minutes a day in each room twice a week. The following plan was cooperatively constructed during the planning session through the leadership efforts of the principal:
>
> The teachers requested that the music consultant arrive at their school each Monday morning at 8:15. Those teachers who wanted the services of the consultant were to meet with her at this time. It was thought that such a provision would help the consultant plan her work in advance around the needs of the teachers. During the morning meetings the teachers could seek help in getting materials which would fit into units that were being taught in social studies and other areas. Specific appointments could be made with the consultant for classroom visitation. Requests could be made for help in teaching songs and dances, or in furthering the music experiences through other activities.
>
> The music consultant was elated with the plans which had been cooperatively developed. She realized that her visits would now have a purpose that would be known to both her and the teachers.[42]

This type of planning between the teachers and the supervisor provides for effective utilization of staff time and results in improved learning experiences for the children. In addition, it should create greater rapport between the teachers and the supervisor. As this team spirit emerges with a common purpose to provide better educational experiences for the pupils, the supervisor should gain acceptance and status while the teachers grow in their ability to accept and utilize his ideas.

THE GENERAL SUPERVISOR

A professional person working out of the central office who deals with improvement of all curricular areas is commonly considered to be a general supervisor. The larger metropolitan school systems may have one or more

---

[42]Albert Shuster and Wilson F. Wetzler, *Leadership in Elementary School Administration and Supervision* (Boston: Houghton Mifflin Company, 1958), p. 165.

general supervisors on their staff who work with the curriculum director. In each county school system if the enrollment is sufficient to warrant a full-time general supervisor one usually is provided. In school systems where the enrollment is not large enough, two or more systems may band together to employ an itinerant general supervisor who shares his services among the schools and works with the administrative staff of each system.

The work of the general supervisor is similar to that of the curriculum director. His major function is to aid the teacher in improving classroom instruction by helping provide appropriate materials and implementing effective instructional plans. This work has been hampered somewhat, particularly among older teachers, by the early days of supervision in which its main purpose was held to be inspectoral and rating in determining the success or failure of each teacher.[43] As a result of this unfortunate use of supervision, many teachers have acquired a "supervisor phobia." This modern concept of supervision, however, is one of democratic leadership geared to promoting desirable pupil outcomes through teacher-supervisor cooperation. Byers and Irish have summed up this situation well in stating, "If teachers can overcome their unwarranted fears of supervisors and accept these skilled people as members of the cooperative team engaged in providing better education for boys and girls, they will find that they receive much professional stimulation."[44]

RESOURCE PERSONNEL ASSIGNED TO THE SCHOOL BUILDING

In many elementary schools there are resource personnel such as the librarian, school nurse, visiting teacher, and guidance counselor who are assigned to a given building to work with the principal and teachers in various capacities. If the individual school building has enough pupils to warrant these resource personnel on a full-time basis such arrangements are usually made. If not, then several smaller schools usually share their services and they are thought of as itinerant resource persons. Each of these persons is a specialist in his field and works under the direction of the principal in cooperation with the classroom teacher to perform his services.

THE SCHOOL LIBRARIAN

One of the persons with whom the classroom teacher works to effect desirable pupil learnings is the school librarian. The modern conception of the

---

[43]Loretta Byers and Elizabeth Irish, *Success in Student Teaching* (Boston: D. C. Heath and Company, 1961), pp. 170-1.
[44]*Ibid.*, p. 171.

librarian is that he is a resource person in charge ot the library or materials center who works with the classroom teacher to undergird the instructional program. In fulfilling this role, the librarian should take his services to the classroom teacher. The benefits derived from the librarian who works in this manner are many. First, he reads widely and knows what materials are available either in the school library or from outside sources such as the state department of education. Second, the teacher is so busy with the minutia of classroom work that he cannot be expected to be well informed on all available materials which would up-grade his classroom instruction. Third, the librarian who works with teachers in a specific location knows what units of study are in progress and which ones are anticipated in the near future. He therefore is in a good position to plan with the teachers how to effect the greatest use of the available instructional media. A fourth reason is that the librarian should be better able to utilize the physical facilities of the library if he takes his services to the teachers to ascertain their needs and then map out a schedule to provide for them. The librarian is truly an assistant to the teacher. They work together to develop a coordinated and well-integrated program of learning experiences for the children.

Since the modern librarian is a resource person who makes the services of the library available to the individual classrooms, he should constantly be on the lookout for ways he can perform his work. Otto has suggested some very practical methods in stating that:

> . . . each classroom can be supplied as frequently as necessary with temporary loan collections of the books which will be in greatest demand by the majority of pupils while a particular unit or activity is in progress. Pictures, bulletins, slides, films, and recordings can be loaned to the classroom for shorter periods of time. These several types of resources will enable the teacher to develop with children the kind of teaching that modern schools desire. The class as a group will not have regularly scheduled periods in the library each week; instead, the whole class will go to the library as the need arises for finding information not available in the classroom collection. Individual pupils and small committees will go to the library whenever their special assignments call for supplementary materials and information. The responsibility for promoting the various objectives in reading, instruction in the use of books and the library, and the guidance of individual children's reading will rest with the classroom teacher, but the teacher will make many demands upon the librarian for assistance in these matters.[45]

The librarian as a resource person should keep abreast of available materials appropriate to the curriculum. As he works with the classroom

---

[45]Otto, *op. cit.*, pp. 409-10.

teacher to develop the instructional program, he should call attention to pertinent materials for a given unit in social studies, science or some other area of the curriculum. In so doing, he moves to fulfill his role as a resource person to the individual teacher as well as the entire staff.

THE SCHOOL NURSE

Another resource person in the elementary school who works with the classroom teachers to provide health education and services is the school nurse. According to Tipple, she works with the entire faculty to accomplish the following school health objectives:

1. To help every child attain the highest state of physical, mental, social, and emotional health of which he is capable.
2. To help every child avail himself fully of his opportunities for education.
3. To utilize the educational facilities of the school to promote the development of sound attitudes, habits, and health knowledge and to help boys and girls become increasingly self-directing in matters pertaining to personal and community health.[46]

The school nurse should work very closely with the teachers, the parents, and the family physicians to effect the attainment of these school health objectives. Her work will involve at least three general areas: (1) she will conduct health screenings in such fields as vision, hearing, and oral hygiene, using the results as a basis for making necessary referrals for professional diagnosis and treatment; (2) she will attempt to determine the health status of the pupils and discover problems which may be utilized for purposes of health education; and (3) she will endeavor to use the various health screenings to serve as educational devices to impress upon students the importance of periodical routine health examinations.[47] In performing these broad general duties, the school nurse will be called upon for many smaller specific activities as part of her job. Some of these duties as enumerated by Tipple are:

1. She develops an acceptable procedure to care for emergencies such as illness and injury which occur under school jurisdiction.
2. She is usually responsible for first-aid instruction to the staff.
3. She emphasizes the health education program to teachers, parents, and students in order to promote positive health practices to prevent and control communicable diseases.

---

[46]Dorothy C. Tipple, "The Changing Role of the School Nurse," *Teachers College Record,* Volume 59, No. 4, (January, 1958), p. 191.
[47]*Ibid.,* p. 192.

4. In working with handicapped children, the nurse shares with others the responsibility for identifying such children and planning necessary medical and educational services. Her primary role is one of interpretation of the health needs of these boys and girls to the parents and school staff.

5. The nurse advises on health aspects of such matters as lighting, heat, ventilation, seating, and cleanliness of buildings in order to provide a good emotional climate for learning.

6. The nurse serves as a consultant or a resource person in the regular program of health instruction. She helps to correlate health service and the program of health education. She serves on curriculum committees to assist in coordinating the over-all health education program and in integrating it with other areas of the curriculum. She may teach specific units or parts of units in areas in which she is especially skilled as a nurse, not as isolated topics but as part of an on going planned health education program.

7. The nurse also serves as a consultant to the administrator and the board of education in many matters pertaining to school health. She may act as the school's representative in community health activities.

8. She assists in planning programs for teacher health and may have specific responsibilities in relation to periodic examinations for school personnel.

9. She participates in in-service education programs for teachers and in adult education programs.

10. The school nurse shares in policy making and program planning. She cooperates with the administrative staff to develop a local health manual of policies and procedures.

11. The nurse is an active participant in school and community health councils, and in other activities to assist in coordination of school health services.[48]

The school nurse is a key staff person on the elementary faculty and provides a vital service to the instructional program. Like the librarian, she should carry her services to the teachers. The teachers in turn should recognize her capacity for assisting them in many educational areas and, therefore, avail themselves of her services.

THE VISITING TEACHER

Many elementary schools are now provided with the services of a visiting teacher. This resource person works closely with the teacher to help problem children make adequate school adjustments. The visiting teacher has the special training and time necessary to deal with problem cases and is the liaison person between the school and the home.

---

[48]*Ibid.*, pp. 192-3.

Whenever the classroom teacher notes that he has a child who is experiencing difficulty in adjusting to the school environment and is unable to remedy the situation, he should refer the problem case through the building principal to the visiting teacher for action. The visiting teacher is in a better position and has more time to work with the home to establish reasons for the pupil's failure to adjust to school life and to chart out a plan of action to alleviate the situation.

The functions of the visiting teacher are varied and many. The American Association of Visiting Teachers, as cited by Shuster and Wetzler, have suggested at least four distinct functions of the position which are: (1) counseling with pupils, (2) counseling with teachers, (3) counseling with parents, and (4) coordinating community agencies as needed to further pupil adjustment.[49]

The elementary classroom teacher should recognize immediately the benefits which are to be derived through working harmoniously with the visiting teacher to achieve improved pupil adjustment. The visiting teacher is in a position to establish a close working relationship between the school and the home, thereby providing valuable assistance to the classroom teacher without assuming the teacher's role in pupil guidance. The visiting teacher also may call for assistance from various community social agencies, such as the Child Guidance Clinic, which are known for their ability to work with special problems that are outside the scope of the school's capacity to solve alone.

THE SCHOOL GUIDANCE COUNSELOR

Regrettably very few elementary schools are provided with the services of a trained guidance counselor. With the emphasis that modern educators are placing on increased early identification of pupil strengths and weaknesses, however, it is logical to assume that more and more guidance counselors will be added to the staffs of the elementary schools in the future.

In the school organization, the guidance counselor has a multiplicity of duties. Seven specific areas over which he has authority for responsibility have been enumerated by Foster as follows:

(1) the over-all school guidance program, (2) counseling, (3) testing and individual analysis, (4) record keeping, (5) provision of occupational and educational information materials, (6) consultant services to other staff members, and (7) general leadership responsibilities for the student personnel program.[50]

---

[49]Shuster and Wetzler, *op. cit.*, p. 296.
[50]Charles Foster, *Guidance for Today's Schools* (New York: Ginn and Company, 1957), p. 21.

The 1955 Yearbook of the Association for Supervision and Curriculum Development identified the following responsibilities of the guidance specialists:

> To help plan and supervise the gathering of such facts as are essential to the understanding and guidance of each individual pupil in the school system.
>
> To help teachers interpret and use these facts (assembled in individual cumulative records) in solving their problems in the guidance of children.
>
> To assume direct responsibility in the guidance of the child only when principals and teachers are unable to solve the child's problems.
>
> To coordinate and integrate the work of the teacher and the various specialists who deal with the child — that is, the guidance consultant should be the liaison worker who unifies all the efforts which school personnel put forth for the child's welfare.
>
> To help teachers and parents plan and carry on a continuous program of education to increase their knowledge and understanding of children.
>
> To help parents and teachers discover the implications and applications of such knowledge for ways of dealing with children in homes and schools.
>
> To help teachers and parents understand the dynamic interrelationships between guidance and instruction, to the end that mutual adjustment of school to pupil and pupil to school may be a continuously evolving process.[51]

Although guidance is primarily the responsibility of the classroom teacher it is supplemented by the specialist who works with individual pupils or teachers, or perhaps with teacher groups, to help them understand child behavior better. The ultimate goal of guidance for both the conselor and the teacher has been well stated by Gordon:

> The focus of elementary guidance is the individual child. The goal is not therapy, but self-development. It is more than just good teaching, because it recognizes and emphasizes the self-development of the child in addition to the increase in skill and knowledge. Its concern is to enable each child to feel worthy, to release his capacity for growth, to come to terms with both himself and his environment.[52]

The guidance counselor should become a vital person in the elementary school. The classroom teacher, by availing himself of his services, can find specialized assistance in pupil counseling, testing and individual analysis, and consultation leading to a deeper understanding of child development.

---

[51]Association for Supervision and Curriculum Development, *Guidance in the Curriculum* (Washington: The Association, 1955), p. 104.

[52]Ira J. Gordon, "Elementary Guidance Just Good Teaching?" *The Instructor.* Volume LXX, Number 7, (March, 1961), p. 113 © 1961 by F. A. Owens Publishing Company; reprinted from *The Instructor* by permission.

CURRICULUM ASSISTANCE FROM THE STATE DEPARTMENT OF EDUCATION

Another type of special service available to the elementary school staff in development of the curriculum is the state curriculum consultant. Basically there are three roles of service provided by a state curriculum consultant: liaison duties between the agency he represents and the local school district, an expert in curriculum development, and a change agent.[53]

STATE CONSULTANT AS A LIAISON PERSON

The curriculum consultant, as a liaison person, assumes a strategic position between the agency which he represents and the local school district. The major portion of all communication between the school district and the state agency concerning curriculum matters is normally channeled through his office. He is thoroughly informed on all state department rules and regulations which will affect the program of studies of the public schools with which he works. He must be able to identify the needs and objectives of the public schools under his jurisdiction and help them bring their plans to fruition in harmony with state department requirements.

This liaison function is a continuous one in which he works with the schools as much as is necessary through the years. The degree to which he works with them may vary, however, depending upon such factors as new programs instituted by the state, the desire of the individual school to upgrade its program and utilize his services, and the amount of time which he has to devote to curriculum improvement.

STATE CONSULTANT AS AN EXPERT

The state curriculum consultant's second role, that of being an expert, is one of special service. He is recognized as being an outside authority who is called in by the local school district to help identify areas wherein curriculum improvements are necesary and to suggest implementation procedures for effecting them. His opinions are considered to be highly objective and his advice weighs heavily upon decisions affecting curricular changes. As long as he does not identify himself with any local group or faction, his status leadership position as an impartial expert will be maintained and his work will be effective.

---

[53]Committee of the Oregon Association for Supervision and Curriculum Development, *Being a Curriculum Consultant,* (Salem, Oregon: State Department of Education, 1960), p. 3.

STATE CONSULTANT AS A CHANGE AGENT

As an agent of change, the consultant works with the local school district on curriculum problems. His work in effecting the solution of these problems is twofold. First, the consultant assists the local school's staff in finding their own solutions to their problems. Second, he suggests, if necessary, experiences calculated to change the concepts and understandings of a given group of individuals as a preliminary condition to curricular change.[54]

Lewin has described change as a three-step process: (1) unfreezing the *status quo*, (2) moving to another level of operation with new ideas, and (3) solidifying operations at the new level.[55] In analyzing these three steps, the role of the curriculum consultant therefore is seen as a multiplicity of functions. He is responsible for disturbing the *status quo* situation by unfreezing the current situation so that new ideas or programs can be instigated. Once this new curricular approach has been established he is the person responsible for re-establishing former stability, thereby insuring some permanency of change.[56]

CURRICULUM ASSISTANCE FROM TEACHER EDUCATION INSTITUTIONS

Teacher education institutions assist the local school district in at least three ways in up-grading their curriculum. First, they prepare prospective teachers in the latest methodology and equip them with up-to-date subject matter in order that they will be able to make a real contribution to the faculty when employed. Second, their professors are available to work as resource persons or consultants with the local school as opportunity permits. Third, many teacher education institutions have curriculum research centers from which the local school system may receive frequent curriculum publications or engage in action or scientific educational research.

EDUCATING PROSPECTIVE TEACHERS

In all likelihood, the greatest influence the teacher education institutions exert upon the improvement of the elementary curriculum is that of providing thoroughly prepared teachers. As these beginning teachers assume their new duties in the schools, they bring with them a wealth of new ideas and an abundance of enthusiasm which are the lifeblood of a dy-

---

[54]*Ibid.*, pp. 4-5.
[55]Kurt Lewin, "Frontiers in Group Dynamics," *Human Relations*, Volume I, Number 1, (1947, pages 1-140), p. 34.
[56]*Ibid.*, p. 5.

namic school program. Generally they are a very adaptable group of individuals amenable to any worthy change in curriculum which the supervisory or administrative staff deems advisable.

PROFESSORS AS CONSULTANTS

Professors from teacher education institutions provide a valuable service to public schools as consultants. Many school systems make it a practice to concentrate annually on at least one phase of the elementary curriculum in such areas as science, arithmetic, reading, or the social studies. In so doing, they frequently engage a professor from the teacher education institution to serve as a consultant in their intensified effort to improve this curricular area. In the larger metropolitan schools there may be several university consultants retained to work with the staff on curriculum improvement problems.

In order that the school system can effect maximum use of the consultant's ideas, time, and experience, careful plans must be mapped out prior to his visit. Bradford has suggested three points to consider in utilizing his services. These preparatory considerations are:

1. Desired results from consultant use.
   a. The group should receive definite assistance in terms of their problems.
   b. The group should be further aided by the consultant in their growth as a group and as individuals in their ability to solve problems.
   c. The consultant should, in recompense for his services, have an opportunity to learn more about the problems of people in the area of his concern and should grow in his ability in the role of the consultant.
2. The role of the consultant.
   a. To help the group uncover problems and to delineate the specific aspects of the problems.
   b. To bring a background of information and experience to the group to aid in the diagnosis and solution of problems.
   c. To bring alternative points of view which may help in the thorough determination of problems and the adequate solution of problems.
   d. To bring specific information to the group where needed.
   e. To help the group test their diagnosis of problems and their tentative solutions.
   f. To help the group evaluate the process of their own group thinking.

Obviously the role of the consultant should not involve:
   a. Setting too high a level of aspiration for the group activity.
   b. Dominating the group by insisting on bringing in information where not needed.

    c. Perverting the group to the consultant's way of thinking.
3. Specific steps in using the consultant.
    a. Opportunities should be planned to enable the group to think through and analyze its problems and to determine exactly the kind of help they wish to secure from the consultant.
    b. Opportunities should be provided for the consultant to be thoroughly prepared in terms of the degree of awareness of these problems, the depth of thinking and total experience of the group.[57]

The university consultant should recognize that his primary function is helping the school staff study its needs and problems, not criticizing existing local practices. Regardless of how well informed the consultant is on education in general, he should at all times realize that the professional staff of the school knows more about their own circumstances and conditions than he does.[58] He therefore should consider his role and function as being purely consultatory.

THE UNIVERSITY CURRICULUM RESEARCH CENTERS

Many teacher education institutions have curriculum research centers to which individual school systems may belong and from which valuable information is obtained for curriculum improvement. An example of these curriculum centers is that of the School of Education of the University of Connecticut. From their Curriculum Center files they have "available to school systems over twelve thousand pamphlets, guides, research studies, and descriptions of practices carried on in schools all over the country."[59] In addition to these services, they conduct upon request curriculum laboratories, clinics, or workshops throughout the state for the local schools in an effort to improve their conditions for learning.[60] Such research centers serve as reservoirs of valuable curriculum materials and research findings which schools may draw upon to give guidance and direction as they seek to up-grade their instructional programs.

Another function of these curriculum centers is educational research. Normally a center will have as its director a university professor who is

---

[57]Leland P. Bradford, "The Use of Psychodrama for Group Consultants," *Sociatry,* A Journal of Group and Intergroup Therapy, Vol. I, pp. 193-4. J. L. Moreno, M.D., Editor: Beacon House, Inc., Publisher.

[58]Edward A. Krug, *Curriculum Planning* (New York: Harper & Brothers, Publishers, 1957), p. 296.

[59]Philo T. Pritzkau, *Dynamics of Curriculum Improvement* (Englewood Cliffs, N. J.: Prentice-Hall, 1959), p. 21.

[60]*Ibid.,* p. 21.

skilled in research. He is provided with a staff of competent researchers which, with the aid of the member school systems, engages in curricular research significant to the membership of the center.

MAXIMIZING AVAILABLE CURRICULUM ASSISTANCE

The wise use of special service personnel in curriculum development rests with each elementary principal and his staff of teachers. As pointed out in this chapter, curriculum assistance is available from the central administrative office, resource personnel assigned to their own building, state department curriculum consultants, and curriculum specialists from teacher education institutions. Each of these special service personnel is qualified to provide a unique curriculum service to the principal and the individual teacher or groups of teachers. The extent to which they are utilized in curriculum improvement will be largely dependent upon the desire of the principal and his teachers to avail themselves of their services.

SUMMARY

In this chapter the premise that "the curriculum should dictate the type of organizational pattern utilized in the elementary school" has been set forth. Varying aspects of this premise were examined. It was pointed out that although this theory is almost universally accepted by educators, more often than not the organizational pattern has dictated the type of curriculum experiences the children will have.

The graded elementary school was examined as to its strengths and weaknesses. Its simplicity of organizational design was studied as one of the prime reasons for its longevity. Its failure to provide a systematic program of continuous pupil progress was carefully scrutinized. Other programs which theoretically insure continuous pupil progress, such as the Platoon Plan, Winnetka and McDade Plans, Dalton Plan, Nongraded Plan, Team Teaching Plan, and the Dual Progress Plan, were thoroughly examined. Research was cited which tended to substantiate the postulate that it is not the organizational pattern which insures satisfactory learning experiences for children, but rather the teachers' acceptance of and identity with that plan and their willingness to make it work which is the more important criterion.

The principal was depicted as the instructional leader of the elementary school. He is currently being thought of more in terms of an instructional supervisor than an administrator. His chief work should deal with the development of the curriculum. As he performs this task in cooperation with his staff he will call on numerous special service personnel for assistance. From the central office he will have the help of the curriculum director, special supervisors, or a general supervisor. Special resource personnel will likely be assigned to his building to aid in curriculum improvement. Most prominent among these resource people are the librarian, school nurse, visiting teacher, and guidance counselor. The principal and his staff may also receive curricular assistance from outside consultants from the state department of education or teacher education institutions.

In the final analysis the extent to which curriculum improvement is effected and a functional plan of organization is adopted will be dependent upon the principal and his teachers. The amount of utilization of special service personnel is likewise in their hands.

QUESTIONS FOR DISCUSSION

1. One of the major goals of the elementary school is to develop a program of continuous pupil progress for each child. Which is more important in attaining this worthy objective, the school's organizational pattern or the types of learning experiences planned for children? Explain.
2. Many educators are agreed that the most effective child guidance service the school provides is rendered by the classroom teacher and not by the guidance counselor. What is meant by this assertion?
3. The nongraded school plan of organization has frequently been attacked by educators who contend that there is no such thing as an ungraded or nongraded organizational pattern. They contend that most so-called "nongraded" programs simply have the grade labels removed and that teachers still use the grade level textbooks in the same manner in which they are used in the graded organizational pattern. What is your interpretation of this issue?
4. Some teachers contend that they teach subject matter. Other teachers contend that they teach children. What different philosophies are inherent in each of these statements? Would a subject matter oriented teacher achieve more success in a departmental plan of organization than would an activity or experience oriented teacher? Conversely would the activity oriented teacher function more effectively in the self-contained classroom than would the subject matter oriented teacher? Explain.
5. What is the relative importance of teacher personality in achieving teaching success in team teaching as compared to other organizational patterns?

TOPICS FOR RESEARCH

1. Devise a flow chart illustrating the types of special service elementary school personnel considered ideal for a maximum program of instruction. Develop job descriptions for each of these personnel.
2. Study schedules in schools whereby the building principal and his teachers have effectively utilized the services of the special service personnel identified in Topic 1.
3. Visit elementary schools which are utilizing the nongraded, team teaching, departmentalized, and self-contained organizational patterns. Determine to what extent these organization plans provide for continuous pupil progress.

BIBLIOGRAPHY

Association for Supervision and Curriculum Development. *Guidance in the Curriculum.* Washington: The Association, 1955.

BRADFORD, LELAND P. "The Use of Psychodrama for Group Consultants," *Sociatry,* Volume 1, Number 2, June, 1947, pp. 193-194.

BROWNELL, JOHN A., AND HARRIS A. TAYLOR. "Theoretical Perspectives for Teaching Teams," *Phi Delta Kappan,* Volume XLIII, Number 4, January, 1962, pp. 151-153.

BYERS, LORETTA, AND ELIZABETH IRISH. *Success in Student Teaching.* Boston: D. C. Heath & Company, 1961.

COOK, DESMOND L. "The Hawthorne Effect in Educational Research," *Phi Delta Kappan.* Volume XLIV, Number 3, December, 1962, pp. 116-8.

CRAMER, ROSCOE V., AND OTTO E. DOMIAN. *Administration and Supervision in the Elementary School.* New York: Harper & Brothers, 1960.

Committee of the Oregon Association for Supervision and Curriculum Development, *Being a Curriculum Consultant.* Salem: Oregon State Department of Education, 1960.

DEAN, STUART E. *Elementary School Administration and Organization: A National Survey of Practices and Policies.* U. S. Department of Health, Education, and Welfare, Office of Education, Bulletin 1960, No. 11. Washington, D.C.; Superintendent of Documents, Government Printing Office, 1960, pp. 30-31.

FOSTER, CHARLES R. *Guidance for Today's Schools.* New York: Ginn and Company, 1957.

GORDON, IRA J. "Elementary Guidance Just Good Teaching?" *The Instructor.* Volume LXX, Number 7, March, 1961, p. 113.

GOODLAD, JOHN I., AND ROBERT H. ANDERSON. *The Nongraded Elementary School.* New York: Harcourt, Brace & World, Inc., 1959.

GOODLAD, JOHN I. "Classroom Organization," *Encyclopedia of Educational Research.* Chester W. Harris (ed.), New York: The Macmillan Company, 1960.

GWYNN, J. MINOR. *Theory and Practice of Supervision.* New York: Dodd, Mead, and Company, 1961.

HAAN, AUBREY. *Elementary School Curriculum: Theory and Research.* Boston: Allyn and Bacon, Inc., 1961.

JARVIS, OSCAR T. *Time Allotments and Pupil Achievement in the Intermediate Elementary Grades.* University of Houston: Bureau of Education Research and Services, Research Study No. 8, November, 1962, Published Doctoral Dissertation.

KRUG, EDWARD A. *Curriculum Planning.* New York: Harper & Brothers Publishers, 1957.

LEWIN, KURT. "Frontiers In Group Dynamics," *Human Relations,* Volume I, Number 1, 1947, pages 1-140, p. 34.

OTTO, HENRY J. *Elementary-School Organization and Administration.* Third edition. New York: Appleton-Century-Crofts, 1954.

PARKHURST, HELEN. "The Dalton Laboratory Plan," *Twenty-Fourth, Yearbook of the National Society for the Study of Education,* Part II, Bloomington, Illinois, Public Schools Publishing Company, 1925, pp. 83-92.

PRITZKAU, PHILO T. *Dynamics of Curriculum Improvement.* Englewood Cliffs, N. J.: Prentice-Hall, 1959.

STODDARD, GEORGE D. *The Dual Progress Plan.* New York: Harper and Brothers, 1961.

SHARP, GEORGE M. "Curriculum Coordinators Study Their Jobs," *Educational Leadership.* Volume XII, Number 8, May, 1955, p. 465.

SHUSTER, ALBERT, AND WILSON F. WETZLER. *Leadership in Elementary School Administration and Supervision.* Boston: Houghton Mifflin Company, 1958.

"The Elementary-School Principalship — Today and Tomorrow," *Twenty-Seventh Yearbook.* Washington D. C.: The National Elementary Principal, National Education Association, September, 1948, pp. 87, 90, 151.

TIPPLE, DOROTHY C. "The Changing Role of the School Nurse," *Teachers College Record.* Volume 59, No. 4, January, 1958, pp. 191-193.

WASHBURNE, C. W. *Adjusting the School to the Child.* New York: World Book Company, 1932.

WASHBURNE, C. W. "Burk's Individual System as Developed at Winnetka," *Twenty-Fourth Yearbook of the National Society for the Study of Education, Part II,* Bloomington, Illinois: Public Schools Publishing Company, 1925, pp. 79-82.

YAUCH, WILBUR A. *Improving Human Relations in Elementary Schools.* New York: Harper & Brothers Publishers, 1949.

If we believe that the prime value of education in our fast-evolving world is its power to enable students to invent and to create new learnings, to prepare them to test, absorb, and use in the future things which nobody knows today, then the goal of the twentieth century teacher must be, more than ever, to implant a love of knowledge and the desire to expand it, and to create in the student a climate of receptivity for knowledge that does not yet exist.

Laurence B. Johnson

The language laboratory represents one of the recent innovations in the elementary school.

Chapter **3**

Innovations in
Elementary School Curriculum

Elementary school systems have great latitude in establishing their individual curriculum in our democratic society. There is no prescribed federal curriculum to which they must subscribe and the requirements set by most of the state boards of education are only minimal. The local system therefore is afforded the opportunity of determining in large measure its own course of study to accomplish certain commonly accepted educational objectives usually referred to in the elementary school as knowledge, understanding, attitudes, appreciations, and skills.

The word "curriculum" means different things to each teacher. Some of them refer to it as the composite subjects which are taught. Others take a more liberal view by holding to the position that the curriculum involves all the experiences which children engage in that are directed by the school. The latter definition is the accepted one for this text. There is no mistaking the point that content is important in curriculum planning. However, the "curriculum includes much more than content," as Ragan has rightly stated; "it includes teacher-pupil relationships, methods of teaching, evaluation procedures, the so-called extracurricular activities — in short, the whole life and program of the school."[1] A modern view of the curriculum therefore suggests that knowledges, competencies, and social amenities necessary for living in our democracy are learned from experiences in the subject matter

---

[1]William B. Ragan, *Teaching America's Children* (New York: Holt, Rinehart & Winston, 1961), p. 96. © 1961, Holt, Rinehart and Winston, Inc. Used by permission of the publishers.

per se and in the activity areas of the curriculum. Any attempt to establish a priority between these areas of the curriculum in today's elementary school would likely be a mistake.

FACTORS INFLUENCING CURRICULUM CHANGE

Theoretically, it would be relatively easy to establish a curriculum for schools in a totalitarian state because all children would learn from the same nationally prescribed course of study. In our democratic society, however, where diversity of opinion is nurtured and the innate rights of each individual are recognized and respected, curriculum planning frequently becomes a complex task. Decisions must be made by teachers in such areas as (1) formulating objectives, (2) choosing an appropriate curriculum pattern, (3) organizing for curriculum development, and (4) planning for continuous program improvement, since all of these factors influence curriculum changes.

FORMULATING CURRICULUM OBJECTIVES

The objectives which the school seeks to accomplish in our society stems from some common sense purposes that are applicable to all levels of learning. The objectives to which a school subscribes should be stressed at each grade level and mastered on a successively higher level as the children progress from one grade to another. These commonly accepted objectives were spelled out well by the Educational Policies Commission of the National Education Association in 1938. Their statement of educational objectives which should be met in the established curriculum was expressed in terms of knowledge, competencies, and social amenities necessary for effective living by the individual in our democracy. Their stated objectives are as follows:

The Objectives of Self-Realization

The Inquiring Mind: The educated person has an appetite for learning.
Speech: The educated person can speak the mother tongue clearly.
Reading: The educated person reads the mother tongue efficiently.
Writing: The educated person writes the mother tongue effectively.
Number: The educated person solves his problems of counting and calculating.
Sight and Hearing: The educated person is skilled in listening and observing.
Health Knowledge: The educated person understands the basic facts concerning health and disease.
Health Habits: The educated person protects his own health and that of his dependents.

Public Health: The educated person works to improve the health of the community.

Recreation: The educated person is participant and spectator in many sports and other pastimes.

Intellectual Interests: The educated person has mental resources for the use of leisure.

Aesthetic Interest: The educated person appreciates beauty.

Character: The educated person gives responsible direction to his own life. He also develops moral and spiritual values.

The Objectives of Human Relationship

Respect for Humanity: The educated person puts human relationships first.

Friendships: The educated person enjoys a rich, sincere, and varied social life.

Cooperation: The educated person can work and play with others.

Appreciation of the Home: The educated person appreciates the family as a social institution.

Conservation of the Home: The educated person conserves family ideals.

Homemaking: The educated person is skilled in homemaking.

Democracy in the Home: The educated person maintains democratic family relationships.

The Objectives of Economic Efficiency

Work: The educated producer knows the satisfaction of good workmanship.

Occupational Information: The educated producer understands the requirements and opportunities for various jobs.

Occupational Choice: The educated producer has selected his occupation.

Occupational Efficiency: The educated producer succeeds in his chosen vocation.

Occupational Adjustment: The educated producer maintains and improves his efficiency.

Occupational Appreciation: The educated producer appreciates the social value of his work.

Personal Economics: The educated consumer plans the economics of his own life.

Consumer Judgment: The educated consumer develops standards for guiding his expenditures.

Efficiency in Buying: The educated consumer is an informed and skillful buyer.

Consumer Protection: The educated consumer takes appropriate measures to safeguard his interests.

The Objectives of Civic Responsibility

Social Justice: The educated citizen is sensitive to the disparities of human circumstance.

Social Activity: The educated citizen acts to correct unsatisfactory conditions.

Social Understanding: The educated citizen seeks to understand social structures and social processes.

Critical Judgment: The educated citizen has defenses against propaganda.

Tolerance: The educated citizen respects honest differences of opinion.

Conservation: The educated citizen has a regard for the nation's resources.

Social Applications of Science: The educated citizen measures scientific advance by its contribution to the general welfare.

World Citizenship: The educated citizen is a cooperating member of the world community.

Law Observance: The educated citizen respects the law.

Economic Literacy: The educated citizen is economically literate.

Political Citizenship: The educated citizen accepts his civic duties.

Devotion to Democracy: The educated citizen acts upon an unswerving loyalty to democratic ideals.[2]

Although this list of objectives is rather comprehensive in nature, it does provide a digest of necessary basic understandings, skills, and attitudes which the teacher should strive to help his pupils achieve. The teacher should not view the formulation of educational objectives as an isolated activity, but rather as an inseparable aspect of curriculum planning.[3] The curriculum should be centered around materials and activities which will accomplish the stated objectives of the school and the teachers.

A more manageable set of elementary school objectives was formulated by the Mid-Century Committee on Outcomes in Elementary Education and published in 1953. The objectives outlined by this group are well within the scope of the school's ability to achieve, adequately measure, and evaluate. They are:

Curriculum Areas

1. Physical development, health, body care
2. Individual social and emotional development
3. Ethical behavior, standards, values
4. Social relations
5. The social world
6. The physical world
7. Esthetic development
8. Communication
9. Quantitative relationships

---

[2]Educational Policies Commission, *The Purposes of Education in American Democracy* (Washington, D. C.: National Education Association, 1938), pp. 51-123.

[3]Ragan, *op. cit.*, p. 97.

Types of Behavioral Change
1. Knowledge and understanding
2. Skill and competence
3. Attitude and interest
4. Action pattern[4]

A larger treatment of these objectives is set forth in Chapter 10 of this text. There the reader will find these objectives interrelated more specifically with elementary school content.

A more recent statement of educational objectives worthy of noting was set forth by The Committee for the White House Conference on Education in 1956. The fourteen objectives which were outlined as being desirable, as cited by Tiegs and Adams, follow:

1. The fundamental skills of education — reading, writing, spelling, as well as other elements of effective oral and written expression; the arithmetical and mathematical skills, including problem solving.
2. Appreciation for our democratic heritage.
3. Civic rights and responsibilities, and knowledge of American institutions.
4. Respect and appreciation for human values and for the beliefs of others.
5. The ability to think and evaluate constructively and creatively.
6. Effective work habits and self-discipline.
7. Social competency as a contributing member of his family and community (Vocational fitness).
8. Ethical behavior based on a sense of moral and spiritual values.
9. Intellectual curiosity and eagerness for life-long learning.
10. Esthetic appreciation and self-expression in the arts.
11. Physical and mental health.
12. Wise use of time including constructive leisure pursuits.
13. Understanding of the physical world and man's relation to it as represented through basic knowledge of the sciences.
14. An awareness of our relationships with the world community.[5]

The individual school is responsible for establishing its own educational objectives. These objectives should be agreed upon by the board of education, administrators, teachers, and parents. The school's statement of educational objectives is generally set forth in their curriculum guides under

---

[4]Nolan C. Kearney, *Elementary School Objectives* (New York: Russell Sage Foundation, 1953), p. 38.
[5]Ernest W. Tiegs and Fay Adams, *Teaching the Social Studies* (New York: Ginn & Company, 1959), p. 35. Reprinted through the courtesy of Blaisdell Publishing Company, a division of Ginn and Company.

such headings as knowledge and understandings to be learned, skills to be developed, and social amenities or attitudes and appreciations to be acquired.

A basic guide for the formulation of educational objectives is needed by the school as it decides upon its goals. A suggested criteria has been devised by Ragan to assist the school in the development of this phase of the curriculum as follows:

1. The objectives of the school are formulated cooperatively by pupils, teachers, parents, and administrators.
2. The objectives of the school are written and placed in the hands of teachers, administrators, and parents.
3. The objectives of the school are stated in terms of desirable growth in behavior.
4. Physical, mental, social, and emotional growth are emphasized.
5. Individual differences in interests, needs, and abilities of pupils are recognized in the statement of objectives.
6. The objectives of the school reflect a belief in democratic living.
7. There is continuous effort to develop an understanding of the objectives of the school by administrators, teachers, and parents.
8. The objectives of the school are subject to continuous study and periodic revision.[6]

The objectives finally adopted by a school should be compatible with its educational philosophy because they should become the guide for the individual teachers as they develop the program of instruction and activities. It would be folly for a school to set objectives in which they placed little or no credence.

CHOOSING AN APPROPRIATE CURRICULUM PATTERN

A second important factor which influences curriculum change is deciding upon an appropriate curriculum pattern. Many school systems select a pattern or design which is in keeping with their philosophy of education embodied in their stated objectives. They develop concomitant curriculum guides and adjust the plan of organization for instruction in the school in a manner which will facilitate the design of the curriculum. It may be said, however, that irrespective of the appropriateness of the local and state curriculum guides available or the curriculum pattern decided upon, in the final analysis the success or failure of the program rests with the teacher. The individual school therefore will do well to choose a curriculum design which meets with wide teacher acceptance.

---

[6]Ragan, *op. cit.*, p. 101.

The curriculum pattern of the earliest schools in America was largely that of separate subjects. This was a natural outgrowth of societal demands and an evolving curriculum. The Colonial legislature of Massachusetts in 1642 decreed that all children under their jurisdiction must be taught to read. Reading therefore became the first and dominant subject in their curriculum. In 1647 the Massachusetts legislature passed another law requiring its constituents who resided in towns of fifty householders or more to provide a teacher at public expense to give instruction in reading and writing. Other states were soon to follow Massachusetts' lead in education and as the frontier moved westward the settlers established schools similar to those which they had left in the Colonial states.

Arithmetic was gradually added to the curriculum of the schools and by 1775 schools were teaching the Three R's. Eventually other subjects and activities evolved such as history, geography, science, music, grammar, spelling, and physical education. These courses were added to the curriculum largely on a separate subject basis.

The separate subject curriculum approach design was utilized extensively by most schools in the nation until around the turn of the present century. Even though today this plan is still used to some extent in America's elementary schools, the trend away from it has increased by larger proportions since the early 1900's. Today with our greater understanding of learning theory, schools are seeking to establish curriculum patterns which are more in keeping with our sophisticated knowledge of child growth and development. Several distinct types of curriculum design have been developed since the turn of the century and are discussed in the following pages of this chapter.

Subjects-In-Isolation

The schools which utilize the subjects-in-isolation pattern are characterized by having rather rigid schedules. Teachers in these schools normally divide the day into enough class periods to accommodate the number of subjects which are included in the curriculum. The amount of time given to each subject area is based on some arbitrary decision. The content of the various subjects, i.e., reading, spelling, handwriting, language, history, geography, civics, arithmetic, science, music, art, physical education and health and safety, therefore is taught in isolation with the subject's own time period as Chart 1 points out. Little if any attempt is made to effect transfer of learning among the different subjects. This situation prompted Beck, Cook and Kearney to state:

> The problems that the children work with [in the subjects-in-isolation approach] are artificial and have little functional relationship to the other

subjects . . . With a separate-subject organization, children may run across geographical discussions of relative humidity or percentage figures relating to population or agricultural production before they have been introduced to such concepts in their science and mathematics. They may be studying about children of Holland or Japan in their geography while their history is dealing with Colonial life. Educators have tried desperately, but have not been able, in the separate-subjects organization, to overcome the barriers in the way of caring for individual and trait differences while integrating learning so that all that is learned may be brought to bear in a meaningful way on thinking and problem solving.[7]

CHART 1

Graphic Portrayal of a Subjects-taught-in-isolation Type of Curriculum

1. Arithmetic
2. Art
3. Assembly Programs
4. Civics
5. Geography
6. Handwriting
7. Health
8. History
9. Homemaking
10. Industrial Arts
11. Language
12. Music
13. Opening Exercises
14. Physical Education
15. Reading
16. Science
17. Special Interest Clubs
18. Spelling

←——————————— Grades 1 Through 6 or 8 ———————————→

Henry J. Otto and David C. Sanders, *Elementary School Organization and Administration,* (fourth edition; New York: Appleton-Century-Crofts, 1964), p. 49. Meredith Publishers Company, © 1964. Reproduced by permission of Appleton-Century-Crofts.

---

[7]Robert H. Beck, Walter W. Cook, and Nolan C. Kearney, *Curriculum in the Modern Elementary School* (second edition; Englewood Cliffs, N. J.: Prentice-Hall, Inc., © 1960), p. 193. Reprinted by permission of Prentice-Hall, Inc.

Under this plan, the textbook frequently becomes the teacher's guide to curriculum development. It is often selected on the basis of its own merits without considering the needs of the children who will be using it. Teachers are prone to make page-by-page daily assignments in the various textbooks as the subjects-in-isolation approach is utilized in curriculum development.

Teaching in such an approach to curriculum development tends to be directed toward the average child with little provision made for the accelerated or slow learners. As a result, many of the bright children are forced to do work which is not challenging while the slow learners are required to do work which is too difficult.

Correlated Subjects

In the early 1900's teachers experimented with the correlated subjects curriculum design in an attempt to escape the highly artificial segmentation of the curriculum.[8] Although there were as many separate courses with their own body of content in the correlated approach as there were in the subjects-in-isolation design, an effort was made to establish a relationship among the various subjects in order that more transfer of learning could be effected for the pupils. Under this plan "reading materials were selected from such fields as science and geography; spelling words were taken from geography, history, and arithmetic; and pupils in language classes wrote themes and presented talks on topics selected from science and geography.[9] Each subject retained its own daily time period as Chart 2 shows. The amount of correlation effected between the disciplines was dependent upon the individual classroom teacher's ability and desire to draw upon content from many subjects in providing unified learning experiences. Within itself, the correlated subjects approach represented no real panacea for all of the ills which beset the subjects-in-isolation pattern, but it did spark a movement toward curricular designs which would be more sensitive to meeting the individual and trait differences of the elementary school children.

Broad Fields

The broad fields curricular pattern is dependent upon the various school subjects for its content. It differs from the subjects-in-isolation and corre-

---

[8]Marie A. Mehl, Hubert H. Mills, and Harl R. Douglass, *Teaching in Elementary School* (second edition; New York: The Ronald Press Company, © 1958), p. 79.
[9]Ragan, *op. cit.*, p. 103.

CHART 2

Graph Portraying Correlated Subjects Curriculum Pattern

1. Reading
2. Language
3. Spelling
4. Handwriting
5. Geography
6. History
7. Civics
8. Science
9. Health
10. Arithmetic
11. Art
12. Music
13. Physical Education
14. Homemaking
15. Industrial Arts
16. Assembly Programs
17. Special Interest Clubs
18. Opening Exercises

◄─────────────── All Elementary Grades ───────────────►

lated approaches by grouping certain courses together in order to provide pupils with more unified learning experiences. These subject groupings are known as broad fields. History, geography, and civics are grouped together in the approach and are known as social studies. The social studies so conceived also utilize content from sociology, anthropology, economics, and political science. Another broad fields grouping is that of science and health. Each of these broad fields, i.e., social studies and science and health, is normally taught through the unit method. In this approach, the unit is developed along the lines of significant problems which the pupils are encountering or will encounter; consequently subject matter lines within the broad field area are disregarded as the materials are covered. The units also may be developed around selected topics to be studied and the content drawn from various subjects in the broad field in order to effect unified learning experiences.

Another example of the broad fields approach of curriculum design is the language arts area. Studies involving communication skills, i.e., oral and written language, spelling, listening, reading, and handwriting, are grouped together into a broad field called language arts. Other broad field areas include the creative and recreative arts and arithmetic.[10] The broad fields curriculum design is graphically portrayed in Chart 3.

CHART 3

Graphic Portrayal of a Broad Fields Curriculum Design for
Elementary Schools

Language Arts	
Social Studies	
Arithmetic	
Science and Health	
Physical Education	Creative and Recreative Arts
Music	
Art and Handicraft	

←———— Grades 1 through 6 or 8 ————→

Adapted from Henry J. Otto and David C. Sanders, *Elementary School Organization and Administration,* (fourth edition; New York: Appleton-Century-Crofts, 1964), p. 52. Meredith Publishing Company, © 1964. Reproduced by permission of Appleton-Century-Crofts.

The broad fields curriculum pattern is characterized by fewer class periods and longer blocks of time in which several subjects are merged. Pupils consequently are afforded the opportunity of more sustained activity in the longer periods which normally results in increased motivation and more meaningful learning experiences.[11]

Core

The core curriculum design lends itself well to the problem solving method of study which teachers frequently utilize in working with elementary children. Under such a plan, information is taken from any reliable source or subject as pupils are engaged in problem solving study. The core may be comprised of either the language arts or the social studies.

---

[10]Henry J. Otto and David C. Sanders, *Elementary School Organization and Administration* (fourth edition; New York: Appleton-Century-Crofts, 1964), p. 52.
[11]Beck, Cook, and Kearney, *op. cit.*, p. 194.

If the social studies is selected as the core, the language arts is integrated with it. Conversely, if the language arts is chosen as the core, the social studies would be merged in similar manner. The social studies and the language arts are not taught as separate subjects in either approach. Normally the social studies becomes the core and the language arts is incorporated as the teacher develops the various units of study during the school year.

The classroom teacher frequently endeavors to relate learning activities in music, art, and physical education with the unit under study in the core program. Science and arithmetic may be correlated with the unit of study in the core as expedient; however, these subjects are also taught as separate subjects. The core program is graphically portrayed in Chart 4.

CHART 4

Graphic Portrayal of a Core Type of Curriculum

1. Arithmetic
2. Art
3. Assembly Programs
4. Health
5. Homemaking
The Core: consisting of History–civics–geography–literature or Social Studies or Social Studies–Science combination including full integration of reading, language, hand-writing, and spelling.
6. Industrial Arts
7. Music
8. Opening Exercises
9. Physical Education
10. Special Interest Clubs

←——————————Grades 1 Through 6 or 8 ——————————→

(Adapted from Henry J. Otto and David C. Sanders, *Elementary School Organization and Administration*, (fourth edition; New York: Appleton-Century-Crofts, 1964), p. 51. Meredith Publishing Company, © 1964. Reproduced by permission of Appleton-Century-Crofts.

The ultimate success or failure of the core program rests with the classroom teacher. He has the responsibility of planning cooperatively with the pupils what units of work they will study in the light of their interests and needs. He also has the responsibility of devising plans whereby the social studies and language arts can be correlated into effective unified learning experiences. Likewise, he has the task of relating the study in music, art, physical education, arithmetic, and science to the unit under study in the core wherever possible. The core curriculum pattern does provide a flexible plan for curriculum development as the teacher seeks to establish unified learning experiences for his pupils.

Learner Centered

The learner or child centered approach to curriculum development first came into prominence in the 1920's and 1930's as an attempt to reject the traditional subjects curriculum patterns. Educators who subscribed to this curriculum pattern contended that the curriculum should emphasize activities, interests, and needs of children rather than subject matter.[12] Ragan stated their philosophy succinctly:

> They regarded childhood as an important period in life, to be lived for itself rather than as a period of preparation for adult life. They had faith that children, when provided with intelligent adult guidance, would select learning activities through which they would develop understandings, skills, and attitudes much more effectively than they would when they were subjected to adult-imposed assignments.[13]

The teacher and pupils jointly plan their objectives, activities, and materials to be covered in the learner centered curriculum pattern. These activities and studies are drawn directly from the children's expressed interests and needs. Subject matter lines are completely disregarded as the activities are developed in the light of joint pupil-teacher planning. Content may be drawn from many subject areas as the children engage in activities which are real to them and meet their immediate needs. If they are studying the importance of the sun to our solar system for instance, they will give little thought to whether pertinent materials are taken from arithmetic, science, or the language arts. Instead they will draw content from many subject areas until they have constructed some unified concepts which satisfy their immediate need to learn why the sun is important to them. Chart 5 vividly outlines the learner centered approach to curriculum development.

12Mehl, Mills, and Douglass, *op. cit.*, p. 80.
13Ragan, *op. cit.*, p. 104.

CHART 5

Circle Graph Portraying the Learner Centered Curriculum Pattern

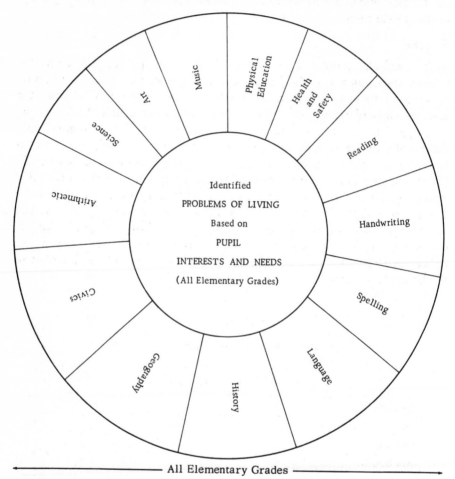

The learner centered approach has never gained widespread use in America's public elementary school. It has been successful, however, in helping to free from rote learning classrooms previously characterized by a dominance of drill and memorization accompanied by excessive dependence upon textbooks.[14]

The learner centered curriculum pattern may one day be utilized in more schools than now. As teachers become more adept in identifying student interests and needs and less fearful of departing from a subject

[14]*Ibid.*, p. 105.

centered approach, recognizing that the here and now is infinitely more important to pupils than some isolated facts they may need in adult living, the learner centered activity program should become increasingly popular in the public school.

Eclectic

The eclectic pattern is a middle-of-the road approach between the subjects-in-isolation and the learner centered programs. It strikes a happy balance for those teachers who are reluctant to deviate too far from the subjects curricular pattern and feel that the learner centered plan is too idealistic. Under this plan, part of the day is devoted to teaching basic skills while the remainder is given over to the units of work or correlated activities in different content areas such as social studies and science as Chart 6 shows. For example, most of the morning hours of the school day would be utilized in teaching reading, handwriting, spelling, and arithmetic. The balance of the day would be used for unit study and related activities in social studies, science, or health and safety. Music, art, and physical education would be worked in sometime during the day when they would either correlate with the unit of work activities or extend the learning in the basic skills studies.

CHART 6

Graph Portraying Eclectic Curriculum Pattern

BASIC SKILLS SUBJECTS AREA
Reading
Handwriting
Spelling
Arithmetic
UNIT STUDY AND RELATED ACTIVITIES
Social Studies
Science
Health and Safety
FINE ARTS AND RECREATION
Art
Music
Recreation

←————————— All Elementary Grades —————————→

The time schedule is very flexible in the eclectic approach. The pupils and teachers can decide daily how much time they will designate for the skills and the activities areas as they deal with the materials they are studying. The eclectic pattern has much to its credit as it provides a method of escaping the artificial segmentation of the subject-in-isolation approach characterized by textbook centered teaching and rote learning. It provides a plan which will enable the teacher to teach the basic skills in a systematic approach and at the same time is flexible enough to allow the teacher and pupils to plan activities for unit study based upon the children's interest and needs.

In the final analysis, it is difficult to completely separate the six types of curriculum patterns previously discussed. Frequently they overlap each other. Good teachers in schools using the subjects-in-isolation approach generally devise methods of relating the subject matter to some extent. Occasionally they defy the prescriptive subject outline as well as the time schedule and create more effective learning situations for their pupils. In terms of actual operation, it also is frequently hard to distinguish among the core, broad fields, and learner centered curricular approaches because many of the elements which characterize each of them are present from time to time in all three programs. The most important decision to make in choosing a given curricular pattern is that it meets with widespread teacher acceptance. The best imaginable curriculum design will fail if teachers are not dedicated to it.

ORGANIZING FOR CURRICULUM DEVELOPMENT

Once a given pattern of curriculum design has been selected, the teacher must determine how to organize his work in curriculum most effectively. Several factors have a direct bearing upon his plans for organizing the curriculum. There are decisions to make concerning an appropriate daily class schedule; fitting the classroom program of instruction into the school schedule; resource personnel; utilizing community resources; and maximizing the use of instructional materials to provide better learning experiences.

The Class Schedule

The daily class schedule that the teacher adopts should be sensitive to the curriculum design which he has chosen. If he has chosen the subjects-in-isolation or correlated subjects design he will have a class schedule characterized by many separate periods. On the other hand if he has chosen the broad feilds, core, learner centered or eclectic pattern, he will have fewer class periods per se and they will be longer. A typically daily classroom schedule which is sensitive to each of the curricular patterns discussed is presented in **Figure 9.**

Subjects-In-Isolation
and
Correlated Subjects

8:30- 9:00	Opening Exercises
9:00-10:00	Reading
10:00-10:15	Handwriting
10:15-10:30	Spelling
10:30-11:00	Physical Education
11:00-11:30	Language
11:30-12:00	Science (M, T, W, Th)
	Health (F)
12:00-12:30	Lunch
12:30- 1:30	Arithmetic
1:30- 2:15	Music (M, W, F) Art (T, Th)
2:15- 2:45	History
2:45- 3:15	Geography
3:15- 3:30	Daily Evaluation

Core

8:30- 9:00	Opening Exercises
9:00-11:30	Social Studies
	(The core of social studies, i.e., history, geography, and civics, will be fully integrated with the study of language arts, i.e., reading, handwriting, spelling and language.)
11:30-12:00	Physical Education
12:00-12:30	Lunch
12:30- 1:30	Arithmetic
1:30- 2:15	Music (M, W, F) Art (T, Th)
2:15- 3:15	Science and Health
3:15- 3:30	Daily Evaluation

Learner Centered

8:30- 9:00	Opening Exercises
9:00-10:15	Interdisciplinary study as planned by pupils and teacher on "problems of living"
10:15-10:45	Physical Education
10:45-12:00	Interdisciplinary study as planned by pupils and teacher on "problems of living"
12:00-12:30	Lunch
12:30- 3:15	Interdisciplinary study as planned by pupils and teacher on "problems of living"
3:15- 3:30	Daily Evaluation

Broad Fields

8:30- 9:00	Opening Exercises
9:00-11:00	Language Arts
11:00-11:30	Physical Education
11:30-12:15	Creative Arts
	(Music M, W, F) Art (T, Th)
12:15-12:45	Lunch
12:45- 1:45	Arithmetic
1:45- 3:15	Social Studies or Science and Health Unit Study
	(These areas will be alternated every 2 to 3 weeks)
3:15- 3:30	Daily Evaluation

Eclectic

8:30- 9:00	Opening Exercises
9:00-11:00	Basic Skills
	Reading 9:00-10:00
	Handwriting 10:00-10:15
	Spelling 10:15-10:30
	Arithmetic 10:30-11:30
11:30- 1:15	Fine Arts and Recreation
	Physical Education 11:30-12:00
	Lunch 12:00-12:30
	Music 12:30- 1:15 (M, W, F)
	Art 12:30- 1:15 (T, Th)
1:15- 3:30	Unit Study and Related Activities -- Social Studies, Science and Health 1:15-2:45
	(These areas will be alternated every 2 to 3 weeks)
	Special Interest Clubs -- Math, science, book, homemaking, industrial arts -- 2:45-3:15
	Daily Evaluation 3:15-3:30

Figure 9. Typical Daily Classroom Schedule Under Different Curricular Patterns.

The amount of time that teachers allocate to the study of the various courses is based largely upon some arbitrary decision. The curricular design decided upon will determine to a great degree time allocations for subjects. Dean's[15] recent national survey has shown, however, that teachers are permitted great latitude in deciding upon how much time they will allot for the teaching of the different courses. He found that 46 per cent of the urban school systems in the nation with scholastic populations of 2,500 or more only suggested the amount of time which their teachers should allocate to the various course offerings as Table 6 shows. He also found that 12 per cent of these systems had no recommended time per subject and that only about 11 per cent of them had definite prescribed time allotment policies.

TABLE 6

Instructional time allocation policy in public elementary school grades 1-6 in urban places with populations above 2,500 by U. S. totals and percentages, 1960.

Policy	United States	
	Per Cent	Schools
Suggested time per subject	46. 1	1, 986
No recommended time per subject	12. 4	533
Prescribed time per subject	10. 7	463
Block time per subject	9. 9	427
Combinations	9. 0	389
Other	1. 5	61
No Answer	10. 4	448
Total	100. 0	4, 307

Adapted from Stuart E. Dean, *Elementary School Administration and Organization*, p. 52. Reproduced by permission of and arrangement with, U. S. Department of Health, Education, and Welfare, Office of Education.

The time allotment schedule of the Tulsa (Oklahoma) public schools is representative of systems which utilize prescribed time periods. Their weekly time schedule is depicted in Table 7.

---

[15]Stuart E. Dean, *Elementary School Administration and Organization* (Washington: U. S. Department of Health, Education, and Welfare, 1960), p. 52.

TABLE 7

Weekly time allotments by subject and grade as found in the Tulsa (Oklahoma) elementary public schools, 1961.

Subject Area	Grade 1	Grade 2	Grade 3	Grade 4	Grade 5	Grade 6
Reading–social studies	570	390	390	360	335	335
Language	75	75	75	90	90	90
Spelling	...	75	75	75	75	75
Handwriting	80	80	80	75	50	50
Arithmetic	75	130	130	150	200	200
Health	...	50	50	50	50	50
Art	140	140	100	100	100	100
Library	175	175	200	200	200	200
Music	85	85	100	100	100	100
Physical education	175	175	200	200	200	200
Science–geography	140	140	100	100	100	100
Speech	85	85	100	100	100	100
Total	1,600	1,600	1,600	1,600	1,600	1,600

Adapted from Beatrice Crump Lee, "Instructional Time Allotment in Elementary Schools," p. 5. Reproduced by permission of, and arrangement with, National Education Association, Research Division, July, 1961.

Schools that utilize the suggested time allotment policy can be illustrated by the time plan of the Houston (Texas) public schools. Under their plan, the Board of Education and the administrative staff suggest to the teacher some time ranges for the courses included in the elementary curriculum, as Table 8 shows. The teacher may use his own discretion in deciding how much time he will assign to each area, keeping in mind the school's suggested policy.

Some teachers feel that the more time one allocates for teaching the subjects the more pupil achievement they can expect. This is not necessarily the case, however. Studies by Daugherty, Denny, and Jarvis[16] have

---

[16]James L. Daugherty, *A Study of Achievement in Sixth Grade Arithmetic in Des Moines Public Schools,* Research Study No. 1 (Unpublished doctoral dissertation, Colorado State College, Greeley, 1955), pp. 80-81; Robert Ray Denny, *A Two-Year Study of the Effects of An Increased Time Allotment Upon Achievement in Arithmetic in the Intermediate Grades,* Field Study No. 1 (Greeley: Colorado State College, 1955), pp. i-vi; Oscar T. Jarvis, *Time Allotments and Pupil Achievement in the Intermediate Elementary Grades.* (University of Houston: Bureau of Education Research and Services, 1962), pp. 57-60.

TABLE 8

Time allocations by subject and grade as practiced in the Houston (Texas) public schools, 1961.

Subject Area	Grade 1	Grade 2	Grade 3	Grade 4	Grade 5	Grade 6
Language arts	160–180 a day	160–180 a day	130–150 a day	130–150 a day	130–150 a day	130–150 a day
Mathematics	20–30 a day	20–30 a day	50–60 a day	50–60 a day	50–60 a day	50–60 a day
History and geography	. . .	. . .	50–60 a day	50–60 a day	50–60 a day	50–60 a day
Science	50–70 a week	50–70 a week	20 a day	20 a day	20 a day	20 a day
Art	40 a week	40 a week	50–70 a week	50–70 a week	50–70 a week	50–70 a week
Music	70–80 a week	70–80 a week	80–100 a week	80–100 a week	80–100 a week	80–100 a week
Health and physical education	150 a week	150 a week	150 a week	150 a week	150 a week	150 a week
Foreign language	. . .	. . .	60 a week	60 a week	60 a week	60 a week
Length of school day (including lunch time)	5 hours	5 hours	6 hours, 10 minutes	6 hours, 10 minutes	6 hours, 10 minutes	6 hours, 50 minutes

Adapted from Beatrice Crump Lee, "Instructional Time Allotment in Elementary Schools," memo 1961-29, p. 6. Reproduced by permission of, and arrangement with, National Education Association Research Division.

shown slight increase in pupil achievement in arithmetic in longer daily class periods. Daugherty and Denny's studies found this to be true in comparing pupil achievement at the sixth grade level in 40 and 50 minute periods. Jarvis also found this to be true at the sixth grade level between children studying in 35-45 minute daily periods and those in a similar group of pupils in periods which were 55-60 minutes long. In all of these studies, however, the achievement differences, although significant, were not great enough to raise any real issue.

Rice found that teachers who allocated more than fifteen minutes per day for teaching spelling were simply wasting valuable time.[17] A study by

---

[17]J. M. Rice, "The Futility of the Spelling Grind," *Forum*, XXIII, (1897), pp. 163-172.

Jarvis comparing the achievement of sixth graders in spelling of 20 and 40 minutes daily did not produce any significant pupil achievement differences.[18]

In language mechanics, Jarvis found that pupil achievement in the sixth grade was greater in 40 to 50 minute daily periods than it was in periods where pupils studied for only 25 to 30 minutes. He also found that there was no substantial difference in pupil achievement in reading among sixth grade students of 60 to 78 minute daily class periods when compared with a similar group who were studying in 40 to 50 minute periods.[19]

It has been said that "education is not to be compared with filling a pot, but with lighting a fire." These research studies tend to point out the wisdom of this statement. It is not necessarily the length of time spent in teaching the subject which is of paramount importance. Rather it is what the teacher does within time allocations afforded him that is the weightier issue. If a teacher views the time allotment as a designated period for dispensing facts, he likely subscribes to the theory that "education is to be compared with filling a pot." If, on the other hand, he places credence in viewing time allotted for teaching a course as a period when information gained by the students can be applied to life situations in a never-ending cycle of study and research, he likely believes that "education is to be compared with lighting a fire" which prompts further learning.

The School Schedule

Another factor which impinges upon the teacher's plans for instruction is the over-all school schedule. Many schools hire special teachers for certain subjects or activities. This is true particularly in music, physical education, and art. In surveying 64 metropolitan elementary schools in 1962, Jarvis found that 44 per cent of them had special teachers in music, 20 per cent in physical education, and 14 per cent in art.[20] Other specialists elementary schools frequently employ whose schedules would also impinge upon the classroom teacher's plans of organization would be such persons as the librarian, speech and hearing therapist, foreign language teacher, instructor in remedial reading, and band director.

---

[18]Oscar T. Jarvis, "How Much Time for Spelling?" *The Instructor*, LXIII, Number 1 (September, 1963), pp. 59, 156.
[19]Jarvis, *Time Allotments and Pupil Achievement in the Intermediate Elementary Grades, op. cit.*, pp. 57-60.
[20]Oscar T. Jarvis, "Teaching Specialists Who Assist Elementary Homeroom Teachers," *The Nation's Schools*, Volume 74, Number 6 (December, 1964), p. 33.

A typical weekly school schedule for teaching specialists in music, art, physical education, and the librarian is shown in Figure 10. This plan is designed for an 18 teacher elementary school with three sections at each grade level and characterizes the impingement of the school schedule upon that of the individual classroom teacher's plans.

To understand fully how the school schedule periodically freezes the classroom schedule, one has only to choose a given section at any grade level presented in Figure 10 and plot the designated periods with the special teachers for a week. For purposes of illustration, let us select section one from the third and sixth grade levels and determine their schedules for a week with the teaching specialists in music, art, physical education, and the librarian. Such a schedule depicted by Figure 11, becomes inflexible or frozen. The classroom teacher knows that the work her students do with these teaching specialists must be at the designated periods. Part of the flexibility of the scheduling in the self-contained classroom therefore is automatically given up when teaching specialists are used in the elementary school in this manner.

The classroom teacher should coordinate his work with the teaching specialists and librarian. He should inform the teaching specialists what unit of study is going on in the social studies or health and safety in order that they might plan music, art, and physical activity experiences which would extend pupil learnings in these areas. The librarian also should select books and other pertinent library materials to be placed in the individual classrooms to enrich pupil learning in the unit of study.

Involving Resource Personnel

Many elementary schools do not have teaching specialists in such areas as music, physical education, art, and foreign language assigned to work extensively in a given building. Instead they employ what may be termed resource personnel or supervisors. These supervisors work with the teachers in many different elementary buildings. Their function is not one of teaching children, but rather of providing ideas and materials for the individual classroom teacher.

These resource personnel make regularly scheduled visits to the schools to which they have been assigned. The classroom teachers are apprised of the visits in advance and are prepared to use the consultative services of these supervisors when they come to their building. The supervisors work extensively with the teachers who need their consultative services. They frequently pass along pertinent information to the classroom teachers through the media of newsletters which are mimeographed in the central office and circulated to the individual elementary buildings.

Music Teacher's Schedule

Time	Mon	Tue	Wed	Thu	Fri
8:00–9:00					
9:00–9:30	1st S-1	1st S-2	1st S-1	1st S-2	1st S-1
9:30–10:00	2nd S-1	2nd S-2	2nd S-1	2nd S-2	2nd S-1
10:00–10:30	3rd S-1	3rd S-2	3rd S-1	3rd S-2	3rd S-1
10:30–11:00	1st S-2	1st S-3	1st S-3	1st S-1	X
11:00–11:30	X	2nd S-3	2nd S-3	2nd S-3	2nd S-2
11:30–12:00	3rd S-3	3rd S-3	X	3rd S-3	3rd S-2
12:00–12:30	Lunch				
12:30–1:00	4th S-1	4th S-2	4th S-1	4th S-2	4th S-1
1:00–1:30	5th S-1	5th S-2	5th S-1	5th S-2	5th S-3
1:30–2:00	6th S-1	6th S-2	6th S-1	6th S-2	6th S-1
2:00–2:30	4th S-2	4th S-2	4th S-3	4th S-3	X
2:30–3:00	X	5th S-3	5th S-3	5th S-3	5th S-2
3:00–3:30	6th S-3	6th S-3	X	6th S-3	6th S-2
3:30–4:00					

Art Teacher's Schedule

Final Preparation for the Activities of the Day

Time	Mon	Tue	Wed	Thu	Fri
9:00–9:45	3rd S-1	3rd S-2	3rd S-1	3rd S-1	3rd S-3
9:45–10:30	3rd S-3	1st S-1	1st S-1	1st S-2	1st S-3
10:30–11:15	1st S-1	2nd S-1	1st S-1	2nd S-1	2nd S-2
11:15–12:00	2nd S-3	2nd S-2	X	2nd S-2	X
12:00–12:30	Lunch				
12:30–1:15	6th S-1	6th S-2	6th S-1	6th S-1	6th S-3
1:15–2:00	6th S-3	5th S-2	4th S-3	5th S-3	4th S-3
2:00–2:45	5th S-1	5th S-1	5th S-1	5th S-1	4th S-1
2:45–3:30	4th S-1	4th S-2	X	4th S-2	X

Physical Education Teacher's Schedule

Time	Mon	Tue	Wed	Thu	Fri
9:00–9:30	X	X	X	1st S-3	2nd S-3
9:30–10:00	2nd S-3	1st S-3	2nd S-3	1st S-3	3rd S-2
10:00–10:30	3rd S-2	2nd S-2	3rd S-2	2nd S-2	1st S-1
10:30–11:00	2nd S-2	1st S-1	1st S-1	1st S-1	1st S-2
11:00–11:30	1st S-2	3rd S-1	3rd S-3	3rd S-3	3rd S-3
11:30–12:00	3rd S-1	3rd S-3	2nd S-1	2nd S-1	2nd S-1
12:30–1:00	5th S-1	4th S-3	5th S-1	4th S-3	5th S-1
1:00–1:30	4th S-3	4th S-2	4th S-1	4th S-2	4th S-1
1:30–2:00	4th S-2	6th S-1	5th S-1	4th S-1	5th S-3
2:00–2:30	5th S-3	5th S-3	6th S-2	5th S-3	6th S-1
2:30–3:00	6th S-3	6th S-2	6th S-2	6th S-3	6th S-1
3:00–3:30	5th S-2	5th S-2	X	X	5th S-1

Librarian's Schedule

Time	Mon	Tue	Wed	Thu	Fri
9:00–9:30	1st S-3	2nd S-1	3rd S-2	4th S-2	5th S-3
9:30–10:00	X	X	X	X	X
10:00–10:30	1st S-2	2nd S-3	3rd S-3	4th S-3	6th S-1
10:30–11:00	X	2nd S-2	X	X	X
11:00–11:30	1st S-1		3rd S-1	5th S-1	6th S-2
11:30–12:00	X	X	4th S-1	5th S-2	6th S-3
12:30–4:00	Unscheduled time for cataloguing, filing, shelving, requisitioning, and working with individual pupils and teachers				

Evaluation of Today's Activities and Initial Planning for Tomorrow

X (Unscheduled)
S (Section)

Figure 10. Typical Weekly Schedule of Special Teachers and Librarian in an 18 Teacher Elementary School.

GRADE 3

Time	Monday	Tuesday	Wednesday	Thursday	Friday
8:30- 9:00	------------------ Opening Exercises --------------------				
9:00- 9:45	Art		Art		
9:45-10:00					
10:00-10:30	Music		Music		Music
10:30-11:00					
11:00-11:30		P. E.		P. E.	Library
11:30-12:00	P. E.				
12:00- 3:30					

GRADE 6

Time	Monday	Tuesday	Wednesday	Thursday	Friday
8:30- 9:00	------------------ Opening Exercises ------------------				
9:00-10:00					Library
10:30-12:30					
12:30- 1:15	Art		Art		
1:30- 2:00	Music	P. E.	Music		Music
2:00- 2:30					
2:30- 3:00				P. E.	P. E.

Figure 11. Typical Weekly Schedule for a Third and Sixth Grade Class*
Depicting Possible Effects of School Schedule of Special Teachers Upon
Classroom Schedule.

These resource personnel or supervisors are vital as change agents for
effecting curriculum innovations and improvements within the local school
system. Normally they are selected to staff a given supervisory position
because they are master teachers in particular specialties. They stay abreast
of curriculum trends through wide professional reading, by attending important conferences, and through visiting other leading school systems. The
individual classroom teacher would do well to recognize the possibilities
for enriching his program of instruction by simply seeking the ideas for
curriculum development which these resource personnel are capable of providing.

Utilizing Community Resources

Community resources which can be utilized by the classroom teacher in
curriculum development can be classified as human and physical. The
resources available to the classroom teacher in any community are as broad

*Classes depicted here are both Section 1 of the third and sixth grades of Figure 10.

or as narrow as its diversity of occupations and industries. Teachers in large communities naturally will have a greater supply of resources than those who teach in small communities.

Human resources are those people residing within the community who are sufficiently versed in a given subject or equipped with a particular skill that the teacher can call upon them to speak to his class or give a demonstration in order to enrich the program of instruction. Physical resources are the industries, businesses, or public facilities to which the teacher can take his children on field trips in order that they might have direct experiences with them.

Some of the human resources which can be employed advantageously in the elementary school have been enumerated by Mehl, Mills, and Douglass as follows:

1. Individuals who have recently made journeys to interesting parts of the country or to foreign countries including, of course, those who have recently come to this country to live.
2. Persons who have unusual information by reason of specialized experience, for example, a forester who is familiar with the wildlife of the country, particularly the local flora and fauna.
3. Individuals who are familiar with the history of the community, and indeed anyone who is well informed along the lines of any of the areas mentioned for study under community survey.
4. Citizens engaged in occupations which may be of interest to the school, for example, an attorney, nurse, architect, farmer, stock raiser, or mail carrier.
5. Persons with interesting or unusual hobbies or collections such as model railroad trains, dolls, stamps, or handiwork of some particular tribe of Indians, or a foreign country.
6. School staff members employed to render some sort of service in connection with projects in the schools — carpenters, electricians, cooks.
7. Individuals who may give educational entertainment, such as a musician, magician, ventriloquist.
8. Possible assistant teachers, for example, in connection with baseball or other games.
9. Individuals to assist teachers in training youngsters in chorus work or choral readings or in marionettes and puppets.
10. Parents.[21]

The teacher can enrich classroom learning greatly by supplementing it periodically with well-planned field trips to selected physical resources of the community. Field trips will be appropriate when they are intended to answer specific questions which have arisen in class, to observe certain

---

[21]Mehl, Mills, and Douglass, *op. cit.*, pp. 255-256.

processes utilized in industry, or for purposes of general exploration.[22] Some trips which the elementary teacher may wish to make together with specific purposes and primary points of emphasis have been suggested by Burr, Harding, and Jacobs as follows:

Destination	Specific Purpose	Primary Emphasis
Wholesale house	to answer specific questions	about how bananas are brought to wholesale houses, cared for, and distributed to re-tailers
Cannery	to observe the process	by which whole ears of corn become cans of corn
Dairy farm	to answer specific questions	about how cows are cared for and milked
Lumber yard	to answer specific questions	about different kinds of build-ing materials
Stone quary	for general exploration	of the excavation, and of how the stone is obtained
Print shop	for general exploration	of how printing is done
Post office	to observe processes	by which letters and packages are received and prepared for distribution
Model home	for general exploration	of modern improvements made possible by technological progress
Department store	for general exploration	of various departments and workers
Radio station	to answer specific questions	about how broadcasts take place
Farm	to answer specific questions	about how baby animals are born and raised
Wharf	to answer specific questions	about freighters: from where they came; products; how unloaded
Dairy	to observe process	by which ice cream is made
House under construction	to answer specific questions	about what various construc-tion workers do
Supermarket	for general exploration	of products sold
Shoe factory	to observe the process	by which leather is made into shoes
Water works	to answer specific questions	about source and quantity of water, and how purified[23]

[22]James B. Burr, Lowry W. Harding, and Leland B. Jacobs, *Student Teaching in the Elementary School* (second edition; New York: Appleton-Century-Crofts, Inc., 1958), pp. 346-347.

[23]James B. Burr, Lowry W. Harding, and Leland B. Jacobs, *Student Teaching In the Elementary School* (second edition; New York: Appleton-Century-Crofts, Inc., 1958), p. 347. © 1950, 1958. Reprinted by permission of Appleton-Century-Crofts.

There are countless other physical resources in the community which can be visited for their educational value which will influence the curriculum. A rather thorough compendium of these resources has been suggested by Mehl, Mills, and Douglass as follows:

Brick yard	Chicken hatchery
Packing plant	Apiary
Rubber factory	Greenhouse
Candy factory	Art gallery
Thermometer factory	Library
Hydroelectric plant	Voting polls
Cotton gin	Political meeting
Mill	Police station
Tapestry weaving shop	Court
Newspaper plant	Assessor's office
Bakery	Flower garden
Photographer's studio	Vegetable garden
Steel plant	Fair
Road under construction	Dog kennels
Building under construction	Grain elevator
Coffee company	Interesting natural scenes
Automobile assembly plant	Various types of houses
Warehouse terminal	Telephone exchange
Oil well	Theater
Church	Zoo
Freight yard	Planetarium
Airport	Park
City hall	Cemetery
Courthouse	Monument
Iron mine	Historical sites
Coal mine	Fire department
Bank	Business college
Hotel	High school
Summer resort	University[24]

A third valuable type of community resource is those materials which the children themselves bring to school. These materials may be specific items which enhance the learning in the social studies or science such as an old flintlock rifle or a barometer. On the other hand, they may not have any direct bearing at all on the unit of study, but may be items which particularly interest the children who believe them to be educational in nature and worthy of presentation at "show and tell" time.

The community resources available to the teacher are many and varied. The teacher can enrich his program of instruction through the proper utilization of these resources. Ragan has rightly stated that "The teacher cannot be a specialist in all fields; he is seldom a scientist, a musician, an

---

[24]Mehl, Mills, and Douglass, *op. cit.*, p. 253.

economist, and a world traveler. His skill lies in guiding the learning of pupils and in bringing them into contact with the educative resources of the community."[25] The teacher therefore should be intelligently informed about community resources and should utilize them effectively.

Maximizing The Use of Instructional Materials

Few schools are blessed with enough financial resources to provide all of the instructional materials needed for each classroom. Even if they could the wisdom of such action would be debatable because some materials are used for a relatively short time each year. To store them at the completion of a given unit of study or learning experience until they are needed next year would be unwise when, through proper scheduling and teacher cooperation, they could be used by other sections at the same grade level or even at other grade levels.

Many schools have established a centrally located curriculum materials room in which instructional items not being used are stored so that they can be requisitioned easily by other teachers. Teachers return materials to this center when finished with them in order that their colleagues can pick them up for use in their rooms.

Customarily the school librarian is responsible for the curriculum materials room since he is working closely with the classroom teachers and knows what units they are studying and which they intend to cover next. The librarian therefore is in a position to advise teachers when the materials will be available and can assist them in long range planning in order that they will have them when necessary. Because he knows present and future study units, the librarian can select appropriate books from his central library to send to the individual classroom libraries. Each individual classroom thus will have access to more of the school's materials as it develops its individual units of study.

Audio-visual education authorities are in general agreement upon what materials influence curriculum development most and are commonly employed in classroom teaching. Gwynn has summarized the materials they feel are most frequently utilized as follows:

> Blackboard and bulletin board; duplicating devices; tack board or felt-board and display
> Visual symbols; cartoons; drawings and sketches; posters, diagrams; flat maps, charts; graphs, comic strips; pictorial statistics
> Still pictures: (1) flat photographs, prints, and postcards (2) projected — opaque and daylight; slides — glass, cellophane, filmstrip, strip film, micro-projection; tachistoscopes; (3) stereoscopes and stereographs

---

[25]Ragan, *op. cit.*, p. 302.

Models and mockups; globes; objects; specimens; exhibits; museums; planetariums demonstrations; dioramas; sand tables, and miniature sets; flash cards

Motion pictures; silent and sound; television; films — educational, theatrical, documentary

Phonographs; records; recordings, transcriptions

Radio, television, dictaphone, loud speaker (public address and inter-communicating)[26]

The classroom atmosphere and method of teacher control should be such that the students view their immediate environs as a learning laboratory. Their environment should be such that they feel free to move around and manipulate, experiment with, and utilize the instructional materials to satisfy their own curiosity and desire to learn. Such a view of utilization of instructional materials is compatible with the modern view of curriculum development which emphasizes working toward meeting the immediate interests and needs of the children. This approach escapes the old theory of elementary teaching which has been characterized well by Beck, Cook, and Kearney's statement:

School-room environments of the past were sometimes highly restricted and needlessly standardized. Learning activities were limited (by the fixed, screwed-down seats, blackboard sidewalls, and cramped quarters) to reciting, reading, writing, and listening. Unnecessary restrictions on communication and movement limited social experiences and social learning. A more unstimulating environment for a group of children is difficult to conceive. In no place outside of school has man duplicated such surroundings for his adult activities.[27]

Through wise planning and scheduling teachers can share their instructional materials, thereby creating better learning situations for every classroom at each grade level. The teachers should cooperate willingly with the school librarian as he endeavors to coordinate the utilization of these materials in a manner that will benefit all children to the maximum degree.

PLANNING FOR CONTINUOUS CURRICULUM IMPROVEMENT

Continuous curriculum improvement can be effected in many ways. Two methods, however, seem to be utilized extensively by elementary schools. They are providing an effective in-service education program and establish-

---

[26]J. Minor Gwynn, *Theory and Practice of Supervision* (New York: Dodd, Mead & Company, © 1961), pp. 107-108. Reprinted by permission of Dodd, Mead & Company, Inc.

[27]Beck, Cook, and Kearney, *op. cit.*, p. 345.

ing a school atmosphere in which teachers feel free to experiment with new media, teaching techniques, and organizational procedures. Each of these practices has enabled the present generation of teachers to break with the *status quo* and provide a continuous curriculum improvement program which is sensitive to the needs of the children.

In-Service Education

The prerequisites for a good elementary teacher are the possession of knowledge, attitudes, and skills. These prerequisites are obtained in large measure by a beginning teacher through his pre-service education programs. The knowledge, attitudes, and skills so acquired must be continually supplemented throughout his professional career, however, if he is to reach his full potentialities in teaching effectiveness. The necessity of in-service education, therefore becomes an integral part of his professional betterment by keeping him abreast of new pedagogical ideas and techniques.

Basically there are two types of in-service education programs which have proven beneficial. They are: (1) cooperative endeavors in which all or groups of teachers participate, and (2) individual projects for improvement. The in-service activities now conducted by the schools under each of these programs are set forth in Figure 12.

While the pre-service programs are an indispensable aspect of general professional education, there are some things about teaching which can be learned only through direct experience with children. In-service education serves a vital function in that it provides both the experienced and inexperienced teacher on-the-job education by linking principles of teaching and learning to the realities of the classroom environment. One cannot expect that the short period of study in pre-service education will provide sufficient knowledge for a lifelong professional career. On the contrary, this knowledge must continually be supplemented through individual and group efforts in in-service education. Although more realistic pre-service educational programs could contribute more to the teacher's preparation, much of the knowledge needed for successful teaching can be acquired only through firsthand experiences with children.[28] In-service education therefore is the agent by which the school continuously prepares its teachers and revises its curriculum to provide a dynamic program of instruction.

Providing For Experimentation

Continuous curriculum improvement is facilitated if the school allows its teachers to experiment. A school which deprives its teacher of this oppor-

---

[28]Mehl, Mills, and Douglass, *op. cit.*, p. 454.

A PROGRAM OF IN-SERVICE EDUCATION FOR THE ELEMENTARY SCHOOL

Type of In-Service Education	Major Purpose to be Achieved	Frequency of Function
Cooperative Enterprises Faculty and staff meetings	Apprise teachers of changes in the school's educational program	As necessity dictates
Teacher council	Recommend changes in curriculum to administrative officials and board of education based upon desires of fellow teachers	Once per month or as occasions demand
Study groups	Teachers within a school study one or more curricular problems	Once each week or more often if necessary
Workshops	Concentrated study upon a given facet of the instructional program such as the "new math"	Summer workshops sponsored by universities may last three to nine weeks; those sponsored by the school are usually three to five days long
Demonstration centers	Teacher observation of modern facilities, teaching techniques, and curricular materials	Demonstration center operates continuously; teachers visit for observation as opportunity permits or occasions demand
Study clinics (conducted by specialized personnel)	To make an intensive study of a significant problem under the guidance of experts	As opportunity permits or necessity dictates
Orientation programs	To inform new teachers about the existing curricular program	At the beginning of the school year in September and at mid-term in January
Group excursions in community	To gain a thorough understanding of the community served by the school	Usually once a year during Business–Education Week

Figure 12. Types of In-Service Education. Adapted with modifications from Marie A. Mehl, Hubert H. Mills, and Harl R. Douglass, *Teaching In Elementary School*, (second edition; New York: The Ronald Press Company, © 1958), p. 458. By permission of the Ronald Press Company.

Type of In-Service Education	Major Purpose to be Achieved	Frequency of Function
Cooperative Enterprises (Cont.)		
Observation of other teachers' work	To see different teaching techniques and instructional aids	As opportunity permits or necessity dictates
Teacher committees	Study curricular problems and recommend needed curriculum revisions	As opportunity permits or necessity dictates
Action research	Scientific investigation of a curricular problem by a group of school personnel	As opportunity permits or necessity dictates
Individual Endeavors		
Graduate work	To increase one's understanding of children, acquire new methods, study new curricular materials, earn an advanced degree	Institutional summer school from three to nine weeks; extension or correspondence courses
Reading -- general and professional	To keep abreast of new developments and trends in the profession and in our contemporary society	As opportunity permits or necessity dictates
Travel	To have direct experience with places and things about which the teacher teaches	As opportunity permits or necessity dictates
Membership and participation in professional organizations	To keep abreast of new policies and practices which can improve the overall instructional program	Most national and state organizations meet one time a year for a period of two to five days; district and local affiliates meet more frequently for day or half-day sessions
Professional writing	To share pertinent curricular information with others through publications	As opportunity permits and promising policies and practices are devised

Figure 12. (Continued)

94

tunity for long will eventually inherit a lifeless program of instruction and a group of teachers who are less than enthusiastic.

Suppose that a school has utilized the self-contained classroom plan of organization, the subjects-in-isolation curricular pattern, and the textbook as the predominant instructional medium for several years. During that period of time, suppose that the school board and administrative staff had repeatedly denied requests from the teachers to try other organizational plans, curriculum patterns, and instructional media. Such a course of action would likely thwart teacher creativity, imagination, resourcefulness, and enthusiasm for the teaching-learning situation.

Contrast that debilitating situation with a school which remains sensitive to sound teacher ideas for experimentation. Such a school realizes that if the teachers are enthusiastic about a new innovation and desire to implement it in their own building, their dedication to the project will likely insure its success. Rather than stifling the desire of the teachers to experiment through rigidly holding to the established program, they are encouraged to try their own ideas for curriculum improvement. Perhaps they desire to experiment with other systems of organization such as team teaching, nongraded primary, or the dual progress plan. Maybe they would like to try the broad fields, core, learner centered, or eclectic curriculum patterns and utilize mass media more extensively. If so, they should be encouraged to experiment when their planning is sound and they are committed to experiment long enough to see if the results they obtain from the new method is superior to the conventional plan.

The elementary schools which have made the largest mark on education at this level in the United States have been those which dared to experiment. Symbolic of these schools are the Winnetka (Illinois) and Dalton (Massachusetts) systems. Experimentation is the lifeblood of a vibrant curriculum.

SHAPING THE CURRICULUM FOR THE DEMANDS OF THE FUTURE

The curriculum of the elementary school is continually changing. This is as it should be. A curriculum which remains impervious to the changing needs of a dynamic society is altogether inappropriate. We are living in an age which is characterized by an explosion of knowledge. It has been said that knowledge is doubling every ten years or less. No longer can a nation or a group of individuals hold a philosophy of isolationism. Men are more than ever interdependent upon one another for the necessities of life. There are therefore many factors which will shape the curriculum of the future.

Among them will be the social conditions of the times, improved instructional media, increased curriculum research, governmental influence, a greater emphasis on individual scholarship and a continuously changing curriculum philosophy.

SOCIAL CONDITIONS

One of the foremost factors which will shape the elementary school curriculum is the prevalent social conditions. The curriculum of the elementary school throughout American history has been the handmaiden of society. As societal needs have changed, the public school curriculum has been altered to take care of the new demands imposed upon the school. Society's changing demands upon the school over the past three hundred years, as outlined by Ragan and modified by Shuster and Ploghoft, are depicted in Figure 13.

One can easily trace the curriculum changes which have taken place in America's elementary schools since the Colonial period right up to our contemporary times through a study of Figure 13. Whereas in 1647 the major purpose of education was religious instruction, it now is social appreciations. The Colonial schools taught the Three R's predominantly, while we presently are teaching the language arts, social studies, arithmetic, science, arts, crafts, health, and physical education. Whereas memorization of facts and rote drill characterized elementary instruction in 1647, experience units with related meaningful drill for skill are now being utilized.

These are but a few of the changes which have taken place in curriculum development over the past three hundred years. It is hard to visualize what the curriculum of the 1970's, 80's, 90's or the twenty-first century will be like, but it is safe to assume that the program of instruction will change in keeping with the needs of society.

IMPROVED INSTRUCTIONAL MEDIA

Teachers have become expert in their use of older instructional media such as films, filmstrips, tapes, slides, recordings, and the opaque projector. In fact, it is hard to find an elementary classroom in which most of these teaching aids are not commonplace. Recent technological advancements have provided us with newer types of instructional media such as television, the overhead projector with its transparencies, and programmed learning which frequently involves the utilization of the teaching machines. Within themselves they are only gadgets, but under the wise direction of a skilled teacher they become effective teaching tools. Elementary school teachers doubtlessly will make greater utilization of these media in the years ahead.

THREE HUNDRED YEARS OF COMMUNITY AND CURRICULUM DEVELOPMENT

Period	Colonial–1647	National–1776	Jacksonian–1800's	Modern–1900's
Purpose of Education	Religious instruction	Appreciate political freedom	Personal and economic advancement	Social appreciations
Content of Curriculum	Reading, writing, spelling, arithmetic, related religious subjects	Reading, writing, spelling, arithmetic, physiology, hygiene, grammar, history, geography, drawing, music, agriculture, deportment	Reading, writing, spelling, arithmetic, physiology, hygiene, English, grammar, language, history, Constitution of the U.S., geography, music, arts and crafts, citizenship, manual training, homemaking, civics, physical education, nature study, literature, deportment	Language arts, social studies, arithmetic, science, arts, crafts, health, physical education
Administrative Organization	Ungraded	Ungraded	Graded, departmental, platoon	Graded, some grade divisions disappearing, ungraded primaries, team teaching
Types of Schools	Dame schools, apprentice schools, reading and writing schools, ciphering schools	Kindergartens, 8 year elementary schools	Nursery schools, kindergartens, 8 year elementary schools	6 and 8 year elementary schools with primary, intermediate, and upper elementary divisions
Methods of Instruction	Emphasis on individual memorization	Monitorial group instruction	Recitation, supervised study, units and project method (individual and group)	Recitation, experience units, group committees

Figure 13. Albert H. Shuster and Milton E. Ploghoft, *The Emerging Elementary Curriculum*, (Columbus, Ohio: Charles E. Merrill Books, Inc., 1963), pp. 14-15, as adapted from William B. Ragan, *Modern Elementary Curriculum*, (revised edition; New York: Henry Holt & Co., 1960) pp. 16-17, Copyright © 1960, Holt, Rinehart and Winston, Inc., by permission of publishers.

THREE HUNDRED YEARS OF COMMUNITY AND CURRICULUM DEVELOPMENT

Period	Colonial–1647	National–1776	Jacksonian–1800's	Modern–1900's
Organization of the Curriculum	Separate subjects	Separate subjects	Separate subjects, correlation, fusion	Separate subjects, correlation, fusion, integration
Teacher Preparation	None	Normal schools	Teachers colleges, schools of education, in-service education	Expanding departments and schools of education experimentation in functional types of teacher education preparation
Control of Curriculum	Local	Local, state	State departments of education, national committees	National committees, state committees, local committees
Materials of Instruction	Hornbook, New England primer	Ungraded textbooks	State adopted texts for separate subjects	Multiple adopted texts, libraries, audio-visual, varied community resources, teaching machines, programmed learning materials

Figure 13. (Continued)

INCREASED CURRICULUM RESEARCH

Another factor which will play an important role in shaping the curriculum of the future is increased curriculum research. Public schools and universities are presently engaged in extensive curriculum research studies. Many of these studies are financed by the U. S. Office of Education, the Ford Foundation, and the Kellogg Foundation. Results of these studies frequently are published in such publications as the *Review of Educational Research* and the *Journal of Education Research*. Teachers can keep abreast of advancement in curriculum research by reading these journals. Many other national publications such as *Educational Leadership, Arithmetic Teacher, Elementary School Journal, National Elementary School Principal, Reading Teacher, Journal of Developmental Reading, School Science and Mathematics,* and *Mathematics Teacher* also carry articles of interest to the elementary teacher.

Perhaps the studies which will do the most good in the final analysis, however, are those action research projects which are carried on within the individual elementary school buildings by teachers. It is at this level that the most far-reaching changes in curriculum are effected. The reason for this is simple; application and implementation of the project findings can be facilitated by those who conduct the research. We can expect to find increased action research in curriculum development in the years ahead within the individual elementary schools since most teachers have learned to view change as a vital element of a dynamic educational program in the Space Age.

GOVERNMENTAL INFLUENCE

The curriculum will be shaped to some degree in the future, as it has in the past, by governmental influence from the state and federal level. The states will continue their minimum foundation programs of financial assistance which guarantees each school certain administrative, supervisory, and teaching personnel for curriculum development in the light of that system's fiscal ability to pay for such professional services. Undoubtedly some schools will make greater effort financially to provide monies for improved curriculum in the future, but it is safe to assume that the state will carry an ever increasing burden of responsibility in this area.

The state department of education in the various states will likely play an increasingly important role in shaping the curriculum to meet the demands of the future in other areas as well. Some of the improved services which they should provide are:

1. A better informed staff of consultants in the different subject matter fields.
2. A better selection of films, filmstrips, and tapes available from the state film library.
3. Improved state curriculum guides for the disciplines included in the elementary instructional program.
4. Increased use of television as a media of instruction with a state department studio and regularly scheduled programs to transmit enrichment lessons given by teaching specialists in such subject matter areas as mathematics and science.
5. Grants-in-aid for teachers in-service who desire to go to summer school and earn a higher degree, extend their proficiencies in their subject areas, or qualify for a fifth or sixth year teaching certificate.
6. Funding pilot projects for curriculum improvement. (An example of this is Georgia's Summer Reading Program in which 6,000 poor readers were taught by 400 teachers in 1964 during a two month term completely financed by the State Department of Education.)[29]

The state has a significant role in helping the local school district provide rich and vital programs of instruction for their constituents. It should assert more aggressive leadership in the future as it works cooperatively with the local school systems to provide enriched curriculum sensitive to the needs of an ever changing complex society.

The federal government actually has no authority delegated to it by the Constitution for control of the public schools in any manner except through the common defense and general welfare clause. Under such conditions in the past, however, it has provided funds to the state to be allocated to the local district for vocational education and school lunch and milk programs. Since 1958, through provisions of the National Defense Education Act, the federal government has exerted influence upon the curriculums of America's schools by pumping funds into the local systems to upgrade the quality of instruction and materials in science, mathematics, foreign language and other programs. There seems to be an ever increasing pressure upon the federal government to allocate grants to insure an adequate and equal educational program in every geographical area of our nation. One cannot predict with certainty the extent of financial assistance from the federal government for curriculum development. It is evident, however, that the government will exert direct influence upon shaping the curriculum of the elemenatry schools in the future if it is in the best interest of the nation to do so in order to promote the common defense or general welfare.

---

[29]"Handbook for Teachers in Summer Reading Program," (Sponsored by Georgia State Department of Education), Athens: University of Georgia's College of Education, 1964), p. 2.

The U. S. Office of Education is an agency of the federal government which assists the states and the local school districts in curriculum development in many ways. Two practices are particularly helpful in curriculum work: (1) providing consultative services of specialists who work with schools on curriculum projects and (2) publishing periodic bulletins which can be used by teachers in curriculum development.[30]

The local school district should not expect the state or federal government to take the initiative in shaping its curriculum to meet the demands of the future. Rather it should exert its own leadership and endeavor to provide more than a minimum program of instruction through local effort supplemented by available governmental assistance.

INCREASED EMPHASIS ON INDIVIDUAL SCHOLARSHIP

Another factor which will likely influence the elementary curriculum of the future is an increased emphasis on individual scholarship, not for just the bright students but for the average and dull as well. Since the potential suregon, bookkeeper, and carpenter sit side-by-side in the elementary classroom, the curriculum of the future must demand the best scholastically from all of the students.

If the instructional program is to accomplish this worthy objective it must be sensitive to some elementary concepts in the teaching-learning situation. First, the curriculum of tomorrow's elementary schools must be aligned with the concept of recognition of the individual uniqueness of each student and of his inalienable right to be afforded educational opportunities which are consistent with his abilities, needs, and desires. Second, standards must be set which will elicit maximum pupil effort. The experiences which are provided in the chemistry laboratory should differ only in kind and not in degree with those provided in the woodworking shop. Third, the curriculum should contain content for the development of appropriate attitudes and appreciations for all of the students. Some of the values which should be taught in the instructional program are honesty, integrity, self-respect, perserverance, responsibility, cooperation, and courage. Finally, the curriculum must provide the individual student with experience which will enable him to learn how to adjust to changing situa-

---

[30]Examples of U. S. Office of Education publications which assist the local school district in curriculum development are the following:

Wilhelmina Hill, *Unit Planning and Teaching in Elementary Social Studies* (Washington, D. C.: U. S. Office of Education, 1963)

————, *Social Studies in the Elementary School Program* (Washington, D. C.: U. S. Office of Education, 1960)

Stuart E. Dean, *Elementary School Administration and Organization* (Washington, D. C.: U. S. Office of Education, 1960)

tions. Schools can encourage individual scholarship by helping students become more self-reliant and not dependent upon preconceived notions or established traditions in dealing with their problems.[31] Students can be taught to apply the scientific method by posing alternate solutions and experimenting with a chosen one until the problems are resolved. In short, individual scholarship demands flexibility of thought and a student willingness to adjust readily to changing situations.

A CHANGING CURRICULUM PHILOSOPHY

The curricular philosophy of any age with which our democratic society has been confronted has been shaped by the requirements of the times. The philosophy of curriculum development during the Colonial Period (1647-1775) was drill for mastery and rote memorization of supposedly necessary skills and subject matter. The Nationalism Period (1776-1799) saw the curriculum philosophy hold to the drill and memorization theory but also incorporate political ideas to teach the perpetuation of a new system of government based on democratic ideals. During the Jacksonian Period (1800-1899) a new philosophy for curriculum emerged which began to stress life adjustment education. The curriculum was modified to include many new subjects as nature study or science, art, music, cooking, sewing, manual training, civics, and geography. The basic philosophy held that each person should receive an education which would enable him to be successful in his chosen vocation.

The curriculum philosophy of the Modern Period (1900-1957) has subscribed to the theory that there are certain knowledge and understandings, attitudes and appreciations, and skills which children should learn to become contributing members of our democratic society. The knowledge and understandings are factual information which every educated person should possess. The attitudes and appreciations are those basic beliefs which are imperative for effective democratic citizenship. The skills involve the mastery of the communicative methods by which man expresses himself or learns from others.

The Modern Period has witnessed a change in the curriculum philosophy of progressive education from a subject approach curriculum to a learner centered theory. As the movement has progressed, the emphasis upon mastery of content, skills, and appreciations has remained constant. Modern Period philosophy, however, dictates that children attain these cultural imperatives through experiences which are more child centered and less formal.

---

[31]Sidney Rosenblum, "Children and Youth in the Space Age," *Educational Leadership*, XXI, No. 7, (April, 1964), pp. 450-451.

What will be the curriculum philosophy of the Space Age (1957-?)? No one can predict with certainly, but we can be sure that it will continually change in order to keep up with the times. A number of educated guesses as to its logical characteristics follow.

Readiness will have to be redefined. Children will be enrolled in public nursery schools beginning at age four and will advance to the public school kindergarten at age five. Completion of this work will be prerequisite to entering the elementary program.

Children will be submitted to a broad range of social experiences and educational media. Programed materials and machines, instructional television, art work, manipulative arithmetic aids, science paraphernalia and specimens, reading readiness materials and other realia will be available to assist children in experimenting and learning at all levels.

The concept of "gradedness" will eventually be disposed of and children will work through enriched curriculum materials as they are ready to handle larger concepts. For example, a mature and able student may be allowed to begin reading at age four or five in the nursery or kindergarten. He will be grouped with other early beginners in subsequent years. Or, a student may not be ready to begin reading even though he has attended both the nursery and kindergarten until he is almost through his first year in the elementary grades. In that event, he will not be rushed into assuming work of which he is not capable until evidences of his readiness to begin it are clearly distinguishable. He will be placed with children of similar age and ability in subsequent years for future instruction.

Through the elementary years children will be working on a nongraded basis in the light of their individual proficiencies. This will start in the primary and eventually spread into the intermediate grades.

There will be an advent of more teaching specialists into the elementary school, particularly for older and more articulate students. Areas likely to be influenced most by these specialists are reading, arithmetic, and science.

The idea that a knowledge of the past is requisite to making intelligent decisions will likely undergo drastic revision in curriculum philosophy. With the mushrooming of new knowledge in the Spage Age, modern philosophy will likely dictate that the teaching of "key concepts" will be more advantageous for students than a shallow and superficial coverage of all of the old understandings as well as the new revelations and discoveries. It has recently been said that man can no longer predict for tomorrow on the criteria of yesterday's experiences altogether because the future is too unpredictable.[32]

---

[32]Hilda Taba, "The Child in a Technological Society," Speech to the 19th Annual ASCD Conference, Miami Beach (April, 1964).

Space Age curriculum philosophy will hold to the idea that the curriculum should be so designed that it will provide experiences which will enable children to become more self-reliant. Fixed thinking will be incompatible with scientific principles of investigation in the Space Age. A forward looking philosophy will hold to the problem solving approach of study and teaching in order to create more autonomous individuals who are capable of meeting unforeseen experiences with an open mind.

SUMMARY

Innovations have taken place in elementary school curriculum in an effort to find a more acceptable method of teaching knowledges and understanding, attitudes and appreciations, and skills to children. The basic objectives which guide the instructional program of the elementary school have changed little in recent years, but a plethora of curricular organizational patterns has evolved, each one reputed to be a panacea for effecting desired student outcomes.

First, there was the *subjects-in-isolation* pattern with each subject being taught as a separate entity. An innovation known as the *correlated subjects* was then devised and utilized in some elementary schools in an attempt to relate learnings between the separate subjects and escape the artificial segmentation of the subjects-in-isolation approach. Eventually a curricular design was created which grouped subjects into common areas such as language arts, social studies, and science and health. This plan became known as *broad fields*.

A fourth innovation was that which was called the *core*. In this approach, social studies or science normally formed the core and full integration was accomplished with the language arts. The balance of the skills subjects, fine arts, and recreational activities were taught separately under this plan. The *learner centered* curricular pattern was another innovation utilized in some schools which desired to develop a curriculum based solely on children's interest and desires. Such an approach to curriculum development centered around basic problems of living or life adjustment education. Under such a plan, the children and the teacher planned together what they would study in an unstructured interdisciplinary manner. The sixth curricular design discussed in this chapter was the *eclectic* approach. This pattern attempts to strike a happy medium between the proponents of the child centered school and the subjects-in-isolation protagonists. The plan provides for a certain segment of the day to be set aside for skills teaching, unit study, and creative and recreative arts.

Each of these curricular patterns has its own unique merits. Regardless of which plan is chosen, teacher acceptance of and dedication to a given pattern is imperative if the basic objectives of the elementary school are to be accomplished.

In organizing for curriculum development, the teacher's daily class schedule will be influenced mainly by two things, (1) the curricular pattern chosen, and (2) the school schedule. If the subjects-in-isolation pattern is utilized, for example, the daily class schedule will be characterized by many periods of short duration as the study of the various subjects of the instructional program unfolds. On the other hand, if the learner centered curricular pattern is utilized there will be decidedly fewer periods with the work concentrating primarily on children's interests and needs in longer blocks of time. Second, if the school utilizes teaching specialists in such areas as music, physical education, or art, the individual classroom teacher will have to build his daily schedule around that of the teaching specialists.

The school which seeks to establish a program of continuous curriculum improvement should provide a dynamic program of in-service education for its teachers. It should also create an environment in which they feel free to experiment with new materials and teaching techniques.

Finally, if the elementary school is to shape its curriculum to meet the needs of boys and girls in the future it should become increasingly research oriented; it should acquire the latest improved instructional media; and it should continually revise its curricular philosophy to keep the instructional program in pace with the times.

QUESTIONS FOR DISCUSSION

1. The term "co-curricular subjects" was used extensively a decade ago. Today it is almost never used. How do you explain this fact?

2. Who determines the curriculum pattern used in the school? To what extent should the individual teacher be permitted to select the type used in his classroom?

3. Should each classroom teacher be permitted to establish time allotments for the subjects he teaches and work out his own daily classroom schedule or should this be uniformly prescribed for all teachers by the school? Why or why not?

4. It has been said that man cannot adequately plan for the future solely on his knowledge of history because things are changing too rapidly in the Space Age. Assuming that this statement is true, what implications does it pose for devising an elementary school curriculum which will prepare children for successful living in our contemporary society?

5. In-service education has been both praised and ridiculed as an instrument for meeting the continuing educational needs of teachers. What is your position on this issue? Under what conditions is the in-service program likely to be most effective? What factors tend to minimize its effectiveness?

6. Should the curriculum pattern dictate the organizational plan of the school or should the organizational plan determine the curriculum pattern used? Why or why not?

TOPICS FOR RESEARCH

1. Read about teaching machines and experiment with them if possible to determine for yourself the possibilities which they afford for innovations in curriculum development.

2. Devise an adequate in-service program for an elementary school for one year selecting some area of the curriculum for major concentration such as the language arts, arithmetic, art, etc.

3. Visit different elementary schools which utilize different curriculum patterns, i.e., subjects-in-isolation, correlated subjects, broad fields, core, learner centered, and eclectic, and determine which of these plans seems to be most desirable in meeting student needs.

BIBLIOGRAPHY

BECK, ROBERT H., WALTER W. COOK AND NOLAN C. KEARNEY. *Curriculum in the Modern Elementary School.* Second edition. Englewood Cliffs, N. J.: Prentice-Hall, Inc., 1960.

BURR, JAMES B., LOWRY W. HARDING AND LELAND B. JACOBS. *Student Teaching in the Elementary School.* Second edition. New York: Appleton-Century-Crofts, Inc., 1958.

DAUGHERTY, JAMES L. A *Study of Achievement in Sixth Grade Arithmetic in Des Moines Public Schools,* Research Study No. 1 (unpublished doctoral dissertation, Colorado State College, Greeley, 1955).

DEAN, STUART E. *Elementary School Administration and Organization.* Washington: U. S. Department of Health, Education, and Welfare, Office of Education, 1960.

DENNY, ROBERT RAY. A *Two-Year Study of the Effects of An Increased Time Allotment Upon Achievement in Arithmetic in the Intermediate Grades,* Field Study No. 1 (Greeley: Colorado State College, 1955).

Educational Policies Commission, *The Purposes of Education in American Democracy. Washington,* D. C.: National Education Association, 1938.

GWYNN, J. MINOR. *Theory and Practice of Supervision.* New York: Dodd, Mead, and Company, 1961.

"Handbook for Teachers in Summer Reading Program," (Sponsored by Georgia State Department of Education), Athens: University of Georgia's College of Education, 1964.

HILL, WILHELMINA. *Social Studies in the Elementary School Program.* Washington, D. C.: U. S. Office of Education, 1960.

HILL, WILHELMINA. *Unit Planning and Teaching in Elementary Social Studies.* Washington, D. C.: U. S. Office of Education, 1963.

JARVIS, OSCAR T. "How Much Time for Spelling?" *The Instructor.* Volume LXIII, Number 1, September, 1963, pp. 59, 156.

JARVIS, OSCAR T. "Teaching Specialists Who Assist Elementary Homeroom Teachers," *The Nation's Schools.* Volume 74, Number 6, December, 1964, p. 33.

JARVIS, OSCAR T. *Time Allotments and Pupil Achievement in the Intermediate Elementary Grades.* University of Houston: Bureau of Education Research and Services, 1962.

KEARNEY, NOLAN C., *Elementary School Objectives.* New York: Russell Sage Foundation, 1953.

LEE, BEATRICE CRUMP. *Instructional Time Allotment in Elementary Schools,* National Education Association Research Division, July, 1961, p. 5, 6.

MEHL, MARIE A., HUBERT H. MILLS AND HARL R. DOUGLASS. *Teaching in Elementary School.* New York: The Ronald Press Company, 1958.

OTTO, HENRY J., AND DAVID C. SANDERS. *Elementary School Organization and Administration.* Fourth edition. New York: Appleton-Century-Crofts, 1964.

RAGAN, WILLIAM B. *Teaching America's Children.* New York: Holt, Rinehart and Winston, 1961.

RICE, J. M. "The Futility of the Spelling Grind," *Forum* XXIII, 1897, pp. 163-172.

ROSEMBLUM, SIDNEY. "Children and Youth in the Space Age," *Educational Leadership.* XXI, No. 7, April, 1964, pp. 450-451.

SHUSTER, ALBERT H., AND MILTON E. PLOGHOFT. *The Emerging Elementary Curriculum.* Charles E. Merrill Books, Inc., 1963.

TABA, HILDA. "The Child in a Technological Society," (Speech), to the 19th Annual ASCD Conference, Miami Beach, April, 1964.

TIEGS, ERNEST W., AND FAY ADAMS. *Teaching the Social Studies.* New York: Ginn and Company, 1959.

The child, the boy, the man should
know no other endeavor but to be at
every stage of development wholly
what that stage calls for. FROEBEL

Part Two

Children and the
Learning Environment

Photo: Wide World Photos

Teacher observation of students at work facilitates understanding of the elementary school child.

Chapter 4

Understanding Elementary School Children

Assuming that the major purpose of education is that of helping all individuals grow into self-directing, productive citizens in a democratic society, it is essential that teachers have a clear understanding of the principal concepts of human growth and development. Also, they should possess some fundamental beliefs about the worth and value of the individual. Effective educational planning must be based upon the belief that the individual grows as a whole with different aspects of his personal development progressing at varied rates. It must be recognized that children are not adults and that they do not think, feel, or react as grown people do. Physically, mentally, and emotionally each child is a growing, changing person with needs and potentialities which are unique.

It is recognized that there are certain skeletal patterns, certain personality types, groups of children that fall within certain intelligence ranges, certain physical stamina categories, and those that achieve within ranges of similarities on certain tests of content and skills. However, the teacher must accept children with the philosophy that each is individually unique and it is his responsibility to provide environment and experiences in which every student can attain his maximum mental, emotional, and physical growth. This means understanding the child first. This comes through accepting the child as he is and for what he may become.

In order that the teacher can understand the child he must know much about him and the circumstances and environment which surround him.

This concept is expressed by Logan and Logan in the following precise expression:

> It means understanding his physical, social, emotional and intellectual growth. It also means knowing his characteristics and needs, his motivations and frustrations, his successes and failures. It means praising him when he achieves and helping him set more realistic goals when he fails. It means knowing his family, his peers, and the social and physical factors that influence his unique personality. It means not being satisfied to evaluate him until all that can be learned about him is known. It means using this knowledge to teach him more effectively in group situations and individually.[1]

The concept of growth as a developmental sequence is important to the teacher. So that he is able to know relatively what to expect of the child at any given time, he should understand the entire growth cycle from infancy to adulthood with particular reference to the years spent from nursery through elementary school. Although children follow an orderly pattern from one stage to the other, each has his own individual pattern. Generally the rapid developer will continue to develop rapidly while the slower developing child will continue at his slow methodical rate. Each has his own limits which the teacher should understand in order that undue pressure is not put on the slower developing child and that the faster developer can be challenged sufficiently.

The teacher must understand that all parts of the child's body and mind do not necessarily develop at the same rate. Many youngsters encounter a period of rapid physical development which consumes their energies and makes them listless and apparently disinterested in school work. The wise teacher will realize that during this period of physical growth the mental processes are developing even though the youngster may not appear to be interested in the academic aspects of living. He should recognize that he can expect no more growth than is in harmony with the child's individual pattern. He should also assist the child to accept himself and use his ability and energies to the best advantage.

The child's needs, motives, and other personal-social drives will develop as the result of living and interacting in his particular environment. Growth is innate and a powerful force which in turn creates expanding needs of the individual. Growth may be accelerated under favorable conditions but academic and cultural accomplishments must be brought about through a continuous program which involves the individual in utilizing his capabili-

---

[1]Lillian M. Logan and Virgil G. Logan, *Teaching the Elementary School Child* (Boston: Houghton Mifflin Company, 1961), p. 29.

ties in a satisfying manner. The teacher should realize that the academic achievement of the child is affected by his physical and social environment as well as factors of personality and physiological development.

The child's initial responses in all phases of development are generalized. The young child responds to stimuli with the whole body. Responses are made with individual parts of the body as these are developed. Early unguided and clumsy responses later develop into skilled and specialized language and motor skills. Every individual normally passes through the various stages of development according to the influences of his own dominant characteristics, needs, health, motives, and personal-social drives.

AGE CHARACTERISTICS AND BEHAVIORAL CHANGES

To help the teacher prepare to understand children, information is provided here which sets forth some of the more important age characteristics and behavioral changes. This is not recommended as a comprehensive grading and listing but as a suggestive presentation to guide the teacher in doing his own cataloguing as he works with children. Particular attention is called to several sources helpful to the teacher in determining age characteristics and behavioral changes of children.[2]

The range of mental ages among children at any grade level is very great. This premise is verified as follows by Beck, Cook and Kearney:

> In a first-grade class made up of a random group of six-year-old children, 2 per cent of the pupils have mental ages of less than four years, and 2 per cent have mental ages of more than eight years. In other words, if we disregard the 2 per cent at both ends of the distribution and consider only the middle 96 per cent of the class, we have a four-year range in mental development . . . When we examine the variability in intelligence and achievement of children at the end of the sixth grade or at the beginning of the seventh grade (twelve-year-olds), we find it to be twice what it was in the first grade (measured in age units). At this level the range of intelligence and achievement (2nd to 98th percentile) is between seven and eight years.[3]

---

[2]See *Curriculum Framework for Georgia Schools,* (Atlanta: State Department of Education, 1954), pp. 7-9; *Child Growth and Development, Characteristics and Needs* (a chart), (District of Columbia, Washington: Public School System, 1946), p. 1; Gladys Gardner Jenkins, *These Are Your Children* (expanded edition; Atlanta: Scott Foresman and Company, 1953), pp. 64-199; Robert J. Havighurst (*Developmental Tasks and Education* (New York: Longmans, Green and Company, 1952).

[3]Robert Beck, Walter Cook and Nolan Kearney, *Curriculum in the Modern Elementary School* (second edition, Englewood Cliffs: Prentice-Hall, Inc., © 1960), pp. 33-34. Reprinted by permission of Prentice-Hall, Inc.

The teacher thus must be aware that within any chronological age group (not to mention grade level) he must be prepared to deal with children of varied maturity. He must realize, however, that there is a sequence of maturational stages through which the child passes at different ages, each covering varying lengths of time. The teacher should determine where each child is on the ladder of maturation and be prepared to help him move to the next rung at the appropriate time.

PRESCHOOL CHILDREN

Preschool children with organized educational experience are in the age range of three to six years. Because of entrance age limits in some states, many children do not enter the elementary school until they are six-and-one-half years old and in many cases the child may be six years eleven months before permitted to enter the first grade or first level in the public school. On the other hand, a few school systems are beginning to use another criterion, that of readiness as determined by standardized tests, as a basis for entrance. Nursery and kindergarten are being added to the educational ladder providing additional years of organized learning experiences. Thus we find that the make-up of the first year in the primary school may vary considerably because of admission and grade level factors.

The childhood years of three to six are characterized by an amazing growth in knowledge, independence, and ability of the child to do things for himself. By the time he is four he has outgrown his baby softness and roundness. He is considerably larger, sturdier, and more self reliant. He has become cognizant of himself as an individual and responds best when treated as an individual. During these years the child thrives on much bodily activity and vigorous outdoor play. Through these, physical growth and body coordination are enhanced.

Probably the most valuable trait of this age child is curiosity even though it may be most annoying to the busy adult. This burning desire to touch, to see inside, and ask why, when met with favorable response by the grownup, opens many doors for the child's development .

By the age of four the child usually is able to communicate with adults well in a reasonable flow of language. He often becomes fascinated with words and repeats nonsensical syllables just for fun. Repetition of toilet words as a rule is a passing attraction that need cause little concern if treated by the parent in a wholesome manner.

Some cooperative play usually begins about the age of three in such games as "house" or "train." He is just starting to share, take turns, and ask for things. He may choose a friend for a limited time, usually not for long.

By four he seems to enjoy another child while being quite noisy in his boasting and bragging. He frequently resorts to name-calling, biting, and tattling. His mother's presence is usually welcome and needed at this stage. It is a time when the child begins to break away from mother for spurts but does not want her too far away for long periods of time. Daddy also begins to enter the picture and his arrival from work is awaited with much expectation.

The five-year-old begins to acquire features and behavior which characterize him as a distinct individual. He is no longer a baby but a child ready to take on some independent activities away from home, such as those in kindergarten, part of the day.

Language facility is growing to the point of his being able to tell about an experience at home or school clearly. He is able at age five, with limited assistance, to do many things on his own such as bathing, dressing, and feeding himself.

It is at five that the child seems to begin to recognize right from wrong and wants to please his parents. Because of this sense of acceptance, kindergarten may be an important element in developing ability for group participation, thus paving the way for a more formal first grade classroom atmosphere.

Some of the pertinent age characteristics of preschool children are as follows:

1. The rate of growth is slow compared to the first 1 1/2 years of life.
2. Lateral-type (broad-built) children develop more rapidly than the linear-type (slender-built).
3. The bones are not completely calcified. Their softness prevents breakage during the child's frequent falls.
4. There is a full set of temporary teeth by three years.
5. Development is confined mainly to the large muscles.
6. Children may lose interest and ability in one skill while acquiring another.
7. The organic system is sufficiently mature so that desirable habits of eating, sleeping, and elimination are fairly well established.
8. Children are interested in the genital organs and their function. Infantile masturbation is often an accompaniment of this interest.
9. Some postural defects may have been established by the age of 5 years.
10. At 5, handedness and eyedness have been established and should normally not be changed. Ninety per cent of children are right-handed.

11. Ages three to six are constantly active; show fatigue more often by being cross or restless; are susceptible to infectious diseases.

12. They have unevenly developed motor skills; have not fully developed accessory muscles that control fingers and hands.

13. They are concerned about health only when they are ill themselves.

14. They are concerned more with adult approval than with approval of their peers.

15. They are beginning to develop socially: 3-year-olds want to play with other children, but in small groups which tend to shift rapidly; are still egocentric (I, me, my, mine); 4-year-olds seek companionship even if it means parental disfavor; 5-year-olds may be jealous of older children, their desire for attention may be seen in all kinds of showing off. (These forms of behavior may alternate with shyness and self-consciousness behavior.)

16. They are increasingly fond of small children and animals.

17. They have generally recognized that others have some rights; physical fighting decreases and verbal criticism increases.

18. They are direct and personal in asking questions.

19. They are not concerned about race, color, sex, or economic status unless influenced by adults.

20. They adopt the manners and social customs of the family.

21. They are amused at noises, grotesque faces and figures, and dramatic situations; have vivid imaginations.

22. They are concerned with themselves, their family, and their own age mates; have no concept of the cultural heritage.[4]

Some of the behavioral changes which preschool children may encounter are as follows:

1. Cooperative play is much enjoyed. A child will play with the same age, younger, or older, but likes to be "bigger than." He shows off, but at times may be shy. He can recognize the skills of others. Boys' and girls' interests are similar.

2. Both locomotor and manipulative play are enjoyed. The use of imagination in play is seen.

3. Laughter is frequent form of communication. Those who do not communicate readily through speech may be unable to achieve close relationships with other children.

4. Children begin to play together (about age 5) in group situations for short periods of time with small numbers of children.

5. They are influenced in speech, language, and social development by environment; thinking and reasoning are becoming more apparent. (Girls develop speech slightly in advance of boys.)

6. There must be a wide variety of activities to develop the muscles of arms and shoulders, the trunk, and the legs and feet. Climbing and

---

[4]See *Curriculum Framework for Georgia Schools.* (Atlanta: State Department of Education, 1954), pp. 7-9; *Child Growth and Development, Characteristics and Needs* (a chart) (District of Columbia, Washington: Public School System, 1946), p. 1.

hanging are essential. Kiddy cars, wagons, scooters, tricycles, and boats are enjoyed. Nail-pounding and block-building are desirable. Additional play may be with sand, toys, dolls, animals.

7. Adults should deal rationally with the child if he exhibits over-interest in the sex organs. Cleanliness, loose clothing, supervision of toilet habits, and substitution of other interests are needed.

8. Children should sleep 11 to 12 hours. Sleep is a prime essential in building sturdy health. Linear-type children need more sleep than laterals. An afternoon nap of 1 to 2 hours is needed.

9. Development of liking for all types of food is a necessity, but should be accomplished without stress and strain. Regularity of mealtime is important.

10. Children should have opportunities to do things for themselves. They like to "help." This takes longer for the adult, but is valuable for children's development.[5]

PRIMARY

The primary school is made up primarily of children of ages six, seven, and eight. The first year in the primary school, age six, is one of extensive transition as the child loses his baby contours and begins to develop adult features. The body is gradually changing in shape with noticeable modification of the face including lengthening of the jaw as baby teeth are replaced by permanent molars. Though less obvious to the observer, rapid change is taking place in the internal organs. The brain has almost reached its full size, the heart is growing rapidly, and the eyes are still developing in shape and size. The tendency toward farsightedness caused by immaturity usually is corrected by age eight.

The teacher will recognize generally that the six-year-old is an active being, often characterized by the expression "he has the wiggles built in." They rush in an out, jump up from their seats, gesture and talk glibly. Each movement of the finer muscles, particularly the hands, is accompanied by movements of the mouth, eyes, and face as well as the body as a whole.

It is only natural for these youngsters to want to be first as can be observed by their dashing, pushing, and quarreling for equipment and materials. Taking turns has to be taught even though it may seemingly have been acquired by the youngster in kindergarten. Bragging about having the best or being the biggest is characteristic of the spirit of keen competition usually prevalent in the age. This is only generally true, however, for there are many who are shy and timid and shrink from the hustle and bustle of the outgoing group.

---

[5]*Ibid.*

Sex differences become evident as girls attire in the dress of their elders and engage in play involving the family. When boys are involved with the girls in such play they usually take the role of the man as father, storekeeper, or policeman. Close friends are ordinarily of the same sex.

Children of this age enjoy dramatization, particularly of the spontaneous type. A story is told with much animation and often bears the marks of creative imagination. The understanding teacher or parent assists the child in gradually distinguishing reality and fancy.

The prolific questioning is indicative of the eagerness to learn, so evident in most six-year-olds. They are interested in the now and near by and try to find clues and answers to their questions. Time and space are of little significance to these children.

The child of six recognizes the adult as someone he wants to please when this person is fair and respectful of him. Thus he will assume minor responsibilities such as straightening the chairs, watering the flowers, and feeding the pets when he is given praise for his accomplishments and limited criticism for his failures. During this period of transition involving his mental, physical, social, and emotional attributes the child needs much reassurance by adults. He often regresses and reacts violently under rigid discipline or too formal procedures. Lack of coordination frustrates him if the adult fails to give a hand when needed or insists upon his hurrying.

The seven-year-old is an active, vigorous person but may remain still for longer periods of time than the six-year-old and is not quite as spasmotic. Usually he has learned to proceed more carefully with more apparent consideration for what is taking place.

Language becomes a strong factor in the development of the seven-year-old as he learns to converse more easily. He is now beginning to use verbalization rather than physical force to express disapproval. Stories, songs, and rhythms have more meaning for him in that he can carry a tune and recognize the correctness of a melody or sequence of a story. Independent reading for pleasure may now occupy some of his time even though he still enjoys being read to. Myths, fairy tales, and poems are of particular interest to the seven-year-old. Stories of real happenings take on more significance as he increasingly seeks to find out more about how things work. Nature stories and series of books about boys and girls capture his attention, with interest in comic books taking a new high. Movies, radio, and television are very stimulating to some children, thus necessitating adults' selection of those programs most desirable for the particular child.

The seven-year-old is a sensitive child usually standing up for his own rights and often the rights of another. He wants to be independent and liked by others of his age group and at the same time meet the approval of adults.

In his effort to please, he often becomes meticulous and over-concerned about correctness in his school work. True values of right and wrong and honesty are still a problem to him, even though he is more aware of ethical behavior and the feelings and attitudes of others. His horizon is reaching out to include experiences beyond his immediate environment as well as more concern for other people. In so doing, he may criticize his playmates and tattle to the teacher and his mother.

The eight-year-old is quite conscious of the adult world and wants to participate more in it. He is enthusiastic and often rushes into situations beyond his wisdom, thus facing many accidents. His desire to find out and try new experiences continues to develop if this spirit has not been squelched by adults. He is still much in need of praise, encouragement, and being reminded of his responsibilities. He is very sensitive, shedding tears when strong discipline is administered and building up resentment when he does not understand the actions of adults.

There is need for exercise of the large muscles in active, outdoor play in order to cope with his boundless energy. Softball, baseball, and other organized games appeal to this age. Such games and gadgets as monopoly, parchesi, erector sets, electric trains, and models of airplanes, ships, cars and trains, hold his attention for countless hours. Girls spend much time in dressing up and playing with dolls at this age.

The eight-year-old begins to cherish the club and gang. He usually picks a best "friend" who may change from time to time and offer a source of satisfaction as well as many arguments. The distinction between boys and girls usually widens at this time; they often gang up against each other for name-calling and teasing.

Dramatic play is a very definite part of the life of the eight-year-old. Boys relive the television programs and movies they see and girls may act out with their dolls scenes which appeal to them. Westerns usually appeal to the boys. Neither boys nor girls at this age care much for love stories. Comic books play a vital role in the interests of the eight-year-old as they read, reread, exchange them with their peers. This age has a natural yen for collecting. This desire may serve as a motivating factor in learning when mother and teacher recognize the child's assortment of bits of paper, string, rocks, bugs, and stamps as important to him. During this age the child's allowance may become significant as he begins to save money to obtain a baseball glove, a tent, or bicycle.

The concept of time is now beginning to take on some significance as he meets the family schedule of meals and work and participates in class-room decisions as to scheduling activities. Observance of special days such as Christmas, Washington's birthday, and Valentine are within his scope of understanding. He still has to be reminded of some routine functions such as bedtime, however, and persists in putting things off.

The eight-year-old recognizes that there is a past and future, that people live and die, and that people lived before him and others will live after him. He is also beginning to realize that children live in other parts of the world, some differently and others much as he does. He is interested in maps and pictures of other places and how people live in these places. As he recognizes other people, their likes and differences, he begins to understand himself better. He is willing to accept the fact that some do better in some ways than he and that he excels in other ways unless the pressure by adults causes him to be overly concerned. He may even be willing to see some of his own mistakes and laugh at them and plan to do better in spite of the fact that he is prone to make excuses for himself.

Some of the pertinent age characteristics of primary children are as follows:

1. An annual growth of 2 or 3 inches and a weight gain of 3 to 6 pounds is expected but there are wide variations, each with its own significance. Some change should be discernible within each 3-month period.

2. At 5 years the legs are lengthening rapidly. The spine has adult curves. The 6-year-old girl is as mature skeletally as the 7-year-old boy.

3. Mental maturity and social adjustment have some correlation with skeletal maturity.

4. The loss of deciduous teeth begins at 5 to 6 years. First permanent teeth to appear are the 6-year molars, important as the keystone to hold the dental arch in place. The central incisors appear next.

5. The large muscles of the arms and legs are more developed than the small muscles of the hands and fingers.

6. Muscular development is uneven and incomplete but motor skills are developing.

7. The lungs are relatively small.

8. The heart is growing rapidly. It is easily damaged by toxins and bacteria and must be protected against strain during convalescence from contagious diseases of childhood.

9. Taxing the heart should be avoided by seeing that children do not compete with those who are stronger or more mature physically.

10. A healthy 6, 7, or 8-year-old has bright eyes, color in his face, straight legs, and great vitality.

11. They are susceptible to fatigue and may withdraw from play when tired.

12. Ages six through eight are generally healthy, strong, and active, but tire easily; enjoy stunts, climbing, jungle gyms; engage in teasing and rough and tumble activities.

13. They grow faster physically but unevenly during the latter part of period; have more control over large muscles near end of period where eye-hand coordination is sufficient for writing, sawing, and other close range activities.
14. They are subject to respiratory diseases.
15. They are short-sighted and have a relatively short interest span — making it difficult to do close work, such as reading, that requires long periods of time.
16. They are disturbed when hurried or pressed by adults.
17. They have fears resulting from insecurity at home and school; need love of family, friendship of teachers, and status with their peers.
18. They are assertive about ideas and desires but do not persist for long; are beginning to form interest or pupose groups — usually of short duration; are concerned about prestige in groups — size, skills; are hurt by ridicule or loss of prestige; are influenced by style of clothes and possessions of their peers.
19. They engage in imaginative and imitative play but without much thought to plot or sequence during earlier stage; resent being disturbed when at play or work; laugh at nonsensical things and like comics.
20. They disagree, boys more than girls, boys engaging in physical force and girls in verbalism; are generally tolerant concerning race and economic status unless influenced by adults; discrimination occurs among neighbors.
21. They play together as sex equals until about eight when they begin to play separately.
22. They are concerned about personal allowances and spending for own choices; interested in earning some money; enjoy collecting and possessing.[6]

Selected behavioral changes of the primary school child may include:

1. Upon entering school there may be a resumption of certain earlier tensional behavior: thumb sucking, nail biting, knee knocking, etc. Occasional toilet lapses may occur.
2. He is eager for action and can be still for only a short time. He is interested in the activity, not in the result. He has a sense of equilibrium. He can stand on one foot, hop, and skip, keep time to music, and bounce and catch a ball. He likes to climb and jump from heights.
3. He is becoming self-dependent. He can brush his teeth, comb his hair, and dress himself. He can perform simple household tasks.
4. The child's questioning attitude extends to problems about sex differences. Knowledge is derived in the home.
5. Nutritional problems may arise when breakfast is hurried or there are frequent purchases of between-meal snacks.

---

[6]*Ibid.*

6. The child can abide by certain safety precautions: cross streets on signals, keep toys from underfoot, avoid hot radiators, stoves, and food cooking. He can understand the necessity for remaining away from those who have contagious diseases.

7. He enjoys making such toys as a wagon and playing with mechanical things that go or make a noise; is beginning to play organized and simple competitive games but not by formal rules.

8. He will test adult rules; have periods of anti-social behavior, as unacceptable language; is resentful of adults, feigns indifference, but needs family approval; has flashes of anger of short duration, but does not hold grudges; may show sympathy almost simultaneously with cruelty.

9. He is more interested in manipulating art materials than in production of realistic pictures during the early period; is becoming concerned with relative size and realisticness near the end of period.

10. He enjoys dramatic presentations of stories; enjoys pets; begins during latter period to prefer things done well; has a growing tendency to stay with a job until it is finished when interested.

11. He is interested in time; as, special days, time to go places, time to do things.

12. He is interested in writing numbers and in counting; learns from experience what halves, quarters and thirds are; can make simple purchases at the store.

13. Expression through movement and noise is necessary for growth. Vigorous exercises will increase the heart action and respiration, thus helping to build endurance. Active, boisterous games with unrestrained running and jumping are needed.

14. It is part of the child's development to play in mud, wade in puddles, fall in snow, walk in fallen leaves, and roll down hills, climb apparatus, play with animals.

15. There must be opportunity to organize simple group play, to skip and dance in small groups.

16. Dramatic activities and rhythmic activities are essential.

17. The withdrawn child must be encouraged gradually to find his place in the group.

18. The child should sleep about 11 hours.

19. Although the child from time to time may reject certain foods because of texture or strong taste, variety in the menu will provide the full protective diet.

20. The child needs training both at home and in school in using the handkerchief, keeping fingers away from mouth and nose, and training in choice of clothing appropriate to weather.[7]

INTERMEDIATE

Ages eight through twelve may appropriately be called intermediate since this is the age beyond childhood and before adolescence. Again the

---

[7]*Ibid.*

teacher must be aware that these ages are generally found in the intermediate school usually thought of as grades four through six; however, only the basic ages of nine through eleven are treated here. Data for the other ages are found in the sections before and after this treatment.

The interests of the nine-year-old, the first basic age of the intermediate school, are more like the ten and eleven age than those of the seven and eight. He often sees those younger than he as babies. This is particularly true of the girl who is nearing the age of puberty. Some few girls may begin menstruation at this age as they move ahead of boys in maturity one to two years. Physically, however, the nine-year-old is just a little larger and more mature than the eight-year-old. The growth plateau which usually precedes the spurt of growth in preadolescence may be reached at this age. The digestive, circulatory, and respiratory systems are not yet fully developed and may be strained if the youngster is allowed to compete physically beyond his strength.

As sex differences show up between the boys and girls more markedly, the boys become more boisterous than the girls and often punch and scuffle with their close friends. The girls usually engage in quieter activities such as skating, rope jumping, and jacks. Both boys and girls engage more in conversation in little huddles on the play grounds and in the building. Often their talking involves planning for their club or gang activities which are important at this age.

The child of nine is now recognized by adults as a boy or girl who is fairly dependable and responsible. He can take instructions and follow directions and express some definite sense of values. He now shows some of his real abilities and expresses his own individuality and personality.

As an individual he now seeks to attain perfection in whatever he does, especially in developing skills. He often corrects his own work because it is not acceptable to him. He will seek help in learning a new skill or technique such as swimming or painting. Reading interests also change at this age as fairy tales, fantasy, and imaginative play are replaced by interest in his community, country, and other countries, even to the extent of concerning himself with world conditions.

A feeling of loyalty and pride for his own country takes on new status as he enjoys studying different parts of his country and their means of subsistence. This is the age of hero worship. The lives of great men and women become significant as he realizes that they are the makers of history who have made unique contributions to society. This often leads him to recognize different points of view on controversial issues and influences him to be outspoken and critical of even the adults he respects most.

He now is capable and interested in participating in the plans of the family and school groups and will accept responsibilities accordingly. He likes to be trusted and to receive recognition for his accomplishments. He often prefers private recognition to public, however, and is usually fair in accepting credit only for that which is truly his. His sense of values has usually developed to the point where he comprehends truth and honesty well and respects the personal and property right of others.

The nine-year-old responds to reasoning and accepts explanations and punishment which are fair when he is faced with the true situation. Because he is still not far from being a child he may revert to dependence upon adults occasionally but will pick up the reins again and move toward greater independence when given the momentary support he needs. Wanting to be like others is a strong pull at this age when the youngster temporarily loses his neat appearance and nice talk to be in with the gang.

By age nine there is considerable interest in small children, particularly their origin. Much discussion of the origin and birth of babies may take place in the gang and club. He is able to understand basic information on the development and function of the human body when he shows he is ready to receive it.

Beyond the age of nine maturity is so varied that it is difficult to describe one age separately from the other. At this point good friends may be suddenly confronted with a spurt in growth by one, leaving the other much the smaller. The development of secondary sex characteristics in one may cause the other to feel immature. Change of interests usually accompanies this rapid maturity. These changes can be met by the individual youngster when he has been informed that each person develops according to his own pattern and that one is not expected to be like another. Boys and girls can discuss and are usually willing at this age to discuss with an understanding adult the many problems and anxieties which may arise when one finds himself more or less physically mature than another of his age.

The ten-year-old who is not changing into puberty is much like the nine-year-old except a little larger, more sturdy, and skillful in his work. He is usually casual and relaxed, but alert to what is going on around him. He is able to take his schoolwork in stride, assuming responsibility for getting things done. At the same time he is a loyal member of his group and gang, knowing how to keep a secret well.

He is friendly and congenial with his parents and affectionate with peers of the same sex, being highly selective in friendships. He is strong on hero worship, greatly admiring the recognized athlete, traveler, and explorer.

The gap between boys and girls is more wide now, with boys taking to the rough and tumble. They still mix in socials and parties even though the girls are more mature and their interests lie in dancing and other social activities which are usually less appealing to the boys.

The picture for the boy or girl entering puberty may be somewhat different. This may come between the ages of nine and fourteen. Most often a plateau is reached when no growth seems evident. This is then followed by a period of rapid growth. During rapid growth strength and coordination of the individual declines, causing him to be listless and apparently in a daze. The attitude may become sullen, resentful, and bullish and change with little warning. He often becomes critical of parents and attaches himself in hero worship to some other adult. During this rapid growth in height and weight the arms and hands become larger. The shoulders of the boys and the hips of the girls broaden. Pubic hair of boys and girls begins to grow and breasts of the girls begin to develop. Since all parts of the body usually do not develop at the same time this is well known as the awkward age. Boys trip and stumble and have difficulty keeping their feet out of the way in school. They tire easily and just do not want to do anything.

Belonging is important to the nine to eleven-year-old. The gang or group has a strong attraction and serves a needed function for both the early or late maturing individual. This is less significant, however, as the individual grows into maturity, the boys holding on to the secret codes and mystery acts longer than the girls. More and more interest is placed on team games with development of skill in sports an important criteria for acceptance by the peers. Pets, television and movies are enjoyed by this age; comics lose some of their attraction. Reading ability may differ four to five years and interests become quite varied. Those who read best will seek more information on science, travel, mechanics, and space. Some enjoy the abridged classics. Girls develop interest in love stories before boys.

Ages nine through eleven in particular need opportunity for letting off steam as they often rebel at adult dominance. They are antagonized by scolding or nagging of adults who become offended by their behavior. They respond, however, to the understanding adult who shows warm affection at the proper time and treats them in an adult manner.

Some pertinent age characteristics of intermediate age children are:

1. Growth in height and weight are normally slow and steady at this age. There will be a lag just prior to pubescence.
2. Some have a spurt of growth at about 10 years. Girls attain skeletal maturity before boys.
3. Permanent dentition continues. Incisors and lower bicuspids appear.
4. This is often a period of dental neglect.

5. Orthodontia (teeth-straightening) is necessary in some cases. The need may be apparent as early as 9 years but treatment may not be initiated until 12 years or later.
6. The small muscles are developing. Manipulative skill is increasing.
7. Muscular coordinations are good. The hand-eye coordinations are continuing to develop.
8. The lungs are not fully developed.
9. At the end of this period the eyes function as well as those of adults. Myopia (nearsightedness) may develop around the age of eight. Many eye defects can be remedied by glasses.
10. Internal changes in glands and body structure are taking place. There is a wide range in the beginning of sexual maturity. The period of rapid growth comes earlier for girls than for boys. It lasts longer in boys.

   Boys: Beginning of puberty cycle: 10-13 yrs. End 14-18 1/2 years.
   Girls: Appearance of menstruation: 9-16 yrs. Average 13 years.
11. Youth of nine through eleven years are usually sturdy though long-legged and rangy in appearance. They seem hurried and untidy and are prone to accidents.
12. The appetite is usually good. They are interested in eating. There now are fewer food preferences and refusals.
13. They usually have good health and boundless energy.
14. They have the widest range of interests of any age group, showing increased interest in realism and facts.
15. They have concern for own personal achievements and are keenly affected by success and failure.
16. They are beginning to show secretiveness; are easily depressed or excited; show rebellion against adult domination.
17. They are growing in ability to make their own decisions and to assume responsibility for consequences.
18. They have a well-developed sense of humor.
19. They show independence, initiative, and interest in fair play.
20. They participate as responsible members of the family group.
21. They recognize human motives quickly and are hard to deceive.
22. They are interested in organized competitive games and sports.
23. They are greatly concerned about group recognition and approbation, but form strong attachments for own sex — interest in opposite sex increases as they approach puberty.
24. They get a certain amount of satisfaction from work done alone, but at the same time enjoy cooperative group enterprises.
25. They are becoming aware of and concerned about other people's ideas and beliefs.
26. They extend interests beyond home and local communities to the nation and to the world.[8]

---

[8]*Ibid.*

Selected behaviorial changes of the intermediate age child may include:

1. The youth of nine through eleven is learning to cooperate better. He plays in self-made groups over a longer period. He is beginning to be interested in teams and will abide by group decisions.
2. He desires prestige and may seek it through size, boasting, and rivalry.
3. The rhythmic sense is much improved.
4. Sex antagonism may be acute. Sex interest is not detailed. Sexual "modesty" appears.
5. He is generally reliable about following instructions in household jobs. He can take care of his own room.
6. He can take responsibility for his own clothing. He is now more aware of his personal hygiene.
7. This youth needs an assured position in a social group. Membership in a gang or a secret club fills this need. He needs a certain amount of freedom in setting up own standards and rules, yet strongly desires understanding and sympathy from adults. Participation in family affairs is important.
8. There must be full opportunity to develop body control, strength, and endurance. He needs activities involving use of the whole body: stunts, throwing and catching, running, "it" games with their accompanying noise, etc. Seasonal play is important: kites, tops, marbles, etc.
9. He needs organized games for team play. He is willing to practice in order to become adequate in skills for games. He gains self-confidence by excelling in some one thing.
10. Encouragement to exercise creativity in rhythms should be given.
11. He should sleep about 10 hours. He usually does not get enough rest. A quiet period in the afternoon, not necessarily bed, may prevent over-fatigue.
12. His increased interest in foods provides a basis for better understanding of the seven basic foods in maintaining good health.
13. The teacher must see that students having visual or aural defects always maintain strategic positions in the class.
14. Close supervision is required to assure properly adjusted furniture and to prevent slumping over desks. Creation of an awareness that good posture and comfortable posture is important.[9]

JUNIOR HIGH

Ages eleven through fifteen are generally associated with junior high school or grades seven through nine. It is well that elementary teachers understand this age in that many elementary schools include at least grades seven and eight. Students retarded one or more grades will be found in

---

[9]*Ibid.*

grades five and six at this age. It is also well for the teacher to know something of the age just above that with which he works in order that he is better able to prepare his students for the next level.

The adolescent is considered dependent and immature but shows surprising maturity and independence at times. He continues to need the help of adults in bridging this developmental span, allowing him to be as independent as possible with the assurance that he can rely upon adult assistance as needed. It is important that he view these years as a part of the natural growth pattern of life and as nothing to be feared.

During this age his moods are varied and changeable. He becomes more withdrawn, especially from his parents, as he seeks to break the bonds of childhood and dependence. Even though he may reject the affection of his parents he still wants their interest and usually recognizes his dependence upon them for support.

There is the constant battle of wanting adult control to rely upon and the rebellion against controls. He may express himself rather frankly and freely at times and withdraw at others. His need to break away from home dependence makes him often critical of home to have an excuse for severing ties. The need is frequently quite acute for venting his feelings without having to suffer the guilt of offending his parents. In the battle with parents he seeks the company and approval of his peers of both sexes. It is essential to him that he look and behave like others of his group and use the same language they do.

In an effort to be accepted the individual often becomes overly concerned about his physical appearance. Since growth is usually uneven his feeling of awkwardness causes fears that his body is not as it should be. Acne, freckles, or any physical difference, even to the color or kind of hair, may cause self-consciousness and deep distress. It is difficult for him to understand and accept the rapid changes of his body.

As he becomes more sure of himself the group or gang is less important and he seeks to become an individual on his own, choosing his friends because of real interest in them. With physical maturity the desire to be accepted by a member of the opposite sex usually comes. Often this becomes paramount, precluding all other interests. It is then that this age needs opportunities for both sexes to be together and engage in common work and play.

During these years youngsters are preparing themselves for moving into the full responsibility of man or womanhood with full acceptance of themselves and realization of their place and function as adults in society. Probably the most crucial responsibility is learning about members of the opposite sex and establishing proper relations with them. During this time the individual is also faced with the problem of selecting and preparing himself for a vocation in order to become a self-supporting and respected adult.

Teen-agers are much more serious than the adult is willing to admit. They are boisterous, rude, thoughtless, and frequently even disinterested in schoolwork, but beneath this they spend much time thinking and day-dreaming. Long hours are spent in talking over their problems, interests, and futures. They will communicate freely with an adult who understands and accepts them as they are. Assignments and responsibilities which make sense to them are entered into with enthusiasm and mastered with dispatch. Current vocational, social, and political problems usually capture their interest. When allowed to participate in planning and initiating an activity they assume firm responsibility and exert a powerful amount of work. Many mistakes will be made in carrying out plans but each opportunity for responsibility is met by growth and encouragement toward maturity, in recognition that the youth responds to guidance and rebels at dominance.

Some pertinent age characteristics of junior high children are:

1. This is a transitional period.
2. During the "pubescent spurt" the rate of growth is very rapid. The lateral-type matures earlier than the linear-type.
3. At 11 or 12 years, girls are usually taller and heavier than boys. Boys' hands and feet appear to be oversized.
4. The lateral-type girl usually reaches adult height at about the age of 14 years. Linear-type girls continue to grow for several years. The lateral-type boy attains adult height at about the age of 16 years. Growth of linear-type boys continues to the age of 20 or later.
5. Permanent dentition of 28 teeth is completed by 13 or 14 years.
6. Muscular growth is very rapid. Restlessness may be concomitant.
7. The muscles of boys become hard and firm. The muscles of girls remain softer.
8. The heart increases greatly in size. Early teen-agers should avoid strenuous competitive sports since the heart and arteries may be out of proportion.
9. The blood pressure may fall. The fatigue point in competitive games should be anticipated. More rest is needed.
10. The puberty cycle is in progress. The reproductive organs are maturing rapidly. Secondary sex characteristics appear. Many girls are embarrassed by the development of breasts and hips. The period of changing voice and initial hair growth on the face is equally embarrassing to boys.
11. The prevalence of active tuberculosis increases in the teenager.
12. Youth of 11 to 16 years are strongly individual. They differ widely in physical maturity and in temperament.

13. Children of 14, 15, or 16 may have reached physiological adult-hood, but lack its experiences. They may exhibit a "know-it-all" atti-tude. They are intensely emotional. They are seeking their own place in the life around them. There may be emotional instability while striving to understand social relationships.

14. Linear-type children may display drooping posture, fatigue, alter-nating alertness and irritability. The lateral-type may display over-weight, slow movements, and placidity.

15. There is a strong interest in sex. These young people may be emotional about bodily changes. Sex-consciousness may cause self-consciousness and shyness with the opposite sex. Teasing may denote sex attraction.

16. A ravenous but capricious appetite may be noted.

17. Adolescents may be overanxious about their health. They appreciate first aid and can give it. To a certain extent they can appreciate group health problems.

18. They show lack of coordination because muscular and skeletal growth take place at different rates of speed.

19. They show energy level fluctuation because of glandular instability.

20. They desire adult privileges, thus trying to prove that they are grow-ing up.

21. They have strong tendency to rebel against authority.

22. They show sensitivity and fear of situations which make them ridicu-lous.

23. They prefer activity and working with materials as a change from working with ideas alone.

24. They are confused when home, peer, and school standards conflict.

25. They desire to conform to peer standards and at the same time to be unique.

26. They show some embarrassment in discussing their own growth and development.

27. They are concerned about normality of their own development and in becoming attractive.[10]

Selected behavioral changes of the junior high age include the follow-ing:

1. For those who need it, orthodontia will improve the appearance and prevent dental decay. The child needs guidance about accepting em-barrassment and discomfort in order to achieve permanent correction.

2. The increase in size and strength of muscles leads to greater interest in outdoor activities.

3. The desire to conform to standards of the age-group is stronger than the response to adult guidance. Many respond more readily to the influence of the teacher than of the parent.

10*Ibid.*

4. Competition is keen. There is respect for good sportsmanship. More highly organized team games are desired. There is a willingness to submerge personal ego for the good of the team or group. The unskilled youth is self-conscious about undertaking new activities.

5. During adolescence there may be close attachment to an almost unlimited admiration of some adult whom he considers to be outstanding.

6. Some youth may initiate too many activities and go beyond the fatigue point. Resultant chronic tension may cause strained relationships. Girls tire more easily than boys.

7. Interest in money-making activities may lead some to work during after-school playtime.

8. Youth of 12 to 16 need unobtrusive adult guidance that does not impinge upon their own feeling of being adults. A balance between security and freedom is needed.

9. Skill is essential for successful group participation. The youth is willing to practice skills in order to gain proficiency, but needs informed guidance.

10. Games of increased organization such as softball, kick ball, modified soccer, ect., are needed on intramural basis. The sedentary or self-protective youth may need encouragement to play out-of-doors.

11. Youth of 12 to 16 need worthy causes in the promulgation of which they may utilize their excess emotions and energy.

12. Special provision must be made for the youth who is reaching his literate capacity and may be able to gain his chief satisfactions from muscular activities.

13. Separate physical education programs for boys and girls should be planned since the difference in strength, maturity, and interests makes it difficult to organize activities beneficial to both. Boys follow youth sports. In addition to group games, girls like smaller group activities, to be carried on by two or more people.

14. It is as important for children to develop good spectatorship as it is for them to develop good sportsmanship.

15. More mature interests must be met by more mature programs. There must be opportunity for many types of social contacts. Club programs, church groups, Boy and Girl Scouts, Y.M.C.A., Campfire Girls, and camping, etc., fill the need for guidance.

16. The rest needs are about 8 to 9 hours or longer.

17. The youth's increasing desire to improve his personal appearance provides excellent opportunity to remedy habitual postural defects and to establish a balanced diet.

18. They need to learn to plan, to do their own share of work, to share praise, and to do the less attractive jobs.[11]

---

[11]*Ibid.*

OBTAINING INFORMATION ABOUT CHILDREN

Schools place much emphasis upon the teacher's getting sufficient and appropriate information about each child in order to understand his behavior. There is much the individual teacher can do to gather data but he must also rely upon resources of the school for help. Certain tests can be administered by the teacher, there can be observation of daily routine, conferences can be held, and visits can be made into the community and children's homes. The classroom teacher, however, is not a trained psychologist nor even a clinician; therefore, clinical and psychological services should be provided. The teacher should use his own techniques for gathering as much data as possible and examining and integrating data already provided, and utilize whatever opportunities are available for gaining a better understanding of each student under his supervision. Five resources usually available for obtaining information about children are (1) surveying the community, (2) studying cumulative records, (3) observing children in many situations, (4) holding conferences with parents, and (5) utilizing student personnel services.

COMMUNITY SURVEY

The community in which each child lives does much to determine the type school he attends and his success in school. The teacher of necessity teaches within these bounds. He therefore is obligated to determine the nature of the community. What he knows about the community his school serves and how he interprets and works within this setting influence his effectiveness within the classroom.

The wise teacher should devise a means whereby he can survey and study early in the year the communities from which his children come. This may be a formal survey using a specific instrument for gathering data or the teacher may follow his own outline. Whatever the guide may be, two areas should receive major emphasis: environmental background and socioeconomic differences. In making the community survey the teacher will do well to keep the following guide in mind as suggested by Mehl, Mills, and Douglass:

1. Racial and national backgrounds of the people.
2. Family make-up such as number, sex, and ages.
3. Historical background of folklore and community beginning.
4. Governmental services such as fire and police.
5. Health and sanitation services.
6. Housing conditions and zoning regulations.
7. Public, private and commercial recreation.
8. Governmental and nongovernmental welfare services.

9. Religious institutions.
10. Educational services such as school, library, and private.
11. Civic organizations.
12. Industries, trades, occupations.
13. Employment types, wages, conditions, and opportunities.[12]

CUMULATIVE RECORDS

The most important aid to the teacher in finding out about children is the cumulative record when the school maintains an adequate and up-to-date system. This depends largely upon the industry and consistency of the entire faculty as data are recorded on the child's forms from year to year. Such forms serve a broader purpose when there are folders in which samples of work can be placed. This is particularly important in that understanding a child involves more than just seeing recorded data. All data placed on the child's record should be carefully examined and sorted beforehand. The teacher must try to understand his reaction to the child and why the child responds to him as he does. Considerable data can be placed in the folder for temporary use. Much of this will be discarded after it has served its function and only the most pertinent recorded.

That which may be classified as most pertinent usually will fall under such headings as the following:

1. Family History
2. Health Data
3. Test Data — Teacher Made and Standardized
4. Interest Inventories
5. Projection Techniques
6. Sociometric Techniques
7. Interviews and Conferences
8. Observational Summaries

The teacher must also keep in mind that data about a child is recorded and subsequently used for a specific purpose. The teacher should thus examine each cumulative folder with a use criteria before him. The following criteria are suggested for using cumulative record data to assist the teacher:

1. Develop security in meeting classroom situations.
2. Plan a varied learning program.
3. Make adjustments in the learning process.
4. Adapt techniques of teaching to children.
5. Choose instructional materials suitable to individuals.

---

[12]Marie A. Mehl, Hubert H. Mills and Harl R. Douglass, *Teaching in the Elementary School* (second edition; New York: Ronald Press Company, © 1958), pp. 250-1.

6. Use group and individual instruction.
7. Help children learn to live together.
8. Help children adjust to people, places, and things outside school.
9. Meet special needs of individual children.
10. Make referrals for diagnosis.

Figure 14 has been prepared as a work sheet to guide the teacher as he reviews periodically the record of each child. He can insert in the appropriate space such data as may serve a purpose in meeting an objective on the criteria above.

Student Name _____ Grade _____ Date _____

TEACHING RELATED TO CHILD STUDY	Family History	Health Data	Test Data	Observational Data	Interest Inventories	Projection Techniques	Sociometric Techniques	Interview and Conferences	
Develop security in meeting classroom situations									
Plan a varied learning program									
Make adjustments in the learning process									
Adapt techniques of teaching to children									
Choose learning materials suitable to individuals									
Use group and individual instruction									
Help children learn to live together									
Help children adjust to people, places, things outside school									
Meet special needs of individual children									
Make referrals for diagnosis and assistance									

Figure 14. Grid for recording data on specific child pertinent to meeting a specific objective.

TEACHER OBSERVATION

Long before our modern methods of evaluating student progress and behavior, the classroom teacher employed observation in guiding students toward personal improvement. This technique is still invaluable in the classroom. The day-to-day observance of the child serves as a guide to the alert teacher in making assignments, selecting materials, and in counseling.

Observation may also be more objective when used in controlled experimental situations, in keeping anecdotal records, and in making a case study. The teacher may structure a situation in order to compare the behavior of one child with that of another under certain conditions.

Notes on an individual child's behavior can be kept over a period of time to determine a pattern or to identify clues to deportment. When carefully recorded such notes are known as anecdotal records.

An observational case study may include the anecdotal record, information from the school records, and general and specific observation by the teacher over an extended period of time. This technique serves as a means of understanding the behavior of an individual and consequently the behavior of children in general after a number of case studies have been made.

TEACHER-PARENT CONFERENCES

In a survey conducted by the National Education Association, 99 per cent of the teachers contacted indicated that they believe conferences with parents contribute to better relations.[13] Through parent-teacher conferences the teacher is able to find out about the aspirations and plans of the parents for their child, information about the child's home, and the response of the child and home to the school. Through this technique the parent is able to share with the teacher something of the behavior of the child at home, his beliefs, attitudes towards right and wrong, and his habits of work. This information should enable the teacher to work with the child at school with more understanding.

The following suggestions for conducting a parent-teacher conference listed by Logan and Logan should be helpful to the teacher:

1. Prepare carefully in advance.
2. Insure privacy and freedom from interruptions.
3. Have an informal setting.
4. Plan a scheduled time limit.
5. Begin on a positive note.
6. Listen with interest, sympathy, and understanding.
7. Establish a friendly feeling with the parent, or parents, and child as the case may be.
8. Encourage the parent to talk.
9. Develop an attitude of mutual need and cooperation.

---

[13]"Teachers View Public Relations," NEA Research Bulletin, 37:35, April, 1959.

10. Let suggestions come from the parent.
11. Build on the parent's suggestions whenever possible.
12. Delay making definite suggestions.
13. Have some of the child's work at hand to talk about.
14. Make future plans cooperatively.
15. End the conference on a friendly note.
16. Make arrangements for a future conference when necessary.
17. Make notes after the parent leaves.[14]

STUDENT PERSONNEL SERVICES

Increasingly the teacher will find invaluable specialized services available to help him better understand the children with whom he works. These are found under the titles of curriculum director, supervisor, guidance counselor, visiting teacher, school psychologist, social worker, clinical attendant, nurse, remedial teacher and many others. These personnel work according to a variety of schedules and channels of administration. The classroom teacher will soon recognize that one of his strong functions is that of coordinator. It is up to him to coordinate the activities and learning experiences of his classroom and to utilize to the best advantage the resources available. One of the teacher's major responsibilities is to determine what services and service personnel are available. He should prepare to call for specific service at the appropriate time.

Home contacts and information about the home and personal record of a child can be provided by the visiting teacher or social worker. Clinical diagnosis and personal counseling can be provided by the student personnel services or arranged for in community, college, university or welfare clinics. Such services may include psychological testing, analysis or remedial work on individual adjustment cases, psychiatric counsel and treatment, speech and hearing correction, reading diagnosis and remedial treatment, and education of the handicapped. These services are an extension of the teacher's skill in dealing with adjustment or problem cases and in discovering information about individuals where he needs additional help.[15]

RECOGNIZING DIFFERENCES — MAINTAINING EFFECTIVE DISCIPLINE

Much emphasis should be placed upon the teacher's knowing how the child grows and develops and in understanding him at various ages under different situations. Knowledge of the developmental behavior of children,

---

[14]Lillian M. Logan and Virgil G. Logan, op. cit. p. 807.
[15]Charles R. Foster, Guidance for Today's Schools, (New York: Ginn and Company, 1957), pp. 28-9.

however, is of little significance unless it is translated into action for helping the child gain the most enjoyment and satisfaction possible during his maturation. Teachers are realizing more and more that their role is one of guidance in helping the child adjust to his developmental needs. It is a matter of recognizing, understanding, and working with the individual in terms of his adherence to or variance from generally expected behavior. Hymes has rightly stated that:

> Youngsters do not get the hang of good behavior right off no (any) more than they get the knack of reading or dancing or typing immediately. . . . Children want to be good, but the ways of behavior — the right things to do, the appropriate actions — are hard to master.
> You have to explain. You have to talk over things. You have to find out what part was not clear. You have to emphasize certain points again. You have to make generalizations clearer. . . You have to give some more examples. You have to talk through with the youngsters what could happen and what might happen and why the right way is best. You have to teach.[16]

Most teaching is slow. When an undesirable behavior is repeated it must be discussed again. Additional plans must be made with the student. The teacher must talk, discuss, analyze, and evaluate a hundred times if necessary. This is what a teacher is for. He is there "to help children see outcomes, to help them search for reasons, to help them think, and to help them decide, to help them make good choices."[17]

This responsibility on the part of the teacher is rather generally referred to as discipline. The point of view taken here is that discipline should be more preventive than corrective. By preventive is meant that when the normal behavior of an individual is recognized and emphasis is placed upon meeting his needs and helping him become a self-supporting, self-directive, responsible citizen, corrective discipline will seldom be needed.

BEHAVIOR CHARACTERISTICS

Basically the child's behavior is characterized in terms of four major categories which are physical, intellectual, emotional, and social. Recognizing these categories and the nature of each as it applies to different ages is imperative for the teacher. The first portion of this chapter is devoted to the characteristics and developmental tasks by age groups in order to provide a basic understanding of the developmental patterns of children.

---

[16]James L. Hymes, Jr. *Behavior and Misbehavior*, (Englewood Cliffs, N. J.: Prentice-Hall, Inc., 1955), pp. 18-19.
[17]*Ibid.*, p. 21.

This treatment will serve as a background for utilizing the taxonomy of characteristics in recognizing specific behavior in terms of the four generally understood categories as presented by Ragan and summarized as follows.[18]

Physical Characteristics

The teacher must recognize that there are two major spurts in the growth of the child which are (1) prenatal, infancy and early childhood and (2) adolescence. The intervening years are characterized by moderate growth. The child usually grows as much during the first five years as he does the next ten. Different parts of the body grow at different rates. The heart and lungs are among the last parts of the body to mature. Periods of awkwardness, lack of coordination, and loss of strength and energy are experienced in pubescence. There is wide variance in growth among individuals of the same age. Girls generally grow and mature faster than boys.

The changing body is subject to fatigue and overexertion which may cause permanent damage to vital organs. These changes are often a source of concern and embarrassment to the individual and as a result he may respond by withdrawing, becoming aggressive, and antagonizing others. The teacher must observe the progressive difference in strength and coordination and varying need for physical activity and letting off steam from early childhood through adolescence.

Intellectual Characteristics

The child is born with an individual intellectual potential, the development of which is influenced largely by the environment in which he is reared. The education and language spoken by his family, the culture of the neighborhood, the attention given to his development by others and his general health are major factors in his readiness for and adaptability to schoolwork. Born into a world of persons, things, and symbols he must gradually develop to the point of manipulating symbols in place of objects as he utilizes his intellectual potential. Although certain standards are recognizable which characterize the intellectuality of the individual and mark him at a certain academic level, there is great variance in the ability of individuals to display mental maturity.

The range of academic maturity increases as children move through the educational ladder. The vocabulary of approximately 2,000 words for

---

[18]William B. Ragan, *Teaching America's Children*, (New York: Holt, Rinehart and Winston, 1961), pp. 72-78. © 1961, Holt, Rinehart and Winston, Inc. Used by permission of the publishers.

the five-year-old may be expected to approximate 9,000 by age 14. **Problems** are solved in the early years at a relatively simple perceptual level by combining objects and counting them. As concepts are developed children are able to solve problems more symbolically. The process of thinking increases with maturity. Children have a wide variety of interests but most are interested in science, social processes and events. Their interests and capabilities change and broaden as they mature.

Children within any group are challenged and confronted by a vast array of competitors and often find it necessary to compete by means other than intellectual processes. Thus the teacher is faced with a wide range of abilities, interests, and means of expression within any age level. In order to cope with this the teacher must be equipped with the understanding set forth by Ragan:

> . . . curiosity is an outstanding characteristic of young children; that children accumulate a vast amount of information on a great variety of subjects by asking questions; that concepts and vocabulary frequently outrun understanding; that thinking involves emotional and personality factors rather than being a purely intellectual process, and that critical thinking manifests itself early and grows gradually.[19]

Emotional Characteristics

Emotional maturity may be associated with the experiences of the early years of a child's life as well as many other factors. Some children are highly sensitive to such stimuli as hunger, discomfort, and strange environments while others react less noticeably. Some accept school tasks as a challenge and enter into the activity with enthusiasm while others reject school as a threat and rebel against its interference in their world of affairs. The young child may react quickly to a situation but his emotional reaction lasts for a relatively short time as compared to that of an adult. As he grows older his emotional outbursts may evolve into moods which continue for considerable time. Fears due to strange objects, noises, falling, and unexpected movements decline during preschool years but fear of the dark, imaginary creatures, or being alone increases. Children differ in their emotional responses and form their own patterns just as they do in other types of behavior. Children with close emotional ties with the home generally find it easier to identify emotionally with the teacher. By the same token emotional disturbances at home may handicap the child's associations and adjustment at school.

As the child grows, other factors such as peer groups, the community, and church enter into developing his personality. The teacher must create

---

[19]*Ibid.,* pp. 238-9.

an emotional climate in the school that accepts the youngster as he is and helps him adjust to changing environments and each new challenge.

Social Characteristics

The swing back and forth in seeking approval of parents and peers during the development of an individual is always a challenge to the home and school. During early childhood the parent and teacher hold paramount status with the child. Their interest in playmates and peers increases with the years in school. The gang stage appearing about the age of nine and continuing into adolescence is a strong status symbol. Clothing, language, and ideals of right and wrong hang heavily upon this symbol of society.

In early childhood one playmate of about the same age usually provides the most acceptable association. There is little attention to sex, intelligence, or color at this time. At the gang stage differences in personal characteristics are recognized and individuals and the opposite sex are often left out. In early childhood boys tease and gang up against the girls. Some sense of values with a knowledge of right and wrong is usually reasonably well established by age ten or twelve, showing considerable interest in social and political affairs of the country.

During the first years of the primary school the child finds it hard to play and work in groups but this gradually improves until by the intermediate grades much good work is done in groups and team games become prominent.

The teacher should recognize that the classroom is a laboratory for improving social behavior and that effective instruction in the fundamentals of education is dependent largely upon the ability to provide satisfactory social behavior of any classroom group. Social behavior in the classroom may be enhanced by encouraging children to appreciate the differences of others through observing each person's unique contributions to the ongoing program. Social behavior can also be improved through helping children understand and accept differences in others such as race, religion, economic status, and language usage by providing activities which utilize the talents of all members of the class.

The teacher must see the foregoing discussion of children's characteristics as general patterns, seek to work acceptably with those who fall within this framework and identify those who fall too far to the left or right. When extreme variances are found, he must look for means of understanding the position of each child and take whatever corrective course is desirable.

BEHAVIOR PROBLEMS AND NEEDS

It is when the behavior chosen by the youth does not agree with the standard set by adults that the youth finds himself in trouble. Four of the chief ways of satisfying these pressures used by children and not approved by adults may be classified as aggressive behavior, submissive behavior, withdrawing type of behavior, and symptoms of illness.[20] The aggressive child reacts to the forces about him by fighting back through name-calling, swearing, loud yelling, domineering talk, statements of what he is going to do to someone or statements indicating resentment toward authority. He may carry on acts of destroying property, soiling and tearing his clothes, or teasing other children.

The submissive child may be one who has met rather severe punishment or defeat and lost his will power. He seems to have little self direction, looks to others to make suggestions, is afraid to meet strangers, easily frightened, rarely fights back, and requires careful and specific directions. He is pushed quite frequently by others, not accepted by the group and is often criticized and picked on. He may blush easily, bite his nails, suck his thumb, or fiddle with his hands or clothes.

The withdrawn type child is neither aggressive nor submissive but leans toward a solitary type of behavior — to withdraw from soicety. He tends to shun contact with his peers, plays by himself, and seems to prefer spectator rather than participatory activity. This type child often develops a specialty such as building model airplanes or fashioning doll costumes, which results in isolation from the group. There are others who want to belong but are not accepted because they are unskilled or awkward or come from "the wrong families."

Some children when frustrated develop a psychosomatic illness. Such illness may include rashes, eczema, cardiovascular disturbances, hypertension, arthritis, migrane headaches, body pains or respiratory disturbances. These persons are not ill enough to be under a doctor's care yet they are not well enough to get along with their age mates and to carry on the learning process. In identifying the four specific types of behavior exemplified by children's actions, Raths has stated:

> This brief account is an attempt to bring to the attention of the alert teacher those behaviors which are more or less characteristic. We want the teacher to be sensitive to the child who is aggressive, submissive, withdrawn, or shows psychosomatic symptoms of illness, if these tend to occur quite often in his school life. Here again we want to say that these behaviors are gross manifestations of possible unmet needs and as yet we have not specified the needs which are not being met. These symptoms should be an alarm to the teacher. They should suggest to her that before this child can live and grow something has to be done in the way of meeting fundamental emotional needs, and we believe the first steps in this

---

[20]Louis E. Raths, *An Application to Education of the Needs Theory,* (Bronxvill, New York: Modern Education Service, 1949), p. 1.

direction must be for you, the teacher, (1) to learn to recognize the symptoms, and (2) to identify those children who, by their daily behavior suggest that these emotional needs have not been met.[21]

In order that the teacher can work effectively with children he must be able not only to identify the major misfits but to identify and classify the more minute needs of the individual. As the teacher learns to identify and classify these needs he will learn to work more effectively with children. He should learn to identify and respond to the following taxonomy of children's needs as suggested by Raths:

1. The need to belong
2. The need for achievement
3. The need for economic security
4. The need for freedom from fear
5. The need for love and affection
6. The need to be free from intense feelings of guilt
7. The need for sharing and self-respect
8. The need for understanding[22]

PRINCIPLES BASIC TO DESIRABLE BEHAVIOR

In consideration of the imposing classification of children's needs, the teacher is faced with the problem of determining how to cope with the divergent behavior of individuals. He must continuously recognize that each person expresses his needs differently and responds to treatment in various ways. The best approach, then, is to follow a sound set of principles as a basis upon which action can be determined to suit the current situation. The following set of basic principles is suggested here as a guide to the teacher in plotting disciplinary action.

1. Human dignity is recognized and respected.
2. Emotions are kept under control.
3. The physical needs of children are respected.
4. Treatment of individuals is consistent.
5. Pupils are respected regardless of race, religion, culture or physical condition.
6. The teacher participates.
7. Courtesy is shown by both the teacher and students.
8. Children's good behavior and achievements are recognized.
9. Cooperation is encouraged.
10. Children are trusted.
11. High standards are encouraged.
12. Distinction is made between the child and his actions.[23]

---

[21]*Ibid.*, p. 6.
[22]*Ibid.*, pp. 6-18.
[23]Bernard G. Kelner, *How to Teach in the Elementary School*, (New York: McGraw-Hill Book Company, Inc., 1958), pp. 69-73.

TECHNIQUES FOR APPROPRIATE BEHAVIOR

Equipped with the knowledge of child growth and development, the understanding of representative types of behavior and with a set of principles to serve as a guide, the teacher then may look at some techniques for maintaining appropriate behavior in the classroom. From the beginning the teacher should keep in mind that first impressions are important with children. The old expression "It is easier to let up than tighten up" has some merit but does not imply that the teacher necessarily shall be stern and tough. A firm start in a pleasant but business-like manner is important. The teacher must help the students understand that the main reason for their being in school is for purposeful work. He also must help them understand that the teacher's duty is to assist each in clarifying his role in schoolwork and in functioning according to his best ability.

This is where getting to know children's capabilities as soon as possible pays off. Work must be assigned in terms of the ability, interest, and achievement of the children involved. After the assignment is made the pattern of work of individuals should be observed and additional assignments made which will challenge but not unduly frustrate them. When help is needed it should be given in terms of the behavior of the individual. Those who are prone to ask for help just to get attention should be recognized early and guided into responsible behavior. Every effort should be made to keep a child working to his capacity and inform him about his progress so that he can achieve success.

It is natural that some children are not going to do their best and some will react negatively to whatever procedure may be followed or responsibility assigned. The teacher who expects this and prepares to meet the situation calmly and give additional time and effort to these individuals will usually be able to cope with special problems.

It is of utmost importance that the teacher follow through on whatever is undertaken. Once a task is initiated or an assignment made it is imperative that both the teacher and student see it through to the end or a point of evaluation wherein a more desirable adjustment can be made. This often calls for courage and consistent and frequent recognition of the bits of progress made. The teacher should allow and watch for signs of self-direction on the part of individuals. When the student sees another way of approaching a problem, encouragement should be given rather than requiring that he stick to the teacher's way.

Teachers often find their chief problem to be talking too much. A youngster with a hearing aid was observed to turn it down while the teacher was talking. When asked about his action he replied that when he got tired hearing the teacher talk he turned the instrument down so he didn't have to listen. The teacher needs to learn to give students simple and clear directions and get out of the way and let them work.

The old adage "nothing succeeds like success" is a good tonic for the classroom. When the teacher adjusts the work schedule so that he feels reasonably comfortable and guides youngsters in planning and reaching attainable goals, it can be expected that a sense of well-being and security may be felt within the classroom.

Wingo and Schorling have prepared specific suggestions concerning discipline for the student teacher which are worthy of consideration by all teachers. These are presented in two sets of ideas, entitled (1) Some Preventive Measures and (2) When Trouble Comes. These helpful guidelines follow.

Some Preventive Measures:

1. At the beginning of the school year, learn the names of the pupils quickly. Social control will be much easier if you can identify a child by his name than if you have to refer to him as "the boy in the blue shirt." Your initial relations with children will be much better if you can identify them as individuals rather than as occupants of desks.

2. Study the seating of the pupils. Insofar as possible, it is desirable for children to sit near those whom they choose. However, it is true that some children do not work very well when they sit near each other. A pupil who is ordinarily a steady worker may, when seated with the wrong neighbor, start the mischievous spirit in both.

3. Keep your eyes open. See what is going on. Remember an important part of your role is to lend support to children to manage themselves. Sometimes only a look from the teacher will serve to help a child get hold of himself. Perhaps moving quietly over to stand near a child will suffice to restore self-control. With young children in kindergarten and the early primary grades, you may need to take a child by the hand and lead him away from a situation which you know will be too much for him.

4. Learn to involve in the activity the pupil whose attention is wandering. If it is a discussion, call for a contribution from the child whose attention is starting to wander. If it is some other kind of activity, introduce some new element — a book, a piece of material or equipment, a comment or question addressed to him.

5. Make every effort to avoid all suggestions of criticism, disorganization, or anger before the group. Make your suggestions for individual improvement in private conference. Maintain an appearance of confidence and poise. Be genuine and hold on to your sense of humor.

6. If a member of the group obstructs the work, the treatment of the case should be calm, dignified, and firm. The sight of a teacher throwing a temper tantrum is never edifying. At the first opportunity

the offense should be dealt with in a private conference. If a pupil is interfering with the work of others, go to him quietly and request his cooperation. When you are not certain what to do, do nothing.

7. Use special occasions to carry over to pupils that you are interested in them as human beings. Hold occasional friendly chats with all children, but especially with those who cause some difficulty.

8. Stop the little things. Anticipate difficulties before they reach the circus stage. The snowball rolling downhill gathers momentum and size. In like manner, many behavior problems that seem insignificant in the early stages may become serious. Proper treatment requires good sense and some other means than a "Don't."

9. Do not draw an issue so closely that somebody has to give in — it may be you.

When Trouble Comes:

1. Isolate a child from the group when he is rapidly "going to pieces." For the time being he is incapable of associating properly with other children; the amount of stimulation is too great for him. Use isolation not for punishment but to relieve both the individual and the group.

2. Do not try to talk with the child until he has "cooled off" enough to talk rationally with you. Avoid making the period of delay an ordeal of mental torture. When he is ready and able to talk calmly about the matter, do it at once. In no case let the matter hang over to the next day.

3. Be frank with a child. State the situation fairly and in a way that he will understand. Be judicial; try to see his side, but do not be "soft" about it. Seek to determine the facts in the case. Get at motives behind the offense.

4. If the child has damaged property, let him propose a method of restitution. If his idea is practicable, let him carry it out, but see that he does what he promises to do.

5. Under no circumstances force a child to apologize to you. If an apology is freely given, accept it with grace, but do not lead a child to feel that you are holding a grudge against him. A forced apology is not a corrective measure or even a punishment. It is a humiliation of both child and teacher.

6. When the matter is settled, drop it. Let the child know that he is restored to full membership in the group and that what went before is "water over the dam." Do not inadvertently help a child to build up a reputation for disorderly behavior. When an individual once has such a reputation, he may tend to do all he can to live up to it.

7. Do not publicize offenses and their treatment before the other children. Never rebuke or punish the whole group for the fault of a few. Do not use sarcasm or ridicule. Never make threats, particularly those you know you will never carry out. Someday somebody may call your bluff. What will you do then?

8. Help children set up their own standards for conduct in various kinds of situations. Remember that all of us are more apt to abide by the rules we help to make.

9. A visit to the home is often effective. Do not overlook the chance to utilize the cooperation of a home in which there is teamwork.

10. Ask for help from your principal and others in the school, but do not wait to do it until you are in extremes. The principal is the educational leader of your staff; he is not the warden of a jail. Do not use his office as a dumping ground for children you want to get rid of, and do not use his name to frighten children by threatening to send them to him.

11. Do not make an issue of something that is trivial. On the campus of the University of Michigan the famous reply of President Angell to the question, "What makes a great administrator?" is still quoted. He said, "You have to be blind in one eye and deaf in one ear." It is not clear how far the beginning teacher can apply this principle, but the experienced teacher will recognize it as very effective. Presumably it will depend on the extent to which the beginning teacher is really in control of the situation.

12. The problem that looms like a mountain of disaster at the end of a tiring day often decreases to molehill significance after a refreshing period of rest. As one beginning teacher, humorously but not irreverently, remarked, "God surely had classroom teachers in mind when He put a night between two days!"[24]

Again, acting upon the principle of individual differences, the teacher must use his good judgment but creative initiative in meeting and coping with each incident. The description of a unique technique employed by one teacher, as recounted by Duane Manning, illustrates the authors' point of view well.

Freddy was a wholesome and mischievous sixth-grade boy. He was sort of a red-blooded All-American type, who fortunately grace all elementary schools with their presence. The schools are infinitely richer because of the Freddies that roam the world, even though they make it difficult for the classroom to remain in the state of tranquility that most teachers prefer. Freddie had a high compression engine and occasionally, when tranquility had rested on his shoulders for too prolonged a period of time, something would have to give.

Freddy's teacher seemed to understand how it was with boys who had high compression engines, and the two of them enjoyed a sturdy sort of relationship. His teacher had taught him a great deal about athletics and seemed to appreciate the fine qualities of the boy, as well as to realistically

---

[24]G. Max Wingo and Raleigh Schorling, *Elementary-School Student Teaching* (second edition; New York: McGraw-Hill Book Company, Inc., 1955), pp. 320-5.

accept those that created difficulty. He always seemed to know when pressures were building up in Freddy and when he was about ready to erupt.

One day the teacher was holding a discussion in social stuides. It was a very special discussion in that it was an example of what the teacher had been trying to achieve with the class for some time. The children were staying on the track, and were talking among themselves without the necessity of involving the teacher each time a child spoke. Things were moving along handsomely. At this delicate point in the proceedings, the teacher glanced over at Freddy and recognized the storm warnings. He was not taking part in the discussion and seemed on the verge of disrupting what was taking place.

The dilemma that confronted the teacher was simply this: he did not wish to do anything to spoil the kind of discussion which had been so painstakingly achieved, but he had to prevent Freddy's disturbance before it occurred. On an impulse, he walked over to his desk and quickly wrote the following note:

Dear Freddy,
    Please do not cause me to come to grips with you today,

                                        Sincerely,
                                        Mr. ....

He then quietly placed the note on Freddy's desk. Freddy unfolded and read the note. He smiled, then shifted unobtrusively into the discussion and helped move it along. A minor crisis was resolved and the discussion was a success.[25]

Certainly this was a masterful stroke of discipline and to be admired but not necessarily copied. The action was bred in the scene of encounter, and the participators were a part of the spirit as well as the ingredients present. That certain blending of the elements and touch of the artist brought the desired effect. A multiplicity of professional traits were involved. A limited listing would include knowledge, skill, understanding, courage, taste, and timing. This incident is only one of the countless strokes of effective discipline employed in the classrooms across the land where individuals who really love, respect, and understand children brighten the portals of learning daily. Its appearance at this point is to encourage teachers to utilize their initiative and all resources available in meeting each new crisis.

---

[25]Duane Manning, *The Qualitative Elementary School,* (New York: Harper and Row, Publishers, 1963), pp. 124-5. Copyright © 1963 by Duane Manning. Reprinted by permission of Harper and Brothers.

SUMMARY

The assumption that each child is different and therefore responds and functions in a unique manner comes into fruition as each teacher learns what children are generally like at each stage of their development. The teacher must know not only the child but the circumstances and environment around him. He must recognize each child's needs, motives and personal-social drives in the light of his living and interacting in his particular environment.

Particular knowledge about children which the teacher needs can be classified as age characteristics and behavioral changes. Realizing that children approach these characteristics and changes at varying ages and stages any taxonomy of them must be treated in a spread of ages rather than any one particular age. A convenient and generally accepted assignment of characteristics and changes by levels is that of (1) preschool, ages three to six; (2) primary, ages five through nine; (3) intermediate, ages eight through twelve; and (4) junior high, ages eleven through fifteen.

A major task of the teacher is obtaining information about children. Five resources usually available are: (1) community surveys, (2) cumulative records, (3) observation, (4) conferences with parents, pupils, and other teachers, and (5) student personnel services.

Effective utilization of available student data is a major function of the teacher. The attitudes of the teacher toward behavior of children usually determines the extent of preventive and corrective discipline. It is imperative that the teacher recognize the four categories of each child's behavior, namely physical, intellectual, emotional, and social, and that he relate these to the different age levels. The effective teacher is sensitive to the symptoms which indicate that children are seeking to satisfy pressures upon them by being aggressive, submissive, withdrawing, or ill. He sees these symptoms as signs of a need felt by the child and should endeavor to help him meet this need. The teacher should continuously review principles basic to effective student behavior and plan the proper course of action for guiding each child toward achieving appropriate conduct.

QUESTIONS FOR DISCUSSION

1. There are certain recognized characteristics of children. How do these differ and compare at the various age levels?
2. How can teaching procedure be related to behavior of children at different ages?
3. Identify sources for gathering information about children. How can information obtained improve the learning situation?

4. What is the role of a teacher in utilizing information about children effectively?
5. Assuming that every individual is different, how can recognition of these differences contribute to effective discipline?
6. Certain principles are recognized as basic to teaching. Which principles can be considered as most conducive to promoting desirable behavior of children?

TOPICS FOR RESEARCH

1. Observe children to identify those who seem to exemplify characteristics usually specified for their age. Observe children to record information on those who do not fit the characteristics usually specified for their age.
2. Determine ways teachers can help children accomplish the developmental tasks identified by Havighurst.
3. Study the relation of socioeconomic conditions to behavior of children in a particular school community.
4. Examine the cumulative records of a class of middle-grade students and give your impressions of the extent to which characteristics of children have been taken into consideration in recording information about them.
5. Observe two or three children from a particular age group whose behavior seems to deviate from that of an average child within that group. Describe how you think you would cope with their variable behavior were you the teacher.

BIBLIOGRAPHY

Curriculum Framework for Georgia Schools. Atlanta: State Department of Education, 1957.

Discipline. Washington, D. C.: Association for Childhood Education International, 1957.

FOSTER, CHARLES R., *Guidance for Today's Children.* Boston: Ginn and Company, 1957.

HAVIGHURST, ROBERT J., *Developmental Tasks and Education.* New York: Longman's, Green and Company, 1952.

HYMES, JAMES L., JR., *Behavior and Misbehavior.* Englewood Cliffs: Prentice-Hall, Inc., 1955.

JENKINS, GLADYS GARDNER, *These Are Your Children.* Expanded edition. Chicago: Scott, Foresman and Company, 1953.

KELNER, BERNARD G., *How to Teach in the Elementary School.* New York: McGraw-Hill Book Company, Inc., 1958.

LOGAN, LILLIAN M., AND VIRGIL G. LOGAN, *Teaching the Elementary School Child.* Boston: Houghton Mifflin Company, 1961.

MANNING, DUANE, *The Qualitative Elementary School*. New York: Harper and Row, Publishers, 1963.

MAUSS, ROLF E., *First-Aid for Classroom Discipline Problems*. New York: Holt, Rinehart and Winston, Inc., 1962.

MEHL, MARIE A., HUBERT H. MILLS, AND HARL R. DOUGLASS, *Teaching in Elementary School*. Second edition. New York: The Ronald Press Company, 1958.

MILLARD, CECIL V., *Child Growth and Development in the Elementary School Years*. Revised edition, Boston: D. C. Heath and Company, 1958.

OLSON, WILLARD C., *How Children Grow and Develop*. Chicago: Science Research Associates, Inc., 1953.

RAGAN, WILLIAM B., *Teaching America's Children*. New York: Holt, Rinehart and Winston, 1961.

RATHS, LOUIS E., *An Application To Education of the Needs Theory*. Bronxville, N. Y.: Modern Education Service, 1950.

WINGO, G. MAX, AND RALEIGH SCHORLING, *Elementary-School Student Teaching*. Second edition. New York: McGraw-Hill Book Company, Inc., 1955.

In education there is nothing so unequal as the equal treatment of unequals.

Charles E. Bish

The individual within the group has his own unique interests and needs.

Chapter 5

Grouping Children
for Effective Learning

Some teachers would agree that the ideal grouping situation in the public elementary school would be one teacher for every child. Such a universal plan of grouping, however, is an impossibility in the United States because our nation is committed to a program of mass education. We have more pupils than we have teachers. Consequently some plan of grouping is necessitated for the instruction of children in America's elementary schools.

Many teachers would challenge the idea that the best grouping plan imaginable would be one teacher for each child because they hold to the idea that children learn from one another. They contend, therefore, that pupils should be allowed the opportunity of close, interpersonal association with their peers in many different learning groups. It is indeed fortunate that most elementary teachers subscribe to this philosophy since our nation's program of education is designed to meet the needs of its divergent masses of students.

Grouping children for instruction is not an easy task. This is an oversimplification of a basic truth because teachers have long known that no two children come to school with exactly the same experiential backgrounds, abilities, aptitudes, skills, or needs. Devising an adequate plan of grouping to meet the various needs of the students therefore becomes a complex endeavor.

If all children possessed similar capabilities and held mutual educational needs, most any plan of grouping would work and "assembly line" teaching techniques with related content would suffice. Children would enter grade one at age six and would progress through the grades emerging from twelve at age eighteen with a high school diploma and a standardized education. Their education would have been achieved much as a car manufacturing plant turns out its finished product. In mass automotive production, from the time the first part is placed on the moving conveyor belt until the final part is added and the finished automobile rolls off the assembly line, each detailed phase of production is handled in the same sterile, standardized method for all cars produced of a particular make. Each child is different, however, and the assembly line technique whereby children progress through the grades with each teacher adding a little more refinement to the process of education in an inflexible program is not compatible with our sophisticated knowledge of child growth and development or individual and trait differences.

Each child differs from other children in his ways of learning and rate of growth and development. Within an average classroom in the elementary school, research has shown that the teacher may expect to find the following ranges of individual differences in reading comprehension and vocabulary, language mechanics, and arithmetic:

—At the first-grade level, the range of achievement is between 3 and 4 years.
—At the fourth-grade level, the range of achievement is between 5 and 6 years.
—At the sixth-grade level, the range of achievement is between 7 and 8 years.[1]

Children are more alike in the first grade from the standpoint of achievement and physical characteristics than they will ever be again. The hazy notion that good teaching should narrow the ranges of individual differences, which some teachers ritualistically hold to, destroys the entire premise upon which a sound educational program is developed. Good teaching should widen, not narrow, the range of individual differences. The farther children progress through the grades under stimulating learning situations, the wider the differences will become as their varying intellects, aptitudes, and desires begin to exert themselves.

Confronted by the wide range of individual differences at any grade level among pupils of comparable chronological age, the school and teachers face the dilemma of designing some plan of grouping which will meet

---

[1] J. Wayne Wrightstone, *What Research Says to the Teacher* (Washington, D. C.: National Education Association, Department of Classroom Teachers and American Educational Research Association, 1961), p. 13.

the instructional needs of all children. Attempts to group children at each grade level so their individual needs can more nearly be met are basically provided for in two ways in the elementary school: (1) intraschool sectioning and (2) intraclass grouping.

GROUPING PROCEDURES WITHIN THE SCHOOL

There are two separate and distinct methods of intraschool grouping of children at the elementary level. The first is that of assigning a grade placement to the individual student. Within itself, this poses little difficulty since it ordinarily is handled on the basis of the individual child's chronological age and number of grades completed in the elementary school. It does, however, constitute a plan of grouping which had its origin in the first graded elementary school established by Philbrick in Boston in 1848 and remains with us to the present day.

The second plan of intraschool grouping is that of sectioning the students. In schools where there are more children to teach at a given grade level than one teacher is capable of teaching, the children may be subdivided into separate sections among two or more teachers. In sectioning students in the elementary school, teachers have attempted to keep the class size as small as possible. Ideally they strive to hold the enrollment in the primary sections to 25 or fewer pupils and the intermediate sections to 30 students or less. Otto has stated the logic behind this reasoning quite succinctly as follows:

> Good elementary schools strive for small classes so that (a) the teacher has more time to spend with each child; (b) classrooms are not crowded; (c) children have more freedom to move around the room; (d) children are under less emotional strain; and (e) children have more opportunity to learn to work in groups.[2]

The basis on which these children are eventually sectioned has been an extremely debatable topic among teachers in the past. Some of the leading practices which have been utilized in formulating these sections have been referred to as mental ability, achievement, cross-class, or heterogeneous grouping. Basically, however, they can be reduced to two major categories designated as homogeneous and heterogeneous since mental ability, achievement, and cross-class grouping plans can be classified as forms of homogeneous grouping.

---

[2]Henry J. Otto, *Elementary-School Organization and Administration* (third edition; New York: Appleton-Century-Crofts, Inc., 1954), p. 207. Reprinted by permission of Appleton-Century-Crofts, Inc.

HOMOGENEOUS GROUPING

Whenever children are placed together in given sections for instruction on the basis of one or more similar and mutually exclusive characteristics they have been grouped homogeneously. In a 1959 study, Dean found that 16.9 per cent of the urban school systems serving cities with populations of 2,500 or more inhabitants utilized homogeneous grouping in some form in grades 1 – 6.[3] The various methods wherby children are homogeneously grouped are subsequently set forth in the following paragraphs of this chapter.

Ability Grouping

Probably the most widely used method of grouping elementary school children into separate sections homogeneously for instructional purposes is on the basis of mental ability. The criteria for establishing the mental ability of children are mental age and I.Q.

Detroit, Michigan, was the first to experiment with ability grouping on a large scale in 1920. They administered intelligence tests to the incoming 10,000 first grade students who were subsequently assigned to X, Y, and Z groups on the basis of the test results. The upper 20 per cent were sectioned into the X group while the lower 20 per cent were assigned to group Z. The remaining middle 60 per cent were sectioned into Y group. The curriculum was differentiated for each group in an effort to meet their varying ranges of ability and interest.[4]

It is difficult to say just how effective mental ability grouping has been in the past. Research findings are often contradictory. Those who extol the virtues of ability grouping hold to the premise that intelligence is an ample predictor of the student's capacity to learn and perform successfully in all areas of the elementary school curriculum. Experience dictates that prediction on the basis of the correlation between intelligence and performance in school is frequently erratic. Wrightstone has found, however, in summarizing the research which has been conducted on ability grouping, that homogeneously grouped students tend to slightly excel heterogeneously grouped children in academic achievement. "The evidence for ability grouping," he concludes, "indicated greatest relative effectiveness in academic learning for dull children, next greatest for average children, and least for

---

[3]Stuart E. Dean, *Elementary School Administration and Organization* (Washington, D. C.: U. S. Department of Health, Education, and Welfare, Office of Education, 1960), p. 68.

[4]Wrightstone, *op. cit.*, p. 6.

bright children."[5] Wrightstone further asserts that "This conclusion must be regarded as tentative."[6]

Teachers who oppose ability grouping take the position that since only slight improvement in academic achievement may be effected by homogeneously sectioned children, much of the social learning which could accrue among heterogeneously grouped pupils is lost. After all, they contend, the prospective surgeon must learn to socialize with the future carpenter and the school is the logical place to accomplish this goal. They also feel that the children who are placed in the slower sections often become stigmatized as the dull group.

Admittedly opinions differ as to the wisdom of sectioning children for instructional purposes on the basis of mental ability. Most would agree, however, that if children are sectioned on the basis of ability, they should have differentiated curriculums. It would be sheer folly to divide the various sections into bright, average, and dull groups and then provide identical curriculum experiences. Research has shown clearly that high-and low-ability students learn differently. Wrightstone summarizes some general characteristics of low-ability pupils, which teachers need to keep in mind as they adapt instruction to meet student needs at this level.

1. Low-ability pupils learn by simple mental processes. They are confused by too many approaches and by complex associations with a topic. The instructional approach should be direct and uncomplicated.

2. Low-ability pupils prefer the concrete in preference to the abstract — the specific rather than the general. Instruction should be focused on the concrete and specific phases of a topic.

3. Low-ability pupils prefer short-time units and specific assignments. In instruction, it is wise to avoid long-range, general, and vague assignments that require a high level of organization.

4. Low-ability pupils possess limited powers of self-criticism. They should have systematic opportunities to discover and correct their errors. The learning process should be so organized that such pupils are not constantly overwhelmed, but are enabled to proceed with order and certainty.[7]

Some of the characteristics of high-ability students which teachers should be cognizant of in adapting instruction to meet their needs have been enumerated by Wrightstone as follows:

---

[5]*Ibid.*, p. 8.
[6]*Ibid.*, p. 8.
[7]*Ibid.*, p. 20.

1. High-ability pupils have superior powers of analysis and general reasoning ability. They can handle complex associations of ideas within a topic.
2. High-ability pupils have a high degree of originality, resourcefulness, initiative, and ability to interpret abstract ideas.
3. High-ability pupils can recognize related material and relate their thoughts, illustrations, and answers to life situations. They can engage in long-range assignments that require a high degree of mental organization.
4. High-ability pupils possess powers of self-criticism. They need opportunities that will challenge their skill in organizing ideas and integrating related ideas into basic but systematic generalizations.[8]

Research evidence is too meager and subjective to say what effect ability grouping has upon the social and emotional development of elementary school children. In schools where students are sectioned on the basis of ability, however, children readily know whether they have been assigned to a bright, average, or dull group. Sometimes children of the dull sections are looked down upon by the brighter students as being intellectually inferior.

Teachers usually prefer ability sectioning unless they are assigned to teach a low-ability section. It is a rare occurrence for a teacher to be completely satisfied to work with a dull section. In general, parents favor the plan unless their children are placed in a dull section.

Achievement Grouping

Assigning children on the basis of previous academic performance to a given section for instruction is commonly referred to as achievement grouping. In sectioning pupils in this manner, the criteria of past achievement test results, students' marks and teachers' judgment are considered. In contrasting the objectives of the ability and achievement sectioning plans, Otto and Sanders have stated that "The objective of ability grouping is to assign to a given class those pupils who *have the capacity* for comparable attainments. The objective of achievement grouping is the formation of classes whose pupils *have past records* of comparable attainment."[9]

The major problem which confronts educators who section children on the basis of academic achievement is selecting an appropriate achievement criterion to supplement the criteria of students' marks and teachers' judgment. Just as pupils have individual differences which are readily

---

[8]*Ibid.*, p. 23.
[9]Henry J. Otto and David C. Sanders, *Elementary School Organization and Administration* (fourth edition; New York: Appleton-Century-Crofts, Inc., © 1964), p. 107.

distinguishable one from the other, so does the individual child have distinguishing trait differences. Beck, Cook, and Kearney have distinguished between individual and trait differences lucidly in their statement:

> The phrase "individual differences" refers to the dissimilarity among the various members of a class or age group in any characteristic such as intelligence, reading ability, spelling ability, and the like; while "trait differences" refers to the variability of a single person with reference to abilities and traits such as his own relative standing in reading, spelling, arithmetic, music, and art.[10]

No one child is equally proficient in all subjects. For example, a third grade student may have grade placement equivalents of 4.5 in reading vocabulary and 6.0 in reading comprehension; 5.0 in arithmetic reasoning and 4.1 in arithmetic fundamentals, and 3.5 in language mechanics and 5.1 in spelling. If reading comprehension were selected as the criterion whereby this student was assigned to a given section, he would doubtlessly be placed in an accelerated group. Consequently he would likely find work in the other academic areas too difficult. Conversely, if he were assigned to a slow section based on his measured proficiency in language mechanics, he would probably find that the work in the other areas would not be challenging enough to meet his needs.

The difficulty of formulating defensible groups in sectioning children which arises from individual trait differences doubtlessly explains why schools do not use homogeneous plans of grouping in the elementary school more than they do. Studies by Hull, Hollingshead, and Burr have shown, as cited by Beck, Cook, and Kearney, that trait differences in the typical student are 80 per cent as great as individual differences within a group of students.[11] Any form of homogeneous grouping, if perfectly done, therefore would reduce the variability of each section of students by only about 20 per cent. An awareness of this truth places the following statement of Wrightstone in proper perspective:

> Studies reveal that, in general, variability in achievement in grades that have three ability groups in each is about 83 percent as great as in normally organized groups. In grades having two ability groups each, the variability of achievement, as measured by standard tests, is about 93 percent as great as in normally organized groups. This difference offers only slight assistance to the teacher in reducing the range of individual differences in his classroom. For a grade organized on three ability levels,

---

[10]Robert H. Beck, Walter W. Cook and Nolan C. Kearney, *Curriculum in the Modern Elementary School* (second edition; Englewood Cliffs: N. J.: Prentice-Hall, Inc., © 1960), p. 31. Reprinted by permission of Prentice-Hall, Inc.
[11]*Ibid.*, pp. 42-43.

the reduction in range is about 15 to 17 percent; for a grade with two ability groups, the reduction in range is 7 to 10 percent.[12]

The data cited here clearly show that homogeneously sectioning children into groups on the basis of mental ability or achievement does not eliminate individual or trait differences. In fact, it only slightly reduces variability within the class by about 17 to 20 per cent when it is perfectly done.

Cross-Class Grouping

A third type of homogeneous grouping plan utilized in the elementary school is cross-class or interclass grouping. It is probably used less frequently than either the ability or achievement plans. Under this technique, children change sections periodically during the school day into different high, average, and low ability groups taught by different teachers in the various subject areas. Available research evidence has shown that such a plan produced no achievement advantages for students in the area of reading when compared with comparable children receiving reading instruction within their regular classes.[13]

As has already been stated, our nation is committed to a program of mass education. The United States has been experiencing a population explosion in recent years and prospects indicate that this trend will grow increasingly worse. In the past, misguided educators have attempted to find simple procedures for formulating homogeneous groups of students in which uniform curriculums with concomitant textbooks, instructional procedures, and achievement standards would meet mass educational needs. The foregoing sections of this chapter, however, have lucidly shown that such a theory is too idealistic because of the divergent needs of the pupils at any grade level. Modern educational philosophy is in firm agreement with Beck, Cook, and Kearney's statement that as teachers we should "Accept the wide range of ability found in all classes as inevitable, accept it as something good, highly desirable, and necessary in this scheme of things. Then set about to find effective ways of meeting the individual needs of children in heterogeneous groups."[14]

The Department of Labor's *Dictionary of Occupations* lists approximately 30,000 different job classifications in the United States. Among these are found engineers, maids, butlers, janitors, lawyers, teachers, and many others. Children will grow up to select one of these given vocations, each

---

[12]Wrightstone, *op. cit.*, pp. 8-9.
[13]*Ibid.*, p. 6.
[14]Beck, Cook, and Kearney, *op. cit.*, p. 49.

with different potentialities, aspirations, interests, and needs. The school has the responsibility of providing them with the type of education which will enable them to achieve happiness and success in their adult years. Static curriculums designed for homogeneously grouped children are not likely to satisfactorily meet this need. On the other hand, differentiated curriculum sensitive to individual and trait differences can accomplish this worthy objective.

HETEROGENEOUS GROUPING

Many educators are fully aware of the research cited in previous sections of this chapter which shows that homogeneous sectioning of children is no real panacea for the wide ranges of individual and trait differences among elementary school students. Perhaps that is why 72.1 per cent of the urban places in the United States with populations of 2,500 or more utilize the heterogeneous plan of grouping.[15]

The heterogeneous sectioning of pupils may be thought of as social grouping. Usually, under this plan, no attempt is made to section children on the basis of likenesses other than chronological age. The children instead are assigned to a given section on the basis of random selection. A frequently used practice is to divide the enrollment cards into two groups on the basis of sex at each grade placement level. Each group of boys' and girls' enrollment cards is alphabetized. Then cards are dealt into as many stacks as there are numbers of sections to be created, keeping a balance of boys and girls in each class. Once the sectioning has been completed, the cards are checked to see if pupil-teacher-parent associations thereby created will likely be compatible. Where known or possible conflicts seem evident, section adjustments are made.

Many educators use a controlled heterogeneous grouping plan, setting up classes or sections which contain approximately 30 students each. They try to place approximately one-third of the upper achieving level, one-third of the middle range, and one-third of the lowest achieving level within each section. The advantages claimed for such a plan of grouping is that it facilitates a good social learning situation in that it approximates more nearly lifelike associations which the students will encounter in out of school hours, and that intraclass groups can be easily formed since there is nearly the same number of bright, average, and dull children.

Where heterogeneous sectioning of pupils is practiced it becomes almost imperative that the individual classroom teacher form intraclass groups. Grouping within the classroom has been a widely accepted practice in

---

[15]Dean, *op. cit.*, p. 68.

recent years because it affords the teacher a vehicle whereby he can adapt the instruction to the level of the group, and, more important, it better enables him to differentiate the curriculum for the individual pupil within the group.

FORMING GROUPS WITHIN THE CLASSROOM

Grouping within the classroom is handled in many different ways. Some of the most widely utilized plans center around ability, interest, friendship, and needs grouping. Many teachers use all of these plans from time to time by employing a program of flexible grouping. Irrespective of the plan selected for grouping children within the classroom, there are some common sense principles which should be followed in forming the group. These guiding principles have been well stated by Ragan as follows:

1. Living in the elementary school is enriched by recognizing differences in children rather than by trying to force them all into one pattern of performance.
2. The child's group should be a situation where each learns from the other and each has a contribution to make to group living.
3. Each child should be permitted to progress at his own rate.
4. The teacher should accept each child as he is and do everything possible to promote his growth in wholesome directions.
5. The plan of grouping should make it feasible for the teacher to know intimately all the children he teaches.
6. The plan of grouping should be flexible enough so that at times the child can be in a group with other children of like ability and maturity and at times in a group with children who differ widely in terms of age, ability, and talents.[16]

INTRACLASS ABILITY GROUPING

Teachers frequently establish ability groups within the classroom for instruction. This practice occurs mostly in reading. Sometimes teachers use ability grouping in arithmetic as well. The problem with intraclass ability grouping is that too often these groups tend to become static. They are recognizable to anyone associated with the class as the bright, average, and dull groups; hence, many times the dull children tend to be stigmatized. The greatest objection to this plan, however, stems from the fact that children's needs vary because of their individual trait differences. Where intraclass ability grouping becomes rigidly fixed, as is so often the case, children frequently will be misgrouped because of their trait differences.

---

[16]William B. Ragan, *Teaching America's Children* (New York: Holt, Rinehart and Winston, 1961), p. 87. © 1961, Holt, Rinehart and Winston, Inc. Used by permission of the publishers.

If ability grouping were to reach its maximum effectiveness, the pupils would have to be reassigned periodically as topics are covered in curriculum development in a manner that would more nearly meet their individual trait differences.

INTRACLASS INTEREST GROUPING

The progressive education movement of the 1900's sparked a drive among teachers to seek newer pedagogical techniques which would be more palatable for elementary school children than the traditional regimented programs. The individual classroom was no longer viewed as a rigidly disciplined place where formalized learning took place in rote manner, but was considered to be a learning center where children felt free to move about and experiment with various media in pursuit of knowledge which interested them. Intraclass interest grouping thus has been a welcome outgrowth of the progressive education movement for teacher and pupil alike.

Interest grouping is a simple procedure. Children with mutual interests group themselves naturally into a unit of pupils to study a given topic. This plan may be utilized in most areas of the curriculum, particularly in social studies and science. Such a plan of grouping has the advantage of being quite flexible. Different students will comprise the groups as topics and interests change. Bright, average, and dull children have rewarding associations with one another while each child makes his own unique contribution to the over-all group study.

INTRACLASS FRIENDSHIP GROUPING

Occasionally children should be allowed to group themselves on the basis of friendship within the classroom for study of selected topics or work on given committees. Friendship grouping has proven practical in formulating different committees such as lunchroom, library, room environment, and playground. In social studies and science unit study, occasional intraclass friendship groupings have stimulated the learning environment and enriched learning experiences also.

INTRACLASS NEEDS GROUPING

Teachers who group on the basis of pupil needs within the elementary school are exercising sound pedagogical technique. Since there are individual and trait differences, student needs are constantly changing. When a teacher groups on the basis of needs he therefore is establishing a plan whereby the level of instruction can be adjusted to pupil level as each new topic is presented during the school year.

Needs grouping is effective in every area of the curriculum, particularly the skills subjects of reading, arithmetic, language, and writing. Once a given topic has been introduced the students can be grouped on the basis of need for differentiated instruction. Groups so formulated remain flexible with different students comprising the membership of different groupings from one topic to another as they progress through their studies.[17]

Under the needs grouping plan, it is unlikely that any child will find himself permanently affixed to a given group. It is likely that he will find grouping situations in which instruction is offered at his achievement level where he can experience learning success and rewarding peer relationships.

REQUISITES OF EFFECTIVE GROUPING PROCEDURE

Every classroom teacher occasionally will follow some plan of grouping. Whether he uses one of those plans discussed here — i.e. ability, interest, friendship, and needs — or some other pattern, he should see that provision is made for each child to (1) attain acceptance, (2) achieve success, and (3) be provided freedom of activity.

GAINING ACCEPTANCE

It is normal for every child to want to be accepted by his peers and his teachers. It is imperative that he be accepted in his group if he is to be expected to do his best work. It is equally important that the child accept his own group; otherwise he may become frustrated, withdraw from the group, and regress in his over-all progress.

Teachers need to be aware of the fact that each child establishes in his own mind two types of groups irrespective of those formed in the classroom. These may be classified as membership and reference. The child surveys his own membership group periodically as he inwardly analyzes with whom he is working, playing, or studying. Mentally he may reject his membership group and wish that he were allowed the privilege of working with his reference group. The child's reference group is that group of individuals in the room with which he mentally identifies himself and desires to be associated. If the child's membership and reference group are the same, he likely will be content with the arrangement and progress satisfactorily. If, on the other hand, his reference group is different from his membership group, the chances are good that he will be discontent with the grouping arrangement.

---

[17]Oscar T. Jarvis, "Grouping to Meet Individual and Trait Differences," *Georgia Education Journal*, December, 1962, Volume LVI, Number 4, p. 13.

The teacher will do well to be constantly on guard to determine if the grouping situations are acceptable to the students. When the teacher determines periodically that the groupings are not acceptable to one or more students, he should ascertain these children's reference groups and reassign them to their chosen group where it is practicable. Above all the teacher must never forget that the individual child should be placed in a group where he can gain acceptance and experience a real sense of belonging. Wherever it is possible, the teacher should allow the child to work in a membership group that is also his reference group.

ACHIEVING SUCCESS

The child should be permitted to work in groups in which he can experience success. Continued failure is frustrating. Continuous success is motivating. The teacher therefore will want to guide the individual child into a group which he accepts and where the level of the work to be done is appropriate to his developmental needs and demonstrated abilities. By working in a group with which he identifies and in which he achieves success, the child's perception of his personal worth is enhanced. He also feels secure and his mind is free to dwell on important curriculum experiences.

FREEDOM OF ACTIVITY

Children should be allowed the privilege of doing their group work in a permissive classroom environment. The teacher should exercise caution not to set up rules which would restrict the purposeful movement of the groups as they are engaged in various study activities. The classroom climate should be such that the students feel free to move around in their groups in the pursuit of knowledge to utilize materials which may be located in different parts of the classroom or the building. They should be permitted to converse at appropriate times as they work together to solve. mutual problems or make their contribution to a collective project.

One of the major purposes for utilizing intraclass groups is to establish a plan whereby students with similar needs can work on mutual problems. If these needs are to be met most expeditiously, the students must be allowed freedom of activity.

This chapter deals primarily with grouping practices. For a more comprehensive treatment of how the teacher works with the group, the reader is advised to examine Chapters 8 and 9.

MAINTAINING FLEXIBILITY IN GROUPING PRACTICES

The ideas and research studies cited in this chapter on the effectiveness of various interclass and intraclass grouping plans have clearly shown that there is no one best plan for sectioning children at their respective grade levels or for forming subgroups within each section once established. The fact that homogeneous grouping of students simply reduces the range of individual differences by about 17 to 20 per cent has been pointed out. Likewise, the point has been adequately made that grouping does not eliminate individual or trait differences but only narrows them slightly. It has also been pointed out that when children have been grouped together into a given section for instruction, a wise grouping plan would be to keep the intraclass groupings flexible. The groups should be formed predominantly on the basis of individual pupil needs with occasional ability, interest, and friendship groupings utilized at appropriate times. The authors of this text are in complete agreement with Veatch's following statement on grouping:

> Groups do not need to be organized upon what is known and commonly understood as ability. Let us hope that eventually all ability grouping as now prevalent in American schools will end. Groups organized upon one and only one specific need are ideal for effective learning; that is a continuation of the principle of *open-ended learning*. The best thing to do, when several children show the same difficulty or interest, is to put them together for a common activity! Put another way, a good practice is to find one common element and then group, rather than to follow the current practice which sets up a group and then seeks to discover a common element among the members. We may take an example from the sports world. Coaches do not group ball players on generalized ability. They group those who need to polish their skills of bunting, of fielding grounders, of catching flies, or kicking field goals, or forward passing, or what have you. This is the way to teach as well as coach![18]

Teachers cannot expect simply to formulate groups and then teach the individual group. Rather they should formulate small groups when specific needs arise that are common to two or more pupils and attempt to teach each individual within the group. This is the real purpose for grouping.

MAKING PROVISIONS FOR THE NEEDS OF EXCEPTIONAL CHILDREN

The manner in which the school provides for its exceptional children is a measure of the quality of instruction for all its students. When one considers the implications of such a statement he is inclined to agree with

---

[18]Jeannette Veatch, "Emphasizing Fundamental Principles for Teaching Basic Skills," *Curriculum for Today's Boys and Girls*. Robert S. Fleming (ed.), (Columbus, Ohio: Charles E. Merrill Books, Inc., 1963), pp. 143-144.

its wisdom because dynamic school programs do make provision for their exceptional students.[19]

Approximately 12 per cent of the students enrolled in America's schools between the ages of five and nineteen years may be classified as exceptional, according to Ragan, and may be referred to as gifted, slow learners, physically handicapped, and social deviates.[20] Each of these classifications of children is in need of special attention if the children are to be expected to progress academically and socially in as normal a manner as circumstances will permit.

GIFTED CHILDREN

Students who are classified as gifted have been defined differently by scholars. Terman, for example, has designated such children as those who possess IQ's of 140 or above.[21] Dechant has stated that children possessing IQ's of 120 and above may be classified as gifted.[22] One can safely say that children who possess IQ's of 125 or above can be classified as gifted learners. In working with this group of pupils, teachers will do well to keep some commonly understood facts about them in mind. Ragan has enumerated them as follows:

1. Mentally gifted children may not require the same amount of drill as other children. Time saved from drill may be used more profitably for other purposes.
2. Gifted children can be expected to do a great deal of planning, executing, and evaluating relative to classroom activities.
3. Higher standards of achievement can ordinarily be set for gifted children.
4. Gifted children should be provided a wealth of reading material.
5. Gifted children should be encouraged to expand their interests and enrich their experiences through participation in special interest clubs.
6. Specialists in various fields should be used, who can bring gifted children information, skills, and insights which the teacher lacks.
7. Special classes composed of gifted children from several grade levels may be organized to study certain subjects.[23]

---

[19]Roy Patrick Wahle, "Methods of Individualization in Elementary School," *Teaching In Elementary School*, Lester D. Crow, Alice Crow, and Walter Murray (ed.), (New York: David McKay Company, Inc., 1961), p. 30.

[20]Ragan, *op. cit.*, pp. 89-90.

[21]Arthur I. Gates, Arthur T. Jersild, T. R. McConnell, and Robert C. Challman, *Educational Psychology* (New York: The Macmillan Company, third edition, 1949), p. 251.

[22]Emerald V. Dechant, *Improving the Teaching of Reading* (Englewood Cliffs, N. J.: Prentice-Hall, Inc., 1964), p. 511.

[23]Ragan, *op. cit.*, p. 91.

The gifted pupils are easily identifiable in any classroom. They tend to be physically superior to other children their age in over-all strength, health, height, and stamina. Likewise, they excel their other age mates mentally in that they ordinarily are astute thinkers and rapid learners. Generally they are well adjusted socially. They possess good leadership abilities and are self-confident, gregarious individuals.

There has been a move within recent years to provide different and enriched learning experiences for the gifted. Frequently they become bored with the programs of minimum instruction offered in many schools and in some cases become disciplinary problems. The gifted are often the underachievers in our schools because, more often than not, the level of instruction is pitched toward the median needs of all the pupils.

Schools have attempted to meet the needs of gifted students primarily through one of two methods, namely vertical acceleration or horizontal enrichment. Under the first plan, the gifted children skip a grade somewhere within their elementary years. The theory behind such a practice holds that they will find the work of the next grade more challenging and better suited to their individual needs. The future progress of the accelerated student is uncertain. He may gravitate to the top of his new grade placement level rapidly and the problem in that event will not be resolved but only temporarily postponed. He may not adjust at all and suffer grievous social and emotional disturbances. Realizing these basic truths, most schools which make provision for the gifted practice horizontal enrichment whereby the child does not skip a grade. Instead they progress normally through the grades along with their peers on an annual promotion basis. Within their sections, the classroom teachers see that they master the essentials expected of all of the children, and then they are given supplementary work to extend their learning and challenge their abilities either individually or in small groups.[24]

SLOW-LEARNING CHILDREN

Students who possess measured IQ's of less than 90 are generally considered to be slow learners. This group of pupils may be subgrouped into the slow learners and feeble-minded classifications.

Most schools consider the slow learners to be those pupils who have IQ's which range from 70 to 90. They customarily are permitted to attend, regular classes with students of higher intelligence. Technically speaking, they are referred to by psychologists and educators as dull normal pupils.

---

[24]Audrey Wrye, *Providing for the Academically Able* (Houston, Texas: Houston Public Schools, Curriculum Bulletin 60CBM46, 1960), Sections 1, 2, and 3.

Teachers should work differently with the slow learners than with the average and bright children. Some of the principles which they should keep in mind in working with this group have been well stated by Ragan:

1. Standards of achievement for slow-learning children should be set up in terms of their ability.
2. Short, frequent drill periods are essential for slow learners.
3. Materials should be divided into short, definite learning units.
4. Visual appeal should be used extensively to stimulate interest.
5. An abundance of easy reading material should be provided.
6. Opportunities to succeed in small understakings should be provided.
7. Slow-learning children frequently need help in making adjustments to group living as well as to school subjects.[25]

Whenever children possess IQ's of less than 70 they are considered to be feeble-minded. They have special educational needs, since they are more trainable than educable. Generally they are removed from the regular classes and are placed in classes of special education. This practice is followed in most of the more progressive urban city school systems. It is not uncommon to find the feeble-minded children sectioned with the normal children in rural areas; however, many rural districts are banning together to form cooperative special education classes for the feeble-minded which are centrally located in order to serve the needs of their region.

The group of students eligible for these special education classes are those with IQ's between 50 and 70. They are commonly referred to as the mentally retarded.. The curriculum for mentally retarded children should not differ greatly from that afforded the normal pupils. The main difference will be that time will vary a great deal more. These children are educable and can master the Three R's, but the length of time required will be considerably longer than for normal children. This is one of the main reasons why they are sectioned differently from normal children.

One cannot expect the feeble-minded to reach the achievement or developmental levels of normal children. However, they need to achieve the goals of self-realization, social and civic competence, and vocational efficiency in accordance with their own capacities.[26]

PHYSICALLY HANDICAPPED CHILDREN

Space will not permit an elaborate treatment of the different types of physically handicapped children. This group would include those who have some sensory defect in hearing, sight, or speech as well as those who may

[25]Ragan, *op. cit.*, p. 91.
[26]Otto, *op. cit.*, p. 502.

be crippled or suffer from epilepsy. Ragan has suggested some guiding principles which will enable the teacher to work more effectively with this group of students as follows:

1. Whenever possible, the physically handicapped child should participate in the normal school experiences with his appropriate age group.
2. The special needs of physically handicapped children are so numerous and varied that they can be met only with the cooperation of the home, school, health agencies, and other community organizations.
3. Blind, deaf, and otherwise severely handicapped children require the services of specialists either in the home or in special clinics.
4. Children with handicaps of hearing or vision need special attention in the regular classroom in such matters as seating arrangement and individual guidance from the teacher.[27]

SOCIAL DEVIATES

A fourth group of exceptional pupils are those who may be termed social deviates. Teachers frequently misunderstand these children and do not deal with them properly in the teaching-learning situation. This group of children may be considered to be those who have emotional disturbances or are maladjusted socially. In working with them, teachers will do well to keep in mind the following principles which have been suggested by Ragan:

1. Children with serious behavior problems should be regarded as objects for study rather than as recipients for punishment.
2. The causes of misbehavior can usually be found in home conditions, community influences, or the school program.
3. Many disturbed children require the presence of normal children in order to develop an image of constructive social behavior.
4. The help of specialists, such as the school psychologist, the guidance counselor, and the social worker is needed with pupils who are severely maladjusted.[28]

America is committed to a program of free public schools for all children. When the needs of these children become so diverse that they cannot be met within the regular classroom, modified programs have to be devised for exceptional children. These need not be totally different educational experiences because the over-all aims of education should be the same for all children. The programs for exceptional children should simply seek to meet the individual needs of their students.

---

[27]Ragan, *op. cit.*, p. 90.
[28]*Ibid.*, p. 91.

SUMMARY

As long as we have more pupils than teachers in America's elementary schools we will have to continue the practice of grouping. Grouping in the past usually has been carried on at four distinct and separate levels in the elementary school with a plan for each level.

The first of these plans is that of assigning children to a given grade level for instruction. This is normally done on the basis of chronological age and number of grades which have been successfully completed. Exceptions occur when children skip a grade, are retained, or are demoted, but these happen infrequently.

Groupings formulated on the basis of sectioning children at a given grade level accounts for the second plan. Once the children have been assigned to a grade level they must be sectioned into as many groups as there are teachers available. This operation generally has been handled on the basis of either homogeneous or heterogeneous groupings. When children are sectioned on the basis of homogeneity, teachers look for common likenesses in such areas as ability or achievement. When they are sectioned heterogeneously, they usually are randomly assigned to a section. Research has shown that homogeneously grouped students do slightly better academically than their heterogeneously grouped counterparts. There are, however, aspects of the elementary curriculum aside from the academics, such as socializing experiences, which are equally important and should be considered when deciding upon a plan of grouping.

Intraclass or within class grouping represents a third plan utilized. These groups are formulated in various ways. Some of the most popular plans are based on ability, interest, friendship or need. Research has shown that trait differences within the individual student are nearly as great as differences between students. The wise teacher should keep the plan within her classroom quite flexible and group predominantly on needs so both the individual and trait differences can be met more effectively. Irrespective of the type of intraclass group which is formulated, the teacher should see that the plan will enable each child to: (1) attain acceptance, (2) achieve success, and (3) be provided freedom of activity.

A fourth program of grouping is one designed to care for exceptional children. These children may be designated as the gifted, slow learners, physically handicapped, and social deviates. Whenever the individual differences of exceptional children deviate to the point that their needs cannot be met in the regular classroom, then it is necessary to establish special education classes for them.

The crux of the grouping issue is that individual or trait differences cannot be eliminated simply by grouping children. It may narrow the range of differences somewhat, but it does not eliminate them. Sound grouping practice would dictate that teachers should form their groups on the basis of student needs within the classroom. Poor procedure would be to set up groups on some arbitrary basis and then attempt to find a common educational need. Probably the most important criterion of all is to keep the grouping plan flexible.

QUESTIONS FOR DISCUSSION

1. What is meant by the statement "the good school should widen individual differences between pupils through good teaching, not narrow them"?
2. Research has shown that trait differences within each student are 80 per cent as great as individual differences between students. How do you explain this fact? What implications does this have for homogeneous and heterogeneous groupings within the classroom?
3. It has often been said that individual differences among elementary chlidren are highly desirable. What is meant by this statement?
4. The individual child recognizes two types of groups in his own mind regardless of the intraschool or intraclass groupings with which he is associated. They are the membership and reference groups. How do you explain the importance of this statement?
5. Most educators are agreed that intraclass groupings should remain flexible. What are the factors which support this contention?

TOPICS FOR RESEARCH

1. Do boys or girls of the same chronological age tend to excel in arithmetic (fundamentals and reasoning), reading (vocabulary and comprehension), and language (punctuation, capitalization, and word usage)? What implications, if any, do these facts present for the classroom teacher?
2. Research has shown that approximately 12 per cent of the scholastic population of the school may be classified as being in need of special education. Survey educational literature to determine the incidence of exceptionality among students by categories and suggest ways in which the school may best meet the needs of these children.
3. Many schools use an intraschool grouping plan which is compatible with a multi-track curriculum. Investigate educational literature to determine

how these programs work. Do they eliminate the need for intraclass groupings? Explain.

BIBLIOGRAPHY

BECK, ROBERT H., WALTER W. COOK, AND NOLAN C. KEARNEY. *Curriculum in the Modern Elementary School.* Second edition. Englewood Cliffs, N. J.: Prentice-Hall, Inc., 1960.

DECHANT, EMERALD V. *Improving the Teaching of Reading.* Englewood Cliffs, N. J.: Prentice-Hall, Inc., 1964.

DEAN, STUART E. *Elementary School Administration and Organization: A National Survey of Practices and Policies.* U. S. Department of Health, Education, and Welfare, Office of Education, Bulletin 1960, No. 11, Washington, D. C.: Superintendent of Documents, Government Printing Office, 1960.

GATES, ARTHUR I., ARTHUR T. JERSILD, T. R. MCCONNELL, AND ROBERT C. CHALLMAN. *Educational Psychology.* New York: The Macmillan Company, 1949.

JARVIS, OSCAR T. "Grouping to Meet Individual and Trait Differences," *Georgia Education Journal,* LVI, No. 4, (December, 1962), p. 13.

OTTO, HENRY J. *Elementary-School Organization and Admin tration.* Third edition. New York: Appleton-Century-Crofts, 1954.

OTTO, HENRY J., AND DAVID C. SANDERS. *Elementary School Organization and Administration.* Fourth edition. New York: Appleton-Century-Crofts, 1964.

RAGAN, WILLIAM B. *Teaching America's Children.* New York: Holt, Rinehart and Winston, 1961.

VEATCH, JEANNETTE. "Emphasizing Fundamental Principles for Teaching Basic Skills," *Curriculum for Today's Boys and Girls.* Robert S. Fleming (ed.) Columbus, Ohio: Charles E. Merrill Books, Inc., 1963.

WAHLE, ROY PATRICK. "Methods of Individualization in Elementary School," *Teaching in Elementary School.* Lester D. Crow, Alice Crow, and Walter Murray (ed.), New York: David McKay Company, Inc., 1961.

WRIGHTSTONE, J. WAYNE. "Class Organization for Instruction," *What Research Says to the Teacher,* Pamphlet #13, Washington, D. C.: National Education Association, 1961.

WRYE, AUDREY. *Providing for the Academically Able.* Curriculum Bulletin 60CBM46, Houston, Texas: Houston Public Schools, 1960.

The classroom environment stimulates and reflects student learning experiences.

Chapter **6**

Creating an Effective Learning Environment

The function of an educational program is to foster, influence, and direct the academic and social growth of young people in such a way that they can master their environment, resulting in profitable living in our democratic society. To achieve this it is both desirable and necessary that young people spend their school hours in a stimulating environment. They must have varied and extensive opportunities for educational experiences and engage cooperatively in activities planned to meet their developmental needs. The school must use all available means to provide the experiences which pupils and teachers jointly and individually employ for profitable learning activities. Whether these activities be for the purpose of discovering new facts, developing appreciations, engaging in constructive or creative work, improving basic skills, promoting language abilities, acquiring desirable health and recreational habits, or enabling students to become socially competent participants in community life, a good learning environment is essential.

The question is appropriately asked, "What is this thing called learning environment?" It has been expressed well in the 1954 yearbook of the Association for Supervision and Curriculum Development as ". . . the atmosphere one senses as he approaches a school or looks in at the open door of a classroom. Everything he experiences, everyone he meets constitutes a learning environment."[1]

---

[1]Association for Supervision and Curriculum Development, *Creating An Environment for Learning* (Washington: The Association, 1954), p. 3.

One is reminded then that the learning environment is constituted by people and things inextricably woven together in an ongoing, active, changing organism. A good learning environment in the school may be characterized by its friendliness, freedom from pressures and strains, busyness and purposefulness. If children are eager to get to school and reluctant to leave in the afternoon; if they ask thoughtful questions and search continually for knowledge they are testing in school, this is strong evidence that the school has an effective learning environment.[2]

Classroom environment not only provides the elements for effective learning but triggers the activity itself and continuously nurtures academic growth. "The best learning environment is the one which stimulates the individual to reach constantly for new horizons, new understandings, new experiences; to ask questions as eagerly at forty as at four."[3]

Any good gardener recognizes that a flower grows best when placed in an environment suited to its particular growth characteristics. Further, he knows that to get the best results the flower must be planted in good soil during the proper season. Appropriate food nutrients, water, sunlight, and cultivation must be administered in the proper amounts and at the right time. In like manner, the educator recognizes that the classroom and its environs provide the educational ingredients which stunt or stimulate the growth of the child. The classroom should be expected to be as attractive as mother's living room and as efficient as dad's workshop.

The classroom environment should be so arranged that it is conducive to developing to the maximum degree the innate potentials of all of the students. The child from a privileged home has the right to expect a classroom with an environment equal to that to which he is accustomed. The child coming from an underprivileged home needs an educational environment better than that in which he lives and one in which he will find stimulation and encouragement to improve his own living conditions.

ENVIRONMENT WHICH STIMULATES ACTIVE ·AND LIFELIKE LEARNING

Too often the school is considered as a place to prepare youth for living through some mechanical process, as if the child were an organism which just exists at the complete will of others until a certain age. At a given signal, which is frequently associated with graduation, the switch is turned and the individual begins to live in a certain manner which meets the approval of other adults. The teacher who stresses this kind of mechanized

---

[2]*Ibid.*, pp. 3-4.
[3]*Ibid.*, p. 5.

learning often exacts from children high academic test scores which impress the lay community. However, this same process which stimulates the development of some academic minded children may keep nonacademic students from doing their best work. In addition, this autocratic environment is not very conducive to teaching the social graces to the students.

The teacher must recognize that when a child is treated as a worthwhile individual he feels accepted and grows into a mature, responsible adult. The child should have opportunities to engage in meaningful life activities in which he is required to make his own decisions and make selections with which he has to live. He should be encouraged to follow through in meeting his own objectives to evaluate his accomplishment and adjust his behavior accordingly.[4]

The child, like the adult, learns as he lives and in the same sense lives as he learns. The attitudes and habits acquired by the child in his educational environment become the attitudes and habits he carries into the adult world. As persistent life situations are taken advantage of for learning purposes in the classroom, the child gradualy accepts more responsibility and broadens his ability to meet problems he will face as an adult. One teacher reported that some time after a sixth grade girl had had the experience of serving on the room environment committee she was observed straightening the books on the classroom shelves. When the teacher commended her for this bit of thoughtfulness, she responded, "It's my room too."

The great challenge to make education lifelike came from Dewey when he wrote: "The educational process has no end beyond itself; it is its own end. . . Since in reality there is nothing to which growth is relative save more growth, there is nothing to which education is subordinate save more education."[5] This point construed in its literal sense challenges the educator to make each day the richest possible for each child, utilizing the experiences as a motivating influence in realizing meaning from the academic skills and tools as they affect life itself. Through lifelike situations children gain experience in the free and openended exploration of problems. They begin to observe the complexity of the world — to search for relationships, causal connections, conditional factors, and implications. They deliberate different points of view and grapple with problems within their scope as they seek to understand how groups and individuals change those things within their power and learn to live with those they cannot change.

---

[4]John L. Childs, "Some Ambiguities in Value Theory." Harold G. Shane (ed.), *The American Elementary School* (New York: Harper and Brothers, 1953), p. 12.

[5]John Dewey, *Democracy and Education* (New York: Macmillan Company, 1916), pp. 59-60.

In essence, the school is a place which makes learning possible for the child rather than a place where something is done to children.

Dewey's expressions in regard to freedom of development by the child have often been criticized. Childs has explicitly shown that it was not Dewey's intention that parents and teachers should adopt a hands-off policy and permit each child to behave according to the promptings of his momentary impulses. Dewey regarded seriously the role of teachers and believed that one of their supreme duties was the responsible guidance of students toward self-directing, resourceful, creative members of society.[6]

It is this point of view as interpreted by Childs that helps us put "lifelike learning" in its proper perspective. To allow the child to operate without any direction or controls is to place him in a very un-lifelike situation. Consequently, the school should provide an environment in which the child can seek new solutions to problems of living and learning. It should provide a situation in which the child can learn as he lives, and at the same time recognize and appreciate the limitations of the society in which he finds himself.

RELAXED ATMOSPHERE

A relaxed atmosphere for effective learning can be developed and maintained within the classroom, in the counselor's office, and in any other areas where groups of elementary students are brought together under the supervision of a person charged with responsibility for their academic and social growth. It is the classroom, however, which bears the major responsibility for creating the effective learning environment. There will be an atmosphere which says a genuine welcome. It will be a place that provides for freedom and, at the same time, respects the rights and privileges of all. Fear, tension, and apprehension will be kept at a minimum. Children will feel that they are accepted for their own worth, that they have a contribution to make to the ongoing activities of the group, and that their strengths and weaknesses are understood and appreciated.

In the relaxed classroom, value is placed upon the individuality of students and the relationships within the group. This atmosphere is developed through the use of warm, understanding words and associations. An unkind word, a disappointing look, a bit of sarcasm or ridicule can be a very humiliating, crushing experience for a child. On the other hand, an informal, friendly atmosphere helps the student feel relaxed and content. It is this type of classroom that is a haven in which he can be his normal self and explore his problems in safety. Out of this exploration may come

---

[6]Childs, *op. cit.*, pp. 22-23.

change and development of new values based upon new ways of seeing or perceiving.[7]

In order that there can be a relaxed atmosphere wherein freedom to explore can take place, a group feeling must be developed by the members of the class. This feeling will come about gradually, but positive steps must be taken to accomplish it. Kimball Wiles suggests the following means of developing a group feeling:

1. Invite pupils to participate in planning.
2. Define clearly for the group the areas in which authority can and will be shared.
3. Extend the range of decisions in which pupils participate.
4. Suggest that group organization be flexible and subject to change in light of evaluation.
5. Encourage individuals and small committees to be responsible to the total class.
6. If the class is large, use a planning committee responsible to the total group as a means of conserving time. Have some meeting of the planning committee before the entire class.
7. Recommend that each work-group be represented on the planning committee.
8. Encourage the desire for self-direction as it becomes evident.
9. Be willing to play a dominating or recessive role as the condition of the group demands.
10. Refer teacher suggestions, as well as pupil suggestions, to the class for examination and decision.
11. Use "we" and "our" rather than "I" and "mine."
12. Allow the class to make a mistake when the results will not seriously harm anyone.
13. Permit the class to experience frustration from time to time and to work out solutions to its problems.
14. Praise the group for standing on its own feet and for solving its own problems.
15. Suggest alternate solutions rather than give answers to a problem.
16. Allow the group itself to face and solve disagreements.
17. Assist the group to devise ways of collecting evidence of its progress.
18. Encourage members to ask for evaluation sessions.
19. Take time at the first meetings to help the group members become acquainted.
20. If possible, have the pupils get together in a social occasion early in their working as a group.
21. Seek to obtain the best possible working environment.
22. Undertake a group project as soon as the class is willing.[8]

---

[7]Association for Supervision and Curriculum Development, *Perceiving Behaving Becoming* (Washington: The Association, 1962), pp. 95-96.

[8]Kimball Wiles, *Teaching for Better Schools* (New York: Prentice-Hall, Inc., © 1952), pp. 141-142. Reprinted by permission of Prentice-Hall, Inc.

When group feeling is established, teaching becomes a matter of considering the curiosity of each person within the group in determining what the subject matter will be. The teacher therefore will be a facilitating person. He will help each child find effective means of getting the information necessary to satisfy his curiosity as well as contribute to the welfare and growth of the group. The room environment must be facilitating and provide an atmosphere in which the student is accepted with warmth and friendliness. It also should be one in which he is helped through planned experiences to satisfy his need to know about himself and his world. It is a safe fortress from which he may venture into unknown and possibly dangerous areas for himself. This environment is one in which vigorous and healthy growth toward adequacy can be achieved for both the individual and the group.[9]

RELEASING CREATIVITY

It is obviously easier for the teacher when all the children are on the same page in the same book at the same time, and to grade each child in terms of the accomplishment of one standard. Such a setting as this, however, has little place for the creative individual. Releasing the creative potential of each pupil does not mean treating all children alike. Providing the same opportunities for all does not mean providing equal opportunities for all. It is only when opportunity is provided for individuals to express themselves differently that creativity may come forth. Some children can never accomplish the academic better than others, but given an opportunity can excel by expressing themselves in a different or unique manner. The teacher must be constantly on the watch for the Jefferson, Edison, or Einstein.

A variety of materials must be available, time allowed in the schedule and permissiveness granted students to do original and creative work. Creativity does not license slothfulness and untidyness. The classroom needs to be so structured and equipped that a variety of activities can be carried on simultaneously. This necessitates proper storage of materials and unfinished projects so that work can be put away and a change of activity made with a minimum of effort.

Providing such an environment for the elementary school child not only sets the stage for creativeness in a wide variety of social and cultural experiences but gives meaning to the fundamentals basic to the education of every productive citizen. In order to accomplish this the teacher and pupils must work together to set the psychological conditions within which

---

[9]Association for Supervision and Curriculum Development, *Perceiving Behaving Becoming, op. cit.,* p. 97.

each child will release his inner responses so that he may receive help in clarifying them. The teacher should help his students promote a group feeling within the classroom which respects the individual's right to create new meanings and translate them into action. The pupil who faces anxieties and fear of reprisal for having thoughts or ideas different from those of his peers, parents, or teacher finds it difficult to be creative. By the same token, the teacher who feels threatened by differences in assignment, activities, and achievement of pupils has difficulty encouraging and stimulating creativity in the classroom.

This implies that there must be mutual respect on the part of the children and teacher as well as the administration and community. The teacher, however, is the one who sets the emotional tone of the classroom and engenders an atmosphere of permissiveness which encourages children to share their experiences, their dreams, and aspirations. In this setting the child has learning experiences which permit him to explore areas of interest which should help him to gain a sense of accomplishment and self-realization.

HEALTHFUL LIVING

The ideal school is built to accommodate the health needs of children and faculty. The effective curriculum provides for healthful living in such a way that the lessons in health are actually practiced. Since conditions change with the times, adjustments have to be made that are not always most desirable. Whatever the condition, the faculty and students must continuously plan to utilize and adjust facilities to the best possible advantage. Factors to which attention must be given are space adjustment, arrangement, and utilization of furniture and equipment.

The child spends most of his time at school in one classroom; therefore, it is desirable that adequate space be provided him to work comfortably and to carry on diversified learning experiences. Even though thirty square feet of floor space, plus storage, place for wraps, and toilet facilities, are considered adequate per child, this is not the only consideration. Furniture must be adjustable to each child. The chair or desk should be such that when he sits with his hips against the back of the chair his thighs will be parallel with the seat and his feet rest flat on the floor. The working space of the desk should be elevated to where the child's arm can move comfortably across the top in a writing position without his having to bend over or raise one shoulder uncomfortably higher than the other.

Classroom lighting should be improved by using lighter colors rather than through quantity of light. Attention should be given to preventing glare and reflection by limiting highly glossy objects and disturbing the light evenly over the room. Chalkboards painted a dull green and yellow chalk should be provided. Venetian blinds should be used for breaking the direct sunlight while letting in sufficient light. There should be properly fitted and installed blinds so that the classroom can be darkened for the showing of films. Blinds or shades need to be adjusted and artificial light regulated as the light outside changes and as necessary for class activities. Children with visual difficulty should be seated so that they can see the board clearly and easily. Regular, consistent recognition of the relation of the children's work habits to their accomplishments will guide the teacher in making appropriate adjustments for the protection of the vision of all.

Central heating with air conditioning, the use of vision-strips instead of windows, and soundproofing are becoming regular features in new elementary school buildings. Whatever the system, the ventilation must be adequate at all times. Even though the major problem of heat control is no longer directly the responsibility of the teacher, the room needs checking to see if it is stuffy and malodorous. The thermometer should be read regularly to determine if the room is too hot or too cold. Restlessness or fatigue on the part of the children often indicates the need for fresh air or change of temperature. A temperature of 68° to 72° at desk height is generally satisfactory. In rooms where windows are to be opened for ventilation, a window board or air deflector eight to ten inches high or an awning type window should be used to keep the air from blowing directly on the children sitting nearby. Temperature and ventilation are integral parts of teaching, since they affect the behavior of children directly.

Even though new buildings are providing a location and arrangement of school facilities such that noise is reduced considerably there are many noise problems which have to be attended to by the school faculty, staff, and children. It is necessary for children to have time for quiet study and relaxation. Arrangement of playground facilities and scheduling play periods to provide the minimum distractions to individual class groups are essential. The seating of children with hearing losses in places where they can best avoid strain due to the acoustics of the room is helpful. The teacher's position in the room while leading discussions, giving directions, or reading to a group can facilitate hearing. Voice modulation, care in pronunciation, and enunciation make it easier for children to hear. Through faculty organization and the cooperative planning of the teacher and each class group, there can be reduction of undesirable noises and acoustical problems.

Even though the major responsibility for the care and cleaning of school plants rests with adults employed for this specific purpose, each teacher and child has a personal and civic obligation to share in this. The effective teacher is continuously attentive to the cleanliness, neatness, and order-liness of his classroom as well as of the total school, plant and grounds. He will be on the watch for better processes and methods of housekeeping such as the care of the chalkboard. The use of an inexpensive eraser vacuum cleaner and the cleaning of chalkboards with clean erasers and a dry cloth, never using water or oil on boards, can curtail the dust problem as well as minimize glare from the boards. Rotating housekeeping committees simpli-fies the care of the room and helps make it more livable. Through the guid-ance of the teacher each child learns to feel and assume a part in the upkeep of his own facilities and builds good habits for living.

The school lunch program is now a fully recognized and accepted part of the learning environment of the child. Valuable lessons are provided in living and in using the fundamental academic skills through an attractive and inviting lunchroom with wholesome and palatable meals. Other aspects of the school which contribute to the healthful learning environment include restroom facilities, water fountains, playground space and equipment, and attention to communicable diseases.

Through cooperative planning, lessons in sanitation, nutrition, com-municable diseases, and the social graces become a vital part of the school curriculum. Through application of the academic processes to these lessons in living, the schoolroom becomes a rich laboratory for helping each child face lifelike situations and solve problems in society.

CHILDREN'S CONTRIBUTION

The school that recognizes each child as a potential contributor to the instructional program has taken advantage of the greatest resource available for providing an effective learning environment. Children, like adults, gain their greatest satisfaction when they contribute to a worthwhile ongoing project. The roadside bird nest in the hands of Jimmy can mean the begin-ning of extensive contributions to the ongoing learning environment of a classroom. When this contribution receives appropriate recognition, it may mean the beginning of a study of wild life, a unit on homes or community resources.

Children can engage an unlimited supply of local resources — human, social, natural, and industrial — on almost any given topic. They can also arrange a classroom conducive to good group working conditions with an artistic appeal to even the most indifferent. When encouraged to feel that the educational setting is their own, young people will take great pride in its development and care.[10]

---

[10]Lutian R. Wootton, "Room Environment Reflects the Instructional Program" *Childhood Education*, (February, 1965), Vol. 41, No. 6, pp. 301-303.

Children may assume responsibility for many duties and functions in the classroom and perform them with ease, charm, and dispatch. They include such activities as greeting visitors to the room, caring for pets and plants, distribution of supplies and equipment, arranging bulletin boards and performing library services. Such performances not only free the teacher from every detail of the day's activities, but provide an invaluable learning experience for the children as they take their turn at these duties. Such experiences also engender feelings of belonging and responsibility with the members of the class and create good relationships with those who visit the room.[11]

TEACHER'S CONTRIBUTION

In the effective learning environment the teacher will see his role as that of a helping person rather than a driver or pusher. He will see himself not only as a resource person but a coordinator of resources, helping boys and girls to find ways they can engage in successful experiences. He must help create situations in which students can find themselves needed and wanted.[12]

The teacher contributes to the learning environment by what he as a professional person brings to the classroom through his personality, attitude, educational preparation, and background of experiences. The personality of the teacher must be one which makes for easy communication with children of the age he works with. It must solicit and maintain the attention and respect of children. The attitude of the teacher toward each experience of the school day will determine to a great extent the outlook of children toward them. When the teacher shows enthusiasm and love for books and the wealth of experiences they contain, the attitude of children toward them will be enhanced.

The teacher's background of experience including his early childhood, his days in the elementary school, and his experiences outside the school in such areas as recreation and travel, will provide an understanding of and appreciation for the aspirations of the children in his classroom. His educational preparation in terms of experiences with children in a variety of situations, and his ability to relate learning and teaching procedures to fundamental skills will help provide situations conducive to effective learning.

The teacher's personality, attitude, background of experience, and educational preparation are personal resources which may or may not con-

---

[11]*Ibid.*
[12]Association for Supervisor nad Curriculum Development, *Op. cit.* p. 95.

tribute to the learning environment depending upon his utilization of these factors. His daily preparation and approach to each activity will free children for learning or inhibit their learning. The following list of actions which promote pupil creativity set forth by Kimball Wiles should serve as a guide to the teacher in providing an effective learning environment:

1. Establish regulations that cover the routine of the classroom.
2. Be permissive enough to enable the student to be honest.
3. Avoid giving own interpretations of events and materials to children.
4. Take class time to give children opportunity to express their interpretations.
5. Be concerned about the feelings, hopes, and aspirations of pupils.
6. Help students value feelings and emotions.
7. Be willing to wait for pupils to arrive at their answers.
8. Stimulate creativeness through brainstorming sessions.
9. Help youngsters with the recording of their feelings.[13]

The teacher who really contributes to an effective learning environment is able to perceive what is going on in the mind of the child and help him to translate this into a learning experience. The teacher who can capture the psychological moment for teaching observes carefully, listens closely, and acts with deliberation. The spring electrical storm may motivate the learning of first aid techniques, or a trip by one of the students in crossing time belts may prompt the investigation of why time is different in the various parts of the world. The alert and informed teacher takes full advantage of circumstantial and environmental factors to enhance and make learning more meaningful.[14]

COMMUNITY'S CONTRIBUTION

The community around the elementary school plays an important part in the learning environment of the child. As the walls of the classroom are extended into the community so the learning experiences of the child become meaningful. All that the child experiences during his waking hours influence his learning. When the experiences of the child in and out of the classroom show him the need for and value of the fundamental tools of reading, writing, speaking, listening, and computation, he is willing to give of himself in mastery of these tools. His contacts with the traffic policeman, the fireman, the postman, and the grocer can be utilized and expanded to increase his knowledge and understanding of their value and to relate academic learning to life situations. Visits to major industries in the com-

---

[13]Kimball Wiles, *Teaching for Better Schools* (Englewood Cliffs: Prentice-Hall, Inc., © 1959), pp. 186-191. Reprinted by permission of Prentice-Hall, Inc.
[14]Wootton, *op. cit.*

munity or to view geographical or historical points of interest help the student begin to evaluate the contributions of his community to the state, the nation, and the world. Interviews with resource people who can bring special talents, skills, training, or hobbies to the attention of the class can help develop appreciation for the abilities of others. Participation in service projects which are appropriate for his age, ability, and interest can contribute to the student's growth. School camping for short periods is recognized as a valuable learning experience in terms of the physical and academic and particularly for the many aspects of democratic behavior that are required in living with other people.

No matter how appealing these experiences may seem, they will be of value only as the underlying purposes are apparent and fully understood by the participants. If the experience is to be effective it should arise from class or school projects, should fulfill a definite purpose, meet a specific need, or solve a particular problem. The class seeking to determine how a letter gets to them from a friend will find a visit to the post office helpful. A group considering the contributions of a particular country to society will find a well-planned visit of an artist from that country a meaningful experience.

The school must recognize that the child spends a relatively small portion of his time in organized school activities; therefore, it must capitalize upon the child's out-of-school experiences. Since the learning process is going on continuously in the child's home, church, and community, the school must seek to build upon these. The teacher will encourage the children to share their experiences, reveal their curiosities, and verbalize their problems. The learnings become a part of the classroom work through activities such as the sharing period, the building of teaching units, in the expression of English themes, and in dramatic play. Recognizing that children learn most readily from firsthand experiences which give them sensory impressions of feeling, seeing, smelling, hearing, and tasting, the school should utilize the community environment with its wealth of potentiality. These out-of-school experiences can stimulate the reading of extensive printed matter for verification, clarification, and the gathering of additional data on topics to suit the varying interests and needs of children. Computation, correct usage, handwriting, and spelling can take on real significance when the child sees these as a means of communication in making a request, solving a problem and recognizing a contribution made for his own gain.[15]

The community itself is a vast resource of learning. Its range of materials can be rich when the teacher and students together constantly search for new resources in their day-to-day contacts. Firsthand experiences can

---

[15]*Ibid.*

be effective when they are directly applicable to the concerns of the moment and related to the community in which the child lives.

PRINCIPAL'S CONTRIBUTION

The administrator is the key to unlocking an environment conducive to learning. The attitudes of the principal affect the creativeness of teachers and children and influence the emotional health of the total school and community. Through his efforts a rich environment of instructional media can be provided. The most effective role of the principal is that of an instructional supervisor and resource person. His knowledge of instruction and how boys and girls learn is essential to unlocking doors for effective learning. The class that sees a field trip as a means of more effective learning can be helped by the principal who is ready to clear the way by giving encouragement, getting the initial policy clearance, and assisting in the preparation and follow-up of the experience. Much will have already been done in preparation for such a trip by the educational tone the administration has set in the community through contact with parents, commercial organization people, and special service people.

The effective principal should assume the position that each teacher is a professional person, expected to exercise professional judgment. He should recognize the fact that each teacher is expected to be expert in applying professional knowledge and skill and alert to the various problems he faces. Further, he should expect teachers to make use of their professional education in a creative, scientific manner. It is his responsibility to free the teacher from the fear of being rated, transferred, dismissed, or denied promotion because he deviates from the routine of past procedures. He should help the teacher and children recognize his position as one of a friend, helper, and resource person who assists the group in accomplishing security and success in their undertakings. The effective administrator serves as a shock absorber in many situations by being a good listener, thereby helping others find solutions to their problems and removing some of the sting from the disappointments, failures, and criticisms which find their way to the schoolroom.

More specifically, the administrator sets the stage and maintains environment conducive to effective learning in the following ways:

1. He makes it possible for the teacher to know the pupil better; to know his abilities, his interests, and his deficiencies well enough to direct his learning experiences.
2. He provides instructional methods and materials with a range of difficulty and content commensurate with the range of abilities and interests of the instructional group.

3. He assumes responsibility for seeing that available research in curriculum is used widely in the school.
4. He is alert to eliminate supervisory or inspectional practices that, no matter how well intended, actually serve to slow down real progress.
5. He is active in developing public understanding through interesting more and more citizens in actual educational planning.[16]

FACILITIES AND EQUIPMENT CONTRIBUTE TO THE LEARNING ENVIRONMENT

The era of two story buildings with spacious halls and winding stairways, cubicle shaped rooms accommodating straight rows of fixed desks, a teacher's desk at the front of the room and two or more walls of blackboard has made its impact upon society. This formal and imposing setting is gradually giving way to one story buildings which open on to outdoor courts with private entrances for each classroom. The classrooms are taking on new shapes with different compartments and work areas within to accommodate the groupings of children as they engage in a variety of activities. In some buildings classrooms are arranged around a central communication area to facilitate the use of mass media. Other designs include a number of cottage type units linked by covered walkways.

Research in the effects of environment upon learning in the classroom is beginning to influence types of equipment for the classroom as well as building designs. Experimentation with a work-center type of furniture through the University of Texas led to the conclusion that "The instructional program in classrooms using the experimental furniture was more in harmony with tenets of modern educational theory than was the instructional program in classrooms using conventional furniture."[17] To carry out this experimentation a "work-center" type of furniture was designed for use in two laboratory schools. Sanders reports that for a classroom of 32 children the following pieces of furniture were included:

1. Two rectangular tables six feet in length.
2. Two round tables three and one-half feet in diameter.
3. Eight table-desks three feet square. These were essentially two one-twelve desks joined back to back. Four book compartments were placed on each of these desks, enough for 32 pupils.
4. Thirty-two pupil chairs.

---

[16]Robert Beck, Walter Cook, and Nolan Kearney, *Curriculum in the Modern Elementary School,* (second edition; Englewood Cliffs: Prentice-Hall, Inc., © 1960), pp. 337-351. Reprinted by permission of Prentice-Hall, Inc.

[17]David C. Sanders, *Innovations in Elementary School Classroom Seating,* (Austin: Bureau of Laboratory Schools, University of Texas, 1958), p. 145.

5. Stuffed (upholstered) furniture consisting of two pupil chairs and a setee large enough to accommodate two children.
6. Two movable book cases four feet long, mounted on rubber casters.
7. Two easels.
8. A teacher's desk and chair.

All the pieces were designed so that they could be easily moved and arranged. Each pupil was provided with an individual book compartment but not individual and permanently assigned work surface. The back of each portable bookshelf was constructed of a teaching surface either chalk board or tack board.[18]

As newer developments arise the teacher should plan with school administrators and architects in providing equipment suited to the instructional program desired. The National Council of Schoolhouse Construction suggests that the classroom needs to provide for these learning activities:

1. Small groups working together.
2. Committee work.
3. Ability grouping for study and work.
4. Play and work activities which bring each child in close contact with every other child in the room.
5. Experimental opportunities.
6. Problem-solving situations.
7. Situations involving the use of visual and audio-visual aids.
8. Activities involving the use of a variety of reference materials.
9. Activities involving the development of cultural skills, such as dramatics, singing, rhythm, dancing, music appreciation, painting, drawing, construction, and modeling.
10. Activities using real-life situations.
11. Group construction.
12. Display of individual and group work.
13. Display of good health habits.
14. Exploring and investigating areas of special interest.
15. Activities planned to develop leadership and followership roles.[19]

Assuming that the activities listed will be carried on in the self-contained classroom, the room must be of ample size and arrangement to permit them. A minimum of 900 square feet, or 30 square feet per student, exclusive of space for toilets and storage materials and wraps, is needed. The rectangular room with a width of 22 to 24 feet is giving way to square, hexagonal, L-shaped, and other variations.

18*Ibid.*, p. 3.
19National Council on Schoolhouse Construction, *Elementary School Planning* (Nashville: The Council, 1958), p. 5.

The classroom should be planned for maximum flexibility in use, with a minimum of fixed equipment. Chalk board, tack boards, sink, storage, and work counters should be placed around the perimeter of the room. Through changeable arrangements of movable equipment, centers can be provided for library reading, science projects, arts and crafts, social studies, language arts, and other activities. An appropriate unit should provide for the teacher's desk, filing cabinet, coat closet, and storage cabinet. Movable children's desks with large working surfaces and of a type desirable for easy grouping should be provided. Adequate storage for books, supplies, equipment, and projects is necessary. Several conveniently located electrical outlets, projection screen, and easily operated darkening devices are essential. Television and radio antennas wired to antenna jacks, a central sound system and a central clock and bell system operating in each classroom are necessary.[20]

The classroom increasingly needs facilities to accommodate the varied educational activities of children. The room must house a great deal of equipment regularly used by the particular group of children. However, the independence of the individual classroom must not reach the point where there are nineteen one-room schools within a building. In order that facilities are readily available, each room should have its own set of encyclopedias, books, a daily newspaper, appropriate magazines, record player with a basic collection of recordings, and a filmstrip and slide projector. It should have its own sets of art materials and easels, basic science equipment and materials, globes and maps, group game equipment such as balls, bats, jump ropes, and puzzles. In addition small group quiet game sets should be provided with a limited number of carpentry tools and other equipment and materials deemed necessary by the particular group. In addition to this equipment, additional sets should be provided from a central library in the school. Other less used and specialized equipment and supplies should be housed in the area of the library, available to each room upon request.[21]

THE ROOM ENVIRONMENT REFLECTS THE INSTRUCTIONAL PROGRAM

A room with effective learning environment tells the visitor the story of what is going on. The arrangement of furniture usually makes obvious whether the lecture or problem solving approach is predominant. The materials tell whether the curriculum is centered around a single textbook or a variety of different level materials which allow for diverse assignments

---

[20]Roscoe V. Cramer and Otto E. Domian, *Administration and Supervision in the Elementary School* (New York: Harper and Brothers, 1960), pp. 445-446.
[21]Wootton, *op. cit.*

and varied group work. The bulletin boards, pictures, displays, and exhibits suggest the topic being studied. The conversation, the recitation, and the general movement of the children in the room tell whether the teacher is doing all of the planning or whether it is done cooperatively with the children.

The various centers in the room should indicate the degree of enrichment through music, drama, art, reading, and science. These areas will likely also reflect the freedom of children to do independent work when they have completed a given class assignment. A visit in the classroom should soon tell whether children are just reading and writing as meaningless drill or whether these activities are considered meaningful by each child or the group. The room environment is also likely to tell if subjects are taught in isolation or if content is taught in relation to lifelike situations, integrating and correlating them.

From observing the classroom environment one can easily tell if standards and rules have been made to fit the children or if children are doing all the adjusting. Likewise, it will tell if each child is in a particular group because it best fits him and it seems likely that he will succeed best there. By observation one can determine if the furniture, equipment and content have been selected for the needs of the particular individual or if the child is moving at the pace that motivates him to do his best and does not overtax his physical and emotional abilities.

SUMMARY

An appropriate environment is essential to effective learning. The learning environment includes the people, things and methods working together in an ongoing ever-changing process. The educator is challenged to provide an environment which stimulates active and lifelike learning, utilizing persistent life situations as a motivating influence in giving meaning to the academic skills and tools. An atmosphere of warmth and friendliness helps children and teachers feel accepted for their own worth. This is realized when positive steps are taken to develop group living.

Creativity enhances the learning environment when children are free to express themselves in different and unique manners in a variety of situations. Effective learning takes place when children live in a healthful environment which recognizes the unique physical needs of the individual and practices elements of living in keeping with the best standards of sanitation, nutrition, communicable disease control, and social graces. The effective teacher recognizes the importance of the contributions of each child to the learning situation and utilizes his potential to the fullest extent.

The teacher contributes effectively to the learning environment as he sees himself in the role of a helping person and as a coordinator of resources and learning activities.

The administrator is the key to unlocking an environment conducive to effective learning by being informed in regard to the instructional program, respecting the teacher as a professional person, and freeing the teacher and children for creative learning. The environment is enhanced as the psychology of learning, which gives attention to providing for individual differences in the classroom, is applied in planning, selecting, and maintenance of facilities and equipment. The room with effective learning environment tells the visitor the story of what is going on. It reflects the image of the school, the teacher, the pupils, and the community.

QUESTIONS FOR DISCUSSION

1. How can classroom learning environment stimulate active and lifelike learning?
2. In what ways do creativity and effective learning environment relate?
3. What are the various roles of the teacher, children, and principal in creating an effective learning environment?
4. How can facilities and equipment contribute to the learning environment for children?
5. In what respects should the room environment reflect the instructional program?

TOPICS FOR RESEARCH

1. Select two classroom situations which you consider to have contrasting learning environment. Seek to determine all aspects of each room which may account for these differences.
2. Compare the attitudes of children in classrooms that have contrasting learning environments.
3. By talking with children at a particular age level find out what children want their classroom environment to be.
4. Develop criteria for evaluating the effectiveness of learning environment.

BIBLIOGRAPHY

Association for Supervision and Curriculum Development, *Creating a Good Environment for Learning.* Washington: The Association, 1954.

Association for Supervision and Curriculum Development, *Perceiving Behaving Becoming.* Washington: The Association, 1962.

BECK, ROBERT, WALTER COOK, NOLAN KEARNEY. *Curriculum in the Modern Elementary School.* Second edition. Englewood Cliffs: Prentice-Hall, Inc., 1960.

BURR, JAMES B., LOWRY W. HARDING, LELAND B. JACOBS. *Student Teaching in the Elementary School.* Second edition. New York: Appleton-Century-Crofts, 1958.

CRAMER, ROSCOE V., OTTO E. DOMAIN. *Administration and Supervision in the Elementary School.* New York: Harper and Brothers, 1960.

DEWEY, JOHN. *Democracy and Education.* New York: Macmillan Company, 1916.

KELNER, BERNARD G. *How to Teach in the Elementary School.* New York: McGraw-Hill Book Company, 1958.

National Council on Schoolhouse Construction. *Guide for Planning School Plants.* Nashville: The Council, 1958.

RAGAN, WILLIAM B. *Teaching America's Children.* New York: Holt, Rinehart, and Winston, 1961.

SANDERS, DAVID C. *Innovations in Elementary School Classroom Seating.* Austin: Bureau of Laboratory Schools, University of Texas, 1958.

SHANE, HAROLD G. (Ed.). *The American Elementary School.* New York: Harper and Brothers, 1953.

WILES, KIMBALL. *Teaching for Better Schools.* New York: Prentice-Hall, Inc., 1952.

WILES, KIMBALL. *Teaching for Better Schools.* Englewood Cliffs: Prentice-Hall, Inc., Second edition, 1959.

Student-teacher conferences are a vital aspect of an effective evaluation program.

Chapter 7

Evaluating, Recording, and Reporting Pupil Progress

Earliest methods of evaluating pupil progress in America's schools centered around the administration of oral examinations to determine how well each child had mastered certain knowledge and skills. Reporting was handled in a very perfunctory method by simply assigning a letter mark. Teachers gave little attention to individual differences among the pupils. They taught by rote and demanded that their students parrot back information word-by-word and fact-by-fact when called upon. Students who were capable of conforming to the regimented classroom routine were rewarded with superior marks and were felt to be progressing satisfactorily by their teachers. Children who were either not capable of mastering the required knowledge and skills or were not willing to conform to the classroom regimentation, were often considered to be performing unsatisfactorily and were issued low marks.

Such a plan of evaluating and reporting pupil progress can be excused on the basis that little was known in Colonial America about theories of learning, individual and trait differences, differentation of instruction, life-adjustment education, or testing instruments. While they may have served their purpose in America's earliest beginnings in public school education, these techniques can hardly be said to be appropriate for the elementary school of today. The subsequent sections of this chapter therefore are given over to a discussion of contemporary practices. The ideas presented here are based upon selected empirical and research data which have been accumulated in America's strivings to provide an improved program of evaluating, recording, and reporting pupil progress in the elementary school.

WHAT IS EVALUATION?

For one to understand fully what is meant when teachers refer to the term "evaluation," he must first comprehend the fact that this is an extremely broad term encompassing several evaluative techniques. Evaluation is dependent, for the most part, upon tests and measurements to appraise the effectiveness of the instructional program as measured by pupil outcomes. The interrelationships among tests, measurement, and evaluation have been stated well by Burr, Harding, and Jacobs as follows:

> A test represents an effort to obtain information. It is any device or procedure for determining the presence, extent, or quality of anything — attitude, knowledge, skill, et cetera. . . A measurement represents an effort to put information into meaningful, useful form. It is a comparison of a particular quantity or score with an appropriate scale or standard. . . An evaluation represents an effort to make use of information in terms of a set of values or principles and purposes. It is a process of judging the amount, quantity, value, or worth of something by appraisal in terms of a system of purposes or values.[1]

Evaluation has been defined differently by various scholars. Some authorities place the emphasis upon measuring and analyzing behavioral change in pupils. Burr, Harding, and Jacobs take this position in stating that, "evaluation is the process of collecting, interpreting, and reporting evidence on changes in pupil behavior as such changes are related to the instructional program."[2] Jameson and Hicks, while emphasing changes in pupil behavior, hold to a somewhat narrower view of evaluation. They have stated that "evaluation consists of collecting and appraising evidence relating to behavioral change in pupils."[3]

Ragan, on the other hand emphasizes the importance of the pupils' previous educational experiences in his statement:

> Evaluation consists of accumulating accurate information about the abilities, status, and problems of pupils, by means of formal as well as informal procedures; it includes also the organizing and interpreting of

---

[1]James B. Burr, Lowry W. Harding, and Leland B. Jacobs, *Student Teaching in the Elementary School* (Second edition; New York: Appleton-Century-Crofts, Inc., 1958), p. 252. © 1950, 1958. Reprinted by permission of Appleton-Century-Crofts, Inc.

[2]*Ibid.*, p. 251.

[3]Marschall C. Jameson and Wm. Vernon Hicks, *Elementary School Curriculum* (New York: American Book Company, 1960), p. 364.

this information in terms of the entire educational background of the pupil.[4]

Michaelis and Dumas have emphasized the fact that evaluation is both quantitative and qualitative. They have stated, "The process of determining the amount and quality of pupil growth and achievement, based on clearly defined purposes, is called evaluation. Evaluation involves making judgments concerning the worth and adequacy of pupil achievement, adjustment, or development."[5]

The fact that evaluation is a continuous involvement has been set forth in Shane and McSwain's statement that it is a "continuous process of inquiry, based upon criteria developed cooperatively in the school-community, and concerned with the study, interpretation, and guidance of socially desirable changes in the behavior of children."[6]

The authors of this text take the position that evaluation is the process whereby teachers gather pupil data continuously to determine what adjustments need to be made in the instructional program in order that acceptable student behavioral changes may be effected in academic achievement, social adjustment, and physical and emotional development Evaluation is the teacher's technique whereby he determines the various instructional levels of the children in order that he can adjust the level of instruction to meet the divergent needs of each member of his class.

WHAT SHOULD BE EVALUATED?

Most elementary schools generally seek to attain the objectives of self-realization, human relationship, economic efficiency, and civic responsibility by every student. Because of individual differences among the pupils, some children will progress more rapidly than others toward the attainment of these objectives. Children do not all learn in exactly the same manner or at the same rate of speed. Periodic evaluation is necessary to determine their individual levels of performance and ascertain how well each of them is achieving in academic, social, physical, and emotional growth.

The objectives of self-realization, human relationship, economic efficiency, and civic responsibility, as outlined in Chapter 3, are very broad. The teacher would find it laborious to make occasional evaluations of each

[4]William B. Ragan, *Teaching America's Children* (New York: Holt, Rinehart and Winston, 1961), p. 317. © 1961, Holt, Rinehart and Winston, Inc. Used by permission of the publishers.

[5]John U. Michaelis and Enoch Dumas, *The Student Teacher in the Elementary School* (second edition; Englewood Cliffs, N. J.: Prentice-Hall, Inc., 1960), p. 311.

[6]Harold G. Shane and E. T. McSwain, *Evaluation and the Elementary Curriculum* (New York: Henry Holt Company, 1951), p. 53.

pupil in his classroom using such an exhaustive criteria. Rothney has suggested a manageable criteria for evaluating pupil progress which has only eleven points as follows:

1. The development of effective methods of thinking
2. The cultivation of useful work habits and study skills
3. The inculcation of constructive social attitudes
4. The acquisition of a wide range of significant interests
5. The development of increased appreciation of music, art, literature, and other esthetic experiences
6. The development of social sensitivity
7. The development of better personal-social adjustment
8. The development of skill in effective communication
9. The acquisition of important information
10. The development of physical health
11. The development of a consistent philosophy of life.[7]

The teacher's primary job in evaluating is to determine how well the individual child is progressing toward these objectives in the light of his own needs, interests, and abilities. In evaluating to determine how nearly each child is measuring up to the attainment of these objectives the teacher will do well to keep the following purposes of evaluation, as suggested by Ragan, in mind. The purposes are:

1. To reveal to teachers what is happening to each child;
2. To motivate learning through furnishing pupils with information concerning success in various areas of the curriculum;
3. To furnish teachers with a means of appraising teaching methods, textbooks, and other instrumentalities of the educative process;
4. To provide a basis for continuous improvement of the curriculum;
5. To give pupils experience in evaluating their own progress;
6. To reveal the progress the school program is making toward the achievement of the accepted objectives.[8]

Evaluation should not be a narrow practice whereby teachers administer periodic tests for the purpose of issuing marks on report cards. The preceding statement of purposes attests to that fact. Evaluation should be the process whereby the teacher takes inventory of individual student strengths and weaknesses and plans a program of instruction which will

---

[7]John W. M. Rothney, "Evaluating and Reporting Pupil Progress," *What Research Says to the Teacher*, Volume 7, Washington, D. C.: National Education Association, Department of Classroom Teachers and American Educational Research Association, 1955, p. 6.

[8]William B. Ragan, *Modern Elementary Curriculum* (revised edition; New York: Henry Holt and Company, 1960), pp. 384-385. Copyright © 1960, Holt, Rinehart and Winston, Inc. By permission of the publishers.

provide a system of learning experiences based on the concept of continuous pupil progress. To put it another way, evaluation enables the teacher to understand the individual child sufficiently so that continuous educative experiences can be planned in the light of his developmental needs and readiness to learn.

WHEN SHOULD EVALUATION BE DONE?

Evaluation in one form or another takes place daily within the elementary classroom. It must be an integral, continuous part of the instructional program. Through frequent evaluation the teacher gathers evidence of accomplishment, growth, and development among his students. Evaluation is the tool which enables him to provide the pupils with learning experiences which are adjusted to their level of development. Otherwise, the teacher would have difficulty in recognizing readiness for learning. This point has been stated succinctly by Rothney as follows:

> Readiness for the next steps does not always emerge at precise days or hours indicated by the calendar or the clock. We must be alert to recognize readiness when it appears lest we lose the golden opportunities when pupils are eager to learn. As classroom teachers, we must recognize lack of readiness, too, lest we require the pupil to study something too soon and actually set him back so that he does not learn it at the usual time. With a plan for continuous evaluation we are more likely to identify readiness (or lack of it) than we are when we depend upon chance.[9]

Most of the evaluation done daily by teacher and pupils is handled on a very informal basis. Occasions where this type of evaluation may occur are:

1. At the beginning of the school day to determine what schedule needs to be set up in order that the day's educational objectives may be accomplished most expeditiously
2. Periodically during the day to determine how effectively work is progressing on different segments of the learning experiences
3. During a regular end-of-day period to determine:
   a. Work which has been completed during the day
   b. Work which remains to be done on given projects
   c. What has been learned during the day and synthesize it
   d. How the teaching-learning situation may be improved
4. Individual pupil-teacher conferences as occasions demand or opportunity permits
5. Whenever a large block of work has been completed
6. At the conclusion of a broad unit of work.

---

[9]Rothney, *op. cit.*, p. 26.

SELECTING APPROPRIATE EVALUATION TECHNIQUES

The teacher will use many different instruments and procedures as he evaluates pupil progress. These, which include standardized and teacher-made tests, need to be selected for utilization on the basis of the fact that they will gather the type of data upon which the teacher can base sound decisions. The criteria of validity, reliability, objectivity, pertinence, appropriateness, practicality, and applicability, as outlined by Burr, Harding, and Jacobs, provide a good basis for selecting instruments and procedures.[10]

VALIDITY

Will the evaluation instrument or procedure yield evidence which will be well founded? Validity refers to the truthfulness of the measuring instrument. For example, a test on arithmetic fundamentals is valid to the extent to which it measures pupil ability in this area rather than other things such as reading comprehension, or general intelligence. In other words, does it measure what it purports to measure? The evaluation instrument is worthless if it is not valid.

RELIABILITY

The reliability of an evaluation instrument or procedure refers to the consistency or accuracy of the results obtained from its administration. That, is, under normal circumstances the measuring device would be considered reliable if it were administered again to an identical or a similar group of students and the same results were obtained making allowance for some pupil improvement resulting from practice.

OBJECTIVITY

When one refers to the objectivity of an evaluation instrument or procedure he is concerned with the degree to which equally competent individuals or groups of pupils show the same results. Objectivity occurs where opportunities for personal opinion, subjective judgment, or bias have been removed. A test which can be scored with a key and which obtains identical results is said to be objective.

PERTINENCE

Tests that adequately measure materials covered in class meet the criterion of pertinence. Any test calling for a knowledge of factual information which has not been studied would definitely be outside the scope of this criterion unless it were a pretest.

---

[10]Burr, Harding, and Jacobs, *op. cit.* pp. 261-262.

APPROPRIATENESS

A test is appropriate when it gathers the type of data desired. Examples of appropriate measuring instruments might be an objective test to evaluate pupil progress in arithmetic fundamentals and essays for evaluating ability of expression in formal writing. A sociogram could be utilized as a means of checking on individual and group adjustment.

PRACTICALITY

The testing instrument should be readily understandable by all students to whom it will be administered. It should be of such length and difficulty that it can be completed by the pupils in a minimum amount of time. Since one of the major purposes of evaluation is simply to measure pupil attainment, brief tests will accomplish this purpose just as effectively as longer ones. In addition they will serve as a basis for determining where learning has taken place and as a guide to decide where there should be more instructional emphasis. Frequent tests or evaluative instruments which are unduly long cannot be justified in the elementary school if they impede teaching and learning.

APPLICABILITY

Evaluation instruments and procedures may be considered applicable if they yield the type of data which will enable the teacher to diagnose pupil strengths and weaknesses, determine the effectiveness of the teaching-learning situation, and serve as a basis for charting a plan of instruction whereby each child can work up to his maximum potential.

METHODS OF EVALUATING ACADEMIC PROGRESS

America's elementary schools utilized oral examinations almost exclusively to measure academic achievement before 1845, when Horace Mann described their limitations and predicted that printed questions with written answers would supplant such a method of measurement in the years ahead.[11] The foresight which Mann exhibited in this statement is staggering when one considers the plethora of standardized testing instruments which are available today to gather pupil data in the elementary school.

There are two basic types of measurement devices utilized in the elementary school to gather data to evaluate pupil progress. They are oral and written examinations. The nomenclature of these measurement tech-

---

11William B. Ragan, *Teaching America's Children*, (New York: Holt, Rinehart and Winston, 1961), p. 321.

niques and devices has been outlined by Ross and Stanley in a manner that makes them easily understandable as follows:

A. Oral.
B. Written.
   1. Informal (nonstandardized).
     a. Essay.
     b. Objective.
   2. Formal (standardized).
     a. Achievement.
       (1) General (survey).
       (2) Specific (diagnostic, practice, etc.).
     b. Intelligence.
       (1) General (individual and group).
       (2) Specific (aptitude or prognosis).
     c. Personality and Interests.[12]

It is easy to distinguish between the two main categories of oral and written examinations. The distinction between the informal or nonstandardized and the formal or standardized written tests has been lucidly made by Ross and Stanley in their statement:

> A formal test often begins as an informal test, which is later subjected to experimental trial and revision, only the best items surviving the process. Formal tests also have carefully worded instructions both for administering and scoring and, usually, norms for interpreting the results.[13]

Teacher-made tests, therefore, are informal, nonstandardized instruments which teachers prepare for use in their own classrooms. On the other hand, most publishers' commercially prepared tests are formal standardized measuring devices which are normed nationally. They provide a means whereby local schools can compare their pupil progress collectively or individually against these norms.

TEACHER-MADE TESTS

The informal teacher-made tests are utilized more extensively in the elementary school for evaluating pupil progress than are the formal standardized tests. The two types of teacher-made tests are essay and objective. The essay test is a discussion type examination where the student writes in detail concerning a given question or point of emphasis. The objective test may take the form of a true-false, multiple-choice, matching,

---

[12]C. C. Ross and Julian C. Stanley, *Measurement in Today's Schools* (third edition, Englewood Cliffs, N. J.: Prentice-Hall, Inc., 1954), p. 23.
[13]*Ibid.*, p. 23.

or completion type question examination. Frequently teachers combine all four types in preparing an objective examination.

Essay Tests

The teacher will do well to remember that since the essay test calls for a great deal of discussion only a few of the critical items concerning a given topic may be included in the examination because of the time factor. Items selected for inclusion in the test therefore should be a representative sample of the materials covered in order that the amount of pupil growth can be accurately measured.

The essay test has a number of weaknesses. Among these is the fact that frequently children fail to stick to the main ideas in answering the questions. In addition they may get carried away with one or more items on the examination and not distribute their time wisely among all of the questions.

The biggest objection to the essay type teacher-made test is its subjectivity. It is hard for the teacher to divorce his knowledge of the student from the written responses while grading the examination. In all probability, if more than one teacher were to grade the same essay test, it would be unlikely that any two of them would assign identical marks. Mehl, Mills, and Douglass have rightly stated:

> Marks in essay tests are quite likely to be measures of composition — of ability to interpret questions, write concisely, and distribute time wisely. These may not be the outcomes which the instructor has been attempting to achieve.[14]

Teachers who use the essay test could overcome their subjectivity somewhat if they prepared an answer key for each item on the examination before grading the tests. This answer key should contain all of the significant points which have been studied. In grading the individual test items, the teacher can use the answer key as a guide for determining how complete and accurate the individual student has been in answering the question. In this manner the essay test can be made more objective.

Some ways in which the essay test can be made more valid and reliable have been suggested by Mehl, Mills, and Douglass. They are:

1. Be specific and clear in stating the topic and the instructions for dealing with it; for example, if learners are asked to "criticize" they should be told upon what basis or with respect to what. Frequently there should be subordinate or supplementing instructions, as in the following;

---

[14]Marie A. Mehl, Hubert H. Mills, and Harl R. Douglass, *Teaching in the Elementary School* (second edition; New York: The Ronald Press Company, © 1958), p. 385.

Discuss farming in the lowlands of southern California with particular reference to the farmer's dependence on irrigation, to the irrigated crops that are grown there, and to the changes brought about in farming as a result of improved farming equipment.

Rarely if ever should pupils be asked to "tell what you know about . . . ."

2. State each question or make each statement so as to measure something besides recall of information, i.e., understanding of the information, its importance, its implications, etc.
3. Estimate the time required by a slow pupil to write out an excellent answer to the question and indicate that amount of time in parentheses after the question.
4. Attempt to keep at a minimum the time required for writing answers. It is of great value in essay examinations to call for short, concise answers so more questions may be asked.
5. Prepare questions which will permit objective scoring as far as possible. Questions so planned can be scored against an inventory of the parts required in a perfect answer.[15]

Objective Tests

The objective tests have two predominant strengths in that they have one correct answer for each test item and they can be scored objectively. Whereas the essay test is limited to only a few items because of the time required for pupils to adequately discuss the questions, the objective test can cover many items more comprehensively.

Primary teachers find that objective tests are more suitable than the essay test for the children they teach because most of the pupils of that age have not developed sufficient vocabularies and methods of expressing themselves in written composition to handle the discussion type examination. Teachers in the intermediate grades also use the objective tests extensively because of the simplicity in grading which gives them more time for lesson preparation, pupil conferences, and the like.

The major drawback to objective tests stems from the fact that pupils sometimes may answer correctly by guessing or through the process of elimination of items which they know to be incorrect. In instances where this occurs, the scores may be somewhat misleading.

Some general rules which teachers should be governed by in devising an objective test have been stated well by Mehl, Mills, and Douglass as follows:

1. Get in mind the outcomes of teaching which constitute the chief objectives of the learning activities; that is, what information, what

---

[15]*Ibid.*, pp. 385-386.

skills or habits, what ideals or attitudes are aimed at in presenting the material to be tested, and which of these is of most worth.

2. Decide how much time is to be given to the test, and estimate how many exercises may be completed by the pupils in the time available.

3. Select about one and one half times as many exercises that test the possession of information, understanding, skills, habits, ideals, or attitudes emphasized, as may be given in the time available, consciously attempting to distribute these over the course somewhat in proportion to the importance of each outcome in the ground covered.

4. Have all the test exercises of one type, true-false, completion, or multiple-response, or, make the examination up of different types. Ordinarily the latter procedure is preferable, since the most effective type of exercise for each item may be chosen on an individual basis. Formulate the items in the types most appropriate to the achievements to be tested. Items not of primary importance and difficult to fit into any form may be tentatively set aside to be used only in case they are needed to give balance or to complete the examination. The shorter the question or exercise, the better.

5. Take care to formulate exercises in such a way that something more than memory is tested. Provide some questions involving reasoning and attitudes.

6. Take care to include some questions which all pupils are likely to answer, and some which very few are likely to answer. The other questions should range in difficulty between these extremes, with a goodly percentage of questions of average or reasonable difficulty.

7. Go over the test exercises carefully, discarding those which are ambiguous or misleading, or which demand elaborate qualification. Reduce the number of test exercises to the desired number, being sure to retain such exercises as will give "range" to the test, and those testing important objectives. Discard those exercises which are least objective and which serve to test powers tested by other questions or exercises. Take care also to preserve proper distribution among the different parts of the material covered.

8. Rearrange the remaining exercises into groups by type; that is, group all the true-false exercises together, all the multiple-choice together, and so on.

9. Rearrange within the groups in the apparent order of difficulty, or in some other logical order. The most difficult exercises should not be placed toward the beginning of the test.

10. In preparing the blank forms for the test, control the position of the answers, allowing for them preferably along one side of the page to facilitate scoring.

11. Prepare a key of correct answers in such form that it may be laid alongside the pupil's paper and thus permit rapid scoring. A cardboard key is very convenient.[16]

---

[16]*Ibid.*, pp. 379-380.

Regardless of whether the teacher administers an essay or an objective test to the pupils in his room, he should apply the following criteria, as devised by Ragan, to the measuring instrument:

1. Does the test represent a comprehensive sampling of the content studied?
2. Do test items range from easy to difficult, with a large number of items geared to the middle group and several items difficult enough to challenge the more capable pupils?
3. Can the test be scored easily and objectively?
4. Does the test require thinking and organizing on the part of the pupils rather than merely recall?
5. Will the test encourage the development of desirable study habits?
6. Does the test foster wholesome teacher-pupil relationships?[17]

COMMERCIALLY PREPARED INSTRUMENTS

The commercially prepared tests afford many advantages for teachers. First, they are valid and reliable instruments having been devised by professional authorities and field tested to select discriminating test items. Second, they have been administered to a sufficiently large number of pupils in different regions of the nation to establish "normal performance" — expectations which are referred to as norms. These norms form the framework whereby the local district can compare its pupil data against the national average. A third advantage of the commercially prepared tests is that they are highly objective. Normally there is only one correct answer, a fact which rules out the teacher's subjective judgment in scoring. This suggests a fourth and equally important advantage of the commercially prepared test; it is easy to score. Lumping all the advantages of the commercially prepared tests together, it is easy to see why they are used in virtually every elementary school system in America today.

Intelligence Tests

The intelligence test is used primarily to determine abstract reasoning ability. These tests purport to measure pupils' general intelligence in different ways reputedly unrelated to what the child has learned at or away from school. Baron and Bernard have suggested a list of abilities which presumably are measured by the intelligence test. This list, as cited by Sowards and Scobey, follows:

1. Memory: immediate or delayed, meaningful or rote
2. Ability to deal with verbal materials (vocabulary)
3. Ability to deal with spatial relationships or to orient the self in space

---

[17]William B. Ragan, *Teaching America's Children* (New York: Holt, Rinehart and Winston, 1961), p. 323.

4. Ability to deal with verbal relationships (analogies, opposites)
5. Ability to deal with numerical materials either as sheer facility with numbers or as ability to reason numerically or quantitatively
6. Ability to find the guiding principle involved in tasks which may be verbal, numerical, spatial, or pictorial in nature
7. Ability to perceive essential details, make fine distinctions, and notice similarities.[18]

There are basically two types of intelligence tests. They are the individual and group mental ability tests. The most widely used individual intelligence tests are the *Stanford-Binet Scale* and the *Wechsler Intelligence Scale for Children*. Widely used group mental ability tests include *Otis Quick-Scoring Mental Ability Tests*, the *California Test of Mental Maturity*, and the *Kuhlmann-Anderson Intelligence Tests*. Normally the individual intelligence tests are administered only in special cases under the direction of a qualified specialist. Group mental ability tests, on the other hand, can be administered to large numbers of children by any competent teacher.

The ability of the individual pupil to do abstract reasoning as measured by the intelligence test is referred to as his intelligence quotient (IQ). The method for computing the IQ is to divide the mental age, which is derived from scores made on the intelligence test, by the chronological age or the number of years the pupil has lived, and multiply the result obtained by 100. Stated in an arithmetical formula it would be written thusly:

$$\frac{\text{Mental Age}}{\text{Chronological Age}} \times 100 = IQ$$

The intelligence tests are reasonably good predictors of academic potential; however, they have their limitations. These limitations have been stated succinctly by Sowards and Scobey as follows:

Intelligence test scores indicate the verbal ability of a child in terms of the English language, and these tests favor children from the American, urban, middle-class culture . . . children from rural areas, bilingual families, or underprivileged urban groups may produce low scores that reflect only their limited experience. Furthermore, mental tests do not measure motivation. Consequently, the usefulness of I. Q. scores in predicting academic success is often overemphasized.[19]

The older children get, the more reliable the intelligence tests results become. IQ scores should therefore not be accepted as a final judgment

[18]G. Wesley Sowards and Mary-Margaret Scobey, *The Changing Curriculum and the Elementary Teacher* (Belmont, California: Wadsworth Publishing Company, Inc., 1961), p. 522.
[19]*Ibid.*, p. 523.

of ability but rather as a guide upon which some likely predictions of academic potential can be made.

The teacher can determine how bright the individual child is by fitting his IQ to the distribution of intelligence in the general population, usually depicted by a bell-shaped curve as shown in Figure 15. If a child had an IQ in excess of 130 he would likely be a very superior pupil capable of doing work in advance of his grade placement. A child with an IQ of 85 would probably be a slow learner and would experience some difficulty in achieving satisfactorily at his assigned placement level.

A test which measures intelligence for certain specific performance areas is referred to as an aptitude test. While the general intelligence test measures the individual's over-all mental capacity, the aptitude test measures those native traits which are necessary to attain proficiency in areas such as music or arithmetic.

Achievement Tests

The achievement test most commonly used in the elementary school is the survey type measuring device. Examples of survey type achievement tests are the *Iowa Tests of Basic Skills, California Achievement Tests, Stanford Achievement Tests,* and *Metropolitan Achievement* Tests. Subject areas which may be included in these survey batteries are reading, arithmetic, language arts, science, and social studies. The *California Achievement Tests*

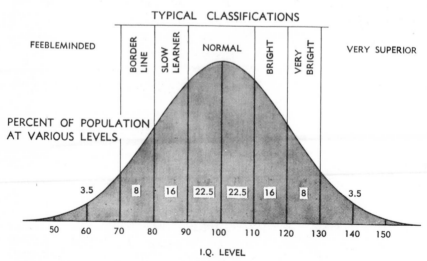

Figure 15. Distribution of Intelligence in the Population. Adapted from R. Murray Thomas, *Judging Student Progress,* (second edition; New York: David McKay Company, 1960), p. 126. Reprinted by permission of David McKay Company.

Complete Battery for grades 4, 5, and 6, for example, tests achievement in six areas: reading vocabulary, reading comprehension, arithmetic reasoning, arithmetic fundamentals, mechanics of English, and spelling.

Raw scores from these achievement tests can be converted into grade placement equivalents. A grade placement equivalent of 4.7 in a given area tested would mean the child is performing at the level of the seventh month of the fourth year of school. By acquiring grade placement equivalents for every subject area tested and plotting them on an individual profile sheet, the teacher may readily ascertain how the student is progressing. The grade placement equivalents derived from the survey achievement tests can enable the teacher to know more expertly:

1. The achievement level of the individual student in the different subject areas
2. How the individual student rates in comparison with the school and national norms
3. The achievement level of the entire class collectively in the different subject areas
4. How the class collectively rates in comparison with the school and national norms.

Another type of achievement test is the diagnostic test which is frequently used to identify specific pupil weaknesses. A third type of achievement test is the readiness test which is utilized to determine whether or not a child has attained sufficient maturity to achieve success in a given subject or skill. The most widely used test of this nature is the reading readiness test which is administered in the first grade.

MEANS OF EVALUATING SOCIAL ADJUSTMENT PROGRESS

There are different measuring techniques which teachers can use to evaluate the progress pupils are making in social adjustment. The most widely utilized technique is that of teacher observation. However, more formalized methods such as the sociogram or personality and interest tests are periodically employed.

PERSONALITY AND INTERESTS TESTS

Standardized personality tests are devised to measure intangible aspects of pupil behavior such as his attitudes, interests, and emotional adjustment. Formal interest inventories seek to establish the degree of interest which pupils possess in such items as occupations, recreation, reading, and activities.[20] These tests are given infrequently in the elementary school. When they are given it would be advisable to have a trained specialist administer them.

SOCIOGRAMS

A technique whereby one studies the relationships which exist in a social group is called sociometry. A sociogram is a diagram of the social relationships within the group. The sociogram can serve the teacher in a number of ways in his role as evaluator. From it he can establish who the leaders are among the pupils as well as determining those children who may be isolates. Furthermore, as the structure of the classroom groups changes with new leaders emerging from time to time, he can determine these happenings by subsequent sociograms.

The manner in which pupil data is obtained for the construction of a sociogram is handled by simply asking the pupils, "With whom would you most like to work on a committee assignment?" Next, the students should be instructed to write their first, second, and third choices on a sheet of paper and hand them in to the teacher. The individual choices of the pupils can then be tabulated in the form shown in Figure 16. In tabulating the total points for each student the choices are weighted as follows:

First choice: 3 points
Second choice: 2 points
Third choice: 1 point

Once the tabulations have been completed the sociogram can be constructed, using geometric shapes to designate sex. Squares were used to represent the boys and circles to signify the girls in the sociogram shown in Figure 17. Letters were used in Figure 17 to designate children; numerals to indicate rank order of preference; arrows to signify direction of choice, and joined arrow heads in center of lines symbolize mutual choices.[21]

In gathering and tabulating data for the sociogram, teachers can enhance its reliability and validity by listing the name of each pupil on the chalkboard in order that children can survey all class members' names before making their choices. This would circumvent children's asking the teacher to spell names and avoid the bias of suggestion. In addition should one or more children be absent, their names would be presented to the class with equal chances for selection. The teacher can expect the boys to select boys and the girls to select girls in the intermediate grades. In the

[20]Sowards and Scobey, *op. cit.*, p. 523.
[21]Burr, Harding, and Jacobs, *op. cit.*, p. 292.

CHOOSERS ↓ / CHOSEN →	Abbott, Samuel (1)	Bishop, Annie (2)	Cobb, Robert (3)	Davis, Betty (4)	Elam, James (5)	Framm, Connie (6)	Goldberg, Israel (7)	Heil, Frank (8)	Irvin, Deborah (9)	Jackson, Edgar (10)	Knight, Elsie (11)	Lang, Charles (12)	Macklin, Fannie (13)	North, Sterl (14)	Ochs, Grace (15)	Pilcher, Homer (16)	Number of 1st Choices	Number of 2nd Choices	Number of 3rd Choices	Total Points (1st-3)	Total times chosen	
1. Abbott, Samuel	×		3	1		2											0	0	0	0	0	Isolate
2. Bishop, Annie		×	1	2									3				0	1	2	4	3	
3. Cobb, Robert		3	×	1							2						1	0	1	4	2	
4. Davis, Betty		2		×	3		1										3	1	1	12	5	Leader
5. Elam, James					×	1			2					3			2	0	1	7	3	
6. Framm, Connie				3		×			2		1						1	3	0	9	4	
7. Goldberg, Israel		3					×	1	2								3	0	1	10	4	Leader
8. Heil, Frank				1		2		×	3								1	0	1	4	2	
9. Irvin, Deborah							3		×		1		2				0	3	2	8	5	
10. Jackson, Edgar					1					×	2					3	0	0	0	0	0	Isolate
11. Knight, Elsie					1	2					×		3				3	3	0	15	6	Leader
12. Lang, Charles							1					×		2		3	2	1	0	8	3	
13. Macklin, Fannie									3		2	1	×				0	1	3	5	4	
14. North, Sterl								3			1			×		2	0	1	1	3	2	
15. Ochs, Grace							1					2			×	3	0	1	0	2	1	
16. Pilcher, Homer												1	3		2	×	0	1	3	5		

Figure 16. Sociogram Data Tabulation Form. Adapted from James B. Burr, Lowry W. Harding, and Leland B. Jacobs, *Student Teaching in the Elementary School,* p. 295. (second edition: New York: Appleton-Century-Crofts, 1958), p. 295, © 1950, 1958. Reprinted by permission of Appleton-Century-Crofts.

primary grades, however, sex is normally not a factor in making choices at the first and second grade levels.[22]

TEACHER OBSERVATION

There are elements of pupil progress which cannot be adequately measured or evaluated by the commercially prepared and teacher-made tests or the sociogram. Some of these elements are individual or group motivation, interests, problems, pressures, or purposes and can be appraised only through continuous teacher observation or judgment.

Teachers with training and experience enter the elementary classroom with a general knowledge of children, but issues arise daily which they

---

[22]*Ibid.,* p. 292.

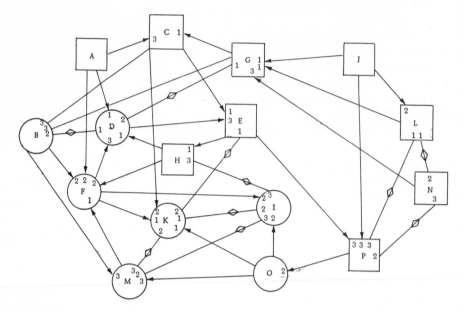

Figure 17. Sociogram. Adapted from James B. Burr, Lowry W. Harding, and Leland B. Jacobs, *Student Teaching in the Elementary School*, p. 294. (second edition; New York: Appleton-Century-Crofts, 1958), p. 294. © 1950, 1958. Reprinted by permission of Appleton-Century-Crofts.

cannot forsee. Hence, through observation they formulate judgments concerning pupil behavior and adjust the instructional program in order that maximum pupil progress in academic and social learning can be effected. It is through the medium of continuous observation that the teacher analyzes how the individual or group accepts responsibility, perfects skills, adjusts socially, attacks problems, meets difficult situations, achieves, in short, how they make behavioral adjustments. Haskew was aware of this fact in rightly asserting that the teacher

> . . . treats behavior as a symptom which gives a clue to background causes. He accepts and loves a child regardless of the child's actions right now. He may encourage or he may curb a child's present behavior, but he is always aware of two facts; first that it is more important to find out why a child acts as he does than to control him right now; and second, that what he does to a child right now — and for that matter all the experiences a child has today — will become part of the set of causes influencing the child's behavior tomorrow. The experienced teacher knows

that a child's reactions — as well as his own actions — are the end product of a complex host of causes. Behavior is caused.[23]

Teachers should be extremely cautious in using the observational technique of evaluating pupil progress or behavior. First, they should be careful to avoid bias and not permanently classify an individual or group of pupils in some manner and then interpret all subsequent behavior on the basis of previous experiences. Second, they should avoid attributing the halo effect to the overconforming children by rewarding them unduly. Third, they should be careful not to deride the nonconforming children, but rather look for causes of seemingly unacceptable behavior. Fourth, they should realize that it is impossible to have all of the facts concerning pupil behavior; therefore, they should not form hasty judgments. Finally, good observational technique would dictate the wisdom of their doing more listening and watching than talking when evaluating.

RECORDING PUPIL PROGRESS

It would be foolish indeed for teachers to engage in the laborious task of measuring and evaluating pupil progress and then fail to record their findings. This would be a mistake for at least two reasons. First, a teacher should not expect to remember all of the important facts he has obtained about the individual student. If such an attempt were made, the teacher would be able to recall only the most vivid impressions he learned about the child. If such impressions were either pleasing or displeasing to the teacher a definite bias would be injected. When a knowledge of past pupil behavior is required to formulate some decision, the previous progress of the pupil may not be accurately recalled and an unwise decision therefore could result. Second, each child will likely be promoted at the end of the academic year and the teachers who work with them next year will need previous records of pupil progress so they can have more accurate knowledge of the backgrounds of their new students and tentatively plan appropriate learning experiences.

CUMULATIVE RECORDS

Teachers accumulate important pupil progress data about the individual student through measurement and evaluation at every grade level in the elementary school. Such data is recorded in the cumulative record folder by the classroom teacher. Pupil progress information which should be collected and recorded in the cumulative record folder includes identifying

---

[23]Laurence D. Haskew, *This Is Teaching* (Chicago: Scott, Foresman and Company, 1956), pp. 55-56.

data, family and school history, attendance and promotion record, special abilities and interests, citizenship traits, testing record, and marks earned in the various subjects, as Figure 18 shows.

Health Record

The health record usually is maintained on a separate card in order that it can be more conveniently used by the school nurse or physician. Although a few elementary schools file the health cards (see Figure 19) in the school nurse's office, most of them file them in the individual cumulative record folders which are maintained in the classroom teacher's file cabinet.

The health record should be kept current in order that the individual child's health status is as accurate as possible. Information which the health card should contain includes medical history, immunization records, and data about the general health status such as height, weight, posture, skin disorders and the like.

Reading Progress Record

Many schools make a practice of keeping a reading progress record card on each student and file it in the cumulative record folder, illustrated in Figure 20. These cards provide a record of the basal and supplementary readers which each child has read a portion of or has completed. Any teacher therefore can survey the child's progress and plan future work without needless replication. A continuous program of reading progress for the individual student can thereby be effected.

Anecdotal Records

The anecdotal record is a recent innovation utilized by most elementary teachers to record pupil progress. Through observation the teacher assesses factual information about his students, makes a brief anecdotal record of critical incidents and files the material in individual cumulative record folders.

Care should be exercised to see that a proper balance of positive and negative anecdotes be included in recording such information. The effectiveness of the anecdotal records has often been lessened by teachers who noted only negative anecdotes about seemingly "unruly" children. Through the teacher's unbiased evaluation of student behavior, he can make anecdotal records of outstanding pupil strengths, normal classroom behavior, and if any, specific weaknesses. Since the anecdotal records are cumulative, the child's pattern of behavior becomes increasingly evident. Whenever breaks occur in the established pattern of behavior, the teacher will have little difficulty in recognizing the deviation.

CUMULATIVE ENROLLMENT RECORD (Every year to be accounted for; include preschool enrollment)
(See material within folder for observational summaries, progress reports, and other pertinent data.)

Tel. No. | Address | Initial or Middle | First Name | Last Name (left margin vertical labels)

YR.	DATE OF ENTRANCE	GR.	SCHOOL	DAYS Pres.	Ab.	TEACHER	REMARKS

Grade											PROMOTION RECORD
Year	19	19	19	19	19	19	19	19	19	19	
Initials of teacher											19
Reading											Sig. of Teacher
Penmanship											19
Arithmetic											Sig. of Teacher
English											19
Spelling											Sig. of Teacher
Social Studies											19
Geography											Sig. of Teacher
History											19
Health											Sig. of Teacher
Science											19
Physical Education											Sig. of Teacher
Music											19
Art											Sig. of Teacher
											19
											Sig. of Teacher

SCHOOL CITIZENSHIP   KEY : S—SUPERIOR, HA—HIGH AVERAGE, A—AVERAGE, LA—LOW AVERAGE, L—LOW

Self-control										REMARKS
Initiative										
Dependability										
Leadership										
Co-operation										
Courtesy										
Makes Wise Use of Time										
Makes Effort										
Uses Materials Carefully										
Works Independently										

ADDITIONAL INFORMATION

Special Abilities	
Remedial Work	
Home Influence	
Notable Accomplishments	
Notable Experiences	

STANDARDIZED TEST RESULTS									WITHDRAWAL RECORD		
DATE	GRADE	NAME OF TEST				MA	CA	GP	IQ	DATE WITHDRAWN	REASON	DATE RETURNED

Figure 18.   Cumulative Record Folder of Clarke County (Georgia) Public
Schools.

PERSONAL

Verification—check when

Date of birth_____certificate is presented_____ Sex _____

Place of birth_____

Residence _____Church preference_____
(If parent does not object)

_____

_____

In case of emergency call Dr._____ Phone_____

FAMILY HISTORY

Maiden_____

Name. Father _____Mother   Guardian_____

Married_____

Names of all children and birth dates: Indicate whether foster, half brothers, etc.
(List in order of birth from oldest to youngest)

_____   _____

_____   _____

_____   _____

Occupation of: Father_____Mother_____   Guardian_____

Firm or Employer   _____   _____   _____

_____   _____   _____

Occupation of older brother or sister:_____

Status or Parents (check) living together_____ divorced_____mother remarried_____

living apart_____ father remarried_____father dead_____

mother dead_____

Indicate important family changes (with dates):_____

_____

_____

Education of Father_____ Mother_____

Health of Father_____Good_____ Poor_____

Mother _____Good_____ Poor_____

If Poor, Indicate Cause_____

Diseases _____

_____

_____

Significant Health Data _____

_____

_____

_____

_____

_____

Figure 18. (Continued)

216

HEALTH RECORD

√ NORMAL   ○ TREATMENT   ⊕ CORRECTED

GRADE											REMARKS
YEAR											
AGE											
HEIGHT											
WEIGHT	ACTUAL										
	NORMAL										
NUTRITION											
POSTURE											
ORTHOPEDIC DEFECTS											
SKIN DISORDERS											
TEETH											
NOSE											
THROAT											
EYES	RIGHT										
	LEFT										
EARS	RIGHT										
	LEFT										
SPEECH DEFECTS											

MEDICAL HISTORY

DISEASE	DATE
MEASLES	
SCARLET FEVER	
DIPHTHERIA	
MUMPS	
WHOOPING COUGH	
CHICKEN POX	
SMALL POX	
MALARIA	
POLIO	
PNEUMONIA	
TYPHOID	
MENINGITIS	
TUBERCULOSIS	

IMMUNIZATION

DISEASE	DATE
SMALL POX	
SMALL POX	
SMALL POX	
TYPHOID	
TYPHOID	
TYPHOID	
TYPHOID	

LAST NAME	FIRST NAME	MIDDLE NAME	SEX		PERMANENT SIGNAL OF PROGRESS							RETARDED — ADVANCED						
			M	F	1	2	3	4	5	6	7	3	2	1	N	1	2	3

Figure 19. Health Record Card of Clarke County (Georgia) Public Schools.

217

Name _____   Houston Independent School District

Date of Birth _____   READING PROGRESS RECORD -- Grades 1-6

	BASAL READER*	PROGRESS**	SUPPLEMENTARY READERS
School _____ Teacher _____ Grade _____			
School _____ Teacher _____ Grade _____			
School _____ Teacher _____ Grade _____			
School _____ Teacher _____ Grade _____			

*List basal readers in the order in which used.
**Indicate book completed or the page number reached.

● Keep up to date.
● Transfer from teacher to teacher.
● Send with record cards in case of transfer.

Figure 20. Reading Progress Record Card — Grades 1-6 — Houston (Texas) Independent School District.

Brief anecdotal remarks concerning important facts revealed in parent-teacher conferences should be recorded and placed in the cumulative record folder. Much valuable information about the child's experiences away from school can be obtained in these conferences which may shed light on his school behavior if good parent-teacher relationships exist.

Samples of Classroom Work

Teachers should include samples of classroom work in the cumulative record folder which give evidence of pupil growth or failure to progress. This information is helpful in ascertaining the developmental profile of the individual child. Too, it is good information to have at one's finger tips for use in parent-teacher conferences if such a record of growth needs discussion.

AN ASSESSMENT OF THE CUMULATIVE RECORDS

The cumulative records of the students will provide the classroom teacher a wealth of information concerning the unique progress status of each child. The helpful information which the cumulative records afford the individual teacher has been stated well by Misner, Schneider, and Keith as follows:

> Family background: names of parents or guardians; occupations of parents or guardians; martial status of parents; with whom the pupil lives; economic conditions of home; number and ages of brothers and sisters; attitude of family toward pupil.
>
> Data about pupil: name; age; appearance; color and race; place of birth; church affiliation; picture of pupil.
>
> General health of pupil: past illnesses; pupil's health habits, such as food in his diet, amount of sleep, and the like; absences and tardinesses; physical examinations; physical handicaps.
>
> Personality traits and work habits: record of developing interests; reports of interviews; teachers' observations of work habits; reports of home visits, and visits and correspondence from parents.
>
> Out-of-class activities: summer activities; hobbies; clubs; spare-time activities.
>
> Work experiences and vocational preferences (entered at junior and high school levels): part-time work activities; summer work; student's expressed goals and purposes.[24]

REPORTING PUPIL PROGRESS

The major goal of evaluation is to determine how well the pupils are progressing and identify ways whereby the school program may be adjusted to more nearly meet individual needs. Evaluation has a secondary purpose, however, namely to report pupil progress to parents.

Reporting in the past has been handled primarily on the basis of periodic marks recorded on a report card. Present day reporting practices include the issuance of marks on report cards, check lists, personal letters, parent-teacher conferences, or a combination of any or all of these.

MARKS AS A METHOD OF REPORTING

The most commonly used marking system in the elementary school is the A-B-C-D-F letters. In this case, A denotes Excellent, B Good, C Average, D Poor, and F Failure. Some schools use the E-S-N-U marking plan where E indicates Excellent, S Satisfactory, N Needs Improvement, and U Unsatisfactory. A few schools use only S and U. Other schools use the Arabic numeral system of 1-2-3-4-5. These numerals customarily carry the same connotations as the A-B-C-D-F plan.

Marks have been misused in the past by too many teachers. They frequently have been employed by teachers to compare pupils. Any experi-

---

[24]Paul J. Misner, Frederick W. Schneider, and Lowell G. Keith, *Elementary School Administration* (Columbus, Ohio: Charles E. Merrill Books, Inc., 1963), p. 284.

enced teacher will agree with the statement that no two children come to the teaching-learning situation with exactly the same background of experiences or identical abilities. Yet some teachers persistently hold to the idea that marks should be used to compare pupil progress. Otto has rightly stated that, "Usually a marking system adds nothing that doesn't already exist without it."[25] The children within each classroom know who can perform best in the subject areas, who excels in athletics, who is cooperative, and who class leaders are. To be told that these facts exist through the issuance of marks by the teacher is an excruciating experience for some elementary children, and informs them of little that they do not already know from personal experience and observation.

Some teachers have attempted to use marks as a motivational device and thereby have misused them in yet another manner. Occasionally they make a statement to their pupils, in an effort to control classroom conduct, such as, "Remember the report cards will be sent home next week and I am sure that you want a high mark in citizenship." Or perhaps they may remark, "Only the brightest children in the room will make A's. Don't you want to be thought of as being bright?" Some teachers have gone so far as to issue low marks on report cards insisting that the pupils will work harder during the next reporting period to raise their marks. Such statements and practices are utilized by teachers who erroneously believe that they have motivational value and will enhance pupil learning.

Research which has been done to determine the relationship between marks and motivation is inconclusive. Tiegs' study, as cited by Otto, has shown that 90 per cent of intermediate grade pupils work harder because of good marks, whereas 97 per cent try harder as a result of poor marks.[26] Otto found, in comparing the prior standardized achievement test results of children in an elementary school who had been receiving letter marks of A-B-C-D-F with their own achievement results for several years, that after the marking system had been abolished altogether there was no drop in the median achievement scores by grades and in most grades there was a slight increase.[27]

The teacher is only fooling himself if he feels that marks of themselves will serve as a panacea to insure that all of the children will continually work up to their maximum capacity. In fact, schools which have abandoned the use of comparative marking systems report that children are highly motivated in more pleasant learning situations and pupil outcomes are quite

[25]Henry J. Otto, *Elementary-School Organization and Administration* (New York: Appleton-Century-Crofts, Inc., third edition, 1954), p. 240.

[26]*Ibid.*, p. 241.

[27]*Ibid.*, p. 241-242.

satisfactory. Most experienced teachers would readily agree with Otto's statement:

> . . . that teaching must be at a low ebb if the marking system is the major motivating device for getting honest effort from students . . . So much competition is ever-present in children's school activities that the presence or absence of a marking system really makes no difference.[28]

The use of marks to report pupil progress to parents has become so entrenched in our elementary schools that it is unlikely we will discontinue this practice in the foreseeable future. Perhaps the E-S-N-U system of marking for reporting purposes is better than either the A-B-C-D-F or the 1-2-3-4-5 plans. At least under the E-S-N-U plan the teacher can evaluate and report how well the child is progressing in the light of his own potentialities instead of assigning a mark on the basis of how his progress compares with that of his peers.

One of the big objections to using marks for reporting to parents is that they do not give the parent a frame of reference for knowing what each mark means. This is particularly true when the A-B-C-D-F or the 1-2-3-4-5 plan is used. An "A" in a room where the mean IQ is 100 would not be the same as an "A" earned in a classroom where the average IQ was 115. This only serves to further point up reasons why more acceptable plans of reporting pupil progress must be developed for the elementary school.

CHECK LISTS FOR REPORTING PUPIL PROGRESS

As has been stated, a few schools have already abolished marks as a means of reporting pupil progress. Some of them have devised comprehensive check lists which cover every area of children's experiences in school. Teachers report to parents by sending these check lists home periodically with many check ($\sqrt{}$) marks in the various curriculum areas to inform the parents if their child is making acceptable progress, needs to improve, or is progressing unsatisfactorily. An illustrative check list can be seen in Figure 21.

PERSONAL LETTERS FOR REPORTING PUPIL PROGRESS

One of the best methods of reporting pupil progress is through a personal letter from the teacher to the parents. This serves a twofold purpose. It reports pupil progress more accurately and it helps to establish good

---

[28]*Ibid.*, pp. 242-243.

					First 9 Weeks			Second 9 Weeks			Third 9 Weeks			Fourth 9 Weeks		
					Is making acceptable progress	Needs Improvement	Is making unsatisfactory progress	Is making acceptable progress	Needs Improvement	Is making unsatisfactory progress	Is making acceptable progress	Needs Improvement	Is making unsatisfactory progress	Is making acceptable progress	Needs Improvement	Is making unsatisfactory progress
ATTENDANCE RECORD																
GRADE PERIOD	1	2	3	4												
Days Present																
Days Absent																
Times Tardy																
PERSONAL GROWTH																
Takes pride in neat and accurate work																
Helps to keep room neat and clean																
Listens to and follows directions																
Works well alone																
Works well with others																
Is courteous																
Finishes work on time																
Makes good use of time																
Practices good conduct																
Practices safety																
Takes care of school property and materials																
Gives and receives criticism in a friendly way																
SOCIAL STUDIES																
Cooperates in activities																
Evaluates and organizes information																
Uses reference materials																
Shares ideas and information																
READING																
Reads and shows interest in good books																
Learns new words																
Understands what is read																
Reads aloud in an interesting manner																
ARITHMETIC																
Knows number facts																
Knows addition processes																
Knows subtraction processes																
Knows multiplication processes																

Figure 21. Pupil Progress Reporting Check List for the Intermediate Grades of Port Arthur Independent School District, Port Arthur, Texas.

PROMOTION RECORD Grade Section Room	First 9 Weeks			Second 9 Weeks			Third 9 Weeks			Fourth 9 Weeks		
	Is making acceptable progress	Needs Improvement	Is making unsatisfactory progress	Is making acceptable progress	Needs Improvement	Is making unsatisfactory progress	Is making acceptable progress	Needs Improvement	Is making unsatisfactory progress	Is making acceptable progress	Needs Improvement	Is making unsatisfactory progress
Knows division processes												
Solves stated problems requiring reasoning												
Works accurately												
SPELLING												
Learns required list of words												
Spells correctly in all written work												
LANGUAGE												
Expresses ideas clearly												
Uses correct forms in speaking and writing												
WRITING												
Writes legibly												
Forms letters correctly												
ART												
Is learning to use materials												
Is learning to express own ideas												
MUSIC												
Responds to simple rhythms												
Participates in group singing												
Is learning music skills												
INSTRUMENTAL MUSIC												
HOMEMAKING AND SHOP												
Learns necessary facts												
Uses facts learned												
PHYSICAL EDUCATION												
Takes part in all activities												
Practices good sportsmanship												
Dresses neatly for gym work												
Takes part in swimming activities												

Figure 21. (Continued)

223

parent-teacher rapport. An excellent illustrative reporting letter, as devised by Burr, Harding, and Jacobs, follows.

Dear Mr. and Mrs. Jackson:

Phillip has made substantial advances in most aspects of his schoolwork during the autumn. While he continues to improve in all areas of academic work except spelling, he needs more study of word composition. To make real progress in spelling, Phillip must accept more responsibility for his own achievement. Skill in reading is steadily developing and Phillip makes excellent use of his free-reading periods. Arithmetic skills are being acquired more slowly, but satisfactorily, although problem-solving is still difficult for him.

Phillip's most gratifying work is in creative writing. In this form of expression his ideas continue to be original, often quite clever, and are beautifully expressed. I am sure that his written reports will become more effective as he determines to make his papers more accurate, neat, and better organized. However, please do not overemphasize this or his grammar, for by doing so we may lose more than we gain.

In his quiet, unassuming way Phillip has a great deal of determination. He is interested in all group undertakings and is assuming an increasingly responsible share of leadership in group control. In physical education, Phillip finds his greatest problems. He cannot seem to get dressed on time, apparently because his participation in group games is not satisfying to him. With patience his motor co-ordination will improve and his muscular skill will come more into balance with his intellectual development. Then we may expect Phillip to be happier and better adjusted socially with the group.

The group selected as a central topic for study the problem of how machines influenced the development of the United States. They titled it "How Machines Helped Our Country," and have had much interesting discussion, enlightening investigation, and fruitful work on various aspects of the topic. In addition to helping unify the group, improve sharing of ideas and co-operation in study, the topic has allowed the children to study at their own levels of ability and improve many skills in functional ways.

Phillip has taken an increasingly active part in music and art. These experiences seem to be particularly enjoyable and relaxing to him.

It has been a pleasure to work with Phillip. We anticipate fine relationships through the year.

Sincerely yours,
Eleanor Moore
Teacher, Sixth Grade[29]

In using the personal letter, the teacher should avoid overly critical or caustic statements. If a critical problem exists with a given child, it should be dealt with in a parent-teacher conference and not treated in a personal letter.

---

[29]Burr, Harding, and Jacobs, *op. cit.*, p. 302.

PARENT-TEACHER CONFERENCES AS A METHOD OF
REPORTING PUPIL PROGRESS

In all likelihood there is no other method as effective as the parent-teacher conference for reporting pupil progress. Under such a plan, the parent and teacher can communicate directly thereby facilitating complete reporting together with concomitant interpretations. The danger of misunderstanding and misinterpretation is greatly lessened by such a plan of reporting. If such conferences are held often enough, the report card bearing marks could be disposed of entirely. The check list form of reporting pupil progress and the parent-teacher conference could be combined to form a good reporting procedure. Coupled with an occasional personal letter from the teacher, the check list and parent-teacher conference could present a highly desirable system of reporting pupil progress.

In planning for a parent-teacher conference, teachers should think out what they are going to say to parents carefully in order to avoid statements which will not accurately report pupil progress or which might lessen existing rapport. If the teacher is going to show student work to the parents, he should select specimens which objectively depict the point he wishes to make.

During the conference the teacher should exhibit a warm spirit of friendship and help the parents to feel at ease. The teacher should allow the parents an opportunity to express themselves by listening courteously when they enter into the conversation. Furthermore, the teacher should avoid the use of educational jargon, speaking in terms which are unmistakably clear to the parents. When the conference is concluded, the teacher should establish the fact diplomatically that future meetings can be set up by the parents or himself as the need arises.

The parent-teacher conference can be facilitated by a check sheet of items to be discussed. This will serve two purposes. First, it will provide a guide for the teacher in conducting the conference, and second it will enable the teacher to speak factually about pupil progress. The check sheet shown in Figure 22, as devised by Jarvis,[30] covers the points of academic aptitude potential, academic achievement record, classwork performance profile, and study habits and attitudes. In using this form, the teacher can tactfully point out to the parents the following things:

1. What type of work the child is capable of doing based on his measured general intelligence
2. What the child's achievement record has been through the years in the various subject areas, and what it is now

---

[30]Oscar T. Jarvis, "Why Not Report All Pupil Progress Facts to Parents?", *Georgia Educational Journal*, LVII, No. 2, October, 1963, p. 17.

Pupil_____School_____ Grade_____ Date_____

GENERAL ACADEMIC APTITUDE POTENTIAL	
High	Pupil is capable of mastering academic school subjects readily
Average	Pupil is capable of accomplishing grade level work with appropriate dedication to his studies
Low	Pupil may encounter learning difficulties in some subjects
Test Dates:	

ACADEMIC ACHIEVEMENT RECORD

Subject Area	1st	2nd	3rd	4th	5th	6th	7th or Above
Reading Vocabulary							
Reading Comprehension							
Arithmetic Reasoning							
Arithmetic Fundamentals							
Language Mechanics							
Spelling							
Test Dates:							

CLASSWORK PERFORMANCE PROFILE				Is overall achievement consistent with the pupil's aptitude potential?	
	Pupil is working:				
Subject	Below Grade Level	At Grade Level	Above Grade Level	Yes	No
Reading					
Arithmetic					
Language					
Spelling					
Writing					
Social Studies					
Science					

PUPIL STUDY HABITS AND ATTITUDES

Criteria	Occasionally	Generally	Always
Assignments completed on time			
Takes pride in neat and accurate work			
Listens and follows directions well			
Works and plays well with others			
Accepts responsibility for own actions			
Uses leisure time wisely			
Shows initiative			
Demonstrates resourcefulness			

TYPES OF PUPIL DATA REVIEWED

	Homework assignments
	Classroom assignments
	Teacher-made test results
	Previous school marks
	Previous achievement test results

Teacher observation comments:

Parent-teacher proposed plan of action:

Parent's Signature _____   Teacher's Signature _____

Figure 22. Teacher-Parent Conference Reporting Form. Adapted from Oscar T. Jarvis, "Why Not Report All Pupil Progress Facts to Parents?" *Georgia Education Journal*, Volume LVII, Number 2, (October, 1963), p. 17. Reprinted by permission of *Georgia Education Journal*.

3. Whether the child is performing above, at, or below grade level and if such performance is consistent with his ability
4. Whether the child has good work and study habits, gets along with his peers, resourceful, et cetera
5. Teacher observations of things which may be influencing pupil behavior
6. A proposed plan of action to extend the educational progress of the child.

Whereas a letter mark on a periodic report card tells parents very little about their child's progress at school, the parent-teacher conference method of reporting renders as complete an accounting as one could desire. It is safe to predict that the future will witness the demise of letter marks on report cards as the primary method of reporting pupil progress. Instead we will find more and more schools reporting by check list, personal letters, parent-teacher conferences or any combination of these plans.

PROMOTION AND RETENTION FACTORS

Teachers have to make decisions about whether or not to promote each child annually. There appear to be at least two different philosophies, the pupil-centered and the subject-centered points of view, which impinge upon promotion and retention decisions.

PUPIL-CENTERED VIEW

The term "social promotion" has come into vogue within recent years in the elementary school. The theory underlying social promotion is that children will develop more normally and naturally if they are advanced each year along with their peers even though they may not master the academics at any grade level. Many teachers feel that children who are retained tend to become stigmatized and frequently develop emotional and mental disturbances. They argue further that the normal range of individual differences at any grade level will necessitate intraclass groupings anyway, and that if they promote each child socially he will find a group in the subsequent grade where instruction is adjusted to his level of development.

The proponents of social promotion have been criticized as do-gooders by teachers who do not subscribe to such a philosophy. However, there is much to be said for the theory of social promotion. One has only to look to the evidence of research to see the wisdom in such a course of action. Research has shown that of the children retained only 20 per cent will do better work the next year, whereas 40 per cent will do the same quality of work which they did the previous year and 40 per cent will actually do poorer work than they had previously done.[31] If one can expect only 20 per cent of the retained children to benefit from retention, then social promotion must be accepted as being a worthwhile practice.

SUBJECT-CENTERED VIEW

Teachers who place credence in the subject-centered point of view concerning promotion or retention take the position that if the child has not mastered the subject matter at his grade level he should be retained. They adhere to the philosophy that the primary task of the teacher is to dispense facts to pupils and insist that they be mastered. These teachers frequently fail to recognize the ranges of individual and trait differences which exist within their rooms. Obviously they are uninformed about the research evidence which shows that over all there is little to be gained through non-promotion.

The practice of annual promotion for every child, with few exceptions, is a wise policy to be followed in the elementary school. It should be continued as long as research evidence shows the practice to be valid.

SUMMARY

Evaluation is the process whereby teachers continuously gather pupil data to determine what adjustments need to be made in the instructional program in order that acceptable student behavioral changes may be effected in academic achievement, social adjustment, and physical and emotional development.

There are at least four good methods of measuring pupil behavior so evaluation may be employed. These methods are commercially prepared tests, teacher-made tests, sociograms, and teacher observation. In selecting measuring devices from the commercially prepared or standardized tests and the teacher-made tests, the teacher should choose measuring instruments which meet the criteria of validity, reliability, objectivity, pertinence, appropriateness, practicality, and applicability.

There are three main types of formal commercially prepared tests which are used in the elementary school. They are the general intelligence, survey achievement batteries, and the aptitudes and interest inventories tests.

Essay and objective type examinations constitute the most commonly utilized types of teacher-made tests presently employed in the elementary school. The oral examination per se is seldom given. The teacher-made objective tests may take the form of true-false, completion, matching or multi-

---

[31]Henry J. Otto and David C. Sanders, *Elementary School Organization and Administration* (fourth edition; New York: Appleton-Century-Crofts, Inc., 1964), p. 141.

ple choice items. Frequently a combination of these type questions is used to formulate a teacher-made objective test.

The cumulative record folder is used for recording significant facts concerning pupil progress. It should include identifying pupil data, school history, standardized test results, health record, anecdotal comments, et cetera. It should be kept up to date by the classroom teacher and passed along to the individual child's subsequent teacher.

There are at least four acceptable methods of reporting pupil progress to parents. They are marks, check lists, personal letters, and parent-teacher conferences. The most widely used method of reporting is that of the issuance of marks on report cards. It also is the most objectionable to progressive minded teachers. A combination of periodic check lists sent home to parents together with personal letters and occasional parent-teacher conferences would provide a thorough and systematic plan of reporting pupil progress, and would be compatible with our sophisticated knowledge of children's individual and trait differences.

Social promotion is a commonly accepted practice in America's elementary schools today. Research has shown that little is to be gained by retaining children. Modern practice embraces the premise that children should be promoted annually with their age mates, and that teachers should form intraclass groups to fit the level of instruction to the developmental needs of all their pupils.

QUESTIONS FOR DISCUSSION

1. What are the major purposes in evaluating student behavioral outcomes?
2. What are the most objective means of evaluating student progress? What are the least objective ways of appraising student progress? What factors should be given consideration in selecting modes of evaluation?
3. What reliance should be placed upon information recorded in students' cumulative record folders? For what purpose should this information be used?
4. Some educators have asserted that marks are meaningless to parents and should not be used in reporting pupil progress. Do you agree with this statement? Why or why not?
5. What is your position on promotion and retention of children? Do you believe social promotion to be an acceptable or unacceptable practice? Explain.

TOPICS FOR RESEARCH

1. Develop a program of systematic testing by means of the administration of standardized instruments for grades one through six.

2. Visit some elementary schools and examine the cumulative record folders to familiarize yourself with the forms being used and the types of data which are being recorded in them.
3. Devise an ideal plan for reporting student progress to parents.

BIBLIOGRAPHY

BURR, JAMES B., LOWRY W. HARDING, AND LELAND B. JACOBS. *Student Teaching in the Elementary School*. Second edition. New York: Appleton-Century-Crofts, Inc., 1958.

HASKEW, LAURENCE D. *This Is Teaching*. Chicago: Scott, Foresman and Company, 1956.

JAMESON, MARSCHALL C., AND WM. VERNON HICKS. *Elementary School Curriculum*. New York: American Book Company, 1960.

JARVIS, OSCAR T. "Why Not Report All Pupil Progress Facts To Parents?" *Georgia Education Journal*. Volume LVII, Number 2, October, 1963.

MEHL, MARIE A., HUBERT H. MILLS, AND HARL R. DOUGLASS. *Teaching in Elementary School*. New York: The Ronald Press Company, Second Edition, 1958.

MICHAELIS, JOHN U., AND ENOCH DUMAS. *The Student Teacher in the Elementary School*. Second Edition. Englewood Cliffs, N. J.: Prentice-Hall, Inc., 1960.

MISNER, PAUL J., FREDERICK W. SCHNEIDER, AND LOWELL G. KEITH, *Elementary School Administration*. Columbus, Ohio: Charles E. Merrill Books, Inc., 1963.

OTTO, HENRY J. *Elementary-School Organization and Administration*. Third edition. New York: Appleton-Century-Crofts, Inc., 1954.

OTTO HENRY J., AND DAVID C. SANDERS. *Elementary School Organization and Administration*. Fourth edition, New York: Appleton-Century-Crofts, Inc., 1964.

RAGAN, WILLIAM B. *Modern Elementary Curriculum*. New York: Henry Holt and Company, 1960.

————. *Teaching America's Children*. New York: Holt, Rinehart and Winston, 1961.

ROSS, C. C., AND JULIAN C. STANLEY. *Measurement in Today's Schools*. Third edition. Englewood Cliffs, N. J.: Prentice-Hall, Inc., 1954.

ROTHNEY, JOHN W. M. "Evaluating and Reporting Pupil Progress," *What Research Says to the Teacher*. Volume 7, Washington, D. C.: National Education Association, 1955.

SHANE, HAROLD G., AND E. T. McSWAIN, *Evaluation and the Elementary Curriculum*. New York: Henry Holt Company, 1951.

SOWARDS, G. WESLEY, AND MARY-MARGARET SCOBEY. *The Changing Curriculum and the Elementary Teacher*. San Francisco: Wadsworth Publishing Company, Inc., 1961.

THOMAS, R. MURRAY. *Judging Student Progress*. Second edition. New York: David McKay Company, 1960.

His (the teacher's) problem is to protect the spirit of inquiry, to keep it from becoming blasé from overexcitement, wooden from routine, fossilized through dogmatic instruction, or dissipated by random exercise upon trivial things. JOHN DEWEY.

Part Three

The Teacher and the Learning Environment

Students' innate curiosities expedite problem solving teaching.

Chapter 8

Teaching and Problem Solving Procedure

The functions of the human mind regarding thought processes are very complex and not as yet fully understood by contemporary man. Through continuous observation and experimentation, we are gradually learning more about the inner workings of the mind, its thought patterns, and its ability to solve problems. The subsequent pages of this chapter are concerned with the thought processes of the individual, which may be called reflective thinking for purposes of definition, and how they relate to the problem solving approach to teaching and learning in the elementary school.

A knowledge of children's thinking which results in problem solving is an essential requisite for the student preparing to enter elementary teaching. This is so because children should be taught *how* to think rather than *what* to think. Brownell expressed this viewpoint years ago in stating that our schools should place emphasis "upon the necessity of having children 'think' instead of 'memorize,' of having them reason out conclusions for themselves rather than complacently and docilely accept conclusions given them by others higher in authority."[1] The day of the autocratic, traditional elementary school teacher who views the curriculum from the standpoint of the subjects-in-isolation approach is drawing to a close. Emerging is a new view of curriculum with the emphasis upon understanding the child

---

[1] William A. Brownell, "Problem Solving," *The Forty-First Yearbook of the National Society for the Study of Education.* Nelson B. Henry, (ed.), (Bloomington, Illinois: Public School Publishing Company, 1942), p. 432.

and developing the materials around his interests and needs. Paramount in importance in this modern approach is the teacher's new found responsibility for helping children to learn how to think effectively rather than telling them what to think.

Progressive minded teachers utilize experience units which cut across subject matter lines in developing the course of study in the light of student interest and needs to provide opportunities for them to apply and correlate concomitant learnings as they engage in problem solving thought processes. This new approach to working with children has been substantiated as a feasible method by educational research findings. Beck, Cook, and Kearney in summarizing Tyler and Wert's studies on the permanency of learning have stated that "learning that involves problem-solving relationships and the operation of the higher mental processes is relatively permanent, whereas learning in which unrelated facts and mere unorganized information is involved is relatively temporary."[2] An understanding of the nature and process of reflective thinking as it relates to problem solving thought as an approach to curriculum development in the elementary school therefore is necessary for the prospective teacher. As one reads the following pages of this chapter, he will do well to keep Brownell's admonition in mind.

> A problem-solving attitude, an inquiring and questioning mind, is a desirable educational outcome, and it is possible of development. The practice of 'learning' by cramming does not produce this outcome, nor does the practice of accepting from others truths and conclusions which ought to be established by the learner himself. The attitude *is* produced by continued experience in solving real problems, one consequence of which is that the learner comes to *expect* new problems and to look for them.[3]

Thorndike has said that, "The more widely the school can reach out beyond the scope of books and classroom, beyond skills and drills and into a variety of areas of experience, the more readily will problems open up to the child."[4] This point of view should serve as a guide to the reader in understanding subsequent ideas presented here.

NATURE OF REFLECTIVE THINKING

The mind of the individual is almost always functioning. Whether awake or asleep, usually some form of thought is coursing through his mind. Some

---

[2]Robert H. Beck, Walter W. Cook, and Nolan C. Kearney, *Curriculum in the Modern Elementary School.* (Englewood Cliffs, N. J.: Prentice-Hall, Inc., 1960), p. 48.

[3]Brownell, *op. cit.*, p. 440.

[4]Robert L. Thorndike, "How Children Learn the Principles and Techniques of Problem-Solving," *The Forty-ninth Yearbook of the National Society for the Study of Education,* Nelson B. Henry (ed.), Part I, (Chicago: The University of Chicago Press, 1950), p. 210.

of this thought may be idle daydreaming during the waking hours, dreaming while asleep, or more purposeful reflective thinking which usually leads to problem solving. This higher order reasoning called "reflective thinking," according to Dewey is "active, persistent, and careful consideration of any belief or supposed form of knowledge in the light of the grounds that support it and the further conclusions to which it tends."[5]

One may prove to his own satisfaction the premise that "the mind of the individual is almost always functioning" simply by purposing not to think. In so doing, he will find that it is impossible not to engage in some type of reverie. One therefore must conclude that there is an endless procession of thought processes taking place within the mind and simply to will not to think is an impossibility. Reflective thinking normally transpires in one of three methods. First, it may be considered to be a continuous chain of related thoughts. Second, reflective thinking may be relegated to things not directly perceived, and third, it may be viewed as being practically synonymous with believing.[6]

REFLECTIVE THINKING AS A CONTINUOUS CHAIN OF THOUGHT PROCESSES

In relationship to the continuous chain theory, reflective thinking on this order involves the conjuring up of all preceding experiences by one's mind in a manner whereby a logical conclusion for a given problem may be drawn. Confronted by a new or different problem the mind of the individual reflects on all previous experiences and constructs feasible hypotheses which could lead to satisfactory solutions. This point has been expressed well by Dewey in stating:

> Reflection involves not simply a sequence of ideas, but a consequence — a consecutive ordering in such a way that each determines the next as its proper outcome, while each outcome in turn leans back on, or refers to, its predecessors. The successive portions of a reflective thought grow out of one another and support one another; they do not come and go in a medley. Each phase is a step from something to something — technically speaking, it is a *term* of thought. Each term leaves a deposit that is utilized in the next term. The stream or flow becomes a train or chain. There are in any reflective thought definite units that are linked together so that there is sustained movement to a common end.[7]

Thus, the continuous chain process type of reflective thinking enables the mind to cope with a new or problem situation on the basis of the inter-

---

[5]John Dewey, *How We Think* (New York: D. C. Heath and Co., 1933), p. 9. Reprinted by permission of D. C. Heath and Company.
[6]*Ibid.*, pp. 4-7.
[7]*Ibid.*, pp. 4-5.

pretation of previous experiences and the application of principles derived
from them.

REFLECTIVE THINKING RELEGATED TO THINGS
NOT DIRECTLY PERCEIVED

Thinking which involves things which have not actually been seen,
heard, touched, smelled or tasted transpires through invention of the mind.
The average student cannot take a trip on a prairie schooner or ride on a
flatboat down the Mississippi River, but through his inventive imagination
he can in effect create a remarkably valid conception of such an experience. In these imaginative enterprises the child establishes a thought
or idea by picturing mentally something not actually present whereby his
reflective thinking establishes a pattern of similarly related successive pictures.[8]

REFLECTIVE THINKING AS PRACTICALLY SYNONYMOUS
WITH BELIEVING

Through exercising one's belief in a given thesis an individual engages
in yet another type of reflective thinking. When one reasons that anything
he throws into the air will come back to earth he is expressing his thoughts
as evidence of his belief in Newton's theory of gravity. When the ancient
Grecians first discovered the colored natives of Africa they thought that
their bodies had been burned by the sun because of the proximity of their
habitat to the equator, which accounted for their skin coloration. Since that
time, however, their early beliefs have been tested and disproved in large
measure by an increased understanding of genetics. Dewey has said that:

> A belief refers to something beyond itself by which its value is tested;
> it makes an assertion about some matter of fact or some principle or law.
> It means that a specified state of fact or law is accepted or rejected, that
> it is something proper to be affirmed or at least acquiesced in. It covers
> all the matters of which we have no sure knowledge and yet which we
> are sufficiently confident of to act upon and also the matters that we now
> accept as certainly true, as knowledge, but which nevertheless may be
> questioned in the future — just as much that passed as knowledge in the
> past has now passed into the limbo of mere opinion or of error.[9]

The mere act of thinking about and giving acquiescence to a commonly
accepted belief does not prove whether or not it is well founded. A person
may say, "I believe that it is possible for man to travel to the moon and

---

[8]*Ibid.*, p. 5.
[9]*Ibid.*, p. 6.

return safely to the earth." Just because the person believes such a feat to be both possible and probable does not establish its validity. In fact, if the person should be challenged to produce specific evidence to support his belief he likely would have meager data to substantiate his assertion. More than likely he has acquired this idea from others because of its current popularity, not because he has made a scientific study of his thesis. In all likelihood his mind has probably acquiesced to what he has heard others say or what he has read. In effect his own mind has done very little in reaching and framing the belief. Concerning this peculiar dilemma, Dewey has said:

> Such thoughts grow up unconsciously. They are picked up — we know not how. From obscure sources and by unnoticed channels they insinuate themselves into the mind and become unconsciously a part of our mental furniture. Tradition, instruction, imitation — all of which depend upon authority in some form, or appeal to our own advantage, or fall in with a strong passion — are responsible for them. Such thoughts are prejudices; that is prejudgments, not conclusions reached as the result of personal mental activity, such as observing, collecting, and examining evidence. Even when they happen to be correct, their correctness is a matter of accident as far as the person who entertains them is concerned.[10]

The three types of reflective thinking discussed vary somewhat in their effect upon the individual's ability to engage in problem solving ventures. In the first two instances mentioned, thought of this nature may actually be harmful to one's mind as a result of the possibility of his attention being distracted from the real world in which he lives. This type of thought, which may be classified as idle daydreaming, is a waste of time. If these thoughts are engaged in judiciously, however, they may provide both enjoyment and needed recreation. Since these types of thinking make no claim to truth, they consequently do not produce ideas which the mind should be willing to accept unquestionably. Conversely, beliefs do involve the mind to a definite commitment on a given issue. In time this belief and commitment must be investigated to determine the grounds upon which they rest. To illustrate, when Columbus conceived the theory that the earth was round, he so expressed his belief. The statement of his thoughts called for a testing of his theory either to prove or disprove his belief. In the investigation of his premise that the earth was round, other concomitant beliefs would of necessity have to be tested. The ideas that circumnavigation was an impossibility because if one traveled too far westward on the Atlantic Ocean he

---

[10]*Ibid.*, p. 7.

would reach a jumping off place and that there were no alternate routes to India would certainly have to be verified.

When Columbus set sail in a westerly direction he placed his belief in the crucible of scientific investigation wherein problem solving thought could occur. Whereas others had been willing to accept as truth what they could see from territories which were familiar to them, Columbus launched out into the unknown to prove or disprove his theory. As a result, because he dared challenge traditional theory by exercising scientific problem solving practices, he kept on thinking until he produced evidence for his belief.[11] Any one of these three kinds of reflective thinking may elicit this type of thought. Dewey said that once this type of problem solving thinking has begun "it includes a conscious and voluntary effort to establish belief upon a firm basis of evidence and rationality."[12]

PROCESSES IN REFLECTIVE THINKING

There are many functional events or processes in reflective thinking. To simply say that children are engaged in or are capable of thinking is indeed a nebulous statement. There are many different types or processes of thinking. The elementary teacher who desires to work effectively with children in developing their abilities to think must be aware of the different processes of thinking. These processes have been catalogued quite well by Russell as (1) perceptual, (2) associative, (3) inductive thinking and concept formation, (4) problem-solving, (5) critical, and (6) creative.[13] Russell's schema of functional events in reflective thinking are depicted in Figure 23.

A study of Figure 23 will lead to the deduction that whenever a conclusion is drawn by an individual there first must have been either an external or internal stimulus which precipitated some type of reflective thinking. As a result of that stimulus, the individual experienced some need to solve an immediate problem. Further study of Russell's schema will lead one to conclude that an individual aroused by a given stimulus to solve an immediate problem is influenced by his emotions, attitudes, habits, and needs in reaching an acceptable solution. In arriving at the solution, the mind conjures up mental images of related experiences by recounting past memories and previously acquired concepts. These percepts, images, memories, and concepts which are the materials of thinking in turn lead to the formulation of a final conclusion through one of the processes in reflective thinking.

---

[11]*Ibid.*, pp. 8-9.
[12]*Ibid.*, p. 9.
[13]David H. Russell, *Children's Thinking.* (Boston: Ginn and Company, 1956), pp. 10-14.

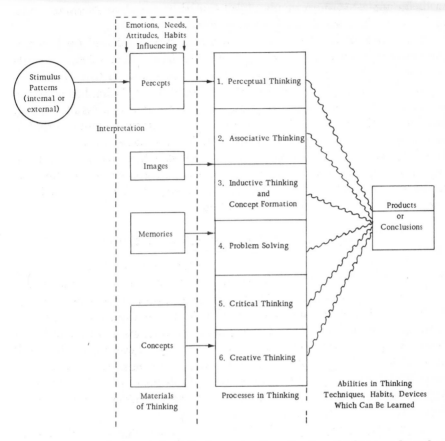

Figure 23. Schema of functional events in reflective thinking. Adapted from David H. Russell, *Children Thinking*. (Boston: Ginn and Company, 1956), p. 10. Reprinted through the courtesy of Blaisdell Publishing Company, a division of Ginn and Company.

PERCEPTUAL THINKING

An individual who responds to a given stimulus which arises from within his own organism or from his immediate environment is likely to engage in perceptual thinking. Perceptual thinking has been defined by Russell as "that type of thinking least directed toward a definite conclusion and most affected by environmental conditions."[14] In other words, when a child employs perceptual thinking he is in actuality engaged in thought patterns

[14]David H. Russell, *Children's Thinking*. (Boston: Ginn and Company, 1956), p. 10. Reprinted through the courtesy of Blaisdell Publishing Company, a division of Ginn and Company.

in their simplest form. A young child may be attracted by the bright blue color of a tricycle and think *blue, tricycle,* or *ride.* Also, he may be attracted by the printed symbol *STOP* on a road sign, but such perceptual thinking rarely leads to higher order problem solving thoughts.

ASSOCIATIVE THINKING

Another type of thought process not directly related to satisfying an immediate goal is associative thinking. Customarily, the child, while engaged in this type of reverie, links an original idea to subsequent thought to formulate a very loosely connected pattern. Seeing the blue tricycle the child may think *tricycle — play — fun — Christmas — birthday* or any number of ideas related to his toy. According to Russell:

> the thinking is not directed toward some particular problem to be solved, but because of certain stimuli . . . the child's reverie moves along a certain path. It is directed toward a goal, but not by the conscious effort of the child. It is a process relying considerably upon memory, influenced by the total setting and the dominant interests of the child. It may taper off to no particular conclusion or be redirected toward some more tangible goal . . . As the child learns the correct response to many school problems, such as the sum of seven and five or the names of the thirteen states originally forming the federation, he may be employing associative thinking.[15]

INDUCTIVE THINKING AND CONCEPT FORMATION

Inductive thinking which leads to concept formation is more directed or highly structured reasoning than either perceptual or associative thinking. When a child sees a dog for the first time, as an example, he forms a mental construct or concept of what a dog looks like. Perhaps this first association was with a small white French poodle. Eventually, however, he sees a German shepherd or a collie. He recognizes that these dogs are much larger of stature than the French poodle and also have different color hair. In this process of inductive thinking, he revises his concept of a dog and formulates a new and different one. As he sees different breeds of dogs in the future, the process will be repeated until he establishes the generalization that dogs may be of many different sizes, color, and breeds.

Through inductive thinking the child formulates concepts upon which he bases his actions and reactions to given problems or stimuli. Through subsequent direct and vicarious experiences he continually revises these mental constructs, normally making them more valid with each revision.

---

[15]*Ibid.*, p. 11.

PROBLEM SOLVING

Problem solving is the most directed type of thinking done by children. It differs from perceptual, associative, and inductive thinking in that the child is confronted by a problem with more than one solution and must choose the best method leading to the most acceptable. After he chooses the preferred solution he applies it to see if it works as well in practice as he theorized. If so, he accepts it. If not, he chooses the next best method and continues his experimentation until an acceptable solution is proven. This process of thinking has been described well by Kilpatrick as follows:

1. Suppose a child faces a situation. First of all there is in him that which makes this a situation for him, and second there is in the environment something that so stirs him that he is moved to act. Only as these things happen together does a child face an actual situation.
2. Facing thus an actual life situation, the second step is to analyze it, partly to set up or clarify ends, partly to get materials for the planning that comes next.
3. The third step is to make one or more plans and choose from among them, for dealing with the situation. In a developing situation the plan will be in process of making from step to step as the situation develops. Planning is clearly an imaginative and creative step, but the imagination is checked and molded by the hard facts of the situation.
4. Then comes the step of putting the plan into operation, watching meanwhile to see how it works, so that if need arise revision may be made.
5. If the plan succeeds, a final stage is the backward look to see what has been done and how it might be done better another time.[16]

Problem solving thinking has unlimited possibilities as a vehicle of methodology for teaching in the elementary school. These possibilities will be treated in greater detail in later sections of this chapter.

CRITICAL THINKING

A synonymous term for critical thinking might well be evaluative thinking. These two terms may well be considered synonymous because whenever a student is involved in problem solving thinking and selects a hypothesis to test to see if it will yield a satisfactory solution, he thinks critically or evaluates the outcome of his trial thesis. However, critical thinking in its broader interpretation according to Russell:

may be more than part of other thinking activities and is frequently advocated as a desirable aim for many school activities in its own right.

---

[16]William Heard Kilpatrick, *Remaking The Curriculum* (New York: Newson & Company, 1936), pp. 48-50. See also Henry J. Hermanowicz, "Problem Solving as Teaching Method," *Educational Leadership,* Volume 18, Number 5, February, 1961, p. 302.

Sometimes the term has been applied specifically to scientific data and sometimes to analysis of propaganda materials . . . It may be applied to a sentence in a textbook, a statement in a radio broadcast, or to the child's own product, in construction, writing, or painting. It is usually applied in problem solving to the hypothesis or temporary solution and, in its turn, may provide material for further thinking.[17]

It is very easy to control man's thought processes in our contemporary society through the media of the press, radio, and television. It seems evident, therefore, that critical thinking affords a unique and promising challenge for effective teaching in the elementary school as children are led to evaluate the ideas of other people as well as their own thoughts and reactions.

CREATIVE THINKING

When a child thinks creatively he is involved in the production of new ideas. Creative thinking differs from critical thinking in that the former deals with new ideas or concepts while the latter is ordinarily concerned with one's reactions to the ideas of others or to his own previous thoughts. Creative thinking is closely related to problem solving. They differ largely from the standpoint that problem solving is a direct process which leads to the attainment of some desired goal, whereas creative thinking enables a person to achieve something new without being coerced into agreeing with previously determined conditions.[18]

All children possess the ability to think creatively; however, some are by nature more creative than others. According to Russell, "the scientist, the inventor, or the painter does not have an ability that other men have never known; he simply has a large share of some particular ability."[19] A worthy goal for any elementary school teacher therefore would be to ascertain the true creative potentialities of each child and endeavor to help him develop his innate talent to the maximum degree.

REFLECTIVE THINKING AND PROBLEM SOLVING

Thinking has been defined "as that operation in which present facts suggest other facts (or truths) in such a way as to induce belief in what is suggested on the ground of real relation in the things themselves."[20] When a child is engaged in purposeful reflective thinking or problem solving

---

[17]Russell, *op. cit.*, p. 13.
[18]*Ibid.*, p. 306.
[19]*Ibid.*, p. 306.
[20]Dewey, *op. cit.*, p. 12.

thought his mind "involves (1) a state of doubt, hesitation, perplexity, mental difficulty, in which thinking originates, and (2) an act of searching, hunting, inquiring, to find material that will resolve the doubt, settle and dispose of the perplexity."[21]

Whenever the individual is confronted with a new problem or perplexity his mind instantly performs certain operations. The functions of the mind when an individual is engaged in problem solving thought may be outlined as follows:

1. *He experiences a felt need to solve a perplexity.* At this stage he is acutely aware of a problem with which he is confronted and which he is motivated to solve.

2. *He locates the difficulty and defines the nature of the problem.* He determines the nature of the perplexity and analyzes the various aspects of the problem.

3. *His mind conjures up various hypotheses which could possibly serve as a solution.* During this phase of thinking, the mind reflects on all previous experiences which bear a relationship to the immediate problem. Consequently, the thought processes suggest several tentative solutions which will enable the individual to solve the perplexity.

4. *He selects the most feasible solution to the problem from all of the posed hypotheses.* The various facets of the problem are analyzed and a commitment is made to the most feasible solution.

5. *He tests the chosen solution to the problem.* If the chosen hypothesis works satisfactorily, the mind will likely accept it. If it does not, the mind customarily reverts back to step three to recall all of the possible hypotheses suggested: selects another feasible one, and tests it to see if it yields a satisfactory solution. This process is continued until the problem is resolved. The individual's mind works religiously in this manner when it is engaged in problem solving thought.

Educators have long been aware of the steps in reflective thinking which the mind utilizes in problem solving thinking. As early as 1910, Dewey spelled out the processes the mind employs. His concept of these steps was:

1. A felt difficulty.
2. Its location and definition.
3. Suggestion of possible solution.
4. Development by reasoning of the bearings of the suggestion.
5. Further observation and experiment leading to its acceptance or rejection, that is, the conclusion of belief or disbelief.[22]

---

[21]*Ibid.*, p. 12.
[22]John Dewey, *How We Think* (Boston: D. C. Heath & Co., © 1910), p. 72. Reprinted by permission of D. C. Heath and Company.

Thorndike's interpretation and amplification of Dewey's five steps in problem solving is most helpful in enabling one to fully grasp the import of this theory. The treatment of these phases in problem solving thought as defined by Thorndike is:

1. *Becoming aware of a problem.* The route to some objective is blocked, routine behavior is not directly successful, and the individual realizes that a problem exists.
2. *Clarifying the problem.* The problem, sensed at first only in general terms, is made more sharp and specific in terms of just what end is to be achieved and just what is known or what resources are available.
3. *Proposing hypotheses for solution of the problem.* Specific proposals are suggested and elaborated for dealing with the problem situation.
4. *Reasoning out implications of hypotheses.* Bringing together the hypothesis and the relevant facts which are known to him, the individual reasons out what follows from the hypothesis which he is considering.
5. *Testing the hypothesis against experience.* The conclusions which follow from the hypothesis are tested against known facts or by experiment and the gathering of new facts, to see if the conclusions are valid and the hypothesis is supported.[23]

Later, Kilpatrick outlined the steps in what he termed the "complete act of thought." In so doing, he illustrated each stage of thinking in problem solving as follows:

1. A situation arouses an impulse or tendency to pursue a certain course of action.

   The baby's crying stirs the mother to seek to relieve him. Unexpected movements in Uranus stir the astronomer to try to explain these movements.
2. A difficulty appears; how to continue the given course is not known; there is no appropriate way of responding known or immediately available.

   The mother does not know what to do for the baby. The astronomer has no satisfactory explanation for the movements of Uranus.
3. An examination of the situation is made to locate and define the difficulty more precisely.

   The mother listens to the baby and considers his movements. The astronomer measures carefully the deviation of Uranus from what had been expected and considers all possible interfering causes. Each is meanwhile considering all the facts with reference to possible solutions.
4. Suggested solutions arise: hypotheses are formed, behavior patterns are suggested.

   The baby is cold or perhaps has colic. Uranus is attracted by some hitherto unknown planet yet more distant from the sun.

---

[23]Thorndike, *op. cit.*, p. 196.

5. Implications (one or more) are drawn from each suggested solution, each hypothesis.
   If the baby is cold, covering him more warmly will relieve his discomfort. If a planet is attracting Uranus, we should see it in such and such part of the sky.
6. Actual trial is made to see where the deduced implications hold.
   Does the baby stop crying when covered? Do we find the new planet where we were told to look, and is it such as to explain the aberrations of Uranus?
7. A solution is accepted in the light of the tests made.[24]

Gray endeavored, in 1935, to set forth the characteristics of problem solving in a larger sense as it pertained to issues of everyday living as opposed to its being relegated solely to academics. In expressing his timely point of view, he listed the following six distinct phases of reflective thought which occur in problem solving:

1. *Sensitivity to problems.* A problem is a difficulty or a situation which demands adjustment . . . A distinguishing characteristic of the educated man is that he is sensitive to problems, i. e., he tries to solve them. Only the ignorant are oblivious to the problems about them.

   Obviously the educator can teach pupils to be more sensitive to problems. School environment should be pregnant with problem situations. Pupils, then, should be free to evolve and formulate their own problems. They cannot learn to recognize problems if the teacher insists on pointing them out. The educator must realize that the entire problem-solving process is learned only when the pupils perform it for themselves.

2. *Knowledge of problem conditions.* Problems can be stated, but they cannot be understood until data have been collected concerning them. It is only when one becomes familiar with the conditions of the problem that it is understood. Such information contains the key to the solution. A thorough knowledge of problem conditions makes further solution behavior less difficult.

   Here again education plays a major role. It enables the problem-solver to recognize significant information. The uneducated individual cannot distinguish facts which are of worth from those which are not. Such ability comes only from experience in problem-solving. One learns to judge the significance of problem data only after he has solved a great many problems. Too much present-day education (so-called) drills the child in fact learning per se. Information is considered as an end in itself instead of an essential means to an end. Knowledge learning is the second step in problem-solving and should not precede the first. Facts have but little significance unless they are learned as a means of solving some problem.

---

[24]William Heard Kilpatrick, *Foundations of Method* (New York: The Macmillan Co., 1930), pp. 242-243.

3. *Suggested solution or hypothesis.* As the data concerning a problem are collected, possible solutions will be suggested. Some will obviously be worthless, but others will appear sufficiently plausible to merit specific statement . . .

If the data are properly interpreted and one of the suggested solutions is accurate (i. e., turns out to be the real solution), the procedure is then called intelligent. The intelligent individual is one who can solve problems with the least number of errors or can predict solutions with the greatest degree of accuracy.

This step is largely neglected in conventional education. Facts are interpreted for the student, and consequently he does not learn to think. The student must be allowed to interpret his own data and formulate his own hypotheses, even though he makes frequent errors. He cannot learn to think by allowing the teacher to think for him. Learning does not take place by proxy. Accurate prediction in problem-solving is learned by experience in doing just that.

4. *Subjective evaluation.* This step is essentially a process of comparing the suggested solution (step 3) with the problem conditions (step 2) to see if it will work. It is an exercise in imagination to "foresee" the problem consequences. Here again, intelligence is essential. But if the problem has been described in detail, if the data are stated accurately and exactly, and if the suggested solution has been applied to the problem conditions with vivid imagination, the probable success of the hypothesis will be evident . . .

The performance of these last two steps constitutes a sort of mental trial-and-error procedure. When an hypothesis is obviously wrong, it is necessary to return to step 3 and formulate a new one. The process of comparing it with the problem conditions is then repeated and it, too, is accepted or rejected.

Proficiency in performing this step depends on one's experience. If the student is encouraged to evaluate hypotheses for himslf, he will soon develop habits of exactness in his thinking and consequent accuracy in his predictions. Again, the teacher must not think for the child.

5. *Objective test.* When a trial solution has passed the scrutiny of subjective evaluation, the next step is to test it out objectively. This may be done by laboratory experiment, controlled observation, historical investigation, etc. . .

The function of education in this step is evident. Students can be trained to accept solutions without test, and become worshippers of authority and tradition, or they can be trained to react critically and doubtfully to solutions which have not been proven of objective worth. Conventional, or old-type, education produces the former type of thinking, while progressive education produces the latter. The former is the method of bigotry and dogmatism, while the latter is the method of science and civilization. Certainly American educators should be concerned with teaching our coming citizenship that untested thought is often wrong and therefore dangerous; that traditional belief is not evidence of truth; and that objective verification of thinking is the most advanced state of social evolution.

6. *Conclusion or generalization.* A very important feature of any behavior is the degree to which it affects future behavior. Education of most worth is that which is most beneficial in later life. We can profit from past experience only when that experience "transfers" to future occasions. In problem-solving behavior, part of this transfer takes place through the data. The same facts may be used in solving two or more problems. Thus the facts learned in one problem situation may have worth in subsequent situations. However, a greater amount of transfer takes place if a generalization (a language description of the common characteristic of a classification) grows out of a problem-solving procedure which applies to future problems.[25]

Although the ideas of Dewey, Kilpatrick, and Gray were expressed several years ago they are just as appropriate today. It is evident that as educators we know a lot more about children's thinking and theories of learning than we utilize in the classroom teaching and learning situation. In short, we know better methods than those we employ. If, however, we are to develop our students academically, socially, and emotionally in order that they can become contributing members in our democratic society, then we must quit spoon-feeding them by oversimplifying every premise included in the curriculum. In so doing, we cut off their desire to engage in problem solving, critical, or creative thinking. These types of thinking are the real attributes of an educational institution and should be the major purposes for its existence. Good teaching involves the creating of problem situations which compel the individual or group to arrive at an acceptable solution to a given problem with a minimum of teacher guidance. Of course it is possible for a teacher to break a problem down into its various components and lead the childern to understand and solve it, but it can hardly be said in that case that they engaged themselves in real problem solving thinking at the highest level.

UTILIZING PROBLEM SOLVING PROCEDURES IN TEACHING

Before a teacher can lead his class into problem solving study and thought he must understand exactly what constitutes a problem and what problem solving actually entails. A problem, according to Russell, may be defined as "a task which a child can understand but for which he does not have an immediate solution," and problem solving "is the process by which the child goes from the task or problem as he sees it to a solution which, for

---

[25]J. Stanley Gray, "What Sort of Education Is Required for Democratic Citizenship?" *School and Society,* Volume 42, Number 1081, (September, 1935), pp. 353-5.

him, meets the demands of the problem."[26] Gates, Jersild, McConnell, and Challman have said that, "A problem exists for an individual when he has a definite goal that he cannot reach by the behavior patterns which he already has available. Problem solving occurs when there is an obstruction of some sort to the attainment of an objective,"[27] and Brownell has stated that, "problem solving becomes the process by which the subject extricates himself from his problem."[28]

For a problem to be worthy of consideration in the teaching and learning situation it must possess two essential characteristics: "first, there must be concern about it, some tension that can only be resolved by the solution of the problem; and second, there must be more than one possible solution so that a choice is involved."[29] When the curiosity of an individual or class has been sufficiently aroused by a problem which is significant and appropriate, problem solving thought may be embarked upon. As an example, consider a sixth grade classroom of students which has been studying the concept of volume in arithmetic. They have learned that to determine the volume of a cylinder they need only to apply the arithmetical formula $V = \pi r^2 h$. Through experimentation they have concluded that this formula will yield the volume of a given amount of liquid or solid contained in any cylinder. The students' thinking to this point has been largely inductive.

Problem solving thinking could be induced by confronting the students with a set of circumstances for which the answer is not evident. In order for them to solve the problem, they must rely upon the application of the principle of volume measurement previously learned. To illustrate, suppose that the students had computed the volume of a given amount of water in a glass beaker. Then suppose the teacher showed them a small rock which he had picked up on the school playground and they were asked if they could compute its volume. Likely the class would look at the ill-shaped rock and immediately recognize that it had no measurable dimensions. At this point, problem solving thinking is called forth. The class would probably hypothesize many ways of figuring the volume of the rock. Some students might conclude that because the rock is without dimension it would be impossible to compute its volume. Through problem solving thought, or trial-and-error activities, the students would work at the prob-

---

[26]Russell, op. cit., p. 251.

[27]Arthur I. Gates, Arthur T. Jersild, T. R. McConnell, and Robert C. Challman, *Educational Psychology.* (third edition; New York: The Macmillan Company, 1949), p. 449.

[28]Brownell, op. cit., p. 416.

[29]Lavone A. Hanna, Gladys L. Potter, and Neva Hagaman, *Unit Teaching in the Elementary School* (revised edition; New York: Holt, Rinehart, and Winston, Inc., 1963), p. 212.

lem until one, several, or all of them formulated the theory that it would be relatively easy to measure the volume of the rock simply by dropping it into a beaker of water for which the volume had been ascertained. Then compute the volume of water in the beaker containing the rock and the difference in these two volumes would be equivalent to the volume of the rock. In essence, this is problem solving thinking in its truest form. This type of problem solving thought has been schematically outlined by Hanna, Potter, and Hagaman as depicted in Figure 24.

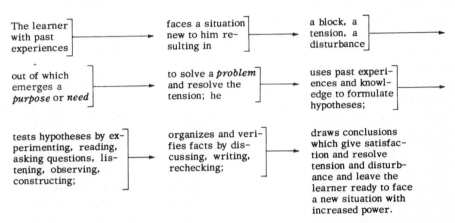

Figure 24. "Flow Chart" of a Complete Living Experience. Adapted from Paul R. Hanna, "Flow Chart" of a complete Living Experience (Stanford University, N.D., mimeographed) by Lavone A. Hanna, Gladys L. Potter, and Neva Hagaman, *Unit Teaching In The Elementary School* (revised edition; New York: Holt, Rinehart and Winston, Inc., 1963) p. 212. Reprinted by permission of Holt, Rinehart and Winston, Inc.

Just as the sixth graders solved the *academic* problem of computing the volume of a rock, it is also possible to solve *social-living* problems. A case in point, as outlined by Tiegs and Adams, concerned a first grade class in a small rural school where every day at lunch time the students were jammed up in cloakroom traffic trying to secure their dinner pails. To alleviate this condition utilizing the problem solving approach:

> The teacher wisely helped the children state the problem as follows: "How can we get our lunch pails without crowding together and trampling on coats and hats that are pulled down?"
> At first no one had any suggestion regarding possible solutions, but the teacher did get the children to talk about the difficulties they experienced. Nevertheless, she refrained from making any suggestions.

Finally the possible solutions began to pop: "Keep pails at our desks"; "have someone pass out the pails"; "let only one pupil at a time get his lunch"; "have pupils go in one door of the cloakroom single file, pick up their pails, and go out the other." At this point there were plenty of suggestions but no agreement on any one suggestion. The class tried out the different suggestions and, needless to say, the last one mentioned above was adopted.[30]

PROBLEM SOLVING AND THE STUDENT

Problem solving involves the application of scientific inquiry techniques by the student in order to prove or disprove a given hypothesis to meet a basic need. Since it is impossible for students to memorize all relevant facts concerning any or all topics in the public school curriculum and then be able to recall them at some later date, it is extremely important that they learn the mechanics of problem solving which will enable them to cope satisfactorily with unknown future circumstances. The mastery of unrelated isolated facts does not constitute good educational theory or practice. The application of these facts to lifelike situations and the other disciplines does, however, represent good pedagogical technique and this approach to teaching and learning is best effected through the utilization of the problem solving procedure. The mastery of facts is not an end within itself; it is only a means to an end. What a student does with the facts after he acquires them is the real test of the success of an educational program.

An elementary curriculum based upon meeting the immediate needs of the students through the problem solving approach is certainly founded on sound educational philosophy. It is evident that any person is far more concerned with his present state of affairs than with unknown future situations. So it is with elementary school children. If their curriculum is based on the here and now — *immediate needs* — and not upon some future eventuality — *deferred needs* — the likelihood of more permanent and fruitful teaching and learning situations is greatly enhanced.

It is possible to develop a curriculum in the elementary school on the basis of meeting the immediate needs of children through the utilization of the problem solving approach without sacrificing the teaching of the basic facts. In fact, the teaching of the basic facts is enhanced by such an approach. This approach to curriculum development and teaching procedure is schematically outlined in Figure 25. This diagram views the problem solving approach as the central core of the curriculum. The subjects which constitute the elementary curriculum content are presented not as separate

[30]Ernest W. Tiegs, and Fay Adams, *Teaching the Social Studies* (New York: Ginn & Co., 1959), pp. 220-221. Reprinted through the courtesy of Blaisdell Publishing Company, a division of Ginn and Company.

entities or unrelated subjects-in-isolation, but rather as a means to an end. In this case, the end is the meeting of immediate needs which eventually will serve as a foundation for meeting deferred needs.

Immediate needs are best met through an unstructured program which is sensitive to the students' interests and requirements. The basic pattern of Figure 25 presents such a program, in effect one which can be tailored specifically to meet immediate student needs and interests. This approach to curriculum development contrasts vividly with the more traditional method of drill and subjects-in-isolation technique whereby the teacher is considered to be a dispenser of facts. Under the subjects-in-isolation technique the curriculum is viewed as possessing certain basic understandings — facts — which will be necessary to the student at some future time in order to meet his deferred needs. The two approaches present quite a contrast. The former is child-centered and the latter is teacher-centered. One technique capitalizes upon student interests in the mastery of curriculum content to meet basic needs, both immediate and future, while the other views the curriculum content as an end in itself, not as a means to an end. In the latter case, mastery of content is of paramount importance and little consideration is given to student interests or immediate needs. The meeting of the curriculum requirements in this instance becomes the immediate problem needing solution rather than allowing the students to identify problems which interest them within the curriculum to engage in scientific problem solving activities. Russell has summarized this point well in stating that "A number of writers have suggested that the typical school hands too many problems to pupils, problems which do not concern them, and for whose solution the only motivation is the teacher's approval. These may be problems to the teacher, but they are not problems to the child."[31]

At this point, the question might well be raised, "How do you utilize the problem solving technique to teaching and learning in the child-centered approach without viewing facts in various subjects as separate entities with each discipline maintaining its own identity with its unique individual body of knowledge?" The answer to this question can best be explained by illustration. First, consider that there are several distinct steps in good problem solving procedure. Let us assume that there are seven basic steps in problem solving endeavor as follows:

1. Environmental conditions which precipitate a problem
2. An awareness of the problem and desire to solve it
3. Analyzing and defining the problem
4. Identifying possible solutions to the problem

---

[31]Russell, *op. cit.*, p. 366.

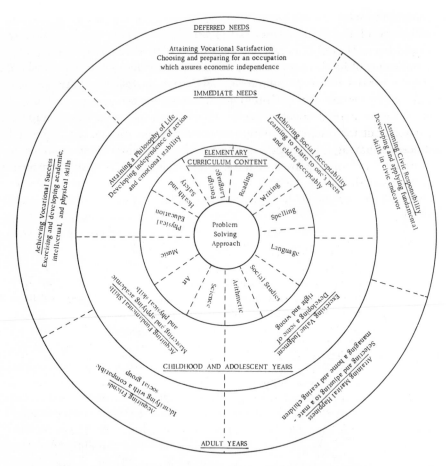

Figure 25. Schema for utilizing problem solving approach in mastery of curriculum through meeting immediate needs and eventually the deferred needs of the students.

5. Collecting and interpreting data related to the problem
6. Testing the most feasible solution to the problem
7. Accepting or rejecting the trial solution

Next, consider that you are an unseen witness in a sixth grade room where the students are just beginning a study of the United Nations. The first thing that you would notice about this child-centered room, which uses the problem solving approach to curriculum development, is the controlled environment. On the bulletin boards you would see thought provoking materials concerning the United Nations. The reading table would contain the latest books, pamphlets, and brochures about the organization and work of the United Nations. At an interest center in the room, you would see a United Nations flag displayed with narratives explaining the significance of its various colors and symbols. The interest center also would contain various filmstrips related to the United Nations' purposes, membership, and program with a filmstrip projector or individual televiewers for group or individual student study. All of this is done to create a proper environment for problem solving. Suppose that the students, stimulated by the environment, identify the problem "Why is the United Nations important to us?" As an unseen witness monitoring the pedagogical techniques of a person skilled in teaching through the problem solving approach, you would likely see the development of a solution to the pupil query as follows:

Step 1: Environmental conditions which precipitate a problem —
Through study, the class would reach the conclusion that for centuries men have differed in opinions concerning such important issues as government, politics, religion, commerce, etc. to the extent that sometimes they have resorted to war to settle their differing points of view.

Step 2: An awareness of the problem and desire to solve it —
As a result of this study, the class might conclude, as world leaders have, that war is not a very humane way to settle differences between nations and purpose to find a more humanistic way of peacefully reconciling differing opinions.

Step 3: Analyzing and defining the problem —
In analyzing the problem the class would probably conclude that too often men have resorted to the brutalities of war to settle their problems and that frequently the greater military power triumphed instead of the matter's being settled by arbitration on the soundness of the philosophical issues involved. The basic problem might be defined as follows:
"Since men for centuries have resorted to war many times to settle their differences, a more acceptable method must be found to reconcile differing points of view."

Step 4: Identifying possible solutions to the problem —
The students would pose several hypotheses which could lead to a settlement of the issue such as:

1. Direct arbitration between the nations involved
2. The act of censorship through aligning other nations sympathetic with the cause of either side (friendship treaties)
3. Appeal to a world court (United Nations)
4. Resort to war itself.

Step 5: Collecting and interpreting data related to the problem —
The class would then gather and analyze significant data con-

cerning the nature and history of arbitration, friendship treaties, world courts and war itself as a means of settling differences between nations.

Step 6: Testing the most feasible solution to the problem —
A study of the data acquired and assimilated in Step 5 should lead the students to deduce that there are many inequities in direct arbitration, friendship treaties, and war itself. Therefore, they would likely conclude that the most equitable and intellectual method of settling differences between countries is the world court as found in the organization of the United Nations. The ability of the United Nations to act as a world court and deter unjust and unwarranted aggression and reconcile differences between countries could be tested by a study of its effect upon world history since its formation on October 24, 1945.

Step 7: Accepting or rejecting the trial solution —
The class will likely accept the United Nations as an acceptable solution for solving disputes between different peoples when they discover that through its efforts issues have been settled over the past two decades with a minimum use of force. Also, since the likelihood of another global war has been greatly reduced as a result of the work accomplished in the United Nations' ability to establish a more peaceful method of settling differences between countries, they should be allowed the privilege of investigating other feasible methods to accomplish the same purpose. In fact, they should be encouraged to do so.

It would be easy for the class to conclude at the end of this problem solving venture that justice, equality, and better prospects for peace in the world community answers their initial problem question, "Why is the United Nations important to us?" Through this discovery approach, the children should be allowed to formulate their own conclusions objectively and unemotionally on the basis of the facts derived from the study.

In answering this problem, the students cut across subject matter boundaries in their quest for an answer. Some of the related outcomes of the problem solving approach to learning follow.

Language Arts

The children developed their reading and research skills as they gathered and analyzed pertinent data. They learned how to use the index of books and developed ability to use the dictionary as they looked up the meanings of words new to them. Hence, they correlated spelling as well as writing with their studies since it was necessary to record data accurately for use in both oral and written reports in connection with their investigation. As a result, grammar was a part of their studies through the problem solving approach.

Arithmetic

Many quantitative concepts had to be applied by the children to reach a solution to their basic problem, which necessitated practical application of arithmetic skills. Such problems as "How many countries were charter members of the United Nations and what is the total membership today"; "What is the per capita annual cost of each United States citizen's share for operating the United Nations and what was the percentage increase or decrease in that cost since its inception in 1945"; "What has been the change in number of troops that the United Nations has had at its disposal from its beginning until now?" These are but a few of the questions which likely arose in the development and solution of the problem. These queries serve as an indicator of how arithmetic can be correlated with the other subject matter areas in problem solving procedure.

Science

This discipline was integrated into this study when the students investigated the work of the Food and Agriculture Organization (FAO) of the United Nations. As a result, they should have learned how this organization works to raise the standard of living in underprivileged nations by providing monetary and technical assistance in helping them to cultivate more and better crops to alleviate hunger and malnutrition. Some of the scientific areas touched upon in the problem solving approach would be an increased understanding of soils and plant propagation, weather, farm machinery, irrigation, and forestry. The students, in seeking a solution to their problem, also would read about the World Health Organization (WHO) of the United Nations and learn of its scientific endeavors to improve the health of people everywhere. They would learn that this organization has carried on extensive campaigns against malaria, tuberculosis, and cholera in the underprivileged nations and that it is continually endeavoring to raise standards of living in environments where these diseases are prevalent.

Music and Art

These areas could have been correlated with the other subject matter in the problem solving study by providing opportunities for the children to learn folk songs of different countries of the United Nations and do art work and handicrafts which depict various aspects of their culture.

A well defined problem such as "Why is the United Nations important to us?" can lead to the correlation and integration of subject matter content from the various disciplines for students in the problem solving approach. It can hardly be said that the traditional lecture method of teaching, which may be called "explanation," could accomplish this wide breadth of integration and application of subject matter content.

The sequence of steps in the problem solving approach to teaching and learning is schematically presented in Figure 26. The diagram portrays that the core of the problem solving processes stems from the environmental conditions which precipitate a problem. The natural outgrowth of the environmental conditions which caused the problem is for man to become aware of it and desire to reach an acceptable solution. The subsequent steps in reflective thinking leading to problem solving are to analyze and define the problem; identify possible solutions; collect and interpret significant related data; test the most feasible solution and, finally, accept or reject the trial solution. Once the problem solving processes have led to an answer of the illustrated problem depicted by Figure 26, "Why is the United Nations important to us?" other related and equally challenging problems will have been identified for further study. In short, the problem solving approach to teaching sets off a chain process of study, investigation, and experimentation leading to the mastery of problems significant to the students themselves to meet their immediate as well as their deferred needs.

Understanding to Be Developed in Problem Solving Thinking

Learning without understanding is empty and futile. A child can be taught that 2 and 2 is 4, but until he understands the number ideas behind the abstract numerals 2 and 4 it can hardly be said that he has experienced learning in its highest form. So it is with problem solving thinking. Students should develop certain understandings in problem solving reverie if they are to become adept thinkers. Understandings which they need to develop in reflective thinking have been defined by Burton, Kimball, and Wing as follows:

1. All statements and conclusions must have a basis in (a) facts, and (b) logically organized sequence of argument.
2. All persons need to learn to be objective and systematic in deriving statements.
3. Rumor, hearsay, gossip, and personal opinion are not evidence and cannot be substituted for facts or logic. Personal experience when properly evaluated produces evidence.
4. Some questions and problems are susceptible to reasonably precise and valid answers — for the time being. Other questions and problems will always have tentative and general answers.
5. Individual differences of interpretation, particularly on nonprecise materials, are inevitable. Certain differences of opinion result from dishonesty in one or more individuals; others are based on wholly honest grounds.

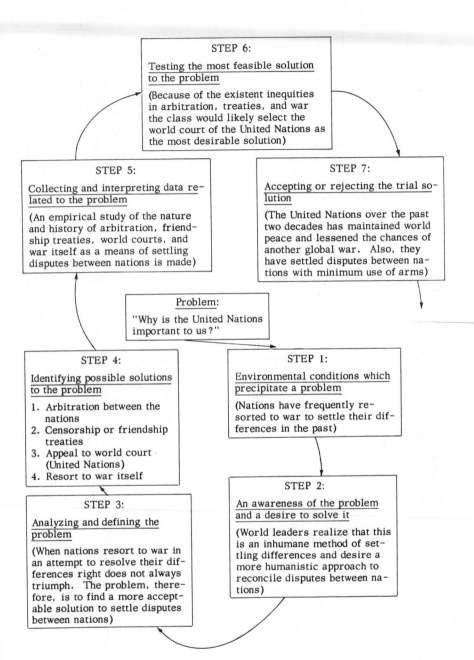

STEP 6:

Testing the most feasible solution to the problem

(Because of the existent inequities in arbitration, treaties, and war the class would likely select the world court of the United Nations as the most desirable solution)

STEP 5:

Collecting and interpreting data related to the problem

(An empirical study of the nature and history of arbitration, friendship treaties, world courts, and war itself as a means of settling disputes between nations is made)

STEP 7:

Accepting or rejecting the trial solution

(The United Nations over the past two decades has maintained world peace and lessened the chances of another global war. Also, they have settled disputes between nations with minimum use of arms)

Problem:

"Why is the United Nations important to us?"

STEP 4:

Identifying possible solutions to the problem

1. Arbitration between the nations
2. Censorship or friendship treaties
3. Appeal to world court (United Nations)
4. Resort to war itself

STEP 1:

Environmental conditions which precipitate a problem

(Nations have frequently resorted to war to settle their differences in the past)

STEP 3:

Analyzing and defining the problem

(When nations resort to war in an attempt to resolve their differences right does not always triumph. The problem, therefore, is to find a more acceptable solution to settle disputes between nations)

STEP 2:

An awareness of the problem and a desire to solve it

(World leaders realize that this is an inhumane method of settling differences and desire a more humanistic approach to reconcile disputes between nations)

Figure 26. Schema of activity cycle in problem solving procedure.

257

6. All interpretations, honest and dishonest, have demonstrable back-grounds and causes.[32]

Thus, it goes without saying that if a child is to develop his abiltiy to do scientific problem solving thought he must maintain a thoroughly objective attitude in interpreting, utilizing, and applying facts. Biases and precon-ceived ideas have no place in problem solving thought because they only tend to distort or hamper the emergence of truth.

Attitudes Which Facilitate Problem Solving Thinking

There are certain attitudes which any student should possess if he is to be an articulate problem solver. It is the duty of the teacher to help his students develop proper attitudes which facilitate problem solving thought. It should be borne in mind by the teacher that just as students differ one from the other in academic and social grace skills so do they vary in the degree to which they possess proper attitudes which are conducive to good problem solving thinking. However, the teacher will do well to remember that these attitudes can be taught to and developed by the students just as can academic and social grace skills. Some of the most important attitudes which will expedite problem solving thinking among elementary students follow.

(CURIOUS.) Children are naturally curious. Enthusiastic teaching can do much to further arouse native curiosity among elementary students. Because children normally wish to know *how* and *why*, their intellectual make-up is uniquely geared for problem solving teaching. This attitude is present to a very large degree when children enter the first grade and should not be squelched. Rather, it should be encouraged through the grades and utilized as a vehicle for curriculum development.

(OBJECTIVE.) The students should remain completely objective in en-gaging in problem solving reverie. They should be helped to develop the belief that they ought to suspend judgment on any issue until all available facts have been analyzed and evaluated.

(OPEN-MINDED.) Children should develop a philosophy that as they look for solutions to various problems they will not be bound by preconceptions or biases. The teacher should help them learn how to utilize all available data relative to the problem. This philosophy of open-mindedness should also embrace the idea that they be willing to give up any decision reached in favor of a new one when sufficient evidence warrants such action.

---

[32]William H. Burton, Roland B. Kimball, and Richard L. Wing, *Education for Effective Thinking* (New York: Appleton-Century-Crofts, Inc., © 1960), pp. 109-110. Reprinted by permission of Appleton-Century-Crofts.

(PERSISTENT.) Once the problem has been identified, the child should be encouraged to stick to the task of searching for evidence upon which a reasonably good plan of action can be formulated.

(DECISIVE.) Problem solving thinkers must be able to reach a decision when all of the facts have been analyzed, evaluated and some tentative solutions have been advanced. The individual must be willing to choose an appropriate course of action from among the alternatives. Once the plan is selected he should stick with it if it proves tenable or until a better course of action is found.

Attitudes Which Impede Problem Solving Thinking

Just as there are certain attitudes which facilitate reflective thinking and result in good problem solving thought there are also detrimental attitudes which impede it. The teacher should be aware of the nature of these harmful attitudes and prepared to deal with them. Some of them are listed following.

(UNCURIOUS.) Since by nature children are curious individuals, whenever the teacher encounters one who is uncurious he must evaluate the situation and take action. If the classroom environment and methodology meet the needs of the other students the teacher may assume that something is organically wrong with the child which may be beyond the scope of the school's authority.

(BIASED.) Students who cannot divorce themselves from their biases or prejudgments are hindered in engaging in effective problem solving thinking. Biased thinking can be overcome through effective teacher guidance and teaching technique utilizing the problem solving procedure.

(NARROW-MINDED.) A student who is not willing to consider all of the facts concerning a given issue curtails his ability to engage in purposeful problem solving thinking at the highest level possible. Regrettably some students desire to look only at data which will support their point of view. Narrow-mindedness on the part of the student also can be overcome through patient and understanding teacher direction.

(LACKING PERSISTENCY.) Some children start well to resolve their problems but are easily discouraged and frustrated. Some of them give up the solution before they complete it. If this is allowed to be repeated too many times the child may begin to lose confidence in his ability to resolve issues and may in fact label himself a "quitter." A major goal of the elementary classroom teacher should be to help children develop persistency in resolving their problems.

(LACKING DECISIVENESS.) Problem solving thinking is impeded when an individual student is either not capable of or willing to make a decision or a definite commitment to a given course of action. Such students need patient but persistent teacher direction in developing their capacities to make a decision once evidence has been gathered and analyzed to support such a course of action.

In summary it may be said that both favorable and unfavorable attitudes affect reflective thinking and one's ability to reason out an issue. Basically the individual's attitudes affect "not only what he sees and hears, what he accepts and rejects, but also the very form and method of his thinking."[33] If thinking and study are to be objective among elementary students, then a scientific attitude must prevail.

Abilities to Be Developed in Problem Solving Thinking

Certain abilities are requisite to good problem solving thinking. The degree to which one exercises the following abilities in reflective thinking largely will determine his proficiency:

1. Recognizes and defines problems, identifies issues.
2. Formulates, extends and verifies feasible hypotheses.
3. Collects, selects, or selectively recalls relevant data, differentiates between reliable and unreliable sources, between factual and nonfactual sources.
4. Recognizes reliable experiments.
5. Draws reasonable inferences regarding cause and effect, logical implication, valid generalization, reliable prediction, and accurate description.
6. Recognizes and evaluates implicit assumptions, uses postulational arguments logically, recognizes relevant value systems and uses them reasonably.
7. Recognizes errors and fallacies.
8. Comes to decisions or conclusions, tests them, applies them to pertinent situations.
9. Applies semantic principles to language employed.[34]

Getting At Facts in Problem Solving

There are many ways for students to obtain facts in problem solving pursuits. The methods are so broad that they range all the way from sensory perceptions to highly controlled scientific investigations. Five methods of getting at the facts have been suggested by Burton, Kimball, and Wing as follows:

1. *Observation via the sense organs* of what we see, hear, taste, and the like.

---

[33]*Ibid.*, p. 41.
[34]*Ibid.*, pp. 267-268.

2. *Observation via instruments of precision,* thermometers, rulers, barometers, altimeters, and many others.
3. *Experimental procedure* for the production of facts to be observed. An artificial situation is set up under controls, with systematic variation of factors and precise measurements of results.
4. *Use of printed sources* such as encyclopedias, statistical reports, historical records, summaries of research, log books, and others.
5. *Use of other persons as sources.* Persons as sources may range all the way from naive, uncritical individuals, from plain liars, to those who are competent and credible witnesses. To be an authoritative source one must:

   a. Have established credibility.
   b. Have special competence in the field.
   c. Be recognized by other competent authorities.[35]

Irrespective of how the students get at the facts they must remain open-minded by considering sufficient evidence on differing points of view before making a final decision on any issue. They need to be made aware of how their own individual interest, prejudices, previous modes of thinking, and incorrect assumptions may impede their recognizing significant evidence. They should learn that alignment with a given individual or group on the basis of false loyalties obscures and denies facts, resulting in further errors in thinking. They need to develop the ability to distinguish between opinion and evidence. Finally, they need to improve their data gathering techniques and become more skillful in detecting the attempts of others to mislead their thinking through mass communication media.[36] Whenever a good thinker listens to or reads a statement, he should keep some basic questions in mind which will assist him in evaluating the material. Some of these questions, as suggested by Burton, Kimball, and Wing, are as follows:

What is the intent of the writer?
What are the main arguments advanced?
Are these arguments supported by facts and reason, given or implied?
Do assumptions, hidden or otherwise, lurk behind statements?
What means of evaluation are used for facts, inferences, assumptions?
Do any obvious fallacies appear; any known methods of checking one's thinking?
Is the language that of an honest thinker, or that of a special pleader, or of a propagandist?
Are terms defined, used consistently; or does meaning shift consciously or unconsciously?
Has the writer supported his conclusion so we can give it belief, or has he failed?[37]

[35]*Ibid.,* p. 79.
[36]Tiegs and Adams, *op. cit.,* p. 230.
[37]Burton, Kimball, and Wing, *op. cit.,* p. 13.

PROBLEM SOLVING AND THE TEACHER

Teachers can aid students immeasurably in developing their ability to engage in problem solving thinking. Through establishing an effective, controlled classroom environment, the teacher can cause his students to identify a suitable problem they are interested in and for which they do not have an immediate solution. With their interests aroused toward solving the perplexity, the teacher's job, according to Parker, is:

> (1) guiding the thinking of the pupils; (2) aiding them when confronted by difficulties that are beyond their powers or which they would waste their time in solving; and (3) eventually making them aware of what good thinking is, so that they may consciously strive for it during their thinking, just as they strive to improve their handwriting or their reading.[38]

The teacher will do well to keep some specific rules in mind in order to perform this threefold job objectively. Parker's outline of these rules serves as a good point of reference.[39]

1. *Define Problem.* The success of problem solving teaching and problem solving thought is dependent from its outset upon the clear definition of the problem under investigation. The teacher has a major responsibility at this stage of the process in helping the students identify just what it is that they want to find out.

2. *Keep Problem In Mind.* An impatient person often says, "get to the point." In effect what he is saying is that he does not wish to be bothered with all of the details and that all he desires are the crucial facts. So it is with problem solving. The teacher can help the students keep the problem in mind by skillfully directing their efforts toward "sticking to the point." If the students do not keep the problem well in mind, there will be lost time and motion which may result in frustration, boredom, or abandonment of the issue.

3. *Stimulate Suggestions.* It takes a great deal of skill on the part of the teacher to stimulate the class to suggest possible solutions for the problem under consideration. He must be careful not to bias their thinking at this critical stage by expressing any of his own hypotheses or beliefs. Also, he has the responsibility for making it possible for all students to be heard concerning their possible solutions to the dilemma. The teacher can stimulate suggestions and facilitate the solution of the problem at this stage by assisting the students in their analysis of the perplexity, recall of previous related experiences, and formulation of intelligent guesses.

---

[38]Samuel Chester Parker, "Problem-Solving or Practice in Thinking. IV." *The Elementary School Journal*, Volume XXI, Number 4, December, 1920, p. 259.
[39]*Ibid.*, pp. 260-267.

(a. *Analysis of the Problem.*) Students need help from the teacher in assessing the defined problem analytically. Perhaps it will be necessary to break the problem down into parts, each requiring its own solution. In that case, the teacher might help the class set up some type of priority on the problems and then assist them in attacking each part separately.

(b. *Recall of Previous Related Experience.*) Since problem solving is largely empirical, the students will have to recall as many previous experiences as they can which are relative to the problem to have a firm foundation upon which to formulate an acceptable solution. The teacher's knowledge of their past experiences as well as their school experiences will enable him to suggest events which will assist them in working out their problem.

(c. *Formulating Intelligent Guesses Which Will Lead to the Solution of the Problem.*) The teacher should encourage his students to make intelligent guesses which might possibly help solve the problem. The teacher also should be aware that intelligent guesses cannot be made where there is a void of student experiences pertaining to the problem. It therefore is imperative that he help the students recall all factors which they can relate to the problem under study.

4. *Evaluate Suggestions.* In evaluating suggested solutions to the problem, the teacher should encourage the students to maintain a sense of open-mindedness; learn to critically evaluate each solution upon its own merits, and to verify their solutions and conclusions before accepting them as proven panaceas.

(a. *Maintaining a Sense of Open-mindedness.*) Our courts have long held that a man is innocent until proven guilty. In like manner, students should be taught by their teacher to suspend judgment on any issue until all of the facts are assessed and the problem is ultimately resolved. Students who can maintain an open mind concerning a given issue will not suffer consequences resulting from hasty decisions. In addition they will develop a sense of "fair play" through examining both sides of an issue before finalizing a belief.

(b. *Critically Evaluate Proposed Solutions.*) The teacher's efforts in helping students learn to evaluate hypothetical solutions to their problems will be amply repaid in time saved. The students need to be taught that before they select a method of attacking a given problem they must reason out the implications of such a procedure. They may find that the solution will work but that there are others which are to be preferred. Students need to be reminded that "haste makes waste."

(c. *Verify Their Solutions and Conclusions.*) Once a solution has been tested and found satisfactory the students need to be reminded that before they accept it as feasible they had better verify their findings. This step is particularly important in scientific problem solving where the rigid control of the variable must be maintained.

5. *Keep Discussion Organized.* Sound organizational practices are imperative in problem solving procedure. The teacher should assist the students in maintaining an outline of the main points concerning the problem; utilizing diagrams and graphs in recording pertinent basic facts so they are easily accessible and assimilable, and summarizing frequently the work accomplished and future steps necessary which will lead to a successful solution.

The general rules suggested here which will aid the teacher in conducting effective problem solving lessons may be reduced to the brief outline form suggested by Parker as follows:

1. Get them to define the problem clearly
2. Aid them to keep the problem in mind
3. Get them to make many suggestions by encouraging them
   (a) to analyze the situation into parts
   (b) to recall previously known similar cases and general rules that apply
   (c) to guess courageously and formulate guesses clearly
4. Get them to evaluate each suggestion carefully by encouraging them
   (a) to maintain a state of doubt or suspended conclusion
   (b) to criticize the suggestion by anticipating objections and consequences
   (c) to verify conclusions by appeal to known facts, miniature experiments, and scientific treatises
5. Get them to organize the material by proceeding
   (a) to build an outline on the board
   (b) to use diagrams and graphs
   (c) to take stock from time to time
   (d) to formulate concise statements of the net outcome of the discussion[40]

The Place of Drill in Problem Solving

The teacher who utilizes the problem solving technique in teaching should recognize that there is also a place for drill in the instructional program. It is evident that mastery of any given fact or concept is enhanced through appropriate drill exercises. Drill and problem solving actually complement one another. Through the problem solving activities in the social studies and science the students will see the need for drill in the areas of reading, spelling, language, handwriting, and arithmetic if they are to effec-

---

[40]*Ibid.,* p. 267.

tively solve problems of interest. They will recognize that if they are to read to acquire data relative to the solution of their problem, they must master the art of reading. The same generalization applies to the other areas of the curriculum wherein drill is deemed indispensable for mastery.

If students are to record data and write reports they must drill for mastery in handwriting. They must learn to spell effectively if their writing is to be correct. Too, they will experience a need for mastery of language or grammar and see the necessity of drill so they can be grammatically correct in their writing and speaking. Many problems will call for the understanding of certain quantitative concepts as an acceptable solution is devised. Students therefore will doubtlessly desire drill exercises in arithmetic which will lead to a mastery of these concepts. Concerning the place of drill in the problem solving approach to teaching and learning, Parker has said:

> . . emphasis on problem-solving should not lead to a neglect of routine drill of the type that prevails in the modern scientific teaching of handwriting, spelling, reading, and arithmetic. The necessity of such drill has been amply demonstrated in scientific investigations; and its presence in the school need not interfere at all with the adequate organization of problem-solving. Both may proceed in the same day without mutual interference, e. g., during the handwriting and spelling periods, the most intense, gainful, effective drills may be carried on, with little or no problem activity, while in some of the history and geography periods the most intense reflective problem-solving may prevail.[41]

In effect the problem solving technique provides the students with a vehicle that will enable them to facilitate transfer of learning as they apply the facts mastered through drill to problematic situations. The acquisition of unrelated and functionless items of knowledge through memorization is meaningless. Facts become meaningful when they are applied to problem situations. What a competent teacher should therefore be doing "is not handing out ideas and conclusions ready-made, to be memorized and passed back, parrotlike, in a recitation, but stimulating pupils to acquire information as a means of bringing about desirable consequences, as a means of solving their own problems."[42] However, one can conclude "that the ability to reason, including the ability to discover relationships and to use previous experience in meeting new situations, develops gradually," according to Gates, Jersild, McConnell, and Challman, and "this suggests that there should be no level of education where learning is exclusively devoted

---

[41]*Ibid.*, p. 268.
[42]Gates, Jersild, McConnell, and Challman, *op. cit.*, p. 479.

to the acquisition of facts or entirely given over to reflective thinking. The two processes should develop together."[43]

Principles to Guide Children's Thinking

Teachers who are proficient in problem solving teaching have been skillful in guiding children's thinking. They have been careful to make their teaching child-centered instead of teacher-centered. They have acquired a good understanding of how children think and have adjusted their instructional programs to promote desired pupil thought. Some general principles which teachers may use for guiding children's thinking are:

1. Provide a permissive classroom atmosphere in which the child is encouraged to ask *why* and *how* in the pursuit of knowledge.
2. Teaching should be of a divergent rather than a convergent nature. In convergent teaching too much emphasis is placed upon having pupils master content as an end in itself. Hence, thinking is curtailed through explanation and drill. In divergent teaching the child confronts a given fact and is curious as to the *why* and *so what* of it. Thus, he is in a position to think about the origin and nature of the fact as well as its possible applications.
3. Children differ markedly in their ability to engage in purposeful reflective thinking. Appropriate provisions should be made for these varying levels of differences.
4. Children's thinking is facilitated through the provision of many direct experiences which will meet some immediate need appropriate to their maturational level.
5. The teacher should exercise precaution in avoiding the pitfall of expecting children to conform to his own preconceived ideas. Children should be allowed to exercise their own judgment thereby releasing their creative potentials.
6. The processes by which children do their thinking cannot be forced upon them. The teacher can, however, help the children discover and develop these thinking processes.
7. The natural inquisitiveness of children should serve as the spontaneous catalyst to motivate elementary school children to do problem solving, critical, and creative thinking.
8. Rarely, if ever, should children's thinking be characterized by students "parroting back" teacher opinions.
9. The mastery of subject matter does not necessarily result in problem solving thinking. Since one's ability to retain and recall facts is relatively short, common sense would dictate that the ability to apply such information is much more important than mere memorization of content. The application of facts to lifelike situations calls forth the best thinking.
10. Children should be provided some time for thinking in which they can reflect on previous direct and vicarious experiences in the light

---

[43]*Ibid.*, p. 448.

of an issue at hand. Also, they need time to read from references which relate to the issue. As they read and recall, if sufficient time is provided, they should be able to formulate intelligent decisions with minimal teacher guidance.

The Teacher and Group Problem Solving

What has been said to this point about problem solving has dealt primarily with the individual student. As the teacher works with his children, however, there will be many occasions to engage in group problem solving ventures. This will be particularly true as the class as a whole develops a unit of work in the social studies or in science. There are a few principles about working with groups in the problem solving process that are helpful to the teacher. Some of these principles, according to Thorndike, are:

1. The group typically brings a broader background of experience to a problem situation than does any single individual.
2. As a reflection of 1, the group is likely to produce more and more varied suggestions for dealing with a problem than will arise from a single individual.
3. The diversity of viewpoints is *likely* to be more representative of the larger population from which they were drawn than is the viewpoint of the single individual.
4. As diversity of background and interest within the group becomes greater, it becomes increasingly difficult to reach a real agreement among the members of the group as to the definition of the problem and the values to be served. Reconciliation of conflicting goals becomes a real problem.
5. Just as a group is likely to produce a greater range of suggestions, so also a group is likely to be more productive in criticisms of proposals and bases for rejecting them.
6. Interstimulation is a distinctive feature of group effort. The suggestion by X, which is criticized by Y, serves as the stimulus to Z for a new and perhaps quite different suggestion.
7. Interpersonal dynamics becomes a significant element. The assertive, the dogmatic, and the persuasive individual — each plays a distinctive role.
8. With increasing size and diversity of group membership, unity and integration of effort are often difficult to achieve. Group members may show a tendency to "ride off in all directions."[44]

Children should learn respect for the views of others and gain a sense of cooperation in teamwork through group problem solving endeavors. The wise teacher should recognize the significance of this possibility and

---

[44]Thorndike, *op. cit.*, p. 209.

utilize this medium effectively to teach not only the academic skills but also the social graces skills so essential to living in a democratic society.

Teacher-Parent Cooperation in Problem Solving Procedure

The wise classroom teacher enlists the parents in helping their children become proficient in problem solving. Through the patient direction of the teacher the parents can become informed on things which facilitate problem solving abilities, as well as those which act as a deterrent to their children. Some of the principles the parent and teacher need to be aware of and things they can do separately or jointly to aid student reflective thinking have been enumerated by Russell as follows:

1. Children and adolescents need to be encouraged to present their own problems, not admonished to think clearly.
2. Success in problem solving, as in much other behavior, depends largely on the child's motivation. The child must feel that the task is important to him, that it is related to some of his other interests and activities. The problem must be *his*.
3. Problem solving as a phase of thinking can be taught, at least in part, because it involves factors which are susceptible to control and to learning through experience.
4. Many children have an active curiosity and an urge to overcome difficulties, both of which attitudes give them a good start as problem solvers, particularly in puzzle situations. The teacher and parent must be aware of the level of difficulty at which the problem can be presented. The individual's and the group's level of aspiration gives clues to the complexity of problems which may be successfully presented.
5. Parents and teachers must avoid providing ready-made solutions to children's problems. Time and patience are not always inexhaustible, but they are certainly desirable when an adult and a child face a problem together.
6. The development of meanings in the problem area is usually a first step toward the solution of problems.
7. Parents and teachers may help the child by calling his attention to any material in the stimulus situation which he does not perceive and to the objective which is to be attained.
8. Pupils can be encouraged to modify an objective as it becomes clearer to them through experience.
9. Parents and teachers can assist pupils in using the inductive-deductive method in cases where definitions, rules, and other generalizations are to be learned.
10. Children and adolescents can be encouraged to raise questions, check sources, and otherwise test the relevancy and worth of ideas suggested. Evaluation is a continuous process in problem solving.

11. Children need opportunities for observation, for using their memory, and time for recollection.
12. Parents and teachers can help children to face, not avoid, basic personal problems by guiding them in their early search for solutions.
13. Older children can be taught to recognize some of the common errors of logic, such as the use of inaccurate analogy or the neglect of negative instances.
14. Inability to solve problems in any particular field may be caused by difficulties with specific techniques. Faulty reading of a problem in social studies or errors in computation in arithmetic may affect solutions unfavorably. Children need to be helped in finding specific causes for their errors.
15. The scientific method may be generalized and verbalized with older children to provide them with a possible series of steps for solving problems and for checking the validity of conclusions.
16. Testing solutions in action provides one of the best antidotes to extreme verbalization in problem solving.[45]

PROBLEM SOLVING AND THE SCHOOL

The previous pages of this chapter have set forth a theory, an ideal in which the school's major responsibility in education is to teach children *how* to think; not *what* to think. Hullfish and Smith have set the issue squarely before us with their cogent question, "If young people do not learn to think while in school, it is fair to ask: *How are they to keep on learning?*"[46] What then is the school's role in teaching students how to think? It may be said with authority that what the school should do is provide a stimulating habitat for reflective thinking so that the students can become less dependent upon the teacher for ideas and more independent and self-directing individually. Dewey recognized this premise and set the issue straight in his statement:

> No one doubts, theoretically, the importance of fostering in school good habits of thinking. But apart from the fact that the acknowledgment is not so great in practice as in theory, there is not adequate theoretical recognition that all which the school can or need do for pupils, so far as their *minds* are concerned (that is, leaving out certain muscular abilities), is to develop their ability to think. The parceling out of instruction among various ends such as acquisition of skill (in reading, spelling, writing, drawing, reciting); acquiring information (in history and geography), and training of thinking is a measure of the ineffective way in which we accomplish all three. Thinking which is not connected with increase of

[45]Russell, *op. cit.*, pp. 376-377.
[46]H. Gordon Hullfish and Philip G. Smith, *Reflective Thinking: The Method of Education.* (New York: Dodd, Mead & Company, 1961), p. 3.

efficiency in action, and with learning more about ourselves and the world in which we live, has something the matter with it . . .[47]

The methods which the average school has utilized in developing the curriculum for its elementary children is in firm contradiction to the theory of developing problem solving thinkers. The average school has done just what Dewey described as the "ineffective way" and has autocratically explained away the concepts inherent in each. The primary method of teaching has largely been assign-study-recite-test, a never ending cycle of frequently unrelated experiences which breeds boredom and frustration. Hullfish and Smith have analyzed the dilemma that the schools find themselves in with their analytical statement:

> Too many of us, in school and out, have assumed that the ability of an individual to repeat the thoughts of others provides evidence that he is an independent thinker. We forget that parrots are not notably reflective. Were we to remember this, we might discover that the time for a teacher to be worried, apart from those moments when facts which are beyond dispute are at issue, is when all in a class agree with him. It is a sad fact that classrooms are frequently intimidated by the tyranny of the right answer, *the answer none dare question*.[48]

Our modern elementary schools must develop an organizational framework which is flexible enough to allow for the development of each child's thinking capactiy in order that he can be "challenged through individual and group activities that will provide him with opportunities to study and analyze facts and data, synthesize related ideas, utilize concepts, reflect on issues, consider differing points of view, and formulate generalizations."[49] In the end, according to Hullfish and Smith:

> The effective way of teaching, once decisions have been made as to which facts should be emphasized at each stage of growth, is the reflective way. It is effective because it is man's sole way of providing for a continuity of learning that will carry beyond the classroom into the continuing affairs of life. When coverage of knowledge and the fostering of thought conflict, therefore, it is but elementary educational wisdom to give the right of way to thinking.[50]

---

[47]John Dewey, *Democracy and Education* (New York: The Macmillan Company, 1930), p. 179.

[48]Hullfish and Smith, *op. cit.*, p. 24.

[49]John U. Michaelis, *Social Studies for Children in a Democracy, Recent Trends and Developments*, (third edition; Englewood Cliffs, N. J.: Prentice-Hall, Inc., 1963), p. 85. Reprinted by permission of Prentice-Hall, Inc.

[50]Hullfish and Smith, *op. cit.*, pp. 228-229.

SUMMARY

Effective teaching in the elementary school may be accomplished through helping children learn *how* to think as opposed to telling them *what* to think. Since education is a continuous process, a student who has been equipped with the tools of learning *how* to think can ferret out necessary solutions to the problems of living as occasions require. Conversely, the student who is taught *what* to think may experience difficulty in resolving subsequent issues as a result of teaching in which he simply learns to parrot back mere facts or the ideas of others.

Basically the processes of children's thinking may be classified as perceptual, associative, inductive, critical, problem solving, or creative. The first three types seldom lead to problem solving per se, whereas the last three normally do.

The problem solving technique of curriculum development lends itself well to teaching children *how* to think. When students are encouraged to seek solutions to problems which interest them they are acquiring the skills of scientific inquiry which will equip them to meet their immediate and deferred needs. As they resolve cogent problems, they will cut across the artificial subject matter boundaries in a quest for knowledge. Hence, subject matter may be more easily correlated and integrated in the problem solving approach to teaching and learning in the elementary school than other plans. Likewise, drill in the fundamental skills of reading, writing, computing, speaking, and listening may be accomplished as a natural outgrowth of problem solving procedure.

Students can be taught how to engage in problem solving thinking. Certain attitudes such as curiosity, objectivity, open-mindedness, persistence, and decisiveness aid the student in engaging in purposeful problem solving pursuits. Conversely, the absence of these attitudes may hinder such thinking. The role of the teacher in problem solving teaching extends far beyond the establishment of proper attitudes, however. He must help children develop the ability to: (1) define a problem, (2) formulate some hypotheses which may lead to its solution, (3) gather and analyze pertinent data, (4) reach a conclusion by accepting one of the hypotheses for trial, (5) test the conclusion with its various possibilities, and (6) evaluate the outcomes.

Teaching children how to think in the elementary school is sound pedagogical technique. Should a conflict arise between the dispensation of knowledge and the engendering of thought, it is only logical to give preeminence to thinking.

QUESTIONS FOR DISCUSSION

1. Contrast teaching by explanation or "telling" and teaching through modes of scientific inquiry. Is it better to tell children "what" to think or to teach them "how" to think? Explain.
2. Explain the term "reflective thinking." Do all educable children engage in reflective thinking? Why?
3. What distinctions can you name which illustrate the different types of thinking of children? How do you account for certain processes of children's thinking that do not ordinarily lead to problem solving while there are other processes of thinking which normally lead to problem solving?
4. Many educators have contended that the school should concern itself primarily with meeting the immediate needs of children and place less emphasis upon their deferred needs. What is your position on this issue? Explain.
5. What are the various mental processes which an individual employs in problem solving thinking? Illustrate your answer by applying these different processes or steps in thinking to a hypothetical problem.
6. What are some of the student attitudes which facilitate problem solving thinking? Discuss them. What are some of the attitudes of learners which impede problem solving thinking? Discuss them.
7. How would you work with children to enable them to become more facile in problem solving thinking? How would you teach them to analyze facts in problem solving procedure?

TOPICS FOR RESEARCH

1. Re-examine the different curriculum patterns discussed in Chapter 3 of this text and determine which of these plans would be most compatible with problem solving teaching.
2. Visit an elementary school and look for evidences of problem solving teaching. Note the children's responses to this method. Compare your findings with those in rooms where you find the explanation or "telling" method being utilized extensively.
3. Read John Dewey's *How We Think* and David Russell's *Children's Thinking* and share the information gained with your fellow students or colleagues.

BIBLIOGRAPHY

BECK, ROBERT H., WALTER W. COOK, AND NOLAN C. KEARNEY. *Curriculum in the Modern Elementary School.* Second edition. Englewood Cliffs, N. J.: Prentice-Hall, Inc., 1960.

BROWNELL, WILLIAM A. "Problem Solving," *The Forty-First Yearbook of the National Society for the Study of Education.* Bloomington, Illinois: Public School Publishing Company, 1942.

BURTON, WILLIAM H., ROLAND B. KIMBALL, AND RICHARD L. WING. *Education for Effective Thinking.* New York: Appleton-Century-Crofts, Inc., 1960.

DEWEY, JOHN. *Democracy and Education.* New York: The Macmillan Company, 1930.

DEWEY, JOHN, *How We Think.* New York: D. C. Heath and Co., 1933.

DEWEY, JOHN. *How We Think.* Boston: D. C. Heath and Co., 1910.

GATES, ARTHUR I., ARTHUR T. JERSILD, T. R. McCONNELL, AND ROBERT C. CHALLMAN. *Educational Psychology.* Third edition. New York: The Macmillan Company, 1949.

GRAY, J. STANLEY. "What Sort of Education Is Required for Democratic Citizenship?" *School and Society,* Volume 42, Number 1081, September, 1935, pp. 353-5.

HANNA, LAVONE A., GLADYS L. POTTER, AND NEVA HAGAMAN. *Unit Teaching of the Elementary School.* Revised edition. New York: Holt, Rinehart, and Winston, Inc., 1963.

HERMANOWICZ, HENRY J. "Problem Solving As Teaching Method," *Educational Leadership,* XVIII, No. 5 (February, 1961), p. 302.

HULLFISH, H. GORDON, AND PHILIP G. SMITH, *Reflective Thinking: The Method of Education.* New York: Dodd, Mead & Company, 1961.

KILPATRICK, WILLIAM HEARD. *Foundations of Method.* New York: The Macmillan Company, 1930.

KILPATRICK, WILLIAM HEARD. *Remaking The Curriculum.* New York: Newsom & Company, 1936.

MICHAELIS, JOHN U. *Social Studies for Children in a Democracy.* Third edition. Englewood Cliffs, N. J.: Prentice-Hall, Inc., 1963.

PARKER, SAMUEL CHESTER. "Problem-Solving or Practice in Thinking. IV," *The Elementary School Journal,* Volume XXI, Number 4 (December, 1920), pp. 257-258.

RUSSELL, DAVID H. *Children's Thinking.* Boston: Ginn & Company, 1956.

THORNDIKE, ROBERT L. "How Children Learn the Principles and Techniques of Problem-Solving." *The Forty-Ninth Yearbook of the National Society for the Study of Education, Part I.* Chicago: The University of Chicago Press, 1950.

TIEGS, ERNEST W., AND FAY ADAMS. *Teaching the Social Studies.* New York: Ginn and Company, 1959.

Children reinforce learning through a culminating experience in a unit of work.

Chapter 9

Teaching Through
Unit Instruction

The problem solving approach to learning is the most commonly utilized method of learning in the adult world. As man faces a need, a concern, or an interest he applies the knowledge, the skills, and the techniques he has acquired to satisfy his human drives. Little attention is given to the category from which he draws this knowledge, skill or technique as he attempts to think through a situation, plot a course of action, and muster up the courage to move ahead. Subjects as organized in the schools of today did not exist until after man had encountered a series of experiences around which he assembled a body of content for easy remembering and future use. These have been organized, classified, and labeled for the convenience of the scholars in transmitting them to subsequent generations. Man has constantly sought better methods of transmittal of this ever-accumulating content to others. Through these efforts educators and psychologists have learned that man learns best in meaningful situations, where he finds the answer to his own questions and problems. Educators therefore have continually endeavored to find a better curriculum vehicle within the framework of the public school for the application of this principle.

The unit of work as an approach to providing for learning in meaningful situations was fostered about 1900 with the advent of the philosophies of Dewey and Kilpatrick. Since then the term, unit of work, has been used in some form and under various names, often synonomously with activity program, centers of interest, or child experiences. The term is generally used to designate all the activities and experiences connected with a chosen theme that will contribute to learning and child growth. As such, the unit cuts across subject matter fields and deals with life problems. Emphasis is centered upon the child's own activity — his search for information and enlightenment, his efforts to plan an enterprise and to evaluate the significance and merits of his work. This activity involves the acquisition of useful information and the development of skills, attitudes, and appreciations.

Other definitions and interpretations of the unit approach to teaching are equally acceptable. Among these are Good's definition which defines the unit as:

> An organization of various activities, experiences, and types of learning around a central problem, or purpose, developed cooperatively by a group of pupils under teacher leadership: involves planning, execution of plans, and evaluation of results.[1]

The particular significance of this understanding of the unit is the matter of involvement of the learner in the three major stimulants to learning which are planning, execution, and evaluation. It is through the application of these that teachers are able to best utilize what is known about children's learning and thereby provide direct learning experiences.

PHILOSOPHY OF UNIT INSTRUCTION

The child is the sum total of his past experiences, his background of culture, his hopes and disappointments, and his knowledge of the world about him — all of which he brings to school with him. He thinks, weighs values, makes choices, and shows enthusiasm or contempt in terms of who he is — a unique individual. In describing the unity of the child Noar has stated that:

> From medicine, psychology, and psychiatry teachers learn that the individual grows, develops, and lives as a total entity. Therefore, they know that he cannot be taught as if his physical, mental, and emotional characteristics and abilities were in separate compartments. From psychiatry and mental hygiene teachers also learn that human behavior is caused — partly from within and partly from without. Therefore, they know that the individual cannot be separated from the environment in which he lives. So, as the teacher's understanding of human growth and development and of the social order increases, he realizes that living and learning in the school must be designed to meet the total needs of the individual. The content and methods must take into account the indi-

---

[1]Carter V. Good, (ed.), *Dictionary of Education* (New York: McGraw-Hill Book Company, 1959), p. 587.

vidual's own background, his immediate family life and the society in which he lives.[2]

To expect the child to master school subjects one by one in isolation is to disregard all that has been learned about the growth and development of the individual. Recognizing these important facts, it is imperative that an appropriate learning situation be provided in the classroom. The unit approach to teaching meets this need in that it emphasizes total patterns of learning rather than isolated bits of knowledge presented in a series of daily assign-study-recite topics. Noar has very vividly explained the feasibility of unit teaching as follows:

> Educators have long agreed that the school is responsible for developing ability to think, to integrate facts and weigh them for relative values, to formulate principles, and to draw valid conclusions. Unit teaching provides maximum opportunity to practice and, therefore, to develop the skills of critical thinking and evaluation. Moreover, in unit teaching emphasis shifts from teaching to learning, from listening to doing, from memorizing facts to using them, from copying to creating, from passive acceptance of the teacher's direction to self-direction in learning.[3]

Even though unit teaching which develops a center of interest has been recognized as a sound psychological approach to instruction for many years, several steps in the improvement of teaching methods had to be effected before it could come into its own. These steps have been depicted by Gwynn in Figure 27 as (1) subject matter, (2) correlation, (3) fusion, (4) center of interest teaching, (5) and experience teaching.[4]

The first step away from the single textbook assign-study-recite method came with the correlation of subject-matter areas with materials from related subject areas. An example of this was the teaching of United States history and geography in the same grade. Each subject retained its own content and separate period but studying the two related areas in proximity was helpful to the student in seeing relationships.

The second step in moving from the strict subject matter arrangement was the interrelation of materials from two or more areas into subject-matter teaching referred to as fusion or broad fields. For example, the subjects of history and geography were combined with civics and current events for teaching an area called social studies as one subject.

---

[2]Gertrude Noar, *Teaching and Learning the Democratic Way* (Englewood Cliffs: Prentice-Hall, Inc., 1963), p. 8.

[3]*Ibid.*, pp. 9-10.

[4]J. Minor Gwynn, *Theory and Practice of Supervision* (New York: Dodd, Mead, and Company, 1961), pp. 63-6.

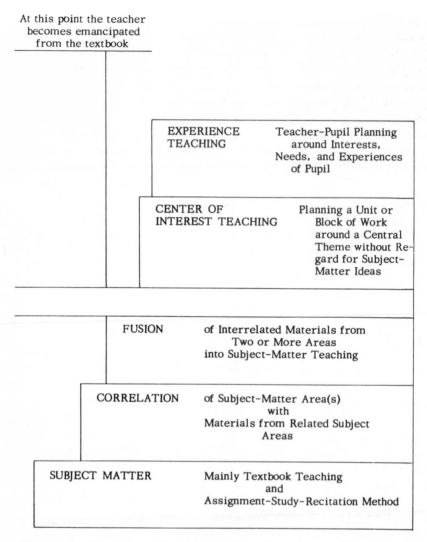

At this point the teacher
becomes emancipated
from the textbook

| EXPERIENCE TEACHING | Teacher-Pupil Planning around Interests, Needs, and Experiences of Pupil |

| CENTER OF INTEREST TEACHING | Planning a Unit or Block of Work around a Central Theme without Regard for Subject-Matter Ideas |

| FUSION | of Interrelated Materials from Two or More Areas into Subject-Matter Teaching |

| CORRELATION | of Subject-Matter Area(s) with Materials from Related Subject Areas |

| SUBJECT MATTER | Mainly Textbook Teaching and Assignment-Study-Recitation Method |

Figure 27. The Steps a Teacher Usually Takes in Going From Textbook Teaching to Teaching Around Centers of Interest by Units. Reprinted from J. Minor Gwynn, *Theory and Practice of Supervision,* © 1961, p. 64. By permission of and arrangement with Dodd, Mead, and Company, New York.

The third step away from subject centeredness involved planning a unit of work around a central theme without regard for subject matter lines. Most often the social studies area served as the base for developing topics that cut across subject matter areas. Content from the various disciplines was drawn upon for the purpose of gaining full understanding of the given topic.

Experience teaching, the fourth move from the single textbook, involving teacher-pupil planning around interests, needs, and experiences of pupils, is recognized as the capstone in educational procedure. In this the problem solving approach seeks to cope with needs and problems that are real to the students within an open schedule and an environment which is rich in instructional media.

Unit teaching is based on sound principles of instruction which guide the educator in providing learning experiences for children. The following principles set forth by Spears serve as a guide to the educator in selecting learning experiences for children:

1. Good teaching is a matter of drawing-out rather than a matter of putting in.
2. Learning is an active and not a passive process.
3. In preparing for citizenship, teaching about democracy isn't nearly as effective as teaching through democratic procedure.
4. Co-operation is a complicated and essential social tool of democracy, the use of which must be taught rather than left to chance or trial and error.
5. The learner cannot be considered aside from his environment.
6. The student who is learning is working for himself rather than for the teacher.
7. We must not mistake conformity for learning.
8. Learning begins where the learner is, not where the teacher is.
9. Learning begins where the child is now, not where he was yesterday or where he will be tomorrow.
10. Growth in school cannot always be measured by a semester or even a year.
11. The teacher cheats the child of part of his education unless he permits him to engage in all three of the closely related aspects of a learning situation, namely, (1) planning the experience, (2) carrying it out, and (3) evaluating it.
12. The child has the right to receive the satisfactions of his schooling here and now, rather than to be promised delivery in the future.
13. Use strengthens and disuse weakens.
14. Praise is a greater educational force than blame.[5]

The foregoing principles, basic to teaching by the unit method, are in keeping with the point of view of Dewey who taught that learning must at all times be purposeful so that the child will achieve understanding and grasp principles. He believed that good teaching was a process of draw-

[5]Harold Spears, *Principles of Teaching* (New York: Prentice-Hall, Inc., 1951) pp. 94-113.

ing out children's abilities rather than imposing ideas on them. He pointed out the dangers of children's memorizing answers to questions propounded by the teacher as the chief teaching technique. He saw interest and effort of the child as complementary rather than opposing forces in learning and education. The motive power back of the effort required to learn, to study, to practice was seen by Dewey as interest. This is contrary to theories of many educators who think that effort is fostered best by difficult and irksome tasks.[6]

The surge of activity and project programs seen in the public schools during the twenties and thirties was a response to Dewey's philosophy and a common sense reaction against the meaningless verbalization and pointless drill that had dominated the schools up to that time. Unfortunately, too many educators got only a smattering of Dewey's philosophy and gained little or none of the technique for carrying out the problem-solving approach to learning in the classroom. Consequently, much aimless and laissez-faire activity went on in the schools which gave the public the wrong image of the "experience" curriculum. In addition to not having teachers prepared for this type teaching, schools were not equipped to provide the variety of different level materials necessary for carrying out the experience program which is basic to problem solving. Also, the general citizenry could not accept so drastic a change from the way they had been educated in the public schools of their day. The ineffectiveness of the movement in the schools was not necessarily an indictment of the educational philosophy but of the preparation for and implementation of the program. Having passed through the stages reviewed, educators, school facilities, and the public are now more ready for an experience type program which implements the unit approach through problem solving.

The term readiness, however, is a relative matter which refers to the general educational front. The readiness of that particular setting for unit instruction must be determined in each school and classroom. The entering new teacher or the old teacher interested in trying a different technique must determine the openness of the learning environment in regard to the proposed approach. Even though the community, the administrative staff, and most of the faculty may be receptive and supportive, the particular group of children may have a background of educational experience entirely different from the proposed approach. In this event, the teacher must move cautiously. He should always assume the positive approach by suggesting leads designed to help individuals and small groups move into

---

[6]Gertrude Hildreth, "Dynamics of Learning in Childhood Education," Harold G. Shane (ed.), *The American Elementary School* (New York: Harper and Brothers, 1953), pp. 32-3.

constructive activities which bring success and a sense of accomplishment. The teacher should always refrain from being critical of procedures followed by other teachers and particularly labeling any approach as being "old fashioned."

Should a group of students not be accustomed to unit teaching involving problem solving and group work, and particularly if the teacher is inexperienced, the group would do well to start with textbook material in which all students have definite assignments. A first step toward problem solving in such a situation might be allowing the class to help decide the order in which certain portions of the textbook content might be used. In providing for the choice, the teacher should select a multiple of content topics for which he is best prepared so that when the study is undertaken he is able to see that the choice of the students brings a sense of accomplishment. During the particular study some students who show special interest in a phase of the topic should be allowed to do independent study to gain additional information, locate a valuable resource, or construct a prop to enhance the class learning situation. With careful guidance from the teacher, the class can move gradually to the point where units of instruction are engaged in and the problem-solving technique is utilized effectively.

THE PROBLEM SOLVING APPROACH

Problem solving is a daily encounter for each person. How well a person meets each new situation, the way he makes decisions, the extent to which he follows through each endeavor will largely determine his academic success. Helping boys and girls learn to solve problems should be the major instructional objective of each teacher and school. The child who learns to think more accurately and to find solutions to problems not only will be in a position to master the tools and skills of learning but will be able to contribute to group welfare as a citizen among his peers in school and in the business and social world.

One of the important values of unit teaching lies in its many opportunities for problem-solving. As a group deals with a center of interest, problems arise in planning, research, group activities, dramatic play, construction, and in evaluating accomplishments. Since the students carry a large share of responsibility in deciding what is to be done, how it is to be done, and evaluating the results, the many problems that arise are recognized as their own which they must solve. The wise teacher guides the children but allows the decisions to be their own in order to teach them effective techniques for the solving of problems.[7]

---

[7]Wilbur H. Dutton and John A. Hockett, *The Modern Elementary School, Curriculum and Methods* (New York: Rinehart and Company, Inc., 1959), pp. 306.

If children are to develop their ability to solve problems, they must be encouraged to experiment, observe, read, discuss, inquire, and make use of all available resources. There is no set area from which a problem should arise, although those of living and working with people are the most likely for identifying problems for classroom solution. The problem may develop from the child's own dilemma or it may be stimulated by the teacher, the textbook, or a curriculum guide. Whatever the source, the important concern is that the child be involved in the process of seeking a solution and realizing satisfactory results from his efforts.

CORRELATING AND INTEGRATING SUBJECT MATTER

The vast explosion of knowledge and scientific data before the youth of today presents a unique challenge to the elementary teacher. The specific challenge is to so correlate and integrate curriculum experiences that the youngster can see relationships among the various subject matter disciplines. It is through this relationship that the youngster should learn to call upon data and acquire skills to meet his present needs and become prepared to live and serve in the society of the future.

Automation, electronic computation, newer methods of communication, new concepts, and new devices all insure the fact that tomorrow's world will be vastly different from today's. Herein lies our concern for a more effective means of helping the learner assimilate greater volumes of information and the know-how to call up vast additional amounts of data on a given subject or problem as the need arises. In essence this calls for a new type of education in which attitude plays a significant role. It calls for creative and original people whose responses are appropriately unique. It calls for people who are able to respond with a wide background of experience without distortion or prejudice. The attitude of a person of this nature must be such that his former experiences are readily available to him and his attitudes toward other people are such that he also has available their experiences.

Bills has found that if teachers have role concepts characterized as molding, directing, moralizing, or manipulating their students are likely to develop negative attitudes toward their schools, their teacher, learning, the administration, and education in general. He also found that the practice of following a single text or workbook slavishly tends to mold, direct, and manipulate students.[8] The student often sees the school standing in

---

[8]Robert E. Bills, "Learner-Curriculum-Morale, Adjusting Curriculum to the Learner" (Athens, Georgia: Address before Georgia Association for Supervision and Curriculum Development, July 7, 1960).

the way of his doing what he wants to do. To avoid this feeling of the student, Bills reported from his study that:

> The teacher must be in psychological contact with the student, that the student must want to learn, that the teacher must have a high regard for the worth of the student, that the teacher must be able to put himself in the shoes of the student, and that the teacher must be willing to share with the student when and as is desired by the student.[9]

This means that provision must be made for the student to participate in identifying his needs, plotting his course of action, and using a wide variety of materials appropriate to his level of understanding. Such a procedure will necessarily cut across subject content lines and levels of materials within content areas. As a topic or problem is selected and developed by a class, materials should be drawn from any subject field that will help the learner achieve his purpose, satisfy his need, or solve his problem. In fact, few problems and needs of children are respecters of subject-matter boundaries. Content areas were developed by scholars primarily for the purpose of classification of information rather than for solving problems of individuals. Frequently such fields as history, geography, health, science, art, and arithmetic may be drawn upon as the learner pursues a particular concern. In the true study of a topic or problem, little attention will be given to the identification of content as a specific discipline except as it may be located in a particular source classified according to a scholar's subject label.

The correlating and integrating of subject matter which comes about as the problem solving technique is applied in unit teaching overcomes the difficulties of fragmented learnings. Hanna, Potter, and Hagaman stress the point that the unit approach to teaching provides opportunities for the learner to act, not just learn about, and causes him to analyze problems, carry on research, experiment, collect data, and arrive at his own answers and generalizations.[10] They further explain the integration of content and learning experiences as follows:

> In a unit of work, each child is given an opportunity to broaden and deepen his learning through a variety of activities and materials that are suited to the individual differences of the children in the group and that challenge each according to his ability and maturational development. Centered on life situations, the unit helps the child to see relationships

---

[9]*Ibid.*

[10]Lavone A. Hanna, Gladys L. Potter, and Neva Hagaman, *Unit Teaching in the Elementary School* (New York: Holt, Rinehart, and Winston, Inc., 1963), pp. 121-2.

between what he learns in school and outside school. Moreover, because the whole child responds to the total situation, unit teaching is as much concerned with the attitudes, appreciations, work habits, skills, and interest the child is developing as with his intellectual progress.[11]

TYPES OF UNITS

Units of instruction are usually classified as subject matter or topical and experience or activity. This classification immediately sets up opposing goals of learning in the education of the child. The subsequent pages of this chapter set forth the premise that the two work hand-in-hand and that each depends upon the other. Little attention is given to differentiating the two classifications of units. As a matter of reference, however, the subject-centered unit is considered as one which focuses primarily on subject matter while the experience-centered unit gives major attention to the process of learning through activities and experiences. Beck, Cook, and Kearney have given the distinction between subject-matter and experience units as follows:

> Subject matter units are of various kinds. During the time when they were more popular they were sometimes characterized as falling into four types: (1) topical units, (2) generalization units, (3) survey units, and (4) problem units. In a topical unit the subject matter concerned itself with a theme such as the French and Indian Wars or the fishing industry in New England. A generalization unit pointed up various conclusions as, "Where the forests are destroyed, floods sweep the lower drainage basins," . . . A survey unit covered a subject such as the cultural resources or the recreational resources of a community. Problem units dealt with such subjects as, "Why did slavery flourish in the South more than in the North?" . . .
>
> An experience unit is a cluster of educative experiences, organized through pupil-teacher planning, placed within the functioning framework of the needs and purposes of the child and his society, and utilizing, to as great a degree as possible, the useful resources to be found in the material and cultural environment, to the end that the democratically determined purposes of the schools may be achieved.[12]

All units that are of real value to the learners must contain subject content, activities, and experiences that further their sequential, developmental education. The content and activities are desirable only as they are suited to the needs, interest, and purposes of the children and equip them with

---

[11]*Ibid.*

[12]Robert Beck, Walter Cook, and Nolan Kearney, *Curriculum in the Modern Elementary School* (second edition; Englewood Cliffs, N. J.: Prentice-Hall, Inc., © 1960), p. 204. Reprinted by permission of Prentice-Hall, Inc.

significant understandings, attitudes, and skills. The most important aspect of the unit is the degree in which it enhances the learning for youngsters and better prepares them to meet life situations. To this end units may be prepared to assist a group of children and the teacher in developing a topic in the form of a resource unit, organizing a teaching unit, or in preparing a descriptive unit. As such, the resource unit is a large body of content and activities planned around a given topic from which a series of learning experiences may be drawn to develop the desired goals of the learners. This is an over-all comprehensive plan from which a teaching unit can be developed.

The teaching unit, then, is that organizational plan which gives direction on a day-to-day basis for carrying out the different learning experiences appropriate to the interests and needs of each learner in the group. The descriptive unit is the record of the unfolding of a particular unit which has been planned, initiated and developed by a group of learners. Copies of many published or mimeographed descriptive units can be obtained as a guide and resource to a group with an interest in a similar topic or problem. Any unit prepared prior to the involvement of the learner can serve only as a guide and resource. Thus, the teacher should realize that the most effective learning takes place when the learner participates in the planning.

PREPARATION FOR TEACHING A UNIT

The term "unit" is used freely among educators that it seems fitting that there be some clarification as to what is actually taking place when the teacher is preparing for or teaching a unit. As a basis for procedure, a unit is a series of carefully developed learning experiences related to a particular topic or problem. On the basis of this, the teacher must start preparation long before the initial planning for the particular unit. This means that prior to the initiation of the unit of study the teacher will have done all in his power to understand the children who will be involved and that an appropriate and stimulating environment for unit teaching will at least be in the making.

In preparation of a unit of work the teacher must keep in mind that whether the idea comes from the children, the teacher, or the course of study, it is his responsibility to see that it answers the needs of the students. The unit should not be forced to cover any area, but the teacher should be prepared to utilize each opportunity presented to develop a skill or content area. It is not necessary that all experiences of the school center around the unit being developed. Other activities in the school day such as the teaching of specific skills, appreciations, and bodies of content, which do not relate to the unit may be provided for as needed outside the framework.

Even though it is necessary for the teacher to prepare very carefully a full outline on any unit to be undertaken in the classroom, the unfolding of the unit of work must follow a pattern of development in keeping with the growth of the children at that time and disregard sequence which is ordinarily logical to adult learning. The teacher must not expect all of the children to seek answers to the same problems and to come up with the same answers. The teacher should prepare to take advantage of these differences by providing for a continuous pooling of ideas, testing of findings and sharing of knowledge between individuals and groups and with the entire class.

SELECTION

Selection of a teaching unit is a cooperative responsibility of the teacher and the learners. It is first the responsibility of the teacher to know what may be expected of children of the age under his supervision and something of the individual differences of this particular group. Next the teacher should know the curriculum objectives of the school, the policies in regard to selection of content, and the availability and use of instructional materials. Equipped with this information, the teacher should take stock of himself to see the relationship he has with this particular group of learners and how ready they are for participating in decision making in selection of instructional blocks of content sufficiently large to be labeled a unit. There should be student participation in activities which relate to the individual, small group, and whole class from the early stages of class organization.

As assurance that the unit selected will offer effective teaching and learning potential, adequate criteria should be applied. The most desirable criteria will be that prepared by the group making the selection. As a guide to the teacher and students in deciding upon an effective unit, the following points should be considered:

1. Contributes to the achievement of the goals of the learners.
2. Provides opportunities for the development of problem-solving skills, democratic behavior, and group action skills.
3. Deals with an important aspect of living which is significant to children.
4. Is related to children's past experiences and broadens their interests.
5. Provides for individual differences within the range of ability of the group.
6. Provides for a variety of activities, materials, and modes of expression.

7. Provides for students to organize, plan, and direct activity.
8. Utilizes the natural devices of children such as curiosity, physical activity, manipulation and construction, creativity and dramatization.
9. Provides for social development.
10. Increases communication skills to higher levels of development.
11. Provides for acquisition of important content, significant concepts, and understandings.
12. Engages children in judging, choosing, and evaluating.
13. Is feasible for development within the framework of the time and instructional resources available.[13]

Three basic means are used to determine the selection of units. These are (1) some form of curriculum framework prepared by a state department of education or a local school administration which suggests specific units for different grades from which teachers may select units suited to needs of their particular class, (2) the selection of units by the teacher and class on the basis of the needs and interests of the particular group, and (3) the dependence upon a series of adopted textbooks which determine the topical content that serves as a basis for subject matter units which may be directed by the teacher.[14]

A well-planned curriculum framework provides for the most logical selection of units in that it offers sequential, developmental units according to the maturity level of the students through the years. The content for each unit is derived from the interests of the children, the nature of the community in which they live, and the demands placed upon them by society. This plan curtails repetition, promotes the provision of appropriate materials for specific units, and prevents the selection of insignificant units. Within the framework of an organized curriculum plan a teacher and his students may find sufficient liberty to allow for individual and group attention to problems utilizing a variety of materials and techniques suited to their specific capabilities.

When appropriate safeguards are utilized, the teacher and pupils may well use the opportunity to select units cooperatively. This is particularly desirable when the selection can grow naturally out of some experience or through discussion and group study. Such an experience helps the pupils to grow in the ability to analyze their needs and competencies and to make decisions about the direction and nature of their learning experiences. Children are generally creative and like to explore and find out about their world. It is therefore recognized that when they participate in unit selec-

---

[13]John U. Michaelis, *Social Studies for Children in a Democracy* (second edition; Englewood Cliffs: Prentice-Hall, Inc., 1956), pp. 130-132. Reprinted by permission of Prentice-Hall, Inc.
[14]*Ibid.*, p. 136.

tion, a greater degree of refreshment and excitement about learning can be expected.

Some effective subject matter units may be developed when using the textbook as a basis for selecting content units but usually when a single textbook series serves as the curriculum guide, other materials are limited and little opportunity is allowed for problem-solving development. However, the textbook is an invaluable tool in teaching when it is used as a guide in determining the selection of skills and the sequence for their development. In this manner it is used primarily as a resource for curriculum development rather than as the curriculum.

Regardless of the means used for selecting the unit of study there are certain factors the teacher should give attention to before deciding the unit to be studied. Some of the more significant factors are the characteristics of the children of that particular age, the capabilities of the group, their educational status and interests, and their emotional and social maturity.

Sources of help to the teacher in becoming knowledgeable on these factors are the principal and supervisor in the school and the curriculum guides adopted by the school. The cumulative records of the pupils provide data as to learning experiences, health, achievement, family background and special conditions and problems. Former teachers of the students can give valuable information as to the interests of the students, their study patterns, and many special characteristics desirable for the teacher to know prior to beginning work with a new group. An understanding of the community including major occupations and industries, cultural activities, recreational facilities and patterns, and general economic and social conditions, is a valuable asset to the teacher in determining what learning experiences seem appropriate.

PREPARATORY ACTIVITIES

The teacher must recognize the importance of his full preparation not only for utilizing the unit approach in teaching but for informing himself as to the content and learning experiences possible in each unit chosen. He should become as well informed as he can about the topic to be studied by collecting resource materials, doing background reading, and acquainting himself with any unit outline which may be available. The teacher should list tentative purposes for teaching the unit, identify concepts which might be acquired by the students during the study, and tentatively decide upon some student activities and experiences to be engaged in.

After taking these preliminary steps, an outline form should be selected as a guide for careful planning of the unit. Using this the teacher should develop plans which are as complete as possible. He should proceed, however, with the understanding that the plans he makes prior to developing the unit are tentative and serve only as a background of information for him and as a guide for the students who actually develop the selected topic. The use of a guide similar to the Georgia plan in Figure 28 can greatly facilitate the efforts of a teacher preparing for the development of a specific unit.

So that a unit outline can be effective, the teacher must see it as an instrument whereby he can organize his preparation for teaching a unit. In so doing he must see the unit as a whole as well as each component

I. Overview. A descriptive paragraph of the scope and content of the unit with a brief table of contents in the form of topics or generalizations to be considered.

II. Objectives.
   A. The appreciations and attitudes to be developed.
   B. The understandings to be developed.
   C. The skills and habits to be developed.

III. Approach Activities. Suggest several activities which the teacher may plan and utilize as a means of arousing interest and setting the stage for introduction of the unit.

IV. Procedure. The procedure constitutes the assimilation or working period of the unit. Here is the crux of the whole unit. List in sequence specific activities that provide for the various levels of maturity, interest, and ability of the members of the class and develop the objectives set forth in the beginning of the unit.

V. Evaluation Techniques. Include samples to illustrate how the teacher intends to gather evidence that the objectives of the unit have been developed or achieved through such media as

   Self-evaluation (teacher, pupils)
   Behavior and anecdotal records
   Activity records
   Checklists and inventories
   Tests

VI. Instructional Aids.
   A. Books useful to the teacher in planning and directing the unit.
   B. Books useful to the children in carrying out the activities of the unit.
   C. Films, slides, exhibits, and recordings available for the use of teacher or children.

Figure 28. Outline for Resource Unit. *Elementary Education Handbook,* (Athens, Georgia: College of Education, University of Georgia, 1964), p. 20. Reproduced by permission.

part, namely overview, objectives, approach activities, procedure, evaluation techniques, and instructional aids. Seeing the plan as a whole, the teacher should visualize it as an umbrella in that the plan that he makes, called a resource unit, is much larger than the teaching unit. It should include all the facets he envisions as well as those which may be engendered by the responses of the students engaged in the learning. Each component part of the unit plan should be treated separately during preparation for the teaching process in order that the teacher can be as well prepared as possible and that adequate and appropriate instructional resources and materials can be made available to the learners.

The teacher should give particular attention to the overview and objectives of the proposed instructional unit during the preparatory stages. It is upon these two phases that all other aspects of the unit are founded. The overview should provide an over-all look at the breadth of the proposed unit and some of the major aspects of the topic which seem feasible for development. This section of the plan should include the grade level for which the unit is being prepared, information as to the importance of the proposed topic, and the length of time which legitimately might be allotted to such a study. A brief table of contents should show something of the direction the unit is to take and the content to be pursued.

Objectives are the compass of the unit of study in that they give direction and plot the boundaries or framework within which the learners can engage in purposeful study. Each of the three types of objectives is significant and requires careful consideration. These are (1) appreciations and attitudes, (2) understandings, and (3) skills and habits. It is under this heading that the knowledge of the teacher in regard to the scope and sequence of the curriculum must come into full focus. It is here that the teacher must envision the extent to which the children of the particular age level can recognize an accomplishment or importance of an aspect of the subject being studied and register appreciations. The teacher must be prepared to determine backgrounds of the students and their readiness for such a study in order to single out specific appreciations which are likely to develop.

Determining understandings to be developed by the learners calls for extensive study on the part of the teacher in identification of the content, the knowledge, and the concepts appropriate to the students. In actuality the understandings are the body of informational learnings that may be acquired by the students during the study. In order that the teacher can be in a position to guide the students in exploring content and plotting solutions to problems which will result in specific understandings, he must read widely and explore extensively many related projects and bodies of content.

He then must record in abbreviated form an extensive array of concepts, generalizations and data which he believes can be understood and mastered by students of the age and calibre he teaches.

Identification of skills and habits appropriate for mastery by students in a selected unit of study also calls for the teacher's thorough knowledge and understanding of the scope and sequence of the curriculum. Each unit of study calls into play certain skills and tends to develop or further certain habits of the students. Thus the teacher should prepare himself for recognizing these natural channels and properly relating the development of appropriate skills to specific phases of the unit of instruction. Particular emphasis should be given to the communication skills of reading, writing, speaking, listening, and computation. In preparation for this relationship, the specific skills and habits expected to be furthered are listed under the appropriate content or skill area in the unit plan. The teacher should always keep in mind that unit work should further these communication skills extensively.

INITIATORY ACTIVITIES

Initiation of any unit of work in the classroom may be the most crucial phase of the learning process. When interest is aroused, curiosity sharpened, and the topic at hand related to the desires of a group of students, there is little problem in getting the study under way. It is imperative that the teacher plan ways to relate the current study to the past experiences of those involved. Current resources of the school and community assist greatly in providing a stimulating classroom environment, which is one of the best means of initiating an effective instructional unit. Thus the teacher must learn what is available, plan activities for initiating the unit, and record these under approach activities as suggested in Section III of Figure 28.

Elements of a stimulating classroom environment which may assist in initiating a new unit of work include a display of books, a collection of pictures, an exhibit of labeled materials, an experiment, a dramatic skit, a guest speaker, a visitor to the school, a motion picture, or a bulletin board. Other factors which may stimulate interest in a special study are the culmination of a previous unit, a talk by an older child, the birthday of a great man or woman, a local happening, a news or magazine article, or a trip by a member of the class or the teacher.

The alert teacher continuously looks for leads to worthwhile activities for individuals and groups. He seeks to develop a feeling of group unity and enthusiasm and shows an interest in the concerns as well as the accomplishments of each individual in the room.

The purpose of the initiatory period is to stimulate interest on the part of children in pursuing new and different areas of learning as they utilize the problem solving approach in gathering pertinent information. During this period the students should be acquainted with the general scope of the unit and each of its major aspects. In preparing for this important phase of the unit the teacher should recognize that the chief function of the initiatory period will have been accomplished when the students begin to ask spontaneous questions which will serve as a study guide for the development of the unit.

DEVELOPMENTAL ACTIVITIES

The teacher should plan so that moving into developmental activities can be done with maximum use of pupil-teacher planning of the learning experiences to be undertaken. Section IV of Figure 28 provides for recording the development of this phase of the unit plan. This in essence is the projected or tentative blueprint of the unit which the teacher prepares in advance. The teacher should proceed on the basis that such a plan can serve only as a guide and resource in teacher-student cooperative development of the real blueprint or teaching unit. Means should be planned whereby children are encouraged to raise questions and name areas about which they have curiosity. Provision is then made whereby these ideas can be clearly stated, recorded, and organized into an outline to be used as a guide for developing a plan of attack.

This step-by-step procedure is the crux of the unit. It should suggest a tentative outline of the unfolding of the unit from the introduction to the culmination. A wide variety of techniques and materials should be utilized in suggested sequential order to depict the total production clearly. This phase of the unit should provide activities such as reading, experimenting, and constructing that are designed to help students determine answers to their questions for future development. In so doing, new and old skills are applied as students select and evaluate information found in reference books, analyze data, weigh values, and decide what applies to the solution of their problems.

CULMINATING ACTIVITIES

The culmination of a unit of instruction not only serves to evaluate what the students have accomplished but provides for the sharing of experiences and information, the summarizing of content and experiences, and the relating of different aspects of learning. Thus, the teacher should make plans whereby each student can participate, identify himself with some activity, and be recognized for his accomplishments. The teacher has the further responsibility of pointing up other areas for examination and study as the unit comes to a close and of leaving the group wanting to do more problem solving through various individual and group activities.

Units of study may be culminated with or without a special occasion involving a display and program. Michaelis suggests that the teacher ask the following questions to determine whether the special occasion type culmination is worthwhile:

1. Will a culminating activity contribute to social learning?
2. Is it worth the time, effort, and expense?
3. Do the children see sense in it?
4. Will it be childlike?
5. Is it a natural outgrowth of preceding activities?
6. Does it suggest a new area of study?
7. Will it help to organize the children's thinking?
8. Does it provide opportunities to apply key learnings?
9. Does it stimulate democratic sharing?
10. Will each child have an opportunity to participate?
11. Will it help to evaluate the achievement of purpose?[15]

Evaluation is a necessary phase of the culmination for which the teacher must plan. Thus, means must be devised from the beginning for the teacher and students to keep records of achievement, change of behavior observed, and the mastery of skills, habits and data acquired. A plan must also be devised for periodic evaluation and appraisal which can be used to improve daily planning, select new materials, clarify needs of individual children, and improve group work. Recognition of values gained through preparation, execution, and evaluation comes into fruition in the culmination of the unit to the extent that careful planning is made for such appraisal in the preparatory stages.

Appropriate instructional materials at the interest and achievement level of the children who are in the learning experience is basic to unit instruction. A listing of resource materials on the topic made available in advance not only prepares the teacher but encourages the students. The students, however, should be encouraged to go far beyond this limited listing as the unit develops.

Recording and evaluating the instructional materials used during the unfolding of a unit is helpful to the teacher in planning future units, in sharing materials with other teachers and in selecting materials for purchase. The form provided in Figure 29 offers valuable assistance to the teacher in keeping a record for the foregoing purposes.

---

[15]*Ibid.*, pp. 147-9.

| Name of Unit | Grade | Teacher | Date |

List materials used under the following headings and in this order:

1 – Books, 2 – Periodicals, 3 – Pamphlets, 4 – Songs, (give name of book and page), 5 – Recordings, 6 – Flat Prints, 7 – Films, 8 – Filmstrips, 9 – Musical Instruments, 10 – Display Materials, 11 – Persons, 12 – Other materials needed but not available. When complete, file in school file for future use.

	Appropriateness			Source of Material			
	EXCELLENT	GOOD	POOR	SCHOOL LIB	CENTRAL	PERSONAL	OTHER
Title Publisher							

Figure 29.   A Form for Recording the Use and Evaluation of Instructional Materials.

IMPLEMENTING A UNIT OF WORK WITH CHILDREN

There are many effective ways of implementing a unit of work but care must be taken in selecting the most desirable approach. The more the teacher relies on the children for assistance in selecting, planning, and initiating their learning experiences the greater the variety of approaches will be in implementing a new unit. When the teacher has prepared carefully he will be well informed about the anticipated subject matter of the unit. He will have collected resource materials, done background reading, and prepared or adapted a resource unit on the subject. Feasibility of the unit in terms of community relationships and socioeconomic background will have been determined. The teacher will be acquainted with the academic achievement and the varied educational experiences of the students who will participate in the study. Also, he will have determined the feasibility of the unit in terms of time factor, materials available, and the relation of the unit to the curriculum.

Drawing upon basic resource units, a teaching plan should be developed with the cooperation of the students involved. This will be done during the initiatory stages of the unit and as it unfolds. Such a plan should rely upon the resource unit for information and guidance but include only that portion which seems appropriate to the students' immediate needs.

Daily lesson plans are a necessity in carrying out the unit in a manner which relates the over-all plans to the ongoing activities and in giving meaning and expression to the needs and interests of the children. These plans should center around four basic elements which are:

1. Purposes — the content, concepts, and skills to be accomplished in the particular lesson.
2. Procedure — the proposed step-by-step movement of all the activities as anticipated they will take place during the instructional period planned.
3. Evaluation and closing — means of identifying the learnings which have taken place during the instructional period as these relate to the objectives set forth and the projection of the learning experiences into the next logical steps.
4. Instructional aids — the materials, tools, props, and gadgets which are planned as aids to learning for the particular situation.

The teacher should make very careful and full lesson plans in the initial stages of the unit and continue to do so throughout its duration to the extent necessary for confident and smooth operation. Better teachers consider that some form of daily lesson plans is always desirable for assuring the most effective growth and accomplishment of each individual. The teacher should realize that daily as well as unit plans should be made flexible and provide for alternate activities to be used as the learning situation dictates.

An excellent organization of data about children which the teacher can secure during orientation for a unit of work, as devised by Noar, is shown in Figure 30. It is not necessary that the teacher have all the proposed information but the more available to him the more likely the unit of work chosen will be appropriate. Noar has suggested that the gathering of the data proposed could serve as a guide for developing the program during the early portion of the term with a group of children, thus building readiness for the implementation of a new unit of work when feasible. The amount of time and the extent to which this is accomplished will be determined by the children's maturity level, emotional stability, concentration and attention spans, relative need for physical activity, manipulative expression and rest periods.[16]

---

[16]Gertrude Noar, *Freedom to Live and Learn* (Philadelphia: Franklin Publishing and Supply Company, 1948), pp. 19-22.

What the Teacher Needs to Know About the Pupils	Experiences that Reveal the Facts	Records to be Consulted

Level of performance in tool subjects	1. Reading lessons
	2. Audience reading
	3. Silent reading
	4. Standardized tests in
	    spelling
	    reading
	    English usage
	    English grammar
	5. Group and individual teacher-made tests on current events, information about history, geography, literature, etc.
	6. Games, quizzes, group contests
		1. Records from previous grades

Scholastic and social abilities and interests. Ability to follow directions·	1. Standardized tests, inventories, questionnaires, interviews 2. "Intimate" creative writing lessons (Autobiography, Three Wishes, My Gripes, What I Would Do with $100, My Favorite Person-book-hobby- etc.) 3. Games 4. Library periods 5. Spontaneous assignments to do things, get information as needs arise, and questions are asked 6. Errands 7. Parties, Picnics, and Trips	
Past experiences, home conditions, economic level, affectional security	1. Intimate writings (as above) 2. Conferences with previous teachers and counselors 3. Making a community survey 4. Party for parents 5. Home visits	1. Clinical records which show facts regarding adjustment to adults 2. Individual and group records of units previously studied 3. Any available community surveys

Figure 30. Preliminary Work During Orientation Period. Gertrude Noar, *Freedom to Live and Learn*, pp. 20-21. Reproduced by permission of and arrangement with Franklin Publishing and Supply Company.

What the Teacher Needs to Know About the Pupils	Experiences that Reveal the Facts	Records to be Consulted
Maturity levels -- physical, social, emotional. Levels of emancipation from adults	1. Discussions: "What is fun? What is beauty?" home life neighborhood problems friendships 2. Interviews with children and parents 3. Conferences with parents 4. Observation of children as they work and play	1. Clinical records
Health problems	1. Questionnaires 2. Interviews with children and parents 3. Observation 4. Discussion of habits of daily hygiene 5. Setting up of health habit charts	1. Records of medical and dental examinations 2. Cumulative records 3. Records made from parental interview when child first entered school
Nicknames, hobbies, after school and in school activities	1. Hobby show 2. Intimate writings (as above) 3. Oral presentations 4. Interviews with children and parents 5. Questionnaires	
Group social pattern (sociometrics), group code, leaders, special roles (bully, clown, etc.), pattern of attractions and rejections	1. Observation of children in and out of classroom 2. Conversation periods 3. Setting up of communities as needed for incidental jobs 4. Games 5. "Guess Who" questionnaires 6. Setting up of experiences 7. Trips 8. Sorting pictures for room decoration 9. Elections 10. Dramatizations 11. Browsing periods	

Figure 30. (Continued)

The knowledge of these important aspects of the group must be skill-fully synthesized and utilized for effective development of a unit of work. The basic approach must rely heavily upon the drives exhibited by the chil-dren. The teacher must recognize the strong inclinations of children to find things out, to create, to experiment, to build, to dramatize, and to experience the security which comes from knowing.

The central focus in developing the learning sequence in the unit should be on problem solving. The teacher has the responsibility for helping the class to deliberate their questions which arise in connection with the unit. A comparable responsibility is planning with the class learning experiences desirable in following through on the students' interests, concerns, and ques-tions. As these particular areas are dealt with, other problems, concerns, and interests are opened up, which tend to keep the students motivated until the area on which the unit is centered has been sufficiently explored.[17]

One must readily recognize the interchange of ideas and expansion of learning as illustrated in Figure 31. This interchange of aspects serves as the drive that causes the interests of a group to become a functioning unit of work. The more the relationship is exercised the greater are the under-standings.

NEEDS AND DESIRES ◀-------▶ EXPERIENCE AND ACTION

Figure 31.   Relation of Basic Aspects of Learning.

ORIENTATION

Let us now visualize a third grade classroom in which the implemen-tation of a unit on communication which we shall label "Sending and Receiving Messages" is taking place[18] Here the teacher has spent time and effort in finding out about available community resources, the school poli-cies and facilities, and has acquainted himself well with the children in the classroom. On the basis of this, the foregoing topic has been tentatively selected for study. The teacher has previously developed a resource unit for the study according to the unit outline described in this chapter. The

---

[17]G. Wesley Sowards and Mary-Margaret Scobey, *The Changing Curriculum and the Elementary Teacher* (San Francisco: Wadsworth Publishing Company, Inc., 1961), pp. 496-7.

[18]Mrs. Helen Bottoms, "Ways of Sending and Receiving Messages." A resource unit prepared in the College of Education, University of Georgia, Athens, Georgia, February, 1963.

teacher capitalized upon the fact that many of his students had traveled during the summer, showing the cards he had received from them to stimulate interest in sending messages. Letters received from two members of the class who had moved to another state and an air mail folder from another who took a foreign tour with her parents also were available for use and display.

The teacher was aware that children often have passing interests in a topic but possess no real or sustained concern about it. Therefore, even though considerable interest was expressed in this initial exhibit, he arranged displays of pictures of several means of communication which seemed likely to arouse more curiosity and provoke questions. He exhibited selected books on the subject which were provocative and within the reading abilities of the children. The filmstrip "Learning About Communication" was shown to let the children see something of what might be gained from such a study.

TEACHER-PUPIL PLANNING

Careful preparation had been made by the teacher in order that the study would blossom into a full-grown unit which could invoke extensive learning experiences in problem solving. As soon as signs of interest were shown each individual was involved in some activity that he could perform successfully. Such activities included bringing cards or letters to class, bringing pictures of telephones, postmen, postal cards, talking with a postman, and visiting a post office as an individual or a team of two or three. Individuals were encouraged to share these materials and experiences during the sharing period. All were encouraged to examine the displays and books and discuss communication in general. When the teacher felt that the time was ripe, a discussion was held to seek to determine the real interest in such a study. The teacher carefully observed the enthusiasm with which the students spoke, the kind of statements they made and the nature of the questions they asked. After the discussion got off to a good start, the teacher began to record on the chalk board "Things We Could Learn About Sending and Receiving Messages." When the ideas from the group began to slow down, the teacher suggested that each person copy in his notebook the problem topics written on the board. The list copied by the students included the following:

1. Ways we send and receive messages.
2. How flags give messages.
3. How letters get from us to our friends.
4. How people sent messages long ago.
5. Why communication is important to us.

6. How messages travel by telegram, telephone, radio, and television.
7. The quickest ways to send messages.
8. Responsibilities we have to our neighbors in using communication facilities.
9. How animals give messages.
10. How we get our newspapers, magazines, and books.
11. Where our language came from.
12. How we improve our ways of talking.
13. Why people in other countries use sounds for words that are different to ours.

After copying the list of things to learn from the board, time was allowed for the students to talk the ideas over with their neighbors in small groups. The children then decided it would be a good plan to take the list of ideas home and talk with their parents about what they could learn from such a study. Everyone was then asked to find out what he could bring from home that would assist in such a study.

The teacher, reflecting upon the overview and objectives of the unit he had previously developed, was now able to evaluate the children's ideas to see if they were in keeping with his proposed plan and to what extent he would need to suggest additional points which the children had not mentioned. He reviewed the section on understandings and the one on skills and attitudes particularly to be sure that he was ready to guide the class in the development of the most important of these. He also reviewed the responses of the group up to this point to see if what he was proposing was suitable and adjusted his thinking and expectations accordingly.

The next day the block of time in the morning, usually known as the sharing period, was given to hearing reactions from the children about the proposed study and what they thought they might offer the class in the way of pictures, books, and realia. The teacher was observing primarily the problems which seemed real to individuals and how each might be involved in activities which would stimulate him to achieve at his maximum learning level. Two lists were put on the board during this period. One was a list of materials that might be brought in by the children. The other was a reorganization of the ideas the children had submitted the first day. The teacher had spent much time after the first listing by the children in seeing the possibilities for providing learning experiences appropriate to the individuals and had made alternate plans of attack. Now he was ready to hear how the children might organize their list of things to learn and was prepared to guide them into an organization of ideas or subtopics which might serve as a guide for developing a comprehensive unit of study based on problem solving endeavor.

At this point the teacher recognized the need for providing content that was definite and tangible for all the class. The social studies text provided a provocative picture and story which all could examine, read, and share. The story, "Messages We See and Hear,"[19] served as a base from which all could work. This definite assignment was made in the social studies text for the purpose of having a minimum body of information understandable by all students. The teacher used this as a springboard for discussion. From this he gained insights into helping each student identify an aspect of the unit or a special interest through which individual and group work might begin to function.

After some discussion of ways to give and receive messages as presented in the text, the teacher began to lead the discussion into consideration of the list of what the students had indicated they would like to know about sending and receiving messages. From this discussion, the first list of things the students had said they wanted to know, and the suggestions which came from talking with their parents, the following major problem areas were agreed upon for study by the group:

1. Why is communication important to us?
2. How does the postman help us?
3. What are some means of communicating with others?
4. How do animals other than human beings, communicate?
5. What were the first methods of communication?
6. How can communication methods be improved?
7. How do books, magazines, and newspapers help us to act intelligently?

After the class agreed upon the foregoing problem areas for study, they decided to record on slips of paper three or four of the areas that each thought he would like to know most about. Then they agreed that each person should list three or four members of the class he would like to work with. After gathering these data, the teacher used all the information he had gained in helping decide topics that might be studied in groups and in determining the kinds of activities that might be feasible for this particular group. He then tentatively assigned individuals to topics for study which might contribute to the development of the unit.

Even though the teacher anticipated involving all students in some rseponsibility for development of the unit, he considered it advisable to limit the number of activities at one time in the early stages. As readiness was shown, he encouraged additional individuals and groups to begin work on new problems.

---

[19]"Messages We See and Hear," Alta McIntire and Wilhelmina Hill, *Working Together* (Chicago: Follett Publishing Company, 1959), pp. 167-9.

RESEARCH AND WORK

Since the children in this particular third grade had participated very little in group work prior to this project, the teacher wisely encouraged everyone to write a paragraph about "My Most Interesting Message." He suggested that this might be related to the problem area in which he was most interested. He then began by letting the students divide into small groups to read their paragraphs to their members. Each group selected one paragraph to be read by the writer to the whole class. Before moving into groups for reading paragraphs, the teacher planned with the class ways of conducting themselves and helped them determine definite objectives. A simple list of four or five reminders was placed on the board. During the work period the teacher moved among the groups to help them work in the manner agreed upon. When necessary, he pointed to the list of objectives or a single point within the list to remind individuals or the group to use their time to better advantage.

Two distinct purposes are important at this stage in development of the unit. Clouser, Robinson, and Neely identify these as the child's purposes and those of the teacher. The child's purpose should be to engage in work that seems worthwhile to him. This purpose furnishes the drive necessary to complete the work successfully. The teacher's purpose should be to develop the child academically, socially, and emotionally through the activity.[20] With these purposes in mind the teacher listened for areas of interest to individual children and considered means whereby this interest could be used to further the learning. The teacher had prepared information on sources as well as specific data appropriate for leading individuals or groups into a facet of the unit at the moment interest was shown in a specific direction.

After reading their paragraphs to one another, some children were guided into developing their paragraphs into longer stories. Others were encouraged to collect pictures showing messages being sent or received and writing what they thought the pictures said to them. Some were able to paint pictures depicting phases of communication while others made their best contributions through reading and sharing with their peers. Finding out how people sent messages long ago became the concern of several. This developed into the preparation of a picture dictionary of messages from the old to the new. Using these initial activities as a starting point, the teacher worked closely with individuals and groups, guiding them as seemed appropriate. Thus, activities were ever changing in keeping with the leads, moods, and needs of the children.

---

[20]Lucy Weller Clouser, Wilma J. Robinson, and Dena Lois Neely, *Educative Experiences Through Activity Units* (Chicago: Lyons and Carnahan, 1932), pp. 26-7.

During some periods all members of the class worked on individual projects. At other periods they worked in groups and at times all read assigned material which was followed by a discussion session. Occasionally, better readers read material to the group too difficult for many to read. Plans were made often by the group for an excursion, an experiment, or construction project. Even though the basic list of things guided the group, new elements were added and some were deleted which did not seem to make a contribution. The teacher was ever cognizant that children's purposes are often revealed through the questions they ask as they work and the ways they go about finding their answers. After sufficient background has been developed, original problems can be re-examined and restated and more problems added to the list. In keeping with this understanding, short periods of whole-class discussion were held regularly throughout the teaching unit to help the students keep their objectives clear and to keep the teacher in tune with the progress being made by the class and groups and individuals within them.

CLASS SCHEDULE

In order to provide for the everchanging activities and to meet the interests and needs of individuals, a schedule which allows for flexibility within large blocks of time must be arranged similar to the one cited in Figure 32. Such a schedule permits children to work without interruption long enough to complete an undertaking. It allows children to share information and experiences they have gained outside the classroom, to try ideas, to search for desired information, and to express feelings of concern and frustration in attempting to pursue an interest or carry out an assignment.

To provide for these ongoing and ever-changing activities there should be a period at the end of each day when children are working on their own while the teacher moves from student to student to see what each has accomplished during the day. He helps each to evaluate his progress and to identify specifically what homework is necessary and what activities to engage in as he enters school the next day. This means that the doors of the classroom are open to every child as he arrives at school each morning so that he can begin his own agreed upon activities or read instructions on the chalkboard and follow them promptly.

In this plan the teacher's first responsibility of the day is to move among the students to observe what is going on and assist children with problems which need immediate attention. He then checks on the availability of resources needed for the day and gives routine but careful attention to record keeping, administrative instruction, and the over-all learning environment. When the teacher has completed these duties and the majority of the

SUGGESTED CLASS SCHEDULE

School	Teacher	Grade

Time	Curriculum Area	Activity
I. 8:30 10:00	Social Studies and Science Activities	Activities performed relate to an interest of a pupil or a group project, pertain to art work, group work, or experience that furthers an interest or solves a problem. Project stems from social studies and science.
II. 10:00 10:30		Physical Education
III. 10:30 11:45	Language Arts Written English Oral English Literature Reading Writing Spelling	Continue work project through experiences in written and oral English; through reading, and study of literature, use of library, and relation of spelling and penmanship to all written work.
IV. 11:45 12:15		Lunch
V. 12:15 1:30	Appreciation Literature Music Health Art Drama Program	Rest immediately following lunch. At same time begin lessons of appreciation by listening to literature and music. Move into interpretation of same. Tie in with the function and relation to the body. Further through program for room, assembly, etc.
VI. 1:30 1:45		Rest and Free Play
VII. 1:45 3:00	Skill Practice Arithmetic English Spelling Reading	Practice in skills based on the findings of the day may be performed in any of the fundamental subjects. Supervise study. Make plans for homework and for activities to be developed at the beginning of the next day.

Figure 32. Class Schedule. Grades One Through Eight. Prepared by L. R. Wootton for use in Alamance County, North Carolina Schools, 1950.

students seem ready, work is stopped and total class sharing, evaluating, and planning are started. During this session the day's agenda is planned. This includes a listing of the major data to be gathered, content to be encountered, skills to be exercised, activities to be pursued and the assign-

ing of responsibilities for each. Those items of importance to most of the
students are identified and an order of procedure for the day is established.

The listing of activities seen in Figure 33 represents an expression of
the third grade students in a planning session of the tasks they recognized
as desirable for accomplishment during one day while working on the
unit "Sending and Receiving Messages." The numbering of activities indi-

---

WORK DETAIL FOR A DAY

6. Answer a letter written by a former member of the class who had
   moved away.
1. Share pictures brought from home.
3. Prepare bulletin board from pictures of animals.
4. Show the filmstrip "Learning About the Community." (Second showing)
10. Work on the song — "A True Story."
7. Read story "Letters and Packages" pages 175-7, *Working Together*.
5. Paint pictures of animals who talk.
2. Share letters members of class brought from home.
11. Make list of people who help us send and receive messages.
8. Find stories about messages and read from books in room library
   and those brought from central library.
9. Figure the cost of postage to send letters to absent classmates.
12. Enter new words in individual spelling notebooks.
13. Arrange reading center in an inviting manner (by committee).

Figure 33. Sample of Agenda Prepared by Third Grade Class Developing
The Unit "Sending and Receiving Messages."

cates the students' designated order of work after all tasks had been listed.
Such a planning session represents a phase of problem solving engaged in
by the whole class and related to the attack made by the individuals and
groups on their respective problems and interests. However, such a listing
or agenda as seen in Figure 33 may be a part of or in addition to the
activities planned by individuals and groups in pursuit of their own interests and projects. With the agenda as a guide, the third grade students
were able to arrange their activties in an order which directed each into the
most appropriate period of the day.

The class schedule in Figure 32 served as a means of organization and
as a guide to over-all planning but was subject to change according to the
needs apparent and opportunities available. By observing this schedule, the
teacher and students were aware of the importance of all areas of the cur-

riculum in providing balance in their learning experiences. The schedule guided the students in arranging their daily agenda in keeping with the over-all curriculum.

The philosophy basic to the schedule in Figure 32 is that this arrangement of curriculum offerings provides for a logical sequence in the day of the elementary school child. When the classroom serves as a laboratory for the child and he feels that it is a place where he can find interesting things, ideas, and information; that he can explore; that he will receive guidance and encouragement; and that he is considered important in the eyes of at least one person, then he will likely enter the classroom most mornings with enthusiasm for learning. This planning and working arrangement makes it important that he be able to enter the room with a purpose and begin to engage in an activity which furthers his goals. Consequently, he can see that he also needs to know what is in the offering during the day and how he can fit into the over-all schedule of activities. When the child recognizes his responsibility in planning and carrying out action in his own interest and sees an outline of definite things to do, he realizes that many of the responsibilities can be met by him at his own study pace and he can use time beyond this in the furtherance of his own peculiar interests.

When the day is started in this manner, the first block of time for the day, as seen in Figure 32, can easily be devoted to working with problems in living which relate primarily to the content areas of social studies, science, civics, health, and geography. The unit on communication cuts across areas, including content from all. It involves problems, experiences, and information outside the classroom which are a natural carry-over to the school day.

In treating interests or problems in living in the before mentioned areas, the communication skills of reading, writing, speaking, listening, and computation serve as the medium of expression. The utilization of these tools and the furtherance of skill in the exercise of these in the communication unit thus become a natural development for the second large block of work, language arts, (Figure 32) in the school day. This is the period at which students write their stories and share them with their peers. They assist each other in correct oral expression and form in writing. They keep their own spelling notebook and learn words required of all for communication about this unit. Simple research techniques become meaningful as the communication skills are applied for greater understanding of how messages are sent and received.

The period following lunch calls for a change of pace and nature of activity as indicated in the third large block of time in Figure 32. It is desirable that this period be more relaxed and reflective. The aesthetic areas of literature, music, art, and drama and the area of physiology related to, applied to, and utilized in the ongoing unit of instruction move the individual gradually from relaxation to active intellectual involvement — from a passive stage of listening to one of creative participation. It is during this period in the unit on communication that the teacher reads to the class such stories as *The Pony Express.*[21] and plays such recordings as *Clear the Line.*[22] Students should be encouraged to read similar stories, listen to other recordings, and dramatize their interpretations.

The fourth and last large block of time in the schedule of the day should be one of catching up, evaluating, and projecting major aspects of the unit and other areas under study outside the unit structure. New skills in arithmetic, English, and spelling may be introduced to the whole class as needed. However, most of the time should be devoted to completion of work undertaken by individuals and groups or assignments on related skills made by the teacher during the first three periods of the day. This work should pertain to practice on a needed skill, mastery of a body of content, or gathering of needed data. The last thirty minutes of the day should be used by the teacher to check the students' purposeful study, research, or reading. He should observe and evaluate the work of each in relation to his responsibilities for the day, his progress toward self-concerned goals, and his attitude toward his work load. Help will be given each student to determine reasonable homework and other activities for the next day in the classroom. After careful interpersonal contact, the teacher should spend a few minutes with the entire class helping them evaluate experiences of the day and make general plans, with particular emphasis upon responsibilities for the next day.

Even though the schedule in Figure 32 calls for such subjects as art and music at certain times, these may be drawn upon at different times to enrich further learning in an interest area. With work centers or nooks provided in the room for art, music, science, reading, and games, the individual can utilize one of these areas whenever he has free time and in so doing he does not disturb others.

EXPERIENCE AND CONTENT

Observance of a block schedule in carrying out the unit "Sending and Receiving Messages" allowed for the unfolding of a unit of work in a manner which provided for the development of children's interests, furthered

---

[21]Samuel Hopkins Adams, *The Pony Express* (Wisconsin: E. M. Hale and Company, 1950).
[22]*Clear the Line* (Recording) Chicago: Silver Burdett Company, 1956.

the learning of content and the mastery of skills necessary for participation in society. The basic list of "Things to Learn About Sending and Receiving Messages" served as a stimulus and guide in keeping the group working toward their objectives. This list was placed in a conspicuous place in the classroom where it could be referred to as needed.

Since the list included a broad coverage of phases of communication, the teacher guided the children in arranging the items so that a limited number of the points would be under study at the time. "How Animals Talk" was chosen as the first phase to develop. "How to Send Letters" was next on the list and was studied with the first listing. The interest in sending letters soon led to planning a trip to the post office. This called for extensive communication such as contacting the post office officials for permission to visit, getting letters of permission from parents, providing for transportation, and planning a code of behavior for the trip.

One can readily see that a trip to the post office involves a number of phases of communication, which might cause the class to undertake more than they are able to cope with satisfactorily. This is a problem of which the teacher must always be aware. When the work is not limited to the group's readiness and ability, opportunity for the children to gain insight into important relationships may be sacrificed, thus causing them to gain only a smattering of knowledge within a broad framework. The teacher should also recognize that children in the primary grades do much of their research work as a whole group with direct help and guidance from the teacher, which necessarily limits the scope of the study undertaken at one time. As the children mature they are able to do research in groups which allows for the study of several phases of the unit at one time.

Third grade children usually are able to assume much responsibility through group work when given the opportunity and practice. By the time the class in point was ready to plan for the trip to the post office, some committees were functioning among them. These included the bulletin board, library, and an exploratory committee which visited the resource agency with the teacher in preparation for the visit by the class. After the excursion to the post office, group work was used in listing "What We Learned at the Post Office." Each of several groups pooled its ideas as to what was gained from the experience. Then, with one person reporting from each group, a common list was prepared by the class with the guidance of the teacher. Letters of appreciation were written to the post office officials and to those who helped with the transportation.

Interest in the post office continued after the visit. The experience had broadened the interest of the group to include the telephone, telegraph, and printed matter seen in the post office such as magazines, newspapers, and different kinds of letters. At this point, research groups were formed to learn more about each of these media. Individuals expressed their preferences for media to study and persons with whom they would like to work.

The teacher recognized that these media, as topics for study, did not lend themselves to extensive research for children of this age. Consequently, he encouraged the students to find information and materials which would be meaningful to them and of such nature that they could share them with others. An example of how the groups worked can be illustrated by observing the work of the one studying the telephone. This group compiled a list of good telephone manners using the kit furnished them by the telephone company. They shared their findings with other members of the class in a skit which contrasted courteous and discourteous telephone use. They also prepared a bulletin board showing development of the telephone through pictures of the earliest to the latest models. A poster was made illustrating courteous use of the telephone and listing good telephone manners. Notebook size copies were duplicated and given to each member of the class with a copy to take home.

From the study of these phases of communication came motivation to learn more about the history of communication and the development and use of the recorder, the radio, television, photography, and motion picture. The whole class made a general study of the history, each person and group sharing information and pictures collected. Grouping for study of the latter phases of communication mentioned was set up with considerable change in group membership based on the children's interests and the observation of the teacher as to how different persons worked together. Activities of the second selection of phases of communication were similar to those carried out in study of the telephone, telegraph, newspapers, magazines, and letters except that the recorder, radio, television, photography, and motion picture provided more graphic material. With the experience of the first study fresh in the minds of the children, participation in the new groups was more free, constructive, and extensive. With the exploration of this second group of elements of communication the unit reached its climax and students were ready to complete this topic and move on.

SUMMARY-EVALUATION

After being involved in a comprehensive study of a topic with any group of students, the teacher is faced with reaching a usable learning climax that will leave the students wanting to know more but having a deep and sincere feeling of accomplishment. Certain types of culminating and evaluating activities affording children opportunities for summarizing their individual and unit learnings with others are desirable. A program, exhibit, or fete of some kind often comes as an outgrowth of the natural ongoing activities. It is desirable from an educational standpoint that any exhibition resulting from a unit of work should be a natural development and assembling of what has actually taken place within the children's learning experiences. Sometimes a simple review of "What We Have Learned and Done" just for the satisfaction of those concerned is all that is desirable. Just to share this with another class near the same grade level or with parents of the particular group of children may bring the desired recognition.

In the unit on communication, as soon as interest was shown in its history it was decided that everyone might contribute in some way. Each person indicated that he would like to know how at least one kind of communication started so this became an assignment for all. Thus, everyone contributed information, pictures, or realia to the project. As a means of summarizing what they had learned, the class decided to name a scrapbook committee to take samples of all their written work and data and put this material in a scrapbook, using pictures they had collected and painted for illustration. An exhibit committee was named to label and display realia and constructed materials. Each person also organized the papers he had written, data gathered, pictures collected, pictures painted, and listed all the stories and books he had read. He then assembled them into a notebook or scrapbook.

As a means of evaluating what had been learned from the unit of study on communication, several debates were set up in which teams tried to prove that one means of communication was more important than another, for example radio or television, and the letter or telegram. A quiz program in which a team of persons posed as experts on one means of communication and was questioned by an interrogator became the favorite activity of the class.

It should be pointed out that culminating activities must come as a result of real study by individuals and the class to solve problems, gain new insight, develop concepts, and experience different and better understandings. The development of an activity for the sake of display accomplishes little and often leaves one with an empty feeling and a sense of wasted effort and time. On the other hand, a culminating activity which results from seeking a better means of visualizing and understanding the answer to a problem, broadening an interest or extending a skill leaves one with a sense of accomplishment. It is this feeling the teacher must strive for in planning, carrying out, and evaluating any unit of work.

Direction and caution given to the student teacher in evaluating performance in group work through unit teaching by Burr, Harding, and Jacobs stands as sound advice to every teacher who seeks to implement the unit approach. Their advice is as follows:

> Children in the elementary school, at each age and grade level, are learning co-operative group work. They begin the process of learning committee work in the kindergarten and they are still learning it when they are in the sixth grade. Even adults in our democracy have much to learn about working co-operatively. As a student teacher, you must expect that the group work will not always go smoothly. You will need to give supervision and guidance to provide frequent discussion of the elements of good committee work and to arrange for periodic evaluation by the committees to the whole group. Through these progress reports and your supervision of the committees at work, waste of time through misdirected effort can be largely avoided.
>
> When children fail in their committee work, it is usually because they have little respect for the job they have undertaken or because they do not have a clear understanding of their group functions and responsibilities. Each of these difficulties can be avoided by careful planning and replanning. You must sit down frequently with each small group guiding them in planning their work, directing them to sources of information, and helping them "to become a group."[23]

SAMPLE RESOURCE UNIT

The resource unit is basic to the development of an effective teaching unit. Its major function is that of preparing the teacher. The resource unit provides the teacher with an over-all understanding of the topic or problem under consideration. It refreshes his mind with basic content and causes him to acquaint himself with current information and instructional materials and media. Preparing a resource unit encourages the teacher to examine the topic in light of its suitableness to the learners. This calls for an understanding of the instructional data and the teaching techniques as well as the skills, attitudes, and appreciations needed by the students.

The format of the resource unit of necessity often appears formal and subject-centered. This, however, does not mean that its development in the classroom shall take this approach. Implementation of any unit depends upon the teacher. A thorough knowledge of the subject and an understanding of the possible directions for development, together with a wide range of learning activities, should tend to give the teacher confidence. It should encourage him to feel free and cause him to foster a permissive, creative learning atmosphere. It is with this interest that the subsequent resource

[23]James S. Burr, Lowry W. Harding, Leland B. Jacobs, *Student Teaching in Elementary School* (second edition; New York: Appleton-Century-Crofts, Inc., 1958), pp. 130-1. Copyright © 1950, 1958. Reprinted by permission of Appleton-Century-Crofts, Inc.

unit "Sending and Receiving Messages" is included. The preceding pages have shown how this unit can serve as a resource for development of a topic area in a problem-solving manner.

Just as the format and content of the resource unit included here is not expected to be followed verbatim, neither is the preceding sample of how a teaching unit can be developed from a resource unit in a problem-solving manner to be adopted as a blueprint for any classroom. It is anticipated, however, that the concepts, samples, and resources presented will stimulate and encourage the classroom teacher to utilize the unit of work as a vehicle for problem-solving. When undertaken in varying degrees, depending upon student readiness and the appropriateness of the learning situation, new avenues toward accomplishment of goals will be forthcoming. The following resource unit developed by Mrs. Helen Bottoms is included as a sample of teacher preparation necessary before undertaking a teaching unit.

SENDING AND RECEIVING MESSAGES: A RESOURCE UNIT[24]

I. Overview

The unit "Sending and Receiving Messages" provides a plan of work for third grade students which should last three to five weeks. Provision is made for guiding students into opportunities and experiences in which they learn about the many ways of sending and receiving messages. The unit also plans for students to learn more about messages we see and hear; how messages were sent long ago; what happens to mail that we take to the post office or put in a mailbox; to learn more about printed messages and why we have so many kinds; to learn more about telephone and telegrams and how to use them; and to learn more about recordings, radio, television, and picture messages.

It is anticipated that this unit will provide opportunities for social interaction, democratic group process, and creative experiences as content is mastered through the problem-solving process. The textbook *Working Together*[25] is utilized as a major reference for content with the purpose of giving objectivity to the unit and a common base of content understandable by all students.

II. Objectives

A. Appreciations and attitudes

1. To increase awareness of the people who help satisfy our needs for communication.
2. To develop a respect for the abilities, responsibilities and skills of others.

---

[24]Mrs. Helen Bottoms (student) College of Education, University of Georgia, Athens, Georgia. February, 1963. Adapted and reproduced by permission of Mrs. Helen Bottoms, 2264 LaVista Road, Toco Hills, Apt. 4, Atlanta, Ga.

[25]Alta McIntire and Wilhelmina Hill, *Working Together* (Chicago: Follett Publishing Company, 1959), pp. 165-196.

3. To develop an attitude of curiousity concerning the world around the child.
4. To appreciate the fact that added facilities of communication have brought about changes in man's way of living.
5. To develop respect for the rights, opinions, and property of other individuals.

B. Understandings to be developed
   1. Communication is very important to us.
      a. It helps us to exchange ideas and information.
      b. It helps us to learn from each other and to work together.
      c. It is essential to our democratic way of life.
   2. There are many messages that we can see and hear.
      a. Language is our basic means of communication.
      b. Animals give messages by making sounds or by making movements.
      c. Man uses many instruments for communication.
   3. Long ago messages were sent in different ways:
      a. The earliest people communicated by drawing pictures on the walls of caves or on rocks.
      b. Later, men began to use signs and letters for writing.
      c. Indians used puffs of smoke or the beating of drums.
   4. Many things happen to mail that we take to the post office or put in a mailbox.
      a. A mailman or mail truck takes the letter from a mailbox to the post office where the mail is sorted.
      b. Letters and packages are taken by airplane, train, or truck to the towns or cities.
      c. The postman then delivers the letters and packages to homes and schools and stores.
      d. Long ago letters were carried by the Pony Express.
      e. Postage stamps help pay for sending mail.
   5. Books, magazines, and newspapers are all printed messages.
      a. Many books are printed each year.
      b. Newspapers give us current news.
      c. People who gather and write news are called reporters.
      d. Magazines have stories, pictures, and sometimes games.
   6. Telegraphed messages are very important to us.
      a. Telegraphed messages travel speedily.
      b. Machines using dots and dashes sent the first telegrams.
      c. Telegrams are called cablegrams when the message travels through cables under the ocean.
   7. Telephones provide a convenient way of communicating.
      a. Telephones help us keep in touch with our friends.
      b. They help us get doctor, policeman, others in a hurry.
      c. We should be polite and not use the telephone too long.
   8. Recordings and radio give messages and much pleasure.
      a. Radio gives us live news.
      b. Recordings give us permanent records of messages.

        c. Programs are planned and timed carefully.

        d. Sound effects make programs seem real.

    9. Television is our newest means of communication.

        a. Pictures and sound come to us from television stations by means of electric waves that travel through the air.

        b. Television brings us pictures and reports of news events.

        c. Television brings us plays, movies, and concerts.

C. Skills and habits to be developed

  1. Reading

    a. Read to answer questions.

    b. Get information from pictures.

    c. Share information.

    d. Apply information.

    e. Locate information in resources such as encyclopedia, dictionary, textbooks, newspapers, and magazines.

    f. Use phonetic analysis when needed.

    g. Select the main thought of a sentence.

    h. Increase sight vocabulary.

    i. New words:

alphabet	signals	collected
photographs	headlines	sports
cartoon	exchange	mouthpiece
operator	announcer	studio
televised	broadcast	electric waves
cancelling	Pony Express	
receiver	microphone	

  2. Listening

    a. Sit still while listening.

    b. Watch the speaker.

    c. Think about what the speaker is saying.

    d. Think of good questions to ask the speaker.

    e. Listen to one another actively.

    f. Listen appreciatively to recordings, to radio, and television programs, and to talks by resource people.

  3. Writing

    a. Express appreciation to someone through a thank-you note.

    b. Improve skills of spelling, punctuation, and capitalization.

    c. Write creative stories about ways pets send messages.

    d. Write simple reports.

  4. Arithmetic

    a. Understand the social significance of money.

    b. Make change in money.

  5. Music

    a. Sing rote songs.

    b. Sing simple rounds and easy descants.

  c. Listen to phonograph recordings, radio, and television and respond creatively.
  d. Create verses for songs.
6. Art
  a. Do creative work in drawing and painting.
  b. Write messages using pictures instead of words.
  c. Draw pictures expressing ideas of early messages.
  d. Develop manual skills through construction of post office.
7. Social living skills
  a. Develop in ability to work with groups.
  b. Develop the use of leisure time.
  c. Develop habit of orderliness.
  d. Develop willingness to take turns and to share.
  e. Refrain from interrupting during discussion.

III. Approach activities
  A. Display letters from students.
  B. Display telephone kit from Bell Telephone Company.
  C. Arrange display of books on communication.
  D. Show and discuss filmstrip "Learning About Communication."[26]
  E. Prepare bulletin board on messages.

IV. Procedure
  A. Discuss approach activities.
  B. Examine and read cards and messages from children who have traveled.
  C. List "Things We Could Learn About Sending and Receiving Messages."
  D. Through group planning organize children's contributions into list that could serve as a tentative guide to study.
  E. Examine ways of giving and receiving messages in pictures of *Working Together*.[27]
  F. Discuss giving messages by talking.
  G. Introduce song "A True Story," *Working Together*.[28]
  H. Read "How Animals Give Messages," *Working Together*.[29]
  I. Locate and read animal stories in library books.
  J. Share animal stories read.
  K. Write stories about sounds made by pets.
  L. Find pictures in magazines about pets and bring to class.
  M. Share in groups stories written.
  N. Talk about the alphabet and what we can write using only twenty-six letters.
  O. Read and report on invention of alphabet.
  P. Show film "Story of Communication."[30]

---

[26]*Learning About Communication*, filmstrip, American Book Company.
[27]Alta McIntire and Wilhelmina Hill, *op. cit.*
[28]*Ibid.*, 170.
[29]*Ibid.*, 171-3.
[30]*Story of Communication*, film. Encyclopedia Britannica Films, Inc., Wilmette, Ill.

Q. Read about sending messages long ago from text and library books.

R. Paint picture stories.

S. Play game writing messages with pictures instead of words.

T. See film "Where Do Our Letters Go?"[31]

U. Read "Letters and Packages."[32] Compare with information in film.

V. Students bring letters from home.

W. Compare stamps, postmarks, addresses, and return addresses on letters.

X. Plan and take trip to post office.

Y. Develop set of behavior guides for trip.

Z. See film strip "Our Post Office."[33]

AA. See filmstrip "The Postman."[34]

BB. Coordinate children's experiences into an experience chart.

CC. Children write story about trip to post office.

DD. Children read or tell about trip and record on tape.

EE. Study voices from tape.

FF. Make list of guides for good listening.

GG. Write thank-you letters to postmaster and others who made trip possible.

HH. Plan construction of post office in classroom.

II. Organize committees to manufacture money, rearrange the physical environment, secure old letters, magazines, and packages to use as mail, construct activity area, draw stamps, make postmark using potato, and any necessary committees that the children might suggest.

JJ. Rotate pupils to various jobs to provide for varied interests and abilities.

KK. Children keep scrapbook of their interpretation of picture of a post office, their story about their trip to the post office and other related work.

LL. Develop mural on messages.

MM. Exhibit materials that give messages in print, books, magazines, etc.

NN. Contrast ways of making books today with ways of long ago.

OO. Visit school library. Learn about all features that are not understood such as withdrawal of books, care of books, return of books, kinds of books available, and courtesy in library.

PP. Write messages in code on telegram forms.

QQ. Read "Telegrams"[35] and other sources on telegrams.

RR. Encourage individual work such as making a telegraph set.

---

[31] *Where Do Our Letters Go?*, film. Coronet Instructional Films, Chicago.
[32] Alta McIntire and Wilhelmina Hill, *op. cit.*, pp. 175-7.
[33] *Our Post Office, filmstrip.* Encyclopedia Britannica Films, Inc.
[34] *The Postman,* filmstrip. Encyclopedia Britannica Films, Inc.
[35] Alta McIntire and Wilhelmina Hill, *op. cit.*, pp. 181-2.

SS. Use telephone kit from Bell Telephone Company for practicing telephoning.

TT. View and discuss the film "Pirro and the Telephone."[36]

UU. Make list of rules for using the telephone.

VV. Encourage children to make own telephone books and list friends' numbers in them. List their telephone rules in books.

WW. See film "Pirro and Phonograph."[37]

XX. Listen to the recording "Clear the Line."[38]

YY. Sing the song "Mail Bags."[39]

ZZ. Record and play back the singing of students.

AAA. Listen to the news on the radio and point out how programs are planned and timed so that they will begin and end at the right time.

BBB. Read "Radio Messages"[40] and other sources on radio.

CCC. View and discuss the filmstrip "Radio Broadcasting Today."[41]

DDD. Make list of television programs children like. Discuss why they like certain ones.

EEE. Plan good ways of watching television.

FFF. View and discuss "Television in Your Community."[42]

GGG. Set up an exhibit on messages. Include stamp collection, toy telephones, letters, old instruments of communication, constructed materials, notebooks, etc.

HHH. Summarize in various ways information gained about communication.

III. Arrange for individuals and groups to share their experiences and accomplishments.

V. Evaluation Techniques
   A. Self-evaluation (Sample questions)
      1. Teacher
         a. Have I provided opportunities for experiences that meet the differing needs of the individuals in the group?
         b. Is there evidence that the children are· gaining in their power of enjoyment?
         c. Is there evidence that children are building those values essential for democratic living?
         d. Is there evidence of growth in the ability to do critical and problem solving thinking?
         e. Do I adequately prepare myself to teach my pupils?

---

[36]*Pirro and the Telephone*, filmstrip. Official Films, Inc., Ridgefield, New Jersey.
[37]*Pirro and the Phonograph*, filmstrip. Official Films, Inc., Ridgefield, New Jersey.
[38]*Clear the Line*, record. Silver Burdett Company, 1956.
[39]"Mail Bags" New Music Horizons, Book III (New York: Silver Burdett, 1944), p. 11.
[40]*Radio Messages*. Alta McIntire and Wilhelmina Hill, *op. cit.*, pp. 186-189.
[41]*Radio Broadcasting Today*, filmstrip. Encyclopedia Britannica Films, Inc.
[42]*Television in Your Community*. Coronet Instructional Films, Chicago, Ill.

       f.   Do I guide group discussions and work rather than dominate?

       g.   Am I preparing an environment conducive to learning?

   2.   Pupil

       a.   What do I know about messages that I did not know before I studied this unit?

       b.   What did I learn about ways of sending messages long ago?

       c.   Did I learn more about how to write thank-you letters and address envelopes?

       d.   Do I know how to use the library and how to care for books?

       e.   Did I learn the right, polite way of using the telephone?

B.   Behavior and anecdotal records

The teacher will make brief notes as incidents arrive and drop them in a folder which will be prepared for each child. Some specific instances that might be recorded are: did not share magazines with others, helped another person with his property, or discussed need for sharing with others.

C.   Charts and check lists

Appropriate charts and check lists will be prepared for periodic self-evaluation by the students. The form in Figure 34 will serve as a guide for developing a form suitable to the situation. This periodic evaluation will be in addition to the day-by-day evaluation. At the end of each day the teacher and class will discuss the extent to which they have met their objectives set for the day, and what over-all accomplishments are recognizable.

D.   Sample questions for written evaluation by students.

   1.   Discussion question: On the lines below, write some "Rules for Good Speaking" and some "Rules for Good Listening."

   2.   Arrange the sentences in order by writing 1 before the sentence that comes first, writing 2 before the ones that come next, and so on.

     ————A cancelling machine marks the stamp.
     ————You put a letter into the mailbox.
     ————A truck takes the letter to the post office.
     ————The letter goes from the mail car to the post office in the town to which it is addressed.
     ————A postman takes your letter to the address you wrote on it.
     ————The letters are sorted in the mail car.
     ————The letter goes to the railroad station in a truck.

   3.   Write the word that belongs in each blank.

       a.   Telegrams are usually ....

                             long — short

Name: _____ Date: _____

School: _____ City: _____

WORKING WELL WITH OTHERS

How do you work with other students in making plans, discussing problems, making things, looking up ideas, and using materials? All of us need to check ourselves to see if we are doing those things that improve group work. Each person should know his good points and shortcomings and consider how to improve himself. Read the statements below and place a check in the square that tells how often you do each item.

How Often Do You Do Each Item Listed Below?	Always	Usually	Some-times	Never
1. I stick to the job until it is finished.				
2. I take part in many different activities.				
3. I work with everyone in the class.				
4. I am eager to try out new ideas and to work on new problems.				
5. I share materials with others.				
6. I help set up plans and directions and follow them.				
7. I work happily without grumbling or losing my temper.				
8. I give in if my ideas conflict with the best interests of the group.				
9. I consider the rights of others.				
10. I am courteous and use good manners.				

Figure 34. Self Evaluation Chart on Working with Others. John A. Michaelis, *Social Studies for Children in a Democracy*. Second Edition. (Englewood Cliffs: Prentice-Hall, Inc., 1956), p. 410. Reprinted by permission of Prentice-Hall, Inc.

        b. I come in an envelope ....
                letter — recording
        c. I carry your voice over wires ....
                telephone — radio
    4. Write a paragraph describing your most interesting experience during your study of sending and receiving messages.

VI. Instructional Aids
    A. Books useful to the teacher in planning and directing this unit:
        1. Jefferson, Blanche, *Teaching Art to Children*. Boston: Allyn and Bacon, Inc., 1959.
        2. Michaelis, John, *Social Studies for Children in a Democracy*. Englewood Cliffs, New Jersey: Prentice-Hall, Inc., 1956.

3. San Bernardino County Schools, *Social Studies for Democracy's Children.* California: Office of the Superintendent of Schools, 1955.

4. Georgia State Department of Education, *Pathways to Music,* Atlanta: Georgia State Department of Education, 1963.

B. Textbooks useful to the children in carrying out the activities of this unit:

1. Cutright, Prudence, and others, *Living In America Today and Yesterday.* New York: The Macmillan Company, 1962.

2. Cutright, Prudence, and others, *Living Together Today and Yesterday.* New York: The Macmillan Company, 1958.

3. Fraser, Dorothy M., and Harry E. Hoy. *Our Community.* New York: American Book Company, 1961.

4. Hanna, Paul R., and others. *In City, Town, and Country,* Chicago: Scott, Foresman, and Company, 1959.

5. McIntire, Alta, and Wilhelmina Hill, *Working Together.* New York: Follett Publishing Company, 1959.

6. Pollock, Thomas, and Florence B. Bowden, *Learning Together.* New York: The Macmillan Company, 1960.

7. Sorensen, Clarence W., *Ways of Our Land.* Atlanta: Silver Burdett Company, 1961.

C. Books useful to the children in independent reading:

1. Adams, Samuel Hopkins, *The Pony Express.* Wisconsin: E. M. Hale and Company, 1950.

2. Anthony, Barbara, and Marcillene Barnes, *Americans All.* Michigan: The Fideler Company, 1941.

3. Batchelor, Christene, *Communication: From Cave Writing to Television.* New York: Harcourt, Brace and Co., 1954.

4. Bolton, Sarah L., *Lives of Poor Boys Who Became Famous.* New York: Studio Publications Company, 1951.

5. Buchheimer, Naomi, *Let's Go to the Post Office.* New York: G. P. Putnam's Sons, 1957.

6. Colonius, Lillian, *At the Library.* New York: Melmont Press, 1955.

7. Eberle, Irmengarde, *Famous Inventors.* New York: A. S. Barnes and Company, 1941.

8. Greene, Carla, *I Want to be a News Reporter.* Chicago: Childrens Press, 1958.

9. Hastings, Evelyn Belmont, *About Postmen.* New York: Melmont Press, 1957.

10. McSpadden, J. W., *How They Sent the News.* New York: Dodd, Mead and Company, 1956.

11. Meyer, Dorothy, *Picture Book of Radio and Television and How They Work.* Chicago: Lothrop, Lee and Shepard Co., 1958.

12. Miner, Irene Serrey, *The True Book of Our Post Office and Its Helpers.* Chicago: Childrens Press, 1955.

13. Parker, Bertha Morris, *The Golden Book Encyclopedia.* New York: Golden Press, 1960.
14. Rogers, Gordon, *Heels, Wheels, and Wire.* Philadelphia: Lippincott, 1956.
15. Schloat, Warren Jr., *Adventures of a Letter.* New York: Charles Scribner's Sons, 1955.
16. Schneider, Ruth, *Your Telephone and How It Works.* New York: McGraw-Hill Book Company, 1958.
17. Shippen, Katherine, *Mr. Bell Invents the Telephone.* New: York: Random House, 1951.
18. Snow, Dorothea J., *Samuel Morse.* New York: Random House, 1955.
19. Stevenson, Augusta, *Ben Franklin: Printer's Boy.* Indianapolis 7: The Bobbs-Merrill Company, 1941.

D. Films useful to the teacher and children
   1. "Pirro and the Telephone." Official Films, Inc., Ridgefield, N. J.
   2. "Pirro and the Phonograph." Official Films, Inc.
   3. "Story of Communication." Encyclopedia Britannica Films., Inc., Wilmette, Ill.
   4. "Television in Your Community." Coronet Instructional Films, Chicago, Ill.
   5. "Where Do Our Letters Go?" Coronet Instructional Films.

E. Filmstrips useful to the teacher and children.
   1. "Learning About the Community." American Book Company, Chicago.
   2. "Learning About Communication." American Book Company.
   3. "Our Post Office." Encyclopedia Britannica Films, Inc.
   4. "Radio Broadcasting Today." Encyclopedia Britannica Films, Inc.
   5. "The Postman." Encyclopedia Britannica Films, Inc.

F. Exhibits useful to the teacher and children
   1. "Telephone Kit." Bell Telephone Company, any local office.

G. Recordings useful to the teacher and children
   1. "Clear the Line." Silver Burdett Company, 1956.
   2. "The Foghorn." Silver Burdett Company, 1956.

SUMMARY

Since man first recognized that learning takes place best in meaningful situations, he has sought to find a means whereby this principle can be utilized best in the classroom. Efforts to use the unit approach to teaching in bringing about meaningful learning originated near the beginning of the twentieth century. This approach was slow to take root, however, in that the times and conditions apparently were not ripe for such divergent classroom procedure.

Gradual steps have been taken through the years to move toward experience teaching from the strictly subject-centered approach. These steps include (1) textbook subject matter, (2) correlation, (3) fusion, (4) center of interest — unit, and (5) experience teaching. Learning theories set forth by Dewey have been reinforced by Spears' principles of teaching which give educators support in providing situations more conducive to learning. Skill in problem solving is now being recognized as essential to all responsible citizens. The unit of work seems the most appropriate vehicle through which this approach to learning can operate effectively.

So that problem solving can take place, individuals must experiment, observe, read, discuss, inquire and make use of all available resources. The important responsibiilty of the teacher is to help students see relationships among bodies of content and be able to apply content and skills in solving problems in our increasingly complex society. More emphasis is being placed upon involving the student in identifying his needs, plotting his course of action, and evaluating his results. In so doing he utilizes a wide variety of instructional materials which cut across subject matter lines. This approach has brought about organization of data into units which range from strict subject matter to experience. The resource unit provides a comprehensive guide to preparation and a major source to be drawn upon by the teacher and class in the development of a problem area.

Extensive preparation by the teacher for effective unit teaching is mandatory. This involves gaining knowledge of children, curriculum, policies, community and school resources, and setting the stage for learning experiences appropriate to the children. Careful selection of problem areas for unit teaching involves both the teacher and the students in applying criteria designed to assist in choosing the most desirable unit for the situation.

After the unit or problem topic has been selected an appropriate outline should be followed in preparing a full resource unit as background information for the teacher. Major aspects of the unit to be prepared by the teacher prior to initiation of the unit include (1) overview, (2) objectives, (3) approach activities, (4) procedure, (5) evaluation techniques, and (6) instructional aids. Using the resource unit outline as a guide, the teacher should plan appropriate activities for initiating the unit. These include bulletin boards, exhibits, displays, films, natural leads from children in the classroom, and special occasions and current events.

The teacher should develop a tentative series of activities pertinent to the unfolding of the unit, realizing that this plan would be subject to the interests and needs of the students and the conditions at hand. Plans should also provide means of focusing on major aspects of the problem area, as well as summarizing and evaluating learner accomplishments.

Careful pre-planning usually results in effective implementation of a unit of work. The success of the unit depends, however, upon the involvement of children in the ongoing procedure. Daily lesson plans prepared by the teacher assist him in projecting the subject under study, serve as a guide for effective teaching, and help him plan each day's work on the basis of preceding accomplishments. The plan should include (1) purpose, (2) procedure, (3) evaluating and closing, and (4) instructional aids.

In order that children may have freedom to work, careful planning by the teacher with the children is required. The major activities of the day must be outlined and observed by all participants. A flexible schedule allowing large blocks of time for the designated areas of the curriculum serves as a framework in which unit teaching may effectively and comfortably function. Within this framework students should identify their problems, outline their courses of action and schedule time to accomplish their objectives. Basic to this, however, is the teacher who should be able to so organize himself that he respects the abilities of others to conduct themselves in such an orderly manner that the students may plan and function on an independent, coherent basis. In so doing they should evaluate at the end of each day the realization of their goals and plan how to begin the next day independently in carrying out their chosen activities.

A major responsibility of the teacher in using the unit approach is to assist and guide students in choosing activities that will stimulate and enrich their interest and strengthen their communication and other basic skills. This must be accomplished by involving each individual in such a manner that he sees the need for basic skills and plans his activities accordingly.

Culminating a unit of work involves activities which summarize and evaluate learning experiences. When these experiences are engaged in as a means of accomplishing student objectives they have meaning for the students and perform worthwhile and appropriate functions in completing the unit.

QUESTIONS FOR DISCUSSION

1. Identify the term "unit teaching." What implications does this term have for teaching?
2. What changes have taken place in the development of teaching procedure from single textbook to unit teaching?

3. How can unit teaching serve as the vehicle for problem solving in the classroom?
4. What are the steps necessary in preparation for teaching a unit? Describe.
5. What are the major aspects of an outline for a resource unit?
6. How do the roles of the teacher and students differ in implementing a unit of work? How do they relate?
7. What aspects of a class schedule involving the teaching of content and skills are conducive to unit teaching? Outline such a schedule.

TOPICS FOR RESEARCH

1. Develop a resource unit observing the guides set forth in this chapter.
2. Observe one or more classrooms in which unit teaching is taking place. Note differences in learning environment and attitudes of children.
3. View films which depict unit teaching. For example view "Effective Learning in the Classroom" distributed by McGraw-Hill Book Company.
4. Through observation and reading delineate the advantages and disadvantages of unit teaching.
5. Devise a desirable approach to unit teaching in a school situation where students and teachers have had little or no experience with it.

BIBLIOGRAPHY

BECK, ROBERT H., WALTER W. COOK AND NOLAN C. KEARNEY. *Curriculum in the Modern Elementary School.* Second edition. Englewood Cliffs: Prentice-Hall, Inc., 1960.

BURR, JAMES S., LOWRY W. HARDING, LELAND B. JACOBS. *Student Teaching in Elementary School.* Second edition. New York: Appleton-Century-Crofts, Inc., 1958.

DUTTON, WILBUR H. AND JOHN A. HOCKETT. *The Modern Elementary School.* New York: Rinehart and Company, Inc., 1959.

GILBOUGH, JOHN W. *How to Organize and Teach Units of Work in Elementary and Secondary Schools.* San Jose, California: Modern Education Publishers, 1957.

GWYNN, J. MINOR. *Theory and Practice of Supervision.* New York: Dodd, Mead and Company, 1961.

HANNA, LAVONE, GLADYS L. POTTER, AND NEVA HAGAMAN. *Unit Teaching in the Elementary School.* New York: Holt, Rinehart, and Winston, Inc., 1963.

HILL, WILHELMINA. *Unit Planning and Teaching in Elementary Social Studies.* Washington, D. C.: U. S. Office of Health, Education, and Welfare, 1963.

MICHAELIS, JOHN U. *Social Studies for Children in a Democracy.* Third edition. Englewood Cliffs: Prentice-Hall, Inc., 1963.

NOAR, GERTRUDE, *Freedom to Live and Learn.* Philadelphia: Franklin Publishing Company, 1948.

NOAR, GERTRUDE. *Teaching and Learning the Democratic Way.* Englewood Cliffs: Prentice-Hall, Inc., 1963.

SHANE, HAROLD G. (Ed.). *The American Elementary School.* New York: Harper and Brothers Publishers, 1953.

SOWARDS, G. WESLEY, AND MARY-MARGARET SCOBEY. *The Changing Curriculum and the Elementary Teacher.* San Francisco: Wadsworth Publishing Company, Inc., 1961.

SPEARS, HAROLD. *Principles of Teaching.* New York: Prentice-Hall, Inc., 1951.

UNIVERSITY OF GEORGIA. *Elementary Education Handbook.* Athens, Georgia: College of Education, University of Georgia, 1964.

Utilization of appropriate content enables students to develop basic skills and acquire necessary knowledge for effective living.

Chapter 10

Extending Basic Skills
With Appropriate Content

After generations of debate and research the question continues to be asked "What shall the schools teach?" Each generation has answered this in its own way, usually with a wide diversity of responses. Three distinct views as to what the schools shall teach today have been set forth by the Project on the Instructional Program of the Public Schools. One view presented limits the responsibilities of the school to the intellectual training of children and restricts the curriculum almost exclusively to academic subjects. A second view takes into account the child's total development. This position emphasizes the pupil's intellectual development as the basic function of the school but recognizes the emotional, social, physical, and vocational aspects of the child's growth and calls on other social institutions and agencies to share with the school in meeting these needs. The most expanded view is that the school should accept full responsibility for the entire range of intellectual, social, physical, and vocational needs of youth served by the particular school and provide an expanded program of instruction and services to meet these needs.[1]

The authors of this publication agree with the position of Project Instruction which states that:

> The education of a child and his experience in school are not synonymous. Family, church, mass media, nonschool recreational facilities, and

[1] Dorothy M. Fraser (ed.) *Deciding What To Teach* (Washington: Project on the Instructional Program of the Public Schools, National Education Association, 1963), p. 87.

social agencies in the community are powerful educational forces in the lives of children and youth. The schooling of young people needs to be studied in relation to these nonschool educational forces. Moreover, this relationship should be re-examined as changes occur in schools, in the non-school agencies, and in the total society.[2]

Being fully cognizant of the imperativeness of the teacher's need for mastery of content and skills as primary to effective teaching, it is expected that mastery of content in the various disciplines will come outside the framework of any course for which this publication might serve as a basic test and before utilization of this textual material. The basic premise maintained and developed here is that use of appropriate content develops and extends basic skills. This point of view places the teacher in the position of determining appropriate curriculum content and guiding children in mastery of skill areas through utilization of content. Four comprehensive skill areas are presented here as the mediums by which teaching can reach the child as he seeks to face problems of living on a sequential developmental basis. These areas are (1) communication skills, (2) socialization skills, (3) environmental understandings, and (4) aesthetic understandings. This chapter thus develops the major topics (1) Determining Curriculum Content, (2) Communication Skills and Content, (3) Socialization Skills and Content, (4) Environmental Understandings and Content, and (5) Aesthetic Understandings.

DETERMINING CURRICULUM CONTENT

As society has expanded and become more complex, pressures upon the school have increased. Additional subjects, services, and modification of curriculum have come as a response to these pressures in many areas formerly considered the responsibility of the home, church, and other segments of the community. These additions and modifications of the school reflect changing patterns of family and community life in regard to out-of-school education in such areas as health, homemaking, recreation, and vocational preparation. Conditions of urban living have made it increasingly necessary that all children learn better ways of living safely and healthfully, making wise consumer choices, using leisure time positively, and practice constructive citizenship.

Changes have also been brought about because of the knowledge explosion. Vast bodies of scientific and technical data have been built up

---

[2]Dorothy M. Fraser (ed.) *Deciding What To Teach* (Washington: Project on the Instructional Program of the Public Schools, National Education Association, 1963) pp. 87-8.

which are easily available for direct transmittal to students through the schools. The changing community and population have challenged the schools with youth of a wider range of abilities and vocational goals. There is increased knowledge in the field of psychology and better understanding of the relation of learning to emotional problems and physical health. It has been recognized that the school must give attention to these factors in order that its intellectual efforts bear full fruition. As a result more explicit attention has been given to character education, civic training, mental health, physical fitness, social development, and occupational guidance through the program of studies, extraclass activities, and special services.

EDUCATIONAL OBJECTIVES

Two renowned statements of educational objectives, the "Seven Cardinal Principles of Education" (1918) and *The Purposes of Education in American Democracy* (1938), have attested to the profession's embracement of the school's responsibility for the social, emotional, and physical development and the specific vocational goals of pupils as well as for intellectual development. Often the inclusion of these broader objectives of education have brought strong criticism that the fundamentals are being replaced by the frills. Nevertheless, schools have continued to include the fundamentals along with the new emphases and subjects. Health education has not replaced English and science, nor has social studies replaced geography and history. These additions have brought new responsibilities and have encouraged more effective ways of inducting youth into society.

Faced with this pressure of added responsibility and concern of the critics, educators have sought to identify attainable objectives which might be amenable to measurement, evaluation, and critical, philosophical analysis. Probably the most extensive effort made to date is that of the Mid-Century Committee on Outcomes in Elementary Education.[3]

The grid depicting educational objectives set forth in Figure 35 presents a picture of elementary school objectives agreed upon by a distinguished group of educators and evaluated by carefully selected critics. The horizontal rows specify the nine major areas of elementary learning: (1) physical development, health and body care, (2) individual social and emotional development, (3) ethical behavior, standards, values, (4) social relations, (5) the social world, (6) the physical world, (7) esthetic development, (8) communication, and (9) quantitative relationships. The vertical columns divide each of the areas of learning into categories that specify (A)

---

[3]Nolan C. Kearney, *Elementary School Objectives* (New York: Russell Sage Foundation, 1953).

knowledge and understanding, (B) skill and competence, (C) attitude and interest, (D) action pattern and (E) determining conditions. The 45 sections of objectives are further subdivided into those aspects obtainable by the end of three levels in the school which are (1) third grade — age 9 (2) sixth grade — age 12 and (3) ninth grade — age 15.[4]

An examination of these objectives reveals that the intellectual as well as the social, emotional, physical, and vocational aspects of the individual have been taken into consideration. It is fully recognized that the optimum results in education can be attained only when a sound core of knowledge,

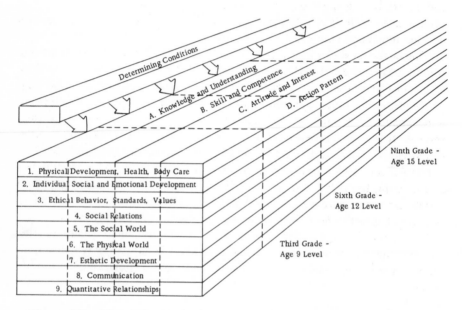

Figure 35. The Behavioral Continuum-Broad Curriculum Areas Intersecting Major Behavior Categories. Nolan C. Kearney, *Elementary School Objectives*, p. 38. Reproduced by permission of Russell Sage Foundation, New York.

understanding, and competence are developed in full consideration of interests, attitudes, and ideals that are wholesome in terms of our democratic ideology and rich cultural tradition. It must be further realized that there is overlapping and duplication between subdivisions and repetition and lack of clarification between items for learning in the categories. This should

---

[4]*Ibid.*, pp. 35-46.

be of minor concern inasmuch as the chief objective of the educator should be to see that major goals of education are provided for and that breadth of opportunities is fully apparent.[5]

CURRICULUM GUIDES

Extensive and sophisticated sets of educational objectives have been set up from time to time by both national and local groups. These objectives, however, are of little value unless they are translated into workable plans with action programs at local level. A major step toward implementation of objectives is the formulation of curriculum guides. The curriculum guide should exhibit a general plan for implementing objectives through an action program. As such, it should serve as a pertinent guide in selecting content and learning experiences at the classroom level.

One of the most significant examples of implementation of objectives into program through a curriculum guide is that of the State Department of Education of Georgia in the *Curriculum Framework for Georgia Schools.*[6] This guide presents a flexible curriculum framework for use by school systems as a reference while making decisions necessary in the ongoing curriculum process. It is considered as a point of departure for the curriculum activities of individual school systems. The guide embraces the objectives of the Educational Policies Commission,[7] presented in Chapter 3 of this publication, as reflecting the beliefs, scope, and details essential to the development of a rich and varied curriculum on local levels in Georgia. Utilizing the characteristics of growth and development of children as the bases for curriculum building, the Georgia guide has provided an organization of educational content from the problems of living with which the individual is faced. This guide for selecting educational experiences includes these basic aspects of living:

1. Achieving and Maintaining Physical and Mental Health
2. Making a Vocational Choice and Earning a Living
3. Performing Responsibilities of Citizenship
4. Conserving and Utilizing Resources
5. Communicating Information and Ideas
6. Expressing Aesthetic Values[8]

---

[5]*Ibid.*
[6]*Curriculum Framework for Georgia Schools, A Guide to Curriculum Planning.* Atlanta: State Department of Education, 1954.
[7]Educational Policies Commission, *The Purposes of Education in American Democracy.* (Washington: National Education Association, 1938), pp. 51-123.
[8]Curriculum Framework for Georgia Schools, *op. cit.*, p. 9.

Using these broad aspects of living as a framework, the Georgia guide has suggested experiences for implementation of objectives in the classroom at different levels. Samples of these experiences are presented here to show the appropriateness of using such a guide in the classroom.

Problems of Living Chart

ACHIEVING AND MAINTAINING PHYSICAL AND MENTAL HEALTH

Kindergarten. (The Immediate Environment. The home, play, nature.)

1. Helping to create and maintain a safe and healthful school-community environment; as, helping in "home and school housekeeping," caring for and arranging flowers.

2. Participating in health services that promote the health of all children and are a continuation of the services for the pre-kindergarten child carried on by the State Department of Health; as, correction of remediable defects, staying home when ill, playing "nurse" and "doctor," telling about visits to doctor and dentist.

Early Elementary: Grades 1 - 2 - 3. (The Immediate Environment. The home, school, community.)

1. Accepting responsibility for helping to create and maintain a healthful school-community environment; as accepting responsibility for keeping home, school, and community clean, attractive and safe.

2. Continuing the promotion of the health of all children, the detection and correction of remediable defects, the prevention and control of preventable diseases; as, cooperating in vision, hearing, and other screening tests, helping to keep own growth chart records.

Later Elementary: Grades 4 - 5 - 6 - 7. (Exploring and adventuring in an expanding environment, local, state, nation, world.)

1. Helping to create and maintain a healthful school community environment; as, assuming a measure of responsibility for regulating heat, light, and ventilation in the classroom, for cleanlines and appearance of classroom, school building, and grounds, cooperating in all programs relating to improving health conditions.

2. Participating in health services for the promotion of the health of all children, the further discovery and correction of physical defects, and the prevention and control of preventable diseases; as, using the public. health and other health personnel as resource persons, visiting dentist regularly.

MAKING A VOCATIONAL CHOICE AND EARNING A LIVING

Kindergarten (The Immediate Environment. The home, play, nature.)

1. Becoming acquainted with people who contribute directly to the comfort, safety and pleasure of the little child; as father, mother, brother, sister, doctor, policeman, maid.

2. Listening to and telling stories of workers with whom the child is familiar.

Early Elementary: Grades 1 - 2 - 3. (The Immediate Environment. The home, school, community.)

1. Becoming acquainted with the contributions of workers in home and community; as, members of the family, policeman, groceryman, milkman, postman, doctors, nurses, farmers.
2. Reading, writing, and telling stories about how people whom they know earn a living.

Later Elementary Grades 4 - 5 - 6 - 7. (Exploring and adventuring in an expanding environment, local, state, nation, world.)

1. Extending knowledge of ways of earning a living in professions, indusdry, arts, crafts and trades; through reading, visitation, creating articles from various materials.
2. Reading biographies of industrial and professional workers who have contributed to social and economic progress.

PERFORMING RESPONSIBILITIES OF CITIZENSHIP

Kindergarten (The Immediate Environment. The home, play, nature.)

1. Making plans for individual and group conduct at school; such as, caring for wraps, respecting the property of others, taking turns, sharing materials and play things, entering and leaving the building.
2. Planning with adults for general welfare and smooth operation of classroom, choosing and following a leader, abiding by group decisions, putting away materials, helping peers, following instructions.

Early Elementary: Grades 1 - 2 - 3 (The Immediate Environment. The home, school, community.)

1. Planning and making decisions cooperatively on matters which affect the group; such as, organizing for living and working together in the room, caring for personal belongings and class projects, participating through representation in a school council.
2. Becoming acquainted by interviews, observation, and discussions with community services: as, fire departments, health department, law enforcement departments, dairy farms, post office.

Later Elementary: Grades 4 - 5 - 6 - 7 (Exploring and adventuring in an expanding environment, local, state, nation, world.)

1. Planning and participating in developing desirable standards for working and playing together in home, school, and community; helping to solve problems through a school council.
2. Finding out how the local government is structured and how it affects the health and welfare of the home, school, and community; identifying and making a time table of important legislation affecting us as citizens.

CONSERVING AND UTILIZING RESOURCES

Kindergarten (The Immediate Environment. The home, play, nature.)

1. Observing trees, plants, grasses in the immediate environment and discussing how they contribute to our welfare.
2. Caring for plants and animals.

Early Elementary: Grades 1 - 2 - 3. (The Immediate Environment. The home, school, community.)

1. Identifying the common uses of the natural resources with which he has contact.
2. Becoming acquainted with wild and domestic animals in the local areas, caring for pets, building bird houses and stations, and growing plants.

Later Elementary: Grades 4 - 5 - 6 - 7. (Exploring and adventuring in an expanding environment, local, state, nation, world.)

1. Utilizing the resources of school and community to meet individual group needs: as, "found materials" for art and science activities.
2. Reading about and observing plants and animals to determine which are harmful to man and how he protects himself against them.

COMMUNICATING INFORMATION AND IDEAS

Kindergarten (The Immediate Environment. The home, play, nature.)

1. Telling about experiences in the home, with pets, visits, T.V.
2. Listening to stories and poems.

Early Elementary: Grades 1 - 2 - 3. (The Immediate Environment. The home, school, community.)

1. Telling about experiences and stories, engaging in discussions of class interests.
2. Listening to stories and poems read or told by individuals.

Later Elementary: Grades 4 - 5 - 6 - 7. (Exploring and adventuring in an expanding environment, local, state, nation, world.)

1. Engaging in oral expressions: as conversations, discussions, reporting, planning of classroom responsibilities and activities.
2. Listening in order to follow directions, discussions, conversation, speeches.

EXPRESSING AESTHETIC VALUES

Kindergarten (The Immediate Environment. The home, play, nature.)

1. Listening to music and singing many songs.
2. Engaging in simple rhythmic games.

Early Elementary: Grades 1 - 2 - 3 (The Immediate Environment. The home, school, community.)

1. Listening to and singing songs relating to a variety of experiences and interests.
2. Participating in rhythmic games and music.

Later Elementary: Grades 4 - 5 - 6 - 7 (Exploring and adventuring in an expanding environment, local, state, nation, world.)
1. Listening to and singing a variety of music — folk, spiritual, seasonal, classical, popular and the like.
2. Playing folk games.[9]

An organization like that just described presumes that education is concerned with the improvement of living, and therefore must derive its content from the problems of living with which the individual must deal. It also recognizes that there are certain bodies of content that have been organized by scholars into categories and labeled according to the interests, knowledge, and skills of the respective scholars. It is from these compilations of data that content and skills can be recognized and drawn upon by the student or the teacher in guiding the individual or groups.

It is in keeping with these realizations that the writers of the *Curriculum Framework for Georgia Schools* related the traditional content areas or disciplines to their selected problems of living classification as follows:

Achieving and Maintaining Physical and Mental Health — personal hygiene, physical education, disease prevention and control, biological science, nutrition, home economics, and fine arts.

Making a Vocational Choice and Earning a Living — economics, business, vocational education, consumer education, resource use, home and family living, social studies, mathematics, the language arts, fine and practical arts.

Performing Responsibilities of Citizenship — social studies, science, the arts, literature, and the language arts.

Conserving and Utilizing Resources — the sciences, the social studies, health, the fine arts and the practical arts.

Communicating Information and Ideas — the language arts, mathematics, social studies, fine arts, the sciences, and certain areas of vocational education.

Expressing aesthetic values — all areas of the curriculum may contribute, as the fine and applied arts, the language arts, social studies, physical and natural sciences, the total environment.[10]

CURRICULUM TRENDS

The school should be aware of the current trends as to what content should be included in the curriculum. This can be noted at local level in

---

[9]*Ibid.*
[10]*Ibid.*, pp. 9-11.

terms of expressions of the people and the emphases currently being supported by them. The teacher, however, should go beyond this by studying current professional literature to determine points of emphasis and shifts in educational trends which affect curriculum content.

Looking at the situation in behalf of the National Education Association, Harold G. Shane pointed out in 1962 that "there has been a distinct trend toward an intellectual or cognitive emphasis in elementary instruction and some withdrawal from the pronounced social emphasis."[11] In view of this he set forth several suggestions with respect to elementary school objectives. Included in these are:

> First, there is nothing inherently wrong with a judicious increase in the tempo of attempts, through education, to improve intellectual powers and extend the information of children. . .
>
> Second, there is a real danger that elementary teachers may become so mesmerized by the magic of technology, the appeal of novel grouping plans, and the respectability of more challenging content that they overlook the fact that these elements are means rather than ends in education.[12]

Shane specifically pointed out that mastery of content per se is relevant to aims only as it motivates the child to continue his education and to use his knowledge, supporting this with Alfred North Whitehead's well-known phrases:

> . . . culture is activity of thought, and receptiveness to beauty and humane feeling. Scraps of information have nothing to do with it. A merely well-informed man is the most useless bore on God's earth. What we would aim at producing is men who possess both culture and expert knowledge in some special direction.[13]

Shane's final suggestion with respect to setting up elementary school objectives stated that

> . . . It is incongruous for elementary education to seek to improve itself by an all-out effort to ape the programs and practices of the junior or senior high schools. Such mimicry is not only foolish but ironic as well during a time when secondary school teaching is being influenced by instructional policies and by research in learning which were initiated in the elementary school.[14]

The most current and succinct views of what should be included in the school program have been set forth by the Project on Instruction as follows:

---

[11]Harold G. Shane, "Elementary Education Objectives," NEA Journal, Vol. 51 (September, 1962), p. 42.
[12]Ibid.
[13]Ibid.
[14]Ibid.

. . . Priorities for the school are the teaching of skills in reading, composition, listening, speaking, (both native and foreign languages), and computation . . . ways of creative and disciplined thinking, including methods of inquiry and application of knowledge . . . competence in self instruction and independent learning . . . fundamental understanding of the humanities and arts, and social sciences and natural sciences, and mathematics . . . appreciation of and discriminating taste in literature, music, and the visual arts . . . instruction in health education and physical education.

Responsibilities best met by joint efforts of the school and other social agencies include development of values and ideals . . . social and civic competence . . . vocational preparation.

. . . To help the student think critically about current issues, the curriculum should provide opportunities for adequate instruction concerning social forces and trends. Attention commensurate with their significance in modern society should be given to issues such as international relations, economic growth, urbanization, population growth, science and technology, and mass media. . . . Rational discussion of controversial issues should be an important part of the school program. The teacher should help students identify relevant information, learn techniques of critical analysis, make independent judgments, and be prepared to present and support them. The teacher should also help students become sensitive to the continuing need for objective re-examination of issues in the light of new information and changing conditions in society.[15]

The writers of this publication recognize the six problems of living identified by the *Curriculum Framework for Georgia Schools* as basic concerns and needs of every individual. They also see these closely allied to the views of what should be included in the school program as set forth by the Project on Instruction. They further attest to the value of the bodies of content and sets of behavior skills which form the background and academic bank from which each individual must draw as he sustains life and makes his place in society. Each of these — problems of living, what the schools should teach, the bodies of content, and sets of skills — is seen as hand and glove in the curriculum of the elementary school. The writers therefore endorse Ragan's point of view in regard to content which is as follows:

The curriculum exists only in the experiences of children; it does not exist in textbooks, in the course of study, or in the plans and intentions of teachers. The course of study has the same relationship to the curriculum that a road map has to the actual experiences involved in taking a trip . . . . The curriculum does not exist in the content to be learned.

[15]Fraser. *op. cit.* pp. 102-3.

The selection of useful, accurate content is a very important responsibility of teachers, but content does not constitute the curriculum until it becomes a part of the experience of the child. The amount of content which becomes curriculum for one child may differ from that which becomes curriculum for another. The teacher-pupil and pupil-pupil relationships, the methods of teaching, and the evaluation procedures used are as much a part of the curriculum as the content to be learned.[16]

SELECTION CRITERIA

The broad approach to determining curriculum content places heavy responsibility upon the individual teacher for guiding children in selecting learning experiences which foster the learning of subject matter content. Because of this the teacher should rely upon curriculum guides adopted by the school system whenever possible, and utilize teacher's guides prepared for adopted textbooks. Basic to the use of any such guides is the knowledge of general criteria for selecting content. A reputable criteria should be at the disposal of every classroom teacher. The criteria should include factors which can be applied not only in determining general content but in selecting content for each curriculum area and for each learning experience. Many factors may be included in such a criteria but some of the more pertinent ones to be used by the teacher are (1) frequency, (2) value, (3) cruciality, (4) scope, (5) recency, and (6) pertinency.

Frequency

The materials which are selected for teaching at any grade level should be those which frequently are used in learning and living in our society, both now and in the future. The knowledges, attitudes, and skills which the teacher desires his students to know will be taught best through materials that all boys and girls customarily study in different regions of our nation.

Value

Although the frequency criterion is extremely important, it needs to be tempered by the closely allied factor of value. Materials which are selected for use in the elementary school should be of such value or quality that they provide challenge and worth for children from both high and low socioeconomic backgrounds. Every curriculum should include some content that is selectively determined as having value for most children. This would

---

[16]William B. Ragan, *Modern Elementary Curriculum,* (revised edition; New York: Henry Holt and Company, 1960), p. 4. Copyright © 1960, Holt, Rinehart and Winston, Inc. By permission of the publishers.

refer particularly to content or skills in the communication area. The curriculum should also include content selected because it is particularly valuable to a given community, region, or people.

Cruciality

There are certain knowledges, attitudes, and skills which should be taught in order that students can make intelligent decisions which demand immediate action. Artificial respiration, how and when to apply a tourniquet, and what to do for a person who has just fainted are illustrative of knowledge concerning crucial events met infrequently by the average citizen which should be taught in the elementary school.

Scope

Knowledges, attitudes, and skills which have been useful for effective citizenship in our society for a long period of time should be selected for inclusion in the instructional program. Care should be exercised by the teachers to avoid too much emphasis upon the local community or geographic area in selecting content and activities. The preponderance of materials selected should have national and universal application potentialities as opposed to only regional or local ones in order to keep the curriculum from becoming too narrow in scope.

Recency

We are living in an age of revolution. New knowledge is accruing in science and technology at a staggering pace. Colonialism is dying and a new spirit of nationalism is arising, particularly on the African continent. Because we are in the early stages of the Space Age and emerging nations are taking their place in the world community, the criterion of recency is extremely important in the selection of instructional materials for the elementary school curriculum. Teachers should exercise sound judgment in choosing those of recent origin to insure their authenticity and value as well as maintaining a proper balance with content previously included in the curriculum because of its common usage.

Pertinency

Pertinent knowledges, attitudes, and skills which children likely will not learn outside of school should be included in the elementary curriculum. When Massachusetts' Colonial legislature enacted its first compulsory school attendance law in 1642 it did so because it felt that parents were neglecting the teaching of their progeny in the home. They therefore acted to provide a system of public education with mandatory attendance regulations, feeling that if the children were not educated properly the state would suffer. The elementary school of today still shoulders the responsibility imposed upon it by this early legislation, with particular attention focused upon providing content and materials which the home, church, or other civic groups fail to provide. In short, where educational shortages exist it becomes the obligation of the school to offer instruction in these areas.

COMMUNICATION SKILLS AND CONTENT

Man is different from other animals basically because of his ability to make meaningful noises and write intelligible scratches on paper. Children are taught to speak and listen so that they can participate in the cultural and intellectual society of which they are a part. They are taught to read, write, and compute so that through commonly accepted written symbols they can be helped to extend their interests and knowledge.

Teachers and educational leaders have long recognized the relationship between language and all aspects of mental, emotional, and social development. The ever-increasing demands which our complex society places upon the individual make the ability to communicate outstandingly important.

During the early part of this century elementary schools were silent schools. Teachers boasted of rooms in which you could "hear a pin drop." Each child worked silently and separately. Language was a "subject" which occupied its little niche in each day's program. There was no real communication among students and between the teacher and students. Lessons were formal and teacher directed.

Now the group process of discussing, planning, and working together is being utilized more and more in our way of life. This necessitates the ability to think and respond quickly and well in situations which call for meeting of the minds. The complexity of life and the demands of most vocations make all of the communication skills essential for day-by-day living. It therefore is not practical to think in terms of teaching isolated skills through meaningless repetition.[17]

Strickland reminds us that "the language of an individual is in a very real sense the mirror of his personality. A child's spontaneity in the use of language is an indication of his feeling of security. The spontaneity, fluency, and control he shows in his speech indicate quite clearly how well his growth is progressing."[18]

---

[17]Ruth Strickland, *The Language Arts in the Elementary School* (Boston: D. C. Heath and Company, 1957), pp. 434-7.
    [18]*Ibid.*, p. 438.

When children are called upon to formulate ideas through the medium of language alone, with only a meager background of experience, their communication is limited and often unintelligible. Talking about changing liquids to gas has little meaning to the child until he actually sees water leave a container in the form of steam after heat has been applied. Previously learned information, the application of knowledgeable skills, the conclusions reached, and the concepts formed then become the new subject matter which is fixed in the child's mind. Through many and varied experiences as just described children learn the important art of communication which includes good thinking, correct oral and written expression, appreciative listening, reading with comprehension and appreciation, the skillful use of books and other instructional media, and the solving of problems. The teacher should accept as his responsibility the development of each of these in every child insofar as the child's ability permits. He should use all known and available means of determining the needs of each child in each skill area.

Basic communication skills for which the teacher should assume responsibility may be classified as receptive, expressive, and manipulative. The receptive skills are listening and reading, the expressive include speaking and writing, and the manipulative deal with those aspects of time, distance, space, and quantity involving computation. These may be recognized in terms of man's developing civilization in the order of listening, speaking, reading, writing, and computation. The child must first associate a sound with an action or an object and then reproduce this sound to communicate. Of course he makes sounds long before he speaks in intelligible communication. Next, in the academic sense, he reads. This begins with the recognition of objects, actions, and symbols which soon become familiar to him as he sees them repeatedly and then perceives them in variable forms. This, of course, is followed by developing understanding of consistent symbolism accepted by others with whom he is communicating. It is only after a consistent set of symbols is understood that the individual can use these symbols to communicate with others in terms of what present day civilization calls writing.

Though listening, speaking, reading, and writing are the generally accepted communication skills, computation is closely associated with them. Much basic computation and problem solving take place within the realm of the individual in terms of behavior as the other communicative skills develop. For example, children early learn to exchange or swap toys. They learn to recognize when one has more than another. They know when "I'm full" of food. Many forms of manipulation and bargaining take place from early childhood, such as bargaining with their parents to let them stay out of bed a little longer, as the beginning of skill in problem solving and computation.

Even though these communication areas may be identified separately they are basic to each experience of every child and should involve the major portion of the child's time. They therefore should be treated as the core of the curriculum rather than a separate subject to be encountered in a brief period during the school day. Specific time should, however, be scheduled to provide for mastery of separate fundamental skills as needed by a class, group, or individual.

LISTENING

The first skill to be developed by the child is that of listening. This is basic to his being able to imitate spoken sounds. This skill should be developed throughout life. Many persons reach the point that they listen more than they read, speak, or write. The use to which the individual puts his listening, and the amount of skill he develops in it, therefore determine to a great extent his ability to learn to live with others.

Schools too long took it for granted that listening developed naturally with age. It is now recognized that listening must be taught like any other skill. It is further recognized that there are types of listening which should be understood by children. These are identified by the Commission on the English Curriculum as (1) passive or marginal, (2) appreciative, (3) attentive, and (4) analytical.[19]

Passive listening is experienced when youngsters study with the radio on. Such may be termed as "tuning out" of one sound while actively engaged in another, then being able to "tune in" when a special program comes on. Appreciative listening is involved when the individual settles down to enjoy a favorite musical selection, a dramatization, or poem being read. Attentive listening is engaged in when need for a specific direction is encountered or desire for entering into a conversation is experiencd. Analytical listening takes place when the listener weighs what is heard in terms of what it says to him as he compares one point of view or set of data with another.[20]

While it is essential for the individual to "tune out" many distracting sounds, the school must concentrate upon the growth of the individual in the appreciative, attentive, and analytical types of listening. It is now recognized that to develop these requires motivation, attention, concentration,

---

[19]Commission on the English Curriculum, National Council of Teachers of English, *Language Arts for Today's Children*, (New York: Appleton-Century-Crofts, Inc., 1954), p. 71.
[20]*Ibid.*

previous acquaintance with the particular vocabulary, and some guided developmental practice.

Because of the passive listening so frequently engaged in by all, the teacher cannot be assured that the child will follow a direction or assimilate a specific point. He must be aware that hearing may be a passive process involving no commitment to action. Only when one has listened in the sense of communicating or assimilating a message can action take place.

Thus certain listening skills should be developed by the individual which he can call up at the appropriate time for each learning experience. The following set of such skills presented by Greene and Petty as adapted from Pratt and Greene should be considered as imperative instruction in the elementary school:

1. Word perception
   a. Recall of word meanings
   b. Deduction of meanings of unknown words
2. Comprehension of ideas
   a. Noting detail
   b. Following directions
   c. Organizing into main and subordinate ideas
   d. Selecting information pertinent to a specific topic
   e. Detecting clues that show the speaker's trend of thought
3. Using ideas to build understandings
   a. Evaluating an expressed point of view or fact in relation to previous learning
   b. Making justifiable inferences[21]

SPEAKING

The child comes to school with some kind of language pattern already established. The pattern may be good or poor depending upon his background of experience at home and otherwise prior to entering school. The school should give him opportunities to express himself through "show-and-tell," in the reading group, and on the playground. The teacher should assist the child in building a wider vocabulary and in the improvement of sentence structure. Form and style should be held as secondary, however, in that the child must have something to say and feel free to say it before the teacher can help him improve his methods of expression.

Speaking and listening according to Ohlsen are two sides of the same coin and are related functionally. Since the chief function of both is social, this can be accomplished when the speaker and listener communicate. Thus,

---

[21]Harry A. Greene and Walter T. Petty, *Developing Language Skills in the Elementary Schools* (Boston: Allyn and Bacon, Inc., 1963), p. 108.

a shift is needed from the major emphasis on structure of the English language to that of more attention to the functional aspects of speaking and listening. In order to accomplish this the teacher must know the following about each child:

1. What the child is doing. What the child's goals are as he sees them.
2. What skills these goals require of him as a speaker or listener.
3. What communication form the speaking or listening takes, such as, discussion, open forum, or interview.[22]

In response to the three vital points set forth, the teacher should find the goals of Herrick and Jacobs as adapted by Sowards and Scobey a helpful guide in providing for children's speaking experiences. They are:

1. Prizing [recognizing the value of] thinking and feeling or through experience [which enables children] to think and feel precisely and sensitively.
2. Valuing effectiveness, or the personal development of language manipulation which will be meaningful to the listener.
3. Aiming for acceptability, or the common use of language in a form which is expected of the educated American.
4. Increasing poise and assurance, or the development of ease, natural self-control in all speaking situations.
5. Developing word sensitiveness, or the development of discrimination in the selection of words from a broad vocabulary.
6. Improving voice qualities, or sensitiveness to varying kinds of voice tone and quality, and skill in the manipulation of one's own voice.
7. Extending language courtesies, or appropriate use of voice, manner, and phrases to be courteous in a social situation.
8. Interrelating speaking and listening, or understanding of the dual relationship of speaking and listening.[23]

The school should be a place where the child is encouraged and challenged to meet these objectives as they apply to him. The teacher must be sensitive to the evidences of readiness for new experiences in language expression. It is imperative that his classroom be one which encourages expression on the part of children. He should see that children's contributions are recognized and appreciated, their efforts valued and their interests, abilities, and needs considered.

Means open for developing oral expression in the primary classroom and the alert teacher include children's own experiences outside school

---

[22]Merle M. Ohlsen, *Modern Methods in Elementary Education* (New York: Henry Holt and Company, Inc., 1959), pp. 258-262.

[23]Sowards, G. Wesley and Mary-Margaret Scobey, *The Changing Curriculum and the Elementary Teacher* (Belmont, Cal.: Wadsworth Publishing Company, Inc., 1961), pp. 250-1.

shared freely in school and informal conversation between small groups on free and planned occasions. Other means are dramatic play, messages, greetings, and introductions, play telephone, planning and evaluating, simple interviews, and telling about work accomplished. Means available for the intermediate grades also include informal speeches; round table discussion; panel discussion; symposium; forum; debate; giving announcements, directions, and explanations, and conducting meetings.

In all instruction the child must know that oral communication is not a one-way street. He must learn that the speaker must not only have something to say but say it in a way that will evoke proper listener response. Elements of the voice available to the speaker for effective presentation include volume, pitch, tone, speed, and emotional reflection. The efficient learning situation will take these vital aspects into account and will provide experiences wherein the learner can develop his potentialities to the maximum.

READING

A child's progress in all areas of the curriculum is dependent upon his ability to read and his success in reading is determined largely by the type of instruction given in developing reading as a skill. The approach to reading therefore should be meaningful to the child and based upon his own experiences. The teacher must recognize that what the child gets from the printed page is decided to a great extent by the experiences, ability, attitude, and interest he brings to the reading situation. Reading therefore should be a natural outgrowth of all social and work situations in the classroom.

Each teacher must recognize his responsibility in helping the child see reading as a useful and meaningful tool that can contribute to and enhance the value of all experiences. In so doing, he should determine the specific skills, vocabulary, and reading activities appropriate for each occasion and motivate the child to get the most from each experience.

Since reading is a highly complex activity involving many specific skills, instruction should be planned leading to specific outcomes. However, the teacher should avoid following a printed set of instructions day by day without thinking much about the meaning and purpose of the procedures. When the teacher understands the purpose underlying a procedure he can decide whether or not it is needed by his pupils and can modify it to fit the circumstances.[24]

---

[24]Albert J. Harris, *Effective Teaching of Reading* (New York: David McKay Company, Inc., 1962), p. 17.

It is the teacher's obligation to know and understand the goals of the reading program as a whole and to be able to detail the broad purposes as needed for each specific lesson plan. Three broad purposes suggested by Harris are (1) developmental reading, (2) functional reading, and (3) recreational reading. An outline of the major skills to be acquired under these purposes is as follows:

I. Developmental reading
    A. The mechanics of reading
        1. Development of a large sight vocabulary
        2. Development of skill in identifying unfamiliar words through use of
            a. Context
            b. Phonics
            c. Structural analysis
            d. Dictionary
        3. Development of good-eye movement habits
        4. Development of good postural habits while reading
        5. Development of oral reading skills
            a. Phrasing and expression
            b. Volume, pitch, and enunciation
        6. Development of speed and fluency in silent reading
    B. Reading comprehension
        1. Acquisition of a rich, extensive, and accurate vocabulary
        2. Learning to interpret thought units of increasing size
            a. The phrase
            b. The sentence
            c. The paragraph
        3. Learning to read for specific purposes
            a. Finding and understanding main ideas
            b. Locating answers to specific questions
            c. Noting and recalling details
            d. Grasping the sequence of events
            e. Anticipating outcomes
            f. Following directions
            g. Grasping the author's plan and intent
            h. Evaluating and criticizing what one reads
            i. Remembering what one reads
        4. Coordinating rate with comprehension
II. Functional reading
    A. Learning to locate information
        1. Mastering alphabetical order
        2. Using an index
        3. Using an encyclopedia
        4. Using other reference works

    B. Developing functional comprehension skills
       1. Learning specialized vocabularies
       2. Applying comprehension skills in content areas
         a. Learning to read textbooks in content subjects
         b. Learning to read independently in content subjects
       3. Developing specialized reading skills needed by special subject matter
         a. Reading arithmetical problems
         b. Interpreting maps, charts, graphs, and diagrams
         c. Reading about scientific experiments
       4. Learning to organize and record what one reads
         a. The formal outline
         b. Summarizing
         c. Note-taking
       5. Learning to remember what one reads
         a. Reciting to oneself
         b. Reviewing
III. Recreational reading
    A. Development of interest in reading
       1. Enjoyment of reading as a voluntary leisure-time activity
       2. Skill in selecting appropriate reading matter for oneself
       3. Satisfaction of present interests and tastes through reading
    B. Improvement and refinement of reading interests
       1. Development of more varied reading interests
       2. Development of more mature reading interests
       3. Achievement of personal development through reading[25]

The teacher should recognize the foregoing outline as one of many good ones and see it as only a basic guide. He should give particular attention to the outline of skills provided by the basal reading text series adopted in his teaching situation and use such as a guide. He should, however, adapt and adjust the details of the guide to the needs of the children. Each daily plan should emphasize a specific skill pertinent to the group. When feasible, more than one skill may be utilized at one time, giving attention to reinforcement of previously introduced reading skills.

The teacher should keep in mind that the teaching of reading skills is developmental and somewhat sequential. Practically all of the skills introduced in the primary grades are developmental. This means that the same skill must be presented many times in a variety of ways and in increasingly more complex situations as an aid to further learning. The teacher should also see that some skills are best introduced only after more easily understood ones have been presented. For example, it is generally accepted that

---

[25]*Ibid.*, pp. 18-19.

the introduction of the initial consonants in words precedes the introduction of the vowels. It is as the developmental skills are mastered that functional reading comes into fruition. This implies that the child uses these skills as tools for learning. This is often called work-type or study-type reading and increases in importance through the grades.

When the child has acquired the desire to read for pleasure or to improve his cultural outlook, taste and appreciation, this may be classified as recreational reading. This should be encouraged by providing time for independent reading as soon as the child is able to read any material on his own.

In order that knowledge of the scope of reading purposes and goals can be translated into teaching effectiveness, it must acquire some form. This should include objectives which coincide more specifically with certain stages or periods within the learning ability of the child. An adapted form of the five stages of reading as established by the National Committee on Reading and generally accepted today include (1) development of reading readiness, (2) beginning reading, (3) rapid skills development, (4) wide reading and (5) refinement of skills, habits, and tastes.[26] These stages serve as a framework of the major reading skills which can be used in implementing the broad purposes or goals of the reading program of the elementary school presented earlier in this chapter.

Reading Readiness

The reading readiness or pre-reading stage begins before the child enters any formal education program. It involves such factors as language development, mental maturity, physical development, auditory perception, visual perception, self-concept, emotional and social readiness, independence and responsibility, and desire to read. It is during this stage that the child has his first association with things, people, and processes.

Through these associations he begins to understand oral language and to speak. Some abilities and skills are developed in auditory perception and visual discrimination. The child begins to interpret pictures, observe sequence in telling about events, follow simple directions, identify colors, and coordinate muscular activities. He learns to discriminate the spoken word from other sounds and to use his voice to communicate his own needs and desires.

---

[26]National Society for the Study of Education, *Report of the National Committee on Reading.* Twenty-Fourth Yearbook, Part I, (Bloomington, Ill.: Public School Publishing Co., 1925), pp. 24-25; Harris, *op. cit.,* p. 20.

Beginning Reading

Beginning reading usually associated with the first grade is the natural outgrowth of the readiness period in the formal school. The child actually begins reading as he looks at pictures, manipulates blocks and symbols, tells experiences in sequence and listens to and discriminates sounds. He becomes aware that the content of reading is ideas and that the sentence is the unit of thought.

With this understanding he develops a sight vocabulary and learns that when grouped in certain ways these words express ideas. Pictures and context clues and word form are the first skills used by the child to unlock meaning from word symbols. As the child achieves a sight vocabulary of from 75 to 125 words, he enters into more formal reading. This includes the use of phonetics which involves hearing and seeing likeness and differences in words, discriminating between letter forms and word forms, and using an initial sound together with oral context to supply an unkown or missing word.

The beginning reading period is one in which the teacher strives to guide the child in positive reading interests and attitudes. An environment is provided which encourages curiosity and the desire to read. The emphasis is on reading for meaning, which includes experiences appropriate to the child's maturity. Materials used include a predominance of pictures designed to support the limited sight vocabulary of the child. A gradual shift is made from the use of many pictures to fewer pictures, with increased verbal content. The move to printed symbols to express communication thus may be accomplished gradually.

Rapid Skills Development

The rapid skills development stage is characterized by increasing independence in reading. The child is now perfecting his means of identifying new words. This stage, usually associated with the second and third grade, is one in which major attention is given to developmental reading and rapid growth in the skills of word recognition, comprehension and interpretation. Phonetic techniques are now adopted and adapted as tools which the individual draws upon at the subconscious or automatic level. Structural analysis is used extensively as the number of polysyllabic words increase. Use of picture clues decreases while sight vocabulary expands with the increasing volume of reading. Use of context clues continues to increase as the child recognizes the importance of getting meaning from what he reads. The dictionary is introduced at this stage as an aid to pronunciation and meaning. Tables of contents and indexes together with simple reference books and encyclopedias become meaningful as resources for locating and selecting content.

Greater enjoyment and more responsibility for reading on their own is seen in children at this stage. Longer units and wider interests demand more mature skills of word recognition, comprehension, and interpretation. Skill is required of the teacher in the adaptation of materials and the pace of learning to the child's development. A wide variety of different level materials is needed as children begin to change their reading to suit their purposes. As they increase their reading range and diversity, they start skimming to locate names, dates, key words, and phrases.

Recreational reading and reading in the content areas of different fields require that the rate of silent reading surpass that of oral reading. At this stage reading matter is related basically to things and events within the immediate environment or experience of the child. This is the critical stage of development and reinforcement of skills. The teacher therefore must constantly use reading material as a means of skill extension. He also must be careful to appraise continuously the strengths and weaknesses of each individual seeking to avoid failure, and correct bad reading habits.

Wide Reading

During the fourth, fifth, and sixth years of school developmental reading continues, but functional and recreational reading take the center of the stage and children read many different kinds of materials. The child enters a reading level of increased power and efficiency, constituting a refinment and perfection of the previous stage. The materials the child deals with carry him beyond the immediate environment to events and activities outside his own personal experience. The vocabulary and language of the material may be beyond the reader's own oral usage but within his level of comprehension.

Research skills are developed as children engage in wide reading. These include use of the dictionary, the encyclopedia, and other library reference books, more elaborate tables of contents, and detailed indexes. Other skills exercised are ability to use the library card catalog and to use diacritical markings. Such specialized skills as skimming, outlining, summarizing, relating ideas in sequence, and reporting on books should be learned by the end of the sixth year in school. The more general skills of comprehension, reading for various purposes at various speeds, ability to shift approach or method according to demands of the materials, reading in the content fields, reading for retention, and reading for enjoyment should become a part of the everyday activities of the child.[27]

Since the child reads in content outside his familiar environment during the intermediate grades his thinking should be creative and imaginative. He should read beyond and between the lines to interpret material. Fruitful reading at this point calls upon the individual to use in a unified manner all he has learned previously. This includes his stored knowledge and skills, experiences and reactions, and attitudes and interests.

During this stage the volume, variety and enjoyment of children's reading increase. Skills and techniques become automatic yet can be used consciously and effectively in trouble spots. The purposes and uses for reading multiply and children are able to fulfill them more satisfactorily. To realize these objectives, however, the school must maintain a program of skill development throughout the elementary school.

Refinement of Skills, Habits, Tastes and Attitudes

The refinement process actually begins in kindergarten and continues throughout life, but the time for giving most attention to it can best be designated as the period including the seventh year of school through high school. By this stage, a wide variety of interests, habits, tastes, and attitudes among youth has been manifested. There is also a great variance in skill. Emphases and experiences provided by the school during this time, when the individual is establishing more or less permanent reading patterns, can greatly help or handicap the youth.

Attempts by the school to force selection of reading or give undue attention to detailed reporting constitute running the risk of preventing children from ever enjoying books at a higher level. When appropriate editorials, syndicated columns, news, and cartoons are allowed to enter the learning environment of the classroom, however, they may be enjoyed and may serve as a basis for refining skills. Magazine reading, including the weekly or bi-weekly news magazines, when discussed by students in the classroom, can establish criteria for evaluating their worth. This is an important skill for use throughout life.

The ability to differentiate between the author's meaning and intent and the reactions of the reader may be well developed through use in the classroom of such magazines as *Harpers, Atlantic, Scientific American* and some professional and trade journals. At this stage attention must be given to increasing skill in appraisal and critical evaluation of the authenticity, perti-

---

[27]Sowards and Scobey, *op. cit.*, pp. 233-234.

nence, internal consistency and general value of material read. Refinement in reading is further developed through activities which show appreciation for style of writing and the use of words to develop setting, mood, rhythm, and balance in prose and poetry. Refinement in reading is also affected by helping children become aware of derivations, extensions, and the difference in meanings of the same word which depend on the context in which it is used.[28]

The reader must be aware at this point that the stages of reading presented here are general and somewhat overlapping. They attempt only to provide the teacher with some base for carrying out a sequential developmental program. This outline of stages may also serve as a framework and guide wherein reading experiences may be planned to help each individual develop his maximum reading skills. Such a guide can only indicate the points at which children appear to be ready for certain attainments and experiences in reading. The teacher must recognize those youngsters who are below or above such a framework and adjust teaching accordingly. It is only as the teacher recognizes landmarks on the road to maturity in reading that he will be able to provide skillful, creative, efficient, and intelligent guidance through content in reading as a communication skill.

An effective reading program should observe the important principles of (1) moving the child from the known to the unknown, (2) moving from the simple to the complex, and (3) recognizing differences in children. Many excellent reading series which observe these learning principles are available. The use of a single series as a flexible basis for the developmental reading program therefore is recommended. Each presents stories that develop vocabulary by the gradual introduction of new words and repetition of these words within material that is familiar and appropriate for the reader.

Teachers' guides prepared for the basal series are carefully developed and contain helpful suggestions for teacher-pupil activities centered around each particular story. When these materials are used by the teacher as a basic guide to developmental reading it can be anticipated that children will learn to read well.

WRITING

The record of civilization has depended upon the communication skill which we know as writing. Writing is done basically for two purposes (1) to send a message when the spoken word cannot easily be transmitted and

---

[28]J. Murray Lee and Doris May Lee, *The Child and His Curriculum* (third edition; New York: Appleton-Century-Crofts, 1960), p. 319.

(2) to make a record of ideas and experiences for future use. Too often man has considered writing as a necessity rather than a privilege or pleasure. It is in this spirit that writing has been taught in school. Thus, according to Strickland, "children have been taught how to write when they had nothing to write, no need for writing other than the teacher's assignment, and no desire for it except to conform to school requirements for the comfort and satisfaction that such conformity may yield."[29]

A third purpose for writing may be called writing for release — to express feelings, to capitalize on ideas, or to portray experiences. Wolfe more succinctly identifies this expressive writing as autobiographical. It is the kind by which the program gives the student invitations to communicate about all patterns of his daily living. The writer contends that "whether or not the child achieves skill in making images or using active verbs is not so vital as the sense of the dignity of his experience, of bringing forth a cup from the deep river of his life . . . ."[30]

When writing becomes a means of release the child will write many stories about his family, his pets, his travels, and his friends. The most important writing will be about himself. How the child begins the day often is a prime topic for his expression. Though he be angry or happy it should be his privilege to express his feeling in writing, knowing that the teacher will read to the class only such writings as he approves for sharing with others.

Writing for this purpose may provide the ideal motivation for incidental teaching of spelling, punctuation, grammar, and penmanship. When given the opportunity and encouragement to express his real feelings about his life experiences, the child's desire not only to write well but correctly will increase. It is in this manner that the child begins to see writing as a tool of communication; recognizes purpose in writing form; and is motivated to acquire skill in spelling, punctuation, grammar, and penmanship.

The real key to teaching writing and its contingencies is well expressed by Wolfe:

> The heart of the language arts program, then, is writing and speaking about those segments of experience which the child knows are most crucial in his day-by-day life. If we can prove to him that we understand what his thoughts and feelings are, we have not only helped him to express himself; we have made him feel that school is a part of life's reality in which he can perform many acts of awakening and awareness that will help him grow . . . . Our opportunity, then, is limitless. All we have to do is to establish an experience program of writing and speaking . . . .

[29]Strickland, *op. cit.*, p. 273.
[30]Don M. Wolfe, *Language Arts and Life Patterns* (New York: The Odyssey Press, Inc., 1961), p. 7.

We should underwrite it with the most realistic kind of educational analysis to determine what boys and girls really want to write about if only they had the chance. This does not mean that we neglect English as a tool subject. When and if we achieve a real experience program, we shall have better spelling and more correct writing in all departments of school life than we had ever thought possible.[31]

It is evident that before the child can begin to write he must have experience in the other communication skills. As children begin to recognize the printed word in terms of recorded symbols for vocal expression and mental ideas, the teacher should provide opportunity and assistance in reconstructing these symbols with pencil and paper. This instruction begins in the first grade according to the readiness of children. Spelling is usually formally introduced in the second grade and the study of the alphabet begun with the introduction of the dictionary in the third grade. Correct grammatical construction begins with oral expression but becomes more direct as writing takes place.

Handwriting

Handwriting is a skill that must be acquired on an individual basis under the careful instruction and guidance of the teacher. The first experience with writing should come in the form of dictation. Often this is at home when the child tells mother what to write grandmother or dictates a letter to Santa Claus or labels a present or card for daddy's birthday. The teacher capitalizes upon this type experience by letting the children tell her what to write when a goldfish, a turtle or white rabbit is brought to the room or when Billy, Mary, or Dick has a birthday. This may even begin in kindergarten as the children tell the teacher what to write to a member of the class who is ill. Many such experiences of dictating may come before children actually begin their copying. This experience should come on an individual basis. Each child should be given the privilege of copying a story written on the board by the teacher, but not required. Since handwriting is a form of art which requires a specific skill, the child should be encouraged to begin this activity only when his muscular development and motivation have reached the point of readiness. Formal writing of any kind, including copying, should begin only when the child feels a need to write. This may come from the desire to identify his possessions or work, to write a letter of thanks or concern for illness of another, or to take a note home to his parents.

---

[31]*Ibid.*, p. 12.

In teaching handwriting as a means of communication meaningless drill should be curtailed and emphasis placed upon producing legible written expression. This is not to overlook but to give meaning to the principle that handwriting is a developmental process that necessitates specific instruction and continuous practice. Specific goals to be achieved in handwriting, such as the ones listed by Greene and Petty following, should serve as a guide to the teacher and children:

1. To encourage pupils to use handwriting as an effective means of expression and thought.
2. To help each child discover how skill in handwriting will serve his needs.
3. To strive for neatness and legibility with moderate speed in all the writing activities of pupils.
4. To establish practice periods which will provide training in the handwriting skills.
5. To analyze handwriting faults of individual pupils and seek their correction.
6. To develop in all pupils a sense of personal pride, self-appraisal and self-improvement in the handwriting skills.
7. To develop correct posture and the proper use of writing tools.[32]

Manuscript writing is generally accepted for use by children in grades one and two. Primary children are better able to make the simple lines and circles required for manuscript writing than they are the more intricate figures of cursive writing. Because of the children's limited control of the fine muscles, manuscript is more readily acceptable. The transfer to cursive writing frequently is made the latter part of the second year; however, many prefer delaying its teaching until the third year.

Grammar

Punctuation and grammar are essential ingredients of writing that are best taught in relation to purposeful expression. When children understand that punctuation is the application of tools which give meaning to written words, just as voice fluctuation does in oral communication, they begin to use it in this manner.

Grammar is so tied in with social usage that to teach sentence structure or word selection in isolation is to waste the students' and teacher's time. Children bring their grammar to school in oral form and inadvertently transfer it to written expression. The teacher should seek to help the child want to change rather than insist upon immediate change. When the individual

---

[32]Harry A. Greene and Walter T. Petty, *Developing Language Skills in the Elementary Schools* (second edition; Boston: Allyn and Bacon, Inc., 1963), p. 117.

becomes too uncomfortable in the change of communication expressions he may withdraw from communicating. This is particularly true with writing in that it involves spelling what the individual hears. Often he speaks so differently from that expected of him that he sees little association with what is spoken and the symbols used in spelling.

Spelling

Spelling is the major tool in writing. It is only when one writes that he needs to spell and his only real need for spelling is when he writes. Thus writing becomes the strongest motivating factor in spelling. The experience of the child in copying a dictated story written on the board or chart paper and that of preparing a manuscript for the school paper involve the same skills. The difference is that the latter experience requires a higher degree of skill. Both involve seeing that the right letters are in the right places to say what is being copied or to express that which the individual is thinking. Basically this act incorporates the simple rudiments expressed by Shane which are "see it (visualize), say it, think it, write it, and check it."[33]

The child should recognize spelling as a sensory-motor skill involving seeing, hearing, saying, and writing. Foundations for good spelling include activities in meaningful situations which lead to growth in ability to listen, observe, and exercise muscular coordination. Much depends, however, upon the individual's attitude toward spelling and its practical application. A good speller is the individual who recognizes the importance of correct spelling, seeks to spell each word he writes correctly, and has the skill to learn to spell new words independently.[34]

Three skills equally important to speaking and spelling and basic to writing are pronunciation, enunciation, and articulation. These generally determine how the child spells and, in turn, writes. The use of rhymes, jingles, poems, and stories fosters auditory skills. Spelling is taught through reading as the child observes the left-to-right direction of word structure, the configuration of words in terms of letter height, shape, and length, and gains the ability to visualize and recall words. All the word attack skills relating to word form and used in reading are vital to mastery of spelling. The child should be taught that spelling is a tool closely associated with effective expression through listening, speaking, reading, and writing, and that writing is particularly dependent upon spelling.

---

[33]Harold G. Shane, Mary E. Reddin, and Margaret C. Gillespie, *Beginning Language Arts Instruction with Children* (Columbus: Charles E. Merrill Books, Inc., 1961), p. 239.
[34]Green and Petty, *op. cit.* p. 278.

In order to encourage effective application of grammar, handwriting, and spelling in writing as a means of communication, the teacher must create an atmosphere in which communication can flow and a variety of speech patterns exist. Moving toward more desirable patterns of expression may well take the line of substituting expressions of informal, simple, acceptable English. The teacher should keep the items for correction as few as possible. Correction by substitution of the right form for any break in proper usage should be encouraged, remembering elementary children develop writing skill more effectively by usage than through drill on the rules of grammar. This position is supported by Pooley as follows:

> Time that is used in teaching children the names of parts of speech and the identification and classification of parts of the sentence is time taken away from the practice of the skills of writing and speaking English.
>
> ....
>
> . . . All the evidence available shows that formal grammar has little or no effect upon the skills of composition in the elementary grades."[35]

The teacher should proceed on the basis that teaching English for the purpose of speaking and writing is not mere instruction in grammar or isolated formal technical skills, principles, and rules of punctuation, capitalization, and sentence structure. Teaching the communication skills emphasizes the practical study of language that relates words and phrases within the sentence structure. According to Sowards and Scobey this approach to teaching grammar for writing "employs an analytical, thoughtful approach that includes knowledge of correct form and understanding of the functions of words and their interrelationship in a sentence."[36]

Children should be encouraged to see that language at school does not necessarily conflict with language at home. This can be achieved by helping them realize that Americans use a variety of language forms, most of them acceptable in some specific situation. Children will be quick to see, for example, that the language used by the news reporter on the radio is different from that used in many situations around the home. The need for and mastery of correct usage will come as the child writes for real purposes.

COMPUTATION

Recognizing computation as a communication skill gives meaning to quantitative activities. It helps the child to see the number system as a

---

[35]Robert G. Pooley, *Teaching English Grammar* (New York: Appleton-Century-Crofts, Inc., 1957), pp. 126-127.
[36]Sowards and Scobey, *op. cit.*, p. 267.

language which man has devised to show quantitative relationships. This language should be a part of the thinking individual such that he possesses a sensitivity and facility in recognizing and coping with computations.

To refer to quantitativeness in terms of computation as a communication skill is not to limit one to manipulation of numbers. Certainly it recognizes that manipulation of a set of symbols is involved but basic to this is understanding, and back of understanding there must be ideas. In fact, it is a system of ideas expressed in symbols which are used as a medium of communication. The factor of major importance is that of bridging the gap between knowledge of the idea and vision of the symbol in expression of an idea.

The most concrete illustration of this returns one to the shepherd pictured by so many writers. Here one visualizes man placing a stone in a certain pile as each sheep leaves the corral to graze in the fields for the day. At night one stone was removed from the pile as each sheep re-entered the corral. The child should recognize that the idea behind this activity was to determine if all the sheep that went into the fields returned in the evening. Each stone in the pile became a symbol for a sheep. The system used was the piling of stones. The Arabic number system serves a related function in the life of society today. Problems encountered are evident because of the degree of abstractness in the system used.

Every effort should be made to return computation — mathematical operations to understanding through concrete experiences. Mathematical understandings are so basic in the lives of every individual that the curriculum must provide for the mathematical needs of the average citizen as well as the professional mathematician.

Beginning in the kindergarten, learning experiences should resemble a widening spiral in which students expand their knowledge of basic concepts by mastering their use in progressively more complex and sophisticated ways. Simply to know mathematical facts is not enough. The student should be continuously faced with problematic situations at his level of development. He should be encouraged to fit a known pattern of operation against each specific problem. If he does not have a pattern he should learn to construct his own. Thus the idea of discovery in problem solving becomes a reality to the child.

When mathematics is considered in this light it must be viewed in terms of the extent to which it fulfills the needs of the individual in becoming a happy, efficient, useful person in society. As the needs of society have changed, the objectives for teaching mathematics have also changed. The

Center for Applied Research in Education now views the computational objectives broadly as mathematical, social, and cultural.[37]

The mathematical objective in teaching arithmetic in the elementary school includes development of elementary mathematical concepts, recognition of structural features, knowledge of basic properties, realization of relationships, and understanding of the rationale of computation. It should also provide for an ever-expanding understanding and insight into the structure and organization of the number system. In meeting this objective the school should strive to develop in the learner a taste and inclination for the subject. It should develop flexibility in thinking, intellectual curiosity and independence. Other mathematical learnings to be gained are an attitude of discovery, creative but orderly thinking, the ability to make judgments, and the ability to analyze and to generalize.[38]

A second objective of mathematics, which is social, involves the application of computation in the interpretation and resolution of quantitative situations in daily living. The individual should become sensitive to numbers in social situations. He should learn to use computation in solving quantitative problems in daily life and grow in appreciation of the needs and use of quantitative ideas in society. The most important aspect of the social objective is helping the learner solve his quantitative problems in the present and future.[39]

Recognition of mathematics as a part of our cultural heritage is an important function of education. The child should learn early to recognize the contributions of mathematics to our past and present civilization. As he develops his mathematical concepts he should associate these with a heritage that has been passed on to him through the efforts and mathematical learnings of others.[40]

Implementation of these major objectives of arithmetic in the elementary school involves understanding some basic features of our language of computation. Some of the features which make mathematics meaningful to children include those expressed by Warner as understanding, discovery, reasonableness, relationship, arithmetic readiness, and social values.[41]

Understanding is basic to learning the number system. This includes appreciating the usefulness of our decimal number system, learning that

---

[37]Frances Flournoy, *Elementary School Mathematics* (Washington: The Center for Applied Research in Education, Inc., © 1964) p. 1-3.

[38]*Ibid.*

[39]*Ibid.*

[40]*Ibid.*

[41]Ruby H. Warner, *The Child and His Elementary School World* (Englewood Cliffs: Prentice-Hall, Inc., 1957) pp. 281-290.

there is more than one way to solve a problem, knowing that every arithmetic problem answers a question, and being able to apply arithmetic skills. Understanding gives meaning to computation.

Children like to handle and manipulate objects. They like to find out for themselves. The discovery approach to problem solving thus curtails the amount of demonstration of process by the teacher and encourages active learning by the student.

The basic processes of addition, subtraction, multiplication, and division should emerge in the experiences of the child in such a way that he sees the practical function of each. He should learn the reasonableness of combinations through estimation. This is accomplished by providing opportunities in which the child rounds off numbers, combines known parts of a number, visualizes groupings, and manipulates objects. During these experiences the child should be encouraged to interpret, explain, discuss, and evaluate computation. Through these intellectual manipulations which initially begin in the kindergarten, the child learns to tell when his answer to a problem is reasonable.

Our number system is structured so that the child can see its orderliness. Relationship can be recognized through decimal structure, frequency, place value, and transformation. The position of numbers in a series helps the child in seeing relationships. For example, two comes after one, eight before nine and so on. This order also pertains to positional names of ones, tens, hundreds, or trillions. Another order of our number system is seen in the fact that place value in a series is determined by the position of the digit in a number. Using only the nine digits and zero our system can express any number from the smallest fraction to infinity. For example, the 3 means three objects when placed in the 1's position; it means thirty objects when in the 10's position, three thousands in the 1,000's position, and 3/10 when in the first decimal position.

The child's readiness for number experiences determines the degree of participation and learning attained. Some children require more experience than others with concrete aids before fully developing meaning. Others require more repetition or practice in an experience before gaining understanding and mastery of a phase of a skill. This concept of readiness applies not only to first grade children but to all levels of education. Much effort must be expended by the teacher in observation and testing to determine every child's readiness for each experience in order to time the introduction of new skills and to use appropriate materials.

When problem solving is used as an avenue for developing mathematical skills, social values are recognized from the outset. Recognizing and coping with human problems naturally involve quantitative relationships. Observing and planning in keeping with the time of day, week, month, and year involve social aspects of mathematics. Planting seed and keeping records of the growth of plants, shopping at the school or community store, recording weather change, measuring cloth for costumes, calculating refreshments for a party, or making the daily lunch report are among the countless opportunities for understanding the social values of mathematics.

The major problem confronting the elementary teacher is selecting and organizing content of the mathematics program. This problem is of such magnitude that it cannot be left to the ingenuity of the individual teacher in each classroom. In order that children can gain understanding of mathematical concepts and mastery of fundamental processes, a sequential developmental organization is necessary. This does not mean that mathematics is to be taught separate and apart from other curriculum areas all the time. It does mean, however, that the teacher must be guided by a systematic professional plan in the introduction of new learnings that are in keeping with the child's progress on a developmental scale.

This makes it imperative that a well prepared course of study or textbook series adopted by a school or system be used as a basic guide by every teacher. Such guides vary from one school system to the other and each commercial textbook series presents content and introduces fundamental processes differently. Nevertheless, when such a guide is carefully selected it will usually provide a desirable scope and sequence that can serve as a framework and safeguard in affording effective computational experiences for children. The following scope and sequence patterns presented by Flournoy should be helpful to the teacher in selecting a more complete guide:

1. NUMBER AND NUMERATION
   Primary grades:
   Understanding 1 — 10 (order: one-to-one correspondence; comparing sets; cardinal and ordinal concepts);
   Writing basic numerals, 0 — 9;
   Understanding and counting the teens, 11 — 19;
   Understanding counting by 10's, 5's, 2's, 3's, 4's;
   Understanding order of counting to 100, to 1,000;
   Understanding base 10, place value, and additive principle to 10,000's;
   Understanding meanings of 0 as no frequency in a place, not any and a reference point;
   Rounding numbers to nearest ten, hundred, thousand;
   Learning Roman numerals through L (50).
   Intermediate grades:
   Extending understanding of place value to hundred thousands, millions, and billions;

Understanding the expression of 100,000 as (10 x 10 x 10 x 10 x 10), 1,000,000 as (10 x 10 x 10 x 10 x 10 x 10), 10,000,000 as (10 x 10 x 10 x 10 x 10 x 10 x 10) and so on;

Introduction to exponential notation, for example, 100 as 10^2, 1,000 as 10^3, 10,000 as 10^4, and so on;

Rounding numbers to the nearest ten thousand, hundred thousand million;

Learning Roman numerals to M (1,000).

2. NUMBER OPERATIONS AND COMPUTATIONAL PROCEDURES WITH WHOLE NUMBERS

Primary grades:

Understanding addition and subtraction as combining and separating operations having an inverse relationship; subtraction as comparing;

Learning the order and grouping properties or principles for addition;

Understanding addition facts to sums of 10 and to sums of 18; related subtraction facts;

Solving simple equations applying addition and subtraction relationships;

Understanding addition and subtraction with two-, three-, and four-digit numerals; with and without regrouping;

Learning column addition to six one-digit addends and four three- and four-digit addends;

Understanding multiplication and division as operations in combining equal sets and separating a set into smaller equal sets, and as having an inverse relationship; division as comparing;

Learning the order, grouping, and distributive properties for multiplication and the distributive property for division;

Learning multiplication facts through sets of five or more and their reverses; related division facts;

Learning multiplication and division with two-, three-, and four-digit numerals by a one-digit multiplier and a one-digit divisor;

Solving simple equations applying multiplication and division relationships;

Understanding uneven division;

Applying skills in problem-solving.

Intermediate grades:

Extending addition and subtraction experiences with properties, facts, and computational exercises;

Learning the remainder of the basic facts of multiplication to multipliers of 9 and reverses; related division facts;

Extending multiplication and division experiences with properties and computational exercises, including two-and three-digit multipliers and divisors;

Extending experience in solving equations applying operational relationships;

Applying skills in problem-solving;

Understanding primes, composites, factors, and multiples.

3. COMMON FRACTIONS

Primary grades:

Understanding halves, thirds, fourths, sixths, and eighths of one whole;

Understanding and finding fractional parts of a group (using partition division);

Understanding simple multiple part fractions as 2/2, 3/4;

Comparing simple fractions and understanding simple equivalent fractions;

Understanding 2/2, 3/3, 4/4, and so on, as names for 1.

Intermediate grades:

Extending understanding of fractional parts of a whole, as tenths, twelfths, sixteenths, and so on; finding fractional part of a group; comparing fractions and expressing equivalent fractions;

Using the terms numerator and denominator;

Understanding the concept of ratio;

Understanding and skill in adding and subtracting fractions with and without like denominators;

Understanding and skill in multiplying and dividing fractions;

Applying skills in problem-solving.

4. MEASUREMENT

Primary grades:

Understanding the concept of measurement as comparison and the meaning of standard measures;

Telling clock time and learning time relationships; understanding hour, day, week, month, year, decade, and century relationships;

Learning the common linear, liquid, dry, weight, and quantity measures and relationships;

Understanding how to read a thermometer, above and below 0°;

Learning to change from one measure to another.

Intermediate grades:

Understanding measurement as approximation;

Extending experiences with common measures and relationships and changing from one measure to another;

Using denominate numbers;

Understanding concept of time zones in the United States and throughout the world;

Interpreting latitude and longitude;

Learning metric measures;

Understanding and finding perimeter and area of rectangular and triangular plane figures;

Understanding and finding volume of three-dimensional rectangular shapes.

5. DECIMAL FRACTIONS AND PER CENT

Primary grades:

Recognizing various coins in our system of money;

Understanding relationship of each coin to cents; of $1 to 100 cents;

Counting money to 50 cents, to $1, to $5, to $10;

Understanding equivalent amounts of money (as a dime is equivalent to two nickels, a half-dollar is equivalent to two quarters);

Making change for various amounts to $10;

Writing cents (such as 25¢); reading and writing dollars and cents (such as $1.55); reading and writing cents with dollar sign and decimal point (such as $.58);

Adding and subtracting simple amounts of money, using dollar sign and decimal point;

Multiplying and dividing simple amounts of money, using dollar sign and decimal point.

Intermediate grades;

Understanding meaning to tenths, hundredths, thousandths, ten-thousandths, hundred-thousandths;

Understanding idea of extending place to right of the one's place with each place 1/10 the value of previous place;

Expressing value of each place; 1/10 x 1), 1/100 as (1/10 x 1/10), 1/1000 as (1/10 x 1/10 x 1/10), 1/10,000 as (1/10 x 1/10 x 1/10 x 1/10);

Reading and writing decimal numerals;

Expressing decimal fractions in equivalent common fraction form; and common fractions in equivalent decimal fraction form;

Rounding decimals to nearest tenth, hundredth, thousandth;

Adding, subtracting, multiplying, and dividing decimal fractions;

Changing per cent to decimal and common fraction forms;

Finding per cent of a number, what per cent one number is of another, and finding a number when it is expressed as a per cent of another;

Applying decimals and per cent in problems.

6. GRAPHS AND SCALE DRAWINGS

Primary grades:

Reading and making simple picture and bar graphs;

Understanding the idea of scale (as, one inch stands for one mile);

Learning to read a simple scale drawing.

Intermediate grades:
Extending experiences with reading and making picture and bar graphs;
Reading and making line graphs and circle graphs;
Making scale drawings.

7. GEOMETRIC CONCEPTS

Primary grades:
Drawing line segments of given length with rulers;
Learning to recognize pictures of line segment, circle, square, rectangle, triangle;
Associating plane shapes with forms in the environment;
Learning characteristics of rectangle; square as a special rectangle;
Measuring length and width and writing dimensions of plane shapes in inches.
Intermediate grades:
Learning the idea of an angle; learning to recognize right angles and right triangles;
Understanding right triangles as half a rectangle with same dimensions;
Recognizing triangles that are not right triangles; learning characteristics of equilateral triangle;
Understanding concept of parallel lines;
Recognizing parallelogram;
Using term quadrilateral for square, rectangle, and parallelogram;
Understanding concept of perpendicular lines;
Learning that the distance from any point on circle to center is same, measuring radius and diameter of circles;
Learning concept of three-dimensional figures as rectangular and triangular prisms.[42]

The point of view toward arithmetic in the elementary school continues to change. Communication today is undergirded by quantitative relationships. Whether it be referred to as computation, mathematics, arithmetic, or quantative relationship it is a language or field vital to effective living in today's society. Warner has described some of the more significant changes well:

The new look in arithmetic has introduced understanding and meaning into arithmetic processes. Through discovery of arithmetic facts, the child is motivated to learn and retains the learning longer. Through estimation and rounding out numbers he determines the reasonableness of his method of computation and of his solution.

---

[42]Frances Flournoy, *Elementary School Mathematics,* © 1964, pp. 9-13. Reprinted by permission of the Center for Applied Research in Education, Inc., Washington, D. C.

The orderliness of our number system is shown through such relationships as the decimal structure of our number system, frequency, place value, and transformation. Arithmetic is taught when a child is ready for it and not before. Provision is made in a balanced program for incidental number teaching, for emphasis upon social values, and for practice in mathematical skills and understandings.[43]

SOCIALIZATION SKILLS AND CONTENT

It must be recognized that social scientists and scholars in related fields have identified some of the basic forces that are influencing the pattern of today's culture. These forces include the continuing development in science, the accelerating technological revolution, the changing patterns of economic growth, the continuing urbanization of our population, the growth of international tensions, the increasing international interdependence, and the exploding world population. Facing and living with these forces of society necessitates the exercise of basic social skills by every individual. The education of youth therefore should include not only acquainting him with these current forces of society but equipping him with such socialization skills that he can live peacefully and productively with others. These skills may be classified as (1) accepting oneself, (2) communicating, (3) participating, (4) cooperating, (5) demonstrating loyalty, and (6) exercising citizenship.

ACCEPTING ONESELF

Each individual lives in a world unto himself. He is made up of certain drives and characteristics which cause him to be unique and apart from any other person. Most of these features, however, are similar to those of other persons. There is however, enough element of difference in each person that when one does not accept his own differences, it makes him feel unacceptable to his peers. The very young child is naturally self-centered and demanding and has little concern for acceptance. As he becomes older, however, he is more aware of himself in relation to others.

Through psychology, mental hygiene, and child development we have learned that only if a person thinks well of himself is he free to recognize and appreciate the merits of others. The individual gets most of his first ideas of his worth and respectability from his family. He soon gets the idea that he is good or bad, ugly or attractive, adequate or inadequate, and wanted or unwanted by people. It is with these impressions of self that the child enters school and challenges the teacher to cope with him as he is or thinks he is.

---

[43]Warner, *op. cit.*, pp. 315-316.

Observing, listening, and interpreting is a continuous challenge to the teacher as he seeks ways of understanding what each child believes, fears, and desires. The wise teacher knows the value of and provides for free play, role play, and creative dramatics. He knows that all persons have good and bad feelings toward themselves and others and helps them release the negative feelings and gain positive feelings. He listens without condemnation to expressions of fear, doubt, and anger and allows the individual to "talk them out" in the appropriate place and time. In so doing, the individual learns the degree to which he is accepted just as he is. He also learns that others have feelings and concerns that need his acceptance and help. The school should offer each child a chance to excel in something and regularly recognize individual accomplishment no matter how small. Gradually the individual is helped to get a picture of himself as a person who can succeed at something and is accepted as a contributor to his society.

As the same time the individual learns to direct, channel, and limit impulses of every kind which conflict with societal norms. This includes control of impulses in destructiveness, intrusiveness, exhibitionism, pride, excessive assertiveness, and inappropriate competitiveness. He then learns the taboo areas as well as those which are open to expression.

COMMUNICATING

As one learns to accept and control himself within the framework of his society he begins to communicate with others. Being able to communicate means more than speaking or interpreting the language of another or even the familiar expressions of his own peers. In order to communicate, one must be able to feel as another feels and to visualize similar images. In essence, it means being able to put himself in the other person's shoes. Freedom to converse requires an acceptance that conversation can be a meaningful and significant end in and of itself. It is one way in which man recognizes his solitude, his freedom, and fraternity with others. The act of conversing is essential to the mental health of each individual. The teacher should therefore provide free and unstructured opportunities for each individual to converse with others.

Successful teachers are empathically understanding of students. They tend to see or attempt to see things as students see them. They tend to be more honest in their expressions to students, behaving in a way which seems to be consistent with how they are thinking or feeling. The greatest barriers to conversation are the reactions of people important to the child. These include parents, peers, and teachers. The more these people respond to the child's conversation with an air of question rather than accepting it as being meaningful and at least momentarily truthful, the more the child fears to express his real self. The more he fears the farther he gets from his personal experience and the greater the lack of communication with others becomes.[44]

Realizing that people constantly judge others in terms of their ability to communicate, Tiegs and Adams have delineated certain skills which students should be given opportunity to develop. These are:

1. Establish rapport with audience
2. Maintain a pleasing appearance
3. Create a favorable impression
4. Handle interruptions
5. Answer questions
6. Accept criticism
7. Reconcile differences
8. Handle critic's errors
9. Defend a report
10. Admit shortcomings
11. Point out shortcomings
12. Handle undeserved praise
13. Set standards for making reports[45]

PARTICIPATION

The extent to which a student participates in an activity influences greatly the learning which comes from the experience. When a child learns through direct experience, he also develops language skill to the extent to which the teacher provides opportunity for him to verbalize his experience. To say that the youngster participates in an activity at school, however, does not mean that he has had desirable learning. According to Dewey, "Everything depends upon the quality of the experience which is had. The quality of any experience has two aspects. There is an immediate aspect of agreeableness, and there is its influence upon later experiences."[46] In this twofold aspect of experience there also must be continuity of experience such "that every experience both takes up something from those which have gone before and modifies in some way the quality of those which come after."[47]

---

[44]Robert E. Bills, "Education is Human Relations," *New Insights and the Curriculum* (1963 Yearbook; Washington: The Association for Supervision and Curriculum Development, 1963), pp. 168-171.

[45]Ernest W. Tiegs and Fay Adams, *Teaching the Social Studies* (New York: Ginn and Company, 1959) pp. 266-269. Reprinted through the courtesy of Blaisdell Publishing Company, a division of Ginn and Company.

[46]John Dewey, *Experience and Education* (New York: The Macmillan Company, 1938), p. 16. Reprinted by the permission of Kappa Delta Pi, an honorary society in education, Box 645, West Lafayette, Indiana.

[47]*Ibid.*, p. 27.

It is the responsibility of the teacher to utilize physical and social sur-roundings in a manner that provides the maximum participation for the child. A fully integrated personality may be developed when successive acts of participation by the child are related and integrated with one an-other. This, of course, assumes that the teacher understands the needs and capacities of the individuals who are involved at a given time and provides for their interaction with the experience. This is the real value of partici-pation.

The child should gain from each experience growth in the ability to enter into a situation in a purposeful and meaningful manner. He should also gain the desire to go on having similar experiences. When this occurs it can be said that the child learns from participation. He then develops an appreciation for worthwhile things. He sees the relative value of his experiences, and learns to apply his new knowledge and to extract meaning from future happenings.

COOPERATION

In order to participate, one must become involved. Involvement implies interaction with things or ideas usually reflecting a social or natural order or interaction with people directly. This then implies that some form of recognition or cooperation must take place. From early childhood the in-dividual is subject to controls and orders laid down by God and man. For example, in playing a game the child recognizes the importance of order and guiding rules. He accepts rules as a part of the game and recognizes violations. However, he is usually willing to change a rule when it is felt the change will improve the game. This indicates that the individual plays the game and submits to changes when necessary because such meets with the approval of his sense of cooperativeness.

Realizing that life is a social process involving "give and take," it is consistent to assume that school experiences are also social and engage the individual in countless autocratic or cooperative activities. Much as the rules of a game have become acceptable to the youngster, so the school can foster his cooperative endeavor. The teacher's greater knowledge of the world, of subject matter, and of individuals serves to arrange conditions that are conducive to cooperation.[48]

In order to develop the cooperative elements of the student, the teacher must survey the capacities and needs of the individuals involved. He then must arrange to provide subject matter or content for experiences that satisfy these needs and develop these capacities. The planning, however,

---

[48]*Ibid.*, p. 64.

must be flexible enough to permit free play for individuality of experiences and yet firm enough to give direction toward continuous development of power. This point of view necessitates the teacher's being a leader of group activities. He has a peculiar responsibility for the conduct of interactions and intercommunications which are the essence of any cooperative group.[49] The teacher should be not only intellectually aware of the capacities, needs, and past experiences of those under his instruction but should permit the suggestions made by individuals to develop into a plan and project. By means of the suggestions a project should be organized into a whole by the members of the group. Thus the plan should become a cooperative enterprise. The development should occur through reciprocal interchange with the teacher as he allows the plan to grow and take shape through the process of social intellectuality.

The foregoing reference to the conduct and acceptance of rules and procedures of an organized game relates to the marks of society in terms of social amenities. It must be recognized that various regions of our nation and world observe these graces in different manners and with different symbols. This, however, does not excuse the lack of such courtesies but places greater responsibility upon the individual to cooperate in the give and take of these conventions. Such cooperation may be identified as mutual accommodation and adaptation.

It is through this mutual accommodation and adaptation of the teacher and children that the child is encouraged to assume greater responsibility for his own behavior and participate in learning activities. It is here that the child becomes aware of group membership and cooperation takes precedence over competition. It is through this process of recognizing differences, as well as likenesses, and making plans in light of the desire and opinions of others that the individual really becomes aware of the spirit of and need for cooperation. From this awareness he examines his own attitudes and actions and strengthens his ability for cooperative endeavor.

LOYALTY OR COMMITMENT

Recognizing and observing conviction and duty to a cause is a quality for which mature individuals aspire. Such a characteristic may be labeled as loyalty or commitment. Loyalty carries with it responsible action. In all societies some form of leadership has always been recognized. The concept of leadership that one holds affects the extent to which he develops a sense of responsibility to the group. Also, the extent to which every individual is recognized as a contributor to society and is given opportunities to partici-

---

[49]*Ibid.,* pp. 64-67.

pate in decision making situations will usually determine the degree to which all students accept responsibility. This point of view implies that if leadership is left to the superior students, the less gifted will be inclined to let them carry the major responsibility, whereas if their ideas are considered the less gifted will seek to make greater contributions.[50]

"The only freedom," says Dewey, "that is of enduring importance is freedom of intelligence, that is to say, freedom of observation and of judgment exercised in behalf of purposes that are intrinsically worthwhile."[51] One may not be able to reject an activity physically but there remains for him the compensation of intellectually and emotionally regarding the action as passé, promptly forgetting the incident and refusing to give his support and loyalty to the leader of the activity. Enforced conformity and acquiescence only prevent students from disclosing their real nature. This in turn causes individuals to operate in irregular and more or less forbidden ways. Freedom of movement, of choice and activity, however, are essential to the development of wholesome attitudes and devotion to cause only when freedom is diverted to constructive action.

Freedom to think results in intellectual growth. This is particularly true when there is reconstruction and remaking of impulses and desires in relation to observation and memory of previous or present experiences. It is in terms of one's studied reactions to these experiences that he formulates his loyalty and commits himself to rsponsible action.

Some means by which the teacher can develop loyalty and responsible action in the classroom include praising the contribution rather than the contributor; centering attention of the class on group achievement and group projects rather than on individual showmanship; and stressing contributions to improvement of living in the classroom. Open membership in service groups to all who want to serve rather than to just those with special skills lessens the idea of status and provides for broader responsibility. The use of the pronouns "we," "us" and "our" when cooperative planning, decision making, and working actually take place serve as a strong force in developing class loyalty. The adoption and use of such terminology encourages individual commitment to responsible action.[52]

CITIZENSHIP

By the very nature of his profession the teacher is obliged to see his present work in terms of the citizenship of his students. He must be aware

---

[50]Kimball Wiles, *Teaching for Better Schools* (New York: Prentice-Hall, Inc., 1952), p. 132.
[51]Dewey, *op. cit.*, p. 69.
[52]Wiles, *op. cit.*, p. 132.

of the potentialities for leading students into fields of service which belong to experiences they have already had. This knowledge should be used as a criterion for selection and arrangement of the conditions that influence students' present experiences which in turn may set the stage for their future.

"Growth," according to Dewey, "depends upon the presence of difficulty to be overcome by the exercise of intelligence."[53] Thus it is the educator's responsibility to see that the problem being studied by youngsters grows out of present conditions and that it is within the range of the capacity of the students. It also should be of such nature that it arouses in the learner an active quest for information and production of new ideas. The new facts and new ideas become the basis for further experiences in which new problems are recognized. Impetus thus is given to further study and activity.[54]

This treatment of problems under the guidance of a skillful teacher may involve the individual not only in basic subject matter but take him into the facts and laws of science which come through everyday social life. Through this process the student comes to understand the economic and industrial problems of current society and determines the relations of human beings and social groups. Through the application of scientific principles man can point the way to measures and policies through which a better social order can be realized. Through the utilization of subject matter acquired by students from the experience approach to teaching, the learner can be carried on to an ever-wider, more refined, and better organized world environment. Through such experience the individual should grow as a citizen, keeping pace with his expanding and complex society.

The student develops in this direction as he learns about the rights and responsibilities of himself and others through working and playing in groups each day. He learns that others have property rights which must be respected. He learns to take turns and to listen and speak at appropriate times. Carrying out responsibilities of the classroom, school and neighborhood becomes a vehicle for application and understanding. Participation in making group decisions, setting up standards, sharing responsibilities for leadership and followership in the classroom and selecting representatives for committees of student council provide firsthand experiences in citizenship.[55]

Development of civic responsibility is a vital part of the education of youth. Through education each should learn to appreciate the contribu-

---

[53]Dewey, *op. cit.*, p. 96.
[54]*Ibid.*, p. 96-97.
[55]Wilhelmina Hill, *Social Studies in the Elementary School Program* (Washington: U. S. Government Office, 1960), p. 32-3.

tions of others. He should learn the feelings of joy, exhilaration, and success which come from sharing one's talents and energy for a worthwhile cause. He should gain respect for constituted authority, the role of the government and operation of civic institutions. Through experiences in the school which encourage the child to exercise the skills of communicating, participating, and supporting he should grow in awareness of his privileges and responsibilities as a citizen. As such he should gain skill in preserving freedom for himself and others and increase his appreciation of the importance of carrying out civic responsibilities.

ENVIRONMENTAL UNDERSTANDING AND CONTENT

A major function of the school is assisting the child in understanding his environment in coping with the problems of living. Through this understanding the individual also learns to appreciate his cultural heritage and apply scientific knowledge in the improvement of society. Even though the present period may be well classified as the scientific age, it must be recognized that many of man's most urgent problems are social. It is upon this premise that the social and natural sciences are herein classified as man's environmental understandings. This approach provides for the treatment of social studies in close association with the sciences. In this manner it is easier for children to learn that all aspects of man's social living are affected by his physical environment and by his skill in manipulating and controlling its various aspects.[56]

The writers are quite aware of the sophisticated array of disciplines from which content is drawn in solving man's problems. Such an array includes economics, political science, history, psychology, sociology, anthropology, philosophy, physics, chemistry, astronomy, geography, and physiology. It is important that the elementary teacher has a strong communicating background in each of these disciplines, but is assumed that this will be attained in the general education and specialized content phases of his preparation. Realizing that any adequate presentation of these disciplines, even in terms of that which is covered by the elementary student, is impractical within one volume, the writers have chosen to deal only with concepts, broad understandings, and skills especially pertinent to teachers of the elementary school.

This approach to gaining environmental understandings is consistent with that of Jarolimek. He points out the value of dealing with concepts rather than subject matter per se very vividly.

---

[56]Robert H. Beck, Walter W. Cook, and Nolan C. Kearney, *Curriculum in the Modern Elementary School* (second edition; Englewood Cliffs: Prentice-Hall, Inc., 1960), p. 268.

There is a growing realization that a heavy emphasis upon subject matter per se is not a proper one. What is important are the basic meanings and learnings which are made possible through the use of subject matter . . . factual data and information can be used to illustrate ways people have coped with environmental factors and forces in the past as contrasted with the ways the same things are done today . . . . Subject matter, therefore, is legitimately used as a means of better understanding man's social and physical world. When information getting or fact gathering become ends in themselves without being related to big, central ideas, the instructional emphasis is misdirected.[57]

A sample of the conceptual approach to using content in developing man's environmental understandings is graphically presented in Figure 36 in order that some understanding of the interlocking of content from the various disciplines can be seen. Figure 37 illustrates how a concept is an extended process, dependent upon repeated experiences in gradually broadening activities.

It is fully recognized that any approach to providing an understanding of man's environment is best developed within the framework of some organized plan. One must be aware that children are going to ask questions and show interests and concerns about themselves, their school, community, state, nation, and world. Knowledge of these expanding and interlocking concerns of youth has led educators to move more and more toward the spiral framework in social sciences. This takes into account the expanding environment and concerns of the child. It adheres to the principles that the child learns first those things which are nearest and of most interest and that the individual moves from the known to the unknown in his learning.

This approach to recognizing the expanding environment of the child may be noted through a listing of themes selected for emphasis by the Hillsborough County, Florida, school system. Their sequence includes:

Junior Primary I — Living in home and school
Junior Primary II — Helping in the community
Junior Primary III — Developing and improving the community
Grade IV — Living in various types of communities
Grade V — Improving life in different regions of the United States
Grade VI — Developing successful ways of living on a world basis[58]

It is easy to see how these broad themes can serve as a guide to developing the child's ever-expanding association with his environment. It

---

[57]John Jarolimek, *Social Studies in Elementary Education* (second edition; New York: The Macmillan Company, 1963), p. 48.

[58]J. Crockett Farnell, Superintendent, *Social Studies for Elementary Children* (Hillsborough County, Florida: County School System, 1960), p. 7.

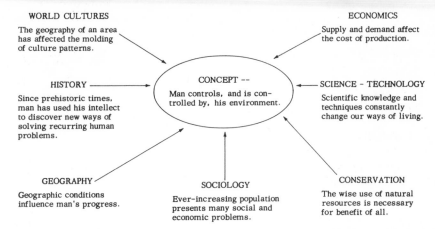

WORLD CULTURES
The geography of an area has affected the molding of culture patterns.

ECONOMICS
Supply and demand affect the cost of production.

HISTORY
Since prehistoric times, man has used his intellect to discover new ways of solving recurring human problems.

CONCEPT --
Man controls, and is controlled by, his environment.

SCIENCE - TECHNOLOGY
Scientific knowledge and techniques constantly change our ways of living.

GEOGRAPHY
Geographic conditions influence man's progress.

SOCIOLOGY
Ever-increasing population presents many social and economic problems.

CONSERVATION
The wise use of natural resources is necessary for benefit of all.

Figure 36. The Concept Approach as Developed Through the Various Social Sciences. Adopted from *Guide to Teaching Social Studies* (Madison, Wisconsin: The Madison Public Schools, 1961), p. 14.

must be recognized, however, that any treatment of topics or themes must not be totally confined to one grade level. Major emphasis should be given to the development of basic understandings and concepts related to the selected theme at the designated level. However, encouragement should be given to any group that is concerned with the solving of an immediate problem, disregarding the grade placement of the topic. In order that balance and continuity can be realized there should be a continuous overlapping and ever-widening range of study. This will provide for depth of concepts and intricacy of experiences which increase with the maturity of the students.

Whatever the framework or point of reference the school and teacher may present, the child should be confronted with the major areas of his envrionmental understandings, including geographical, historical, political, and scientific. The succeeding treatment of these areas is presented as suggestive data to which the basic ideas set forth in the preceding pages can be applied.

GEOGRAPHICAL UNDERSTANDINGS

The need for geographical understandings becomes increasingly more crucial in the space age. Radio and television take the youngster vicariously to all parts of the globe and into an understanding of planetary associations. Concepts of time and distance assume new meaning as advanced speed crafts and vehicles convey individuals swiftly from continent to continent.

As it relates to current happenings in the world geography becomes a major vehicle for guiding the student in gaining information about geographic factors. Ohlsen has succinctly expressed this point of view as follows:

> Geography in the elementary school should not be descriptive study; it should be a causal study. It should be a study of how man and his natural environment are interrelated; of what men do and why they do it; of the patterns of human use of geographic environment.[59]

In this approach to teaching geography the children analyze the operation of geographic influences which they can see, beginning with a study of "home geography" in the fourth grade. The fifth and sixth grades study the geography of our world. Particular emphasis is given to the study of geographical patterns of entire continents. This approach gives attention to distances from the equator of the area under study. It surveys and analyzes mountain masses, rainfall, natural resources, and cultivable land. These factors are studied for a continent as a whole in relation to historical forces of friendships, enmities, racial agglomerations, and the like. No attempt is made to consider all the details of the geography of each country. Most of the time is spent on study of the larger countries which are most involved with the problems of peace in our present world, utilizing historical facts and data as they help to make the present situation intelligible.[60]

The approach to teaching geography suggested here presumes the acquisition of skills in using such instructional tools as charts, graphs, globes, maps, and date lines. It assumes that geographical concepts begin in the first grade as the child determines, through appropriate guidance, the location of the school in relation to his home, and recognizes transportation as a means of getting to and from school.

This approach also includes the acquisition of certain skills which may be classified as geographical but also apply to historical. Such skills have been classified by Tiegs and Adams as those having to do with maps, globes, and time. For the primary grades they include:

1. The development of map readiness
2. Landscape form and concepts
3. Directional concepts
4. Locational concepts and skills
5. Distance concepts and skills

---

[59]Merle M. Ohlsen, *Modern Methods in Elementary Education* (New York: Henry Holt and Company, Inc., 1959) p. 312.

[60]*Ibid.*, pp. 312-316.

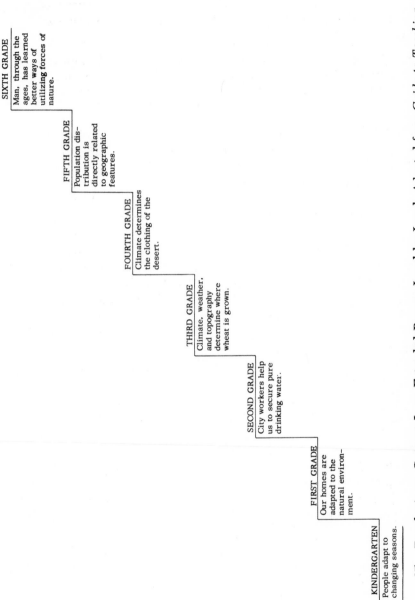

SIXTH GRADE

Man, through the ages, has learned better ways of utilizing forces of nature.

FIFTH GRADE

Population distribution is directly related to geographic features.

FOURTH GRADE

Climate determines the clothing of the desert.

THIRD GRADE

Climate, weather, and topography determine where wheat is grown.

SECOND GRADE

City workers help us to secure pure drinking water.

FIRST GRADE

Our homes are adapted to the natural environment.

KINDERGARTEN

People adapt to changing seasons.

Figure 37. Developing a Concept Is an Extended Process Level by Level. Adopted from *Guide to Teaching Social Studies*, (Madison, Wisconsin: The Madison Public Schools, 1961), p. 15.

377

6. Time concepts and skills
7. Understanding the calendar
8. Learning to tell time.[61]

Skills and concepts for grades 4, 5, and 6 as set forth by Tiegs and Adams include all those listed for the primary grades with these additional ones:

1. Relating globes and maps
2. Extending global concepts and skills
3. Simple grid system
4. Latitude
5. Land forms and visualization
6. Distance and area concepts and skills
7. Map symbols and map readings
8. Making inferences from maps.[62]

For the junior high students, Tiegs and Adams have proposed the extension of all skills set forth in previous grades and added to those the understanding of (1) revolution and the seasons and (2) relating time, distance, and longitude.[63] The teacher should realize that the communication skills as presented in a preceding section are fully applicable to developing environmental understandings. In fact their most direct application should be realized in dealing with the environmental factors of man pertinent to both geography and history.

A set of environmental factors appropriate for such treatment has been well delineated by the State Department of Education in Georgia under two categories which are (1) physical geography and (2) cultural geography. The listing of factors or generalizations which follows provides an adequate base for developing a social science program which cuts across and draws upon content from a wide range of disciplines.

Physical Geographic Factors.
1. Life on the earth is influenced by the earth's shape, its size, and set of motions.
2. The shape of the earth causes the unequal distribution of sunlight and differentiates climates and natural vegetation into regional types.
3. Earth movements of rotation and revolution are basic to understanding climate and time — night and day, as well as seasons.
4. Weather, climate, and earth crustal movements affect the surface of the earth and cause regional differences in landforms, minerals, drainage, soils, vegetation.

---

[61]Tiegs and Adams, *op. cit.*, pp. 281-290.
[62]*Ibid.*, pp. 291-306.
[63]*Ibid.*, pp. 306-318.

5. Climate is determined by sunlight, temperature, humidity, precipitation, winds, atmosphere pressure, unequal rates of heating and cooling of land and sea, ocean currents, mountains.
6. The crust of the earth consists of various types of rocks that influence topography. Soils are altered by nature and man.
7. Major climatic regions coincide approximately with major vegetation as related to climatic conditions.
8. Soil, water, solar energy, and air are the natural resources most indispensable to man. Natural vegetation is a great resource utilized by man.
9. The earth is divided into climatic regions; these classifications are a means of organizing information about the earth.
10. The physical elements of the earth are a unit and no part can be understood fully except in terms of its relationship to the whole.

Cultural Geographic Factors.

1. Man constantly seeks to satisfy his needs; in so doing he tries to adapt, shape, utilize, and exploit the earth to his own end. Some aspects of the natural environment, however, are not significantly altered or utilized by man.
2. The natural environment may set the broad limits of economic life within, but it is man who determines its specific character within the limits of his culture.
3. To exist, man must utilize natural resources. Human change may depend upon the nature and extent of man's available supply of energy and his ability to control it.
4. Man's utilization of natural resources is related to his desires and his level of technology.
5. The economic processes of production, exchange, distribution, and consumption of goods are economic concepts which have·a geographic orientation and vary in part according to geographic influence. The nature of the organization of economic processes within an area results from the kinds of resources, the stage of technology and the socio-political attitudes prevailing.
6. Land has a dominant position in the location of production. Since people prefer to live near their work, the location of production becomes significant in the location of people.
7. The kinds of climate, soil, native vegetation, animals, and minerals influence the nature and extent of man's achievements within each region. The amount and kind of food needed for health varies with climatic conditions and man's technology.
8. Factors of production, including technology, are subject to change; therefore, geography is concerned with changing patterns and land use.
9. Understanding the location of political or other social institutions is not complete without an understanding of the economics of the area.

Since understanding of the economy of the area depends in part upon understanding the natural environment of that area, it follows that political and social institutions are related to the natural environment.

10. The sequence of human activities and culture patterns are related to the geographic accessibility, location, and the particular time in which human beings live. People in different stages of civilization react differently to similar environments.

11. Man may, by his activities, upset the balance of nature; man may do something to correct the problem.

12. Competition for the acquisition of the earth's natural resources sometimes results in political strife and even war.

13. Geographic positions of nation states are also related to political co-operation and strife.[64]

Thus we recognize geography as an integral part of the environmental understandings which the child must gain. He must recognize how geography plays a part in all other environmental factors and learn to apply his geographical skills in coping with man's numerous problems. The student should understand that geography is fluid in that its various factors affect man and he in turn learns to cope with them.

HISTORICAL UNDERSTANDINGS

It has been traditionally accepted that history is taught in order to provide a basis for understanding the future. A knowledge of history gives man insight, appreciation, and understanding of current problems related to those of previous generations. Through study of our history the child may grow to love and appreciate his country as he understands the struggle and accomplishments of those before him in building the nation. A knowledge of history may provide opportunities for the individual to identify himself as a person with the historical past. As these historical understandings become the experience of individual children they become the common background of the general population.[65]

Even though contemporary man is living in a unique society, his set of values and problems of living are basically the same and are of relative importance to those of any preceding generation. He is engaged today, as in all generations, in spending most of his time securing food, clothing, and shelter, protecting his young and seeking personal happiness and security. Children are better able to interpret the factors which lead to historical events when they understand that history is a record of the living as well

---

[64]*Social Science for All Grades* (Atlanta: State Department of Education, 1961), pp. 91-2.
[65]Jarolimek, *op. cit.*, pp. 300-303.

as of the dead and that they are living during a history making period also. They then can see that a date in history extends before and after it.

This can be exemplified by the historical events related to the date of December 7, 1941. In order to understand the Korean incident one must be familiar with events following World War II. In turn, one must go back to World War I in order to grasp the significance of World War II. Eventually he gains some understanding of the series of events which led to December 7, 1941. It can be seen that history is a continuous story of man's activities which cannot be categorized only by dates.[66]

The teaching of historical understandings fits well into the framework set forth in Chapters 8 and 9 since they set forth the teaching unit as a vehicle for problem solving. Historical elements are a major portion of the vehicle for learning to be accomplished by youth through the unit approach to teaching. One objective in education should be that of helping the child to develop an understanding and appreciation of man's achievement through the years. This goal should be approached with the idea of helping the child understand the past in terms of the people who lived during those times, their problems, ways of living, and means of meeting their basic needs.

In the great push toward scientific and technological developments it is quite easy to laud the current power of our machinery and to forget the heritage of our civilization. There is great need for an understanding of the history of our nation. The melting pot from which our population is formed provides one of the richest and most varied cultural backgrounds in the world.[67]

It is imperative that as our young people meet more people from other countries they understand and respect their own cultural and historical backgrounds and are able to interpret it to those with whom they are associated. It is also necessary that they understand other countries with emphasis on similarities in current educational, economic, political, and cultural problems. This is believed to be of vital importance in cultivating and maintaining good relations among our world citizens.

Recognition of the values of each succeeding generation in terms of the culture of each geographical and political setting is crucial to the development of historical understandings. Members of the recent national project on the Instructional Program of the Public Schools, being well aware of this, identified six fundamental values they believed should serve as criteria for improvement of our schools. These values have been adopted here as guidelines for studying the history of civilization. They are:

---

[66]*Ibid.*
[67]Hill, *op. cit.,* p. 39.

1. Respect for the worth and dignity of every individual
2. Encouragement of variability
3. Equality of opportunity
4. Faith in man's ability to make rational decisions
5. Shared responsibility for common good
6. Respect for moral and spiritual values and ethical standards of conduct[68]

When the acts of man through the years are reviewed with such a set of values in mind, historical places, dates, and events take on different meanings. The child can visualize each incident in its setting and in terms of the conditions and personalities involved. He then can begin to see the reason for certain actions of his present society and consequently will become more interested in gaining broader historical and geographical understandings. The generalizations presented under the headings "Physical Geographic Factors" and "Cultural Geographic Factors" also are pertinent and therefore should be considered again at this point.

Regardless of whether the teacher and children have free range in selecting topics for history units or only the privilege of supplementing the text with resource material, the teacher has certain responsibilities. He must make sure that what is selected for study is within the comprehension of the children and appropriate to the topic and learners. The Jarolimek criteria following may be helpful to him.

1. Is the historical material to be studied directly related to experiences children have had or are having?
2. Is the historical material such as to appeal to the natural interests of the children with whom it is to be used?
3. Will the historical material enrich and extend some important social studies concept, generalization, understanding, or attitude?
4. Are the appropriate materials of instruction available — books, films, recordings, slides, pictures?
5. Can the basic historical concepts contained in the material be simplified to the extent that young children will be able to understand them?
6. Does the material lend itself to active participation by the children as they learn it?[69]

The teacher thus has the opportunity to help children gain historical understanding and in so doing appreciate the culture that is theirs to enjoy. He may deny this appreciation and understanding by setting up a barricade of dates and facts over which the youngsters may never pass. The volume of material is staggering, but when children are able to identify themselves

---

[68]Fraser, *op. cit.*, p. 216.
[69]Jarolimek, *op. cit.*, p. 304.

within the stream of history and learn to use the proper educational skills history can be intriguing and stimulating.

POLITICAL UNDERSTANDINGS

A fast growing area of content is herein classified as political and defined as those understandings having to do with citizens or government. In keeping with the problem solving approach to teaching, political understandings become significant to youth as they are manifested in current emphases, problems, and concerns. This will engage children in seeing happenings involving status leadership and conflicts between persons and parties in control of power. This will invoke controversial issues.

The teacher must remain as objective as possible, trying diligently to guide the youngsters in having access to the most current and authentic information possible. He will refrain from stating his views and beliefs on such issues in any manner which may tend to directly prejudice those under his supervision.

In order that the youngster can have as rich learning opportunities as possible, learning experiences should be provided so that each individual grows in his ability to:

1. Understand important developments in key areas in world affairs; this would include a study of significant geographical and historical factors, recent economic and political developments and intellectual and ideological developments.
2. Understand the development of foreign policies of the United States and the role of the United States in international affairs.
3. Have a better understanding of the appropriate role of the military in a democratic society and in world affairs.
4. Understand the different political ideologies and the merits and limitation of each.
5. Become increasingly aware of the effects of technology on the social, economic, and political aspects of modern society and their potentialities for change in the future.
6. Understand the role of innovations in human institutions to meet new problems in economic political and human affairs.[70]

Jarolimek has well described the need of our society in regard to political understandings as follows:

If the United States is to protect and maintain its freedom and the right to self-government, the citizens must know their political institutions and how they function; they must also face up to the responsibilities and duties which are a part of a representative government such as ours.[71]

---

[70]*Social Studies for All Grades, op. cit.,* p. 50.
[71]Jarolimek, *op. cit.,* pp. 327-8.

Equipping children with basic political understandings is a function of the elementary school beginning with the first year. Sample understandings which can be gained by children as selected from Jarolimek's list are:

Grades one, two, and three:

1. We help make rules and live by them.
2. Policemen work for the community and are paid by the community.
3. People in our country choose who their leaders are.
4. When we choose someone for a leader we give him certain powers.
5. The flag stands for our country.

Grade four:

1. In our country we have several governments; the community, the state, and the government of our whole country.
2. The people of a state choose persons to make the state laws.
3. The place where the state government has its offices is the state capitol.
4. State governments have much to do with our everyday affairs of living.
5. It is important that the best people possible be chosen for positions in government.

Fifth Grade:

1. The major European nations in Columbus's time were ruled by kings and queens.
2. Many people came to the new world to gain freedom.
3. The first plan of government of the United States was based on the Articles of Confederation.
4. Representatives from the states developed a new plan of government; it is described in the Constitution.
5. The Supreme Court helps protect the rights that citizens have under the Constitution.

Sixth Grade:

1. All countries have some type of government.
2. The earliest group of people was the family; from this grew larger groups such as tribes, which had leaders.
3. As people acquired more property, there was need for more laws.
4. Democracy as a system of government was developed by the Greeks.
5. Many of our ideas about government and law have come to us from the Romans.
6. Not all nations of the world allow citizens to have anything to say about how they are governed.[72]

The schools not only should provide for development of direct political understandings but also give attention to other areas vital and complementary to the political framework in which the individual finds himself.

---

[72]*Ibid.*, pp. 330-334.

These areas are economic, religious, educational, recreational, and family. They are completely intermeshed because they function in a culture and are complex and call upon several disciplines for comprehension. It is not necessary, however, to teach these as separate subjects. When chlidren study occupations in the community as a part of a unit of instruction they touch upon economics. As they study a primitive society they see how hunting may involve not only economic but recreational and religious principles.[73]

In helping children understand the political aspects of our society the elements of change, courage, integrity, preservation, and extension should be related to our democratic ideals. The child must understand that it is through our organized institutions, be they the 4-H Club or the federal government, that society develops. It is within this environment that the individual has rights, privileges, and responsibilities. The attitudes he displays and the energy he expends in relation to these institutions to a large extent determine his happiness and effectiveness.

SCIENTIFIC UNDERSTANDINGS

Science teaching in the contemporary elementary school curriculum has risen above the designation of nature study assigned to it in the recent past. Teachers now recognize the hunger of children for understanding and truth about the world in which they live. They realize that children are keen observers. They determine likenesses and differences easily and with guidance soon learn to perform elementary analysis and reach generalizations.

The alert teacher captures these innate qualities of youth and develops their capacity for scientific thinking. The increasing bodies of content assembled under a multiplicity of disciplines make it difficult for educators to agree upon the specfic subject matter to be included in the elementary school science curriculum. There is general agreement, however, that more emphasis is being placed upon the process of discovery. Children are being encouraged to find out for themselves and to use resources to better advantage.

In this age of discovery the teacher has the responsibility of guiding students in acquiring the skill and habit of utilizing some organized approach so that his time and energy may bring the most rewarding results. The approach most commonly recognized is referred to as the scientific approach. The general aspects of the scientific approach as set forth in problem solving have been described fully in Chapter 8. Specific steps identified with gaining scientific understandings through problem solving as presented

---

[73]*Ibid.*, pp. 318-320.

at this point include (1) curiosity, (2) observation, (3) formulating an hypothesis or hunch, (4) testing hypothesis, (5) drawing conclusions, and (6) correlation or integration.

All children want to find out. They want to see, to open, to touch, to hear, to smell. This innate urge, known as curiosity, motivates the individual to action and constitutes the first step in learning.

When freedom and encouragement are given, the element of curiosity easily moves to observation in varying forms. It may be pulling the wheels off a toy car, tearing apart the petals of a flower, or pushing an electric switch just to see what will happen. Guidance in approaching such acts in a systematic manner can aid the child in more fruitful observation. It can teach him to stop and look from many angles and to apply all his senses before the impulse to act is energized. While doing this he may have a hunch or supposition that will move him to formulate an intelligent opinion.

Such an opinion, or sophisticated guess, is classified as an hypothesis. The individual thus constructs his ideas into an "if and what" statement, that is, he predicts that if certain conditions are met and certain actions are taken he will expect to get some specified results.

After formulating such an hypothesis the individual sets up a situation and provides the conditions and actions to determine if his guess or opinion is correct. This then is the act of testing the hypothesis. He utilizes all means possible to make the testing objective and to record his finding in clear and precise manner.

When all data have been collected his next step is to analyze them. He examines them under every possible circumstance and seeks to summarize the findings. Utilizing these findings he checks his hypothesis to see if what he had supposed would happen actually took place. Looking at all aspects of the findings he draws whatever conclusions are evident.

The scientific approach may logically stop at this point but the practical citizen has one other responsibility, that is, he must see how his conclusions coincide with his previous beliefs, see how this involves others and what values it holds for future study and developments. In essence he must relate the new findings and new self to the present and past. He then adjusts his own thinking and actions as the situation applies to his previous understandings and to the next appropriate level of operation.

The foregoing point of view in regard to learning by discovery utilizing the scientific approach implies that children should work within the realm of scientific interests and potential. It also infers that the teacher should be well informed in regard to generally accepted scientific objectives and current understandings. The following set of objectives for teaching scientific understandings in the elementary school as adapted from Blough and Schwartz should prove of aid to the teacher.

1. Help students come to understand some generalizations or "big meanings" or scientific principles that they can use in solving problems in their environment.
2. Help students to grow in ability to solve problems.
3. Help students develop a scientific attitude.
4. Help students develop skill in handling scientific materials.
5. Create in children an interest in and an appreciation for the world in which they live.[74]

The child should be assisted in recognizing the interdependence between man and his environment. Through this he should see how geographical and historical understandings are related to scientific understandings, that is, as environment affects man he learns to use it better through scientific discoveries. The child should be led to see how many scientific problems develop as man lives in his environment. Some of the most pertinent problems are concerned with health and physical development. Recognizing this the child should learn how man's bodily functions can be improved through scientific diet, exercise, rest, and medication.

Re-emphasizing the relationship of geography and science, the child should recognize the earth on which he lives as a huge sphere surrounded by atmosphere which sustains man. He should learn the importance of water that has been provided for him in quantities that cover more of the earth's surface than the land. He should also find out about the great wealth of other resources stored in the earth for man's use. Through this approach to scientific understanding the child should come to appreciate the fact that man's culture is related to the environmental conditions under which he lives and that the increase in man's scientific knowledge greatly affects his culture.[75]

Implementation of the problem-solving approach to learning relies heavily upon the interests of children. It also recognizes the teacher as a strong member of the group which gives guidance to the program, making available his knowledge of resources and content.

This assumes that scientific understandings will be developed through scientific experiences and that these experiences will be planned coopera-

---

[74]Glenn O. Blough and Julius Schwartz, *Elementary School Science and How to Teach It* (third edition; New York: Holt, Rinehart and Winston, 1964). pp. 13-21.
[75]Robert Beck, Walter Cook, and Nolan Kearney, *Curriculum in the Modern Elementary School* (second edition; Englewood Cliffs: Prentice-Hall, Inc., © 1960), pp. 313-315.

tively by the students and teacher. Care must be given, however, to the selection of such scientific experiences that established science guides are utilized to the best advantage. In selection of these experiences the teacher can rely upon a criteria presented by Shuster and Ploghoft which suggests that each should:

1. Be based upon sequence as it is related to the maturity level of the learner and provides the necessary continuity from kindergarten through grade six.
2. Provide for the differing ability levels of the children to insure continuous growth of all.
3. Be based upon problems which are within the comprehension range of the members of the class.
4. Provide the kind of experiments which are rudimentary in nature and natural for children to carry out in the classroom.
5. Contribute to helping children achieve the objectives of science education which will insure growth in critical thinking and result in a better understanding of the scientific method as a process for solving problems in everyday life.
6. Aid the children in developing favorable attitudes, appreciations, skills, and habits related to developing a "democratic personality."
7. Develop skill in analyzing, appraising, and evaluating evidence before reaching decisions.
8. Help children to become familiar with and recognize the value of utilizing many kinds of resources both human and physical in seeking solutions to purposeful problems.[76]

In addition to using such a criteria as the foregoing the teacher should avail himself of one of the many scope and sequence charts for selecting science content that have been prepared at local, state or national levels. The local school or school system usually will have adopted a prepared outline, developed their own, or will rely upon an adopted series of science texts to serve as their guide. A source of national repute which may guide the teacher in selection of science content is the Forty-Sixth Yearbook for the Study of Education. It suggests that planned experiences for children each year should include opportunities for growth in six broad areas of the physical and biological environment. These areas are (1) the universe, (2) the earth, (3) conditions necessary for life, (4) living things, (5) physical and chemical phenomena, and (6) man's attempt to control his environment.[77]

---

[76]Albert H. Shuster and Milton E. Ploghoft, *The Emerging Elementary Curriculum* (Columbus: Charles E. Merrill Books, Inc., 1963), pp. 309-310.
[77]National Society for the Study of Education, *Science Education in American Schools,* Forty-Sixth Yearbook, Part I (Chicago: University of Chicago Press, 1947), pp. 75-76.

Realizing that this is a broad coverage which presents a serious problem of selection for the teacher he should also utilize a reputable professional elementary science textbook. One of the most comprehensive resources of this type is Blough and Schwartz's *Elementary School Science and How To Teach It.*[78] This source gives basic science information in nineteen pertinent areas. It also provides suggestions prepared especially to aid the teacher in guiding children's experiences in understanding each particular body of content. These areas cover the six broad areas of physical and biological environment suggested by the National Society for the Study of Education.

Again it must be pointed out that some more specific guide should be available to the teacher and students in making their selection of science experiences. An example of this is found in *Science for Georgia Schools*, Volumes I and II.[79] This source presents suggested principles for the science curriculum in eleven integrative themes which are also consistent with the science areas presented by the National Society for the Study of Education. This scope and sequence guide was designed to be used by the teacher in guiding students toward scientific understandings. Supplementary to this resource are three volumes of *Science Aids Through the Grades* by Alex F. Perrodin.[80] These volumes give specific examples by grades of how each principle set forth in *Science for Georgia Schools* can be taught in the classroom.

Selected principles from each grade level for the theme "Living Matter" as found in *Science for Georgia Schools* are presented here to show how the teaching of scientific understandings can be developmental.

Grade One:
1. All matter is either living or nonliving.
2. All living matter is either plant or animal.
3. Plants and animals need food, air, water and light to maintain life and to grow.

Grade Two:
1. Animals are equipped to get their food in different ways.
2. Animals depend upon plants and/or other animals for food.
3. Chlorophyll-bearing plants make their own food.

Grade Three:
1. Plants store food in roots, stems, leaves, bulbs, and seeds.
2. Plants and animals use food for growth and release of energy.
3. Animals store food in their bodies and in their special hiding places.

---

[78]Glenn D. Blough and Julius Schwartz, *Elementary School Science and How to Teach It* (third edition; New York: Holt, Rinehart and Winston, 1964).

[79]*Science for Georgia Schools* (Volume I for Grades 1-3) Atlanta: State Department of Education, 1958); ———— Science for Georgia Schools (Volume II for Grades 4-8 (Atlanta: State Department of Education, 1958).

[80]Alex F. Perrodin, *Science Aids Through the Grades* (Parts I, II, and III) Athens: College of Education, University of Georgia, 1960-1961.

Grade Four:

1. Some plants and animals live in communities and depend upon each other.
2. Chlorophyll-bearing plants release oxygen and provide food and shelter for some animals.
3. Different animals help plants in different ways.

Grade Five:

1. The cells of all plants and animals are made up of a living substance called protoplasm.
2. Plants and animals are constantly changing.
3. Organisms grow, develop and pass through life cycles according to the inherited pattern present in their genes.

Grade Six:

1. Changes are constantly occurring in communities of living things.
2. Living things compete in a struggle for existence.
3. The living world maintains a natural balance through cycles. (Life to decay, decay to life.)

Grade Seven:

1. The energy in foods is made available to an organism through the process of metabolism, involving digestion, assimilation, and oxidation. Wastes are disposed of through the process of excretion.
2. Each species has its own special requirements for food essential to its best growth.
3. Growth is essentially the increase in size and multiplication and differentiation of cells.

Grade Eight:

1. Every living cell depends upon the movement of water and dissolved materials through its membrane and/or cell wall, (osmosis).
2. Each organism must have certain materials for life and whatever essential ones it cannot build it must acquire.
3. Each species of living organisms is adapted, or is in the process of being adapted, both structurally and functionally, to live where it is found.[81]

In the elementary school, science has emerged from the nature study of rock collecting and insect gathering to a way of thinking, a way of working and a mode of living. Relationships between science and social studies are now understandably overlapping as the school seeks to extend the basic skills of the child through his scientific environment. It is increasingly more difficult to provide a course of study that selects specific content for each grade level. The scientific approach to teaching can now utilize the innate capacity of youth for scientific thinking. Through the process of discovery

---

[81]*Science for Georgia Schools, op. cit.*, pp. 2-4.

separate doors can be opened for individual children, allowing them to pursue their interests and capabilities to broader understanding. The child is led to understand how man's culture is related to his environment. He learns how he can participate in planning and developing his own environment, utilizing a wide variety of resources.

Prepared guides including scope and sequence charts serve as a resource for the teacher but by no means limit the program of scientific experiences available. More and more the teacher must be freed from the pressure of specific content required for all children. He must be equipped and encouraged to utilize the avenues of the child's immediate scientific environment and native curiosity. Through this approach, the child can be prepared to live in a world which is becoming increasingly more complex and technical by developing his own technique of scientific inquiry.

AESTHETIC UNDERSTANDINGS

Man's basic means of communication are reading, writing, speaking, listening, and computation. Mastery of skill in using these media is, logically, the chief objective of education. Communication through use of these tools involves utilizing content related to man's historical, geographical, political, and scientific environment. Without man's natural instincts and tendencies toward socialization and aesthetic appreciation, however, these experiences would be of little avail.

It is easy for society to recognize the foregoing needs of the individual for living and communicating with his fellow man. This is especially true with the communication skills and the environmental understandings. The skills do not share the same respect but have been increasingly accepted.

The grouping of children's needs known as elements of enrichment or aesthetic understandings has had spasmodic acceptance and emphasis. These include physical fitness, moral and spiritual values, music, and art. A changing emphasis in regard to this area permits this grouping to be classified as aesthetic understandings. The position set forth here agrees with Montgomery in that this relation refers to experiences which provide for development of the senses of the individual so that he understands something of the possibilities before him. It seeks to open up means whereby the individual can enjoy those things which he can use and share through creative construction. It includes such emotional responses as "whole-souled enjoyment, wonder, and devoting all levels of one's consciousness to an action."[82] It goes beyond the utilitarian in that it seeks for

---

[82]Chandler Montgomery, "Sensing and Responding to the World: Aesthetic Development," Robert S. Fleming (ed.), *Curriculum for Today's Boys and Girls* (Columbus: Charles E. Merrill Books, Inc., 1963), pp. 375-379.

the individual a full rich life including more than what one can eat or sell. It goes beyond the understanding which comes from correctly naming, analyzing, and generalizing. It leads to the quality of understanding achieved by giving oneself to an experience generously, wholly, and without gainful intent. In essence, it means the development of one's own perceptions of qualitative, sensed differences. Through this approach to aesthetic understandings the individual's own creative planning, choosing, changing, and evaluating are separately and collectively stimulated and modified.[83]

PHYSICAL FITNESS

From the beginning of time man has depended upon his physical body for sustenance. The physical body is the house or temple in which man lives. Man is most productive and acceptable to others when his body is fully functional. The individual thus must early learn the importance of developing his body to its maximum as well as protecting it from the hazards of society. With this understanding, the child should learn how to help his body grow and how to use it in such a manner that it will be able to do the things he wants to do.

The child soon learns that his feelings of comfort and readiness for activity are determined by bodily functions. These needs are expressed in terms of food, warmth, rest, exercise, and the like. As they are met, the child should learn that the body develops into a specimen which is not only functional but is attractive to others in terms of form movement and hygienic conditions. The body as the house of the individual presents an image of the real self. Its appearance gives others an indication of what the individual is and what can be expected of him. The body, as a human specimen may call for respect from others or it may cause others to reject the individual.

When teachers understand the human body in this light they will recognize the child's need for a variety of rigorous, meaningful physical activities in keeping with the developmental stage of each individual. The teacher should recognize the body movement skills as fundamental to the child's physical growth. He should also see these in relation to the child's thinking, manner and means of expression, getting along with self and others, and problem solving. He therefore should provide for development of each child's physiological endurance, strength, agility, and kinesthetic reactions. Beginning in the primary school these should be opportunities for boys and girls to discover, learn, develop, and exercise physical skills which they will utilize the rest of their lives.

---

[83]*Ibid.*

Activities should be provided that will help the child find out what his body can do. These should help him gain skill in maintaining balance and equilibrium, transferring weight, controlling objects and equipment, sensing speed and rhythm, and adapting to space. Movements fundamental to all skill patterns should be a regular part of the experiences of every ·child. These include walking, jumping, hopping, running, leaping, bending, stretching, twisting, turning, skating, bouncing, pushing, pulling, and swinging. Development and exercise of these skills are found in organized activities such as games, sports, stunts, swimming, and rhythms. During skill development the child should encounter many conditions which further habits and attitudes conducive to the best skill implementation. Experiences which the child should encounter for this purpose include trial and error, success, persistence, encouragement, understanding, value judgments, decision making, and following rules and directions.[84]

Physical activity is more easily recognized as a contributor to the development and maintenance of the functional body than to bodily health. Essential to physical fitness, however, are proper ˙health habits and practices which prepare the body for physical activity. The major responsibility for this outside the home resides with the classroom teacher who may in turn call for the assistance of specialized school personnel such as the nurse or physician. Through the instructional program and the utilization of other services, the teacher should help the child to gain understandings in proper nutrition, adequate rest and sleep, opportunities for physical activity, and protection from disease and accidents. The instructional program also should help the child gain understandings and appreciations that encourage the proper care of the body. Other personal needs of the child to which the instructional program may contribute include acceptance, security, love, success, recognition, intellectual stimulation, and a sense of personal worth.

The school should be aware of the array of topics relevant to the development of individuals whose bodies are well prepared for rich and productive living. In keeping with the approach to other basic areas of the curriculum, experiences must be provided which are pertinent to the children involved. The instructional program is the vital instrument for developing the fully functioning individual, but much depends upon the total environment, instructional facilities, and policies of the school. Those of major consideration include ample play space and equipment, heatlhful

---

[84]See Gladys Andrews, *Creative Rhythmic Movement for Children* (Englewood Cliffs, N. J.: Prentice-Hall, Inc., 1954), pp. 37-43; Jeanette Veatch, "Developing Skills in Various Subject Areas," Robert S. Fleming (ed.) *Curriculum for Today's Boys and Girls* (Columbus: Charles E. Merrill Books, Inc., 1963), pp. 224-8.

toilet facilities, lunch facilities, safety devices, permissive schedule, periodic health examinations, health record system, attention to prevention and control of diseases, and provision for emergencies in sickness and accidents.

MORAL AND SPIRITUAL VALUES

The United States of America has long been recognized as a God-fearing nation with high moral standards and devotion to spiritual values. Its Constitution provides for basic freedoms of man including religion. It has, however, specified that the church and state are to be separate. Recognizing the dangers inherent in a state religion it has left the teaching of the issues and doctrines of religion to the home, church, and synagogue. In recent rulings of the Supreme Court it has been decreed that the schools may teach *about* religion. This places a great responsibility upon the school in providing appropriate content. In order that the child can gain meaning from the vast background of the development of the religions of man, he must be able to recognize the values that have grown out of man's commitment to moral standards, religion, and democracy which have made our country what it is.

Foshay has succinctly appraised the position of the schools in teaching *about* religion as follows:

> If we suceed in teaching in the public schools the values that grow out of religious commitment (without dealing directly with the nature of specific religious commitments) then the meaning of the religions the children are learning *about* will at least have a chance — and perhaps a good chance — of being apparent to them. It matters what religions one adheres to, and it matters whether one adheres to a religion or not. If we teach about religion, and leave it at that, it will seem only to matter politically and culturally. But if we teach this material and at the same time teach the values we all hold, it will become apparent that religion matters not only politically and culturally, but that it matters morally and spiritually as well.[85]

Through appropriate experiences in group living boys and girls learn the significance of living according to moral and spiritual values generally prized in our culture. In assuming responsibilities for the welfare of others and in sharing materials, facilities, and ideas they gradually move from the realm of selfish impulsiveness to the realm of weighing values in light of conscience, reason, and experience. The study of great men in relation to values held by them gives the child some basis for developing his own set of values. The study of many religions and what these religions have

---

[85]Arthur W. Foshay, "Teaching About Religion in School" (address; Atlanta: Atlanta Institute on Public Education and Religion, October 23, 1964).

meant to people enables the child to see values in religion and thus determine a basis for his beliefs and actions.

Havighurst has found that there are five stages through which the ordinary person goes in the process of developing moral character. These stages include:

1. The amoral, impulsive stage, during which the person follows his impulse and has no morality.
2. The egocentric, expedient stage, during which the person has learned to control his impulses for the sake of his safety and so as to make a good impression.
3. The conforming state, during which the prime principle of behavior is to conform to the demands and expectations of the social group in which one lives.
4. The irrational conscience stage, during which the strongest principle of behavior is the inner moral conscience which has been absorbed without change or criticism from the moral teachings of parents and others.
5. The rational conscience stage, during which adolescents become emotionally and intellectually independent of the older generation.[86]

It has been found that by the time he reaches his teens, every person has in his make-up some of all five of these aspects of moral character. Each person, however, is likely to show sufficient evidence of one or more of the stages to classify him according to a specific type of moral motivation. The teacher should be able to recognize these as sequential developmental stages and help the child to see that the rational conscience stage is the highest type and the one especially valuable in our changing society.[87]

Two important ways the school can help the child in moving toward the rational conscious stage, the essence in moral character, are (1) to provide models for character development that boys and girls in the early grades can follow and (2) to provide more opportunities for reflective thinking in regard to moral matters. This recognizes the fact that character is learned by children from those who are important in their eyes. Seeing the teacher take a stand on a moral issue should encourage the child to make his own moral decisions. Reflective thinking may start in the kindergarten as the children are permitted to make choices and analyze the results. Content in history, literature, and general reading matter of children through the grades presents numerous situations to which moral principles can be applied to human behavior.[88]

---

[86]Robert J. Havighurst, "What Research Says About Developing Moral Character," *NEA Journal*, Volume 51 (January, 1962) pp. 29-30.
[87]*Ibid.*
[88]*Ibid.*

To fail to teach moral and spiritual values in the schools is to deny responsibility for teaching the whole child. Knowledge without character or principle is dangerous. The individual without purpose has no commitment. Without commitment he lacks the motivation necessary for making full use of educational opportunities which otherwise may be at his disposal.

MUSIC

Recognizing that music is a universal medium of communication, the program in the elementary school should be concerned with the musical needs of children. Music experiences should provide for creativity and a variety of experiences. Music is a means of expressing joy, devotion, sorrow, and patriotism. As such it depicts the history of man through the ages.

Ways in which the individual responds and expresses himself through music include singing, dancing, playing an instrument, listening, and composing. Reading and feeling or sensing music are skills essential to the full expression of the individual. The teacher must be cognizant of these skills and modes of expression as objectives for the music program are determined. The development of appreciation and enjoyment of music as an integral part of daily living is the major objective of a sound program. With this in mind the six aims of school music expressed by Logan and Logan should serve as a guide for the music program of the school. These aims are:

1. To dvelop creativity and to awaken a sense of beauty.
2. To provide a means of recreation now and in later life.
3. To develop discrimination in music.
4. To develop the imagination.
5. To provide the child with musical skill.
6. To develop the child's voice.[89]

The major means of music expression and the one most accessible to all is the voice. Man has devised many other instruments for music expression including the piano, organ, and those of the orchestra and band. The child should have opportunity to be acquainted with many of these instruments and acquire skill in the use of those for which he is suited. Music has a way of appealing to the human emotions causing the individual to move portions of his body in rhythm. This phase of music expression, which includes many kinds of dance from the simple march to the intricate polka, allows the individual to express himself through bodily movement.

---

[89]Lillian M. Logan and Virgil G. Logan, *Teaching the Elementary School Child* (Boston: Houghton Mifflin Company, 1961). pp. 556-7.

Opportunities for utilizing the elements of music which arise from any connection with learning experiences in other areas of the curriculum should be taken. Singing songs that children already know serves as a good base for stimulating their interest in new songs and those related to a current emphasis. The teacher should have a repertoire of songs at his disposal appropriate to the children's ages and curriculum content. Graded series of music books approved for use in the school by a local or state textbook committee provide a basic resource for songs in the classroom. Some instrument for pitching songs should be used so that the songs can be sung in tune. Recordings provided by basic music series publishers are effective in teaching new songs, especially when the teacher lacks a desirable singing voice. Use of the piano should be limited so that the child can hear his voice with other voices and get the "feel" of relative tones. The piano is always helpful, however, when used by a creative pianist to motivate interest and enjoyment in singing together.

Listening is basic to all music. It is no longer the passive skill it once was assumed to be. In order to sing, play an instrument, or express oneself rhythmically, there must be careful listening. Listening is more than sitting while the teacher plays recordings he considers "good for children to know." The child should be allowed to listen in his own way. Some children listen by letting the tones surround them so that they relax and enjoy the sensation of sound. Other children listen to enjoy the story the music presents. Others visualize actions and scenes the music brings to mind. Some children follow the shifting instruments or changing themes in the score. Many listen to enjoy the simple melody and counter melodies. Listening, then, is an active process which involves determining the appropriate moods and movements suited to particular music. The child should recognize that listening to music in any form not only provides enjoyment but contributes to the growth and development of his aural powers. This enables him to be more selective in other areas of appreciation, especially in the development of reading and speaking.[90]

Music reading may come with ease and pleasure when it is related to songs children have memorized, or the skill is related to the child's desire to create songs and to play an instrument. Many graded music books present music reading in an attractive manner. With a little initiative and creativeness on the part of teachers, children gradually learn to associate sounds with notes on a music score and in turn reproduce these notes in sounds with the voice or an instrument.

---

[90]Alfred Ellison, *Music With Children* (New York: McGraw-Hill Book Company, 1959), p. 199-201.

The wise music teacher recognizes that there is readiness for reading music on the part of children just as there is readiness for other skills in the curriculum. The teacher should recognize, however, that formal teaching of music reading below the fourth grade and even below junior high school is questionable unless a wealth of experience in music is provided in the primary grades. It has been found that delay until the sixth grade in teaching note reading seems to do no damage to the ultimate ability of pupils to read music from the score.[91]

Rhythmic expression is natural to the very essence of the individual and thus an intricate part of the music program. Almost all movement in life, including the heart beat, breathing, and digestion, functions on a rhythmic basis in its natural form. Man's ability to move in rhythm has contributed to his power to do certain types of work more easily. Many of the early folk songs portray working movements characteristic of certain types of manual labor. Response to music through rhythm is natural with children. Many of their activities involve total bodily movement. The individual may express himself through movement when he is unable to verbalize. The teacher should capitalize upon this and encourage physical response to various kinds of stimuli. In so responding, the shy or retiring child may make contacts not permissible otherwise. In addition, the aggressive child may relieve excess energies and the tense child may find relaxation through music. The following basic understandings of rhythm as adapted from Ellison should guide the teacher in providing rhythmic experiences for children:

1. Patterns of living are characterized in function by rhythm.
2. Music has the power to modify natural body rhythms.
3. A rhythmic program involving bodily movement provides for expression of emotion through motion.
4. Formal rhythms may serve as a good introduction to bodily movement of the stereotyped child.
5. Creative rhythms involve those physical activities of children which freely express their feelings.
6. Creative rhythms allow children to interpret their feelings about the music which they hear.
7. Creative rhythms may allow for children's rhythmic bodily movement to be based on their feelings with the music following the children rather than the children following the music.
8. Rhythmic dramatic pantomime is an important aspect of creative rhythms.

---

[91]See Alfred Ellison, *op. cit.*, p. 41; Jeanette Veatch, "Developing Skills in Various Subject Areas." Robert S. Fleming (ed.) *Curriculum for Today's Boys and Girls* (Columbus; Charles E. Merrill Books, Inc., 1963), p. 205.

9. Since no two people hear music in exactly the same way, no two people, therefore, should necessarily interpret it physically in exactly the same way.
10. In creative rhythms the major task is to bring an element of conscious approach to movement, while maintaining the spontaneous free out-burst of motion which characterizes movement in play.[92]

Music composition, usually associated with the professional, may begin in the early grades as the group or an individual recognizes a need for a musical expression not found in print. Writing down sounds in musical notes may give the child real satisfaction. The act of composing by the teacher and group may provide a means of expression needed in rounding out the study of a content unit. Such an experience usually is rare but the possibilities for it should not be overlooked. The child who is especially gifted in this area should be encouraged. Guidance should be given by either the classroom teacher or music resource person in developing, analyzing, criticizing, and evaluating any such contribution.

The extent of the music experiences and opportunities of each child is determined largely by the leadership and permissiveness of the classroom teacher. The teacher must understand the objectives of the music program and have sufficient knowledge of music, children, and materials to provide a variety of appropriate experiences. The program should emphasize the pleasure and appreciation which come from participation in a music experience. It should include carefully selected songs, singing games, rhythms and dances, instruments to play, music for listening, and basic skills in reading and performing. It should contribute to the well-being and growth of each individual.

ART

The child continuously seeks to express himself through experiences which allow him to cope with visual and concrete materials. He wants to create. It is in this sense that art provide for the fulfillment of his needs. If the child receives satisfaction through building, molding, cutting, and painting and the environment is conducive to pursuing these expressions, he will grow in his ability and enthusiasm for developing greater skills in these media. These constructive expressions, fortunately, seem to have appeal for almost all children including the slow learner, the average, and the gifted. Reasons given by Logan and Logan for this appeal include:

1. It helps children develop creative expression.
2. It helps children acquire artistic skills.

---

[92]Ellison, *op. cit.,* pp. 120-122.

3. It helps children gain understanding of their environment as they depict their experiences.
4. It helps children develop taste through contact with a variety of media and techniques.
5. It helps in the development of intellectual discipline.
6. It provides initial experiences for future avocational interests.[93]

The basic point of view to keep in mind in working with the young child is that art is self-expression. It is play to him. The wise teacher will help him maintain this feeling as he encourages the child to put into his art the thoughts and feelings that are important to him. The child who is uninhibited will sing as he paints a picture, molds a clay boat, or builds a block airport tower. It is only when adults begin to react to his "play" that he becomes self-conscious and unsure of himself.[94]

The teacher should be aware that very few if any of the children who pass through his classroom doors will ever be renowned artists. However, he can be assured that every individual, through his own creativeness and ingenuity, may help to make the spot where he lives more functional for himself and inviting to others. He can assist the child in feeling his own adequacy and ability to grow through self-expression. Four basic ingredients are necessary for true self-expression, namely encouragement, stimulating environment, appropriate and adequate materials, and time.

The teacher, concerned with the growth and development of children, studies each child and helps him to find his aptitudes. He also recognizes each accomplishment of the individual. The teacher sets the stage for children's expression by exposing them to many stimulating experiences through story telling, pictures, films, dramatizations, and excursions. A wealth of materials should be available to the classroom with free access given to children to try, experiment, examine, compare, and combine. These ingredients, however, will be to no avail unless adequate time is allowed for the child to utilize them according to his own play-work pattern and pace.

As in other fields, it is desirable that sequential planning be provided in the field of art. This should afford three kinds of art activities in the classroom. These are (1) art learning activities, (2) self-directed art activities, and (3) integrated art activities. It is in the first of these that particular attention should be given to developmental skills. A summary of the sequential learnings desirable for primary children suggested by McFee includes:

1. Experiences that increase their visual awareness; motivation to observe, to watch for relationship, and to look for detail.

---

[93]Logan and Logan, *op. cit.*, pp. 579-580.
[94]Warner, *op. cit.*, pp. 180-181.

2. Encouragement to maintain and develop curiosity and creativeness through opportunities and rewards for inquisitiveness, flexibility, and originality.
3. Learning that there are different ways of working in different situations. Overcome stereotyped ideas about work and play.
4. Increasing means of creative expression by exploring media.
5. Paralleling visual language with verbal language in the learning of similarities and differences.
6. Relating own work to art in their environment and in other cultures and periods. Begin to make aesthetic judgments.[95]

Experience has shown that there is a lessening of emphasis on art in the intermediate grades. At this time, individualities become more distinct, the range in art abilities widens, and there is a greater press from other curricular areas. Because of these factors it is imperative that there be a continuation of the same types of art experiences from the primary grades on through the elementary school. The primary learnings should serve as a base for developing the finer and more intricate skills. Understandings that should be given greater emphasis in the intermediate grades include:

1. Developing taste. Levels of aesthetic taste can be raised by exposure to, and training in, the fine arts and superior product design advertising.
2. Learning the artist's role in society. Explore role of designer through visits to the studios of architects and city planners.
3. Perceptual training. Paralleled cognitive and perceptual training. Associate verbal skills with pictorial symbols in communication experiences.
4. Handling complexity. Increase the number and kinds of systems the children can use for organizing complex visual experiences. Look for obvious patterns in painting and then the more subtle. Translate what is seen in visual space into written descriptions.
5. Cognitive and visual learnings. Explore the way forms, colors, and shapes change as they move in space and light.
6. Develop creativity. Encourage and reward independence. Study lives of great men and women whose contributions to our way of life have been an outgrowth of their independent creative thinking and action.
7. Increase skills. Introduce more complex printing methods, paper sculpture, weaving, pottery, mosaics, and a variety of paints and means of applying paints.[96]

Self-directed activities of children should begin as early as the teacher can allow a child to pursue his own impulses and interests in an art medium.

---

[95]June King McFee, *Preparation for Art* (Belmont, Cal.: Wadsworth Publishing Company, Inc., 1961), p. 214.
[96]*Ibid.*, pp. 230-237.

Some time should be provided in the schedule for independent activities when the teacher is free to move about helping individuals. Media and materials should be accessible to the child who has the urge to express himself visually upon completion of assignments ahead of other children. Strong encouragement, individual assistance and recognition should be given those who engage in self-directed activities.

Art takes on a richer meaning for children as they engage in experiences which integrate it with other phases of the curriculum. Through this means, relationships of the various units of learning can be shown. Sequences in learning can be recognized and summaries of content and basic understanding can be organized and presented. Involvement of children in art media for this purpose will depend upon their previous art learnings. It will also take into consideration their maturity for utilization of the media which the integrative experience might suggest.

SUMMARY

The responsibiilty of educators for determining what to teach and through what means skills are to be developed is continuous. Major devices that should be used in determining what to teach include educational objectives, curriculum guides, curriculum trends, and selection criteria. The position is maintained that learning skills can be developed through the use of appropriate content. Skill areas basic to the needs of the child include communication, socialization, environment, and aesthetic.

The ability to use the communication skills is what distinguishes man from other animals. As he develops the skills of listening, speaking, reading, writing, and computation, he increases his ability to communicate and to improve his living and learning environment. It is now recognized that listening is a skill that must be taught if it is to function effectively. The school which curbs purposeful pupil communication is a deterrent to developing the art of speaking. Many types of experiences should be provided so that the child can learn to speak effectively. It is recognized that speaking and listening are related functionally as a social need.

All areas of the curriculum are dependent upon the ability of the child to read. Reading therefore should be taught as a functional skill. It is recognized that learning to read is developmental. Each individual passes through several stages which are usually identified as reading readiness, beginning reading, rapid skills development, wide reading, and refinement in reading techniques.

The record of civilization depends upon the skill of writing. Writing is used to send messages, to record information for the future, and to express feelings and ideas. Handwriting, grammar, and spelling are tools necessary for writing.

Computation is a language expressed through a number system man has devised for showing quantitative relationships. The newer approach to mathematics seeks to return computation — mathematical operations — to understanding through concrete experiences. This involves development of mathematical concepts, recognition of structural features, knowledge of basic properties, realization of relationships, and understanding the rationale of computation.

Growth of society, urbanization of people, exploding world population, and other factors demand that man develop socialization skills that will enable him to live peacefully and productively with others. These include accepting oneself, communicating, participating, cooperating, demonstrating loyalty, and exercising citizenship. Each individual must recognize that he is different from others, learn to accept his differences, and use them to the best advantage.

The child should learn the rewards which come from giving of himself as he participates in an activity and cooperates with others. Recognizing and observing duty to a cause involve skill characterized as loyalty. Daily experiences in school should be of such nature as to develop in each child the social skill of citizenship.

A major function of the school is to assist the child in understanding his environment and thus coping with the problems of living. The social and natural sciences are treated together as man's environmental understandings so children can learn that all aspects of man's social living are affected by his environment. Areas included in this classification are geographical, historical, political, and scientific.

As it relates to current happenings in the world, geography can serve as a major vehicle for guiding the student toward information about other environmental factors. Historical understandings help the child develop an understanding and appreciation of man's achievement. It should be approached with the idea of helping the child understand the past in terms of the people who lived then. It also should help the child see how history gives man insight into current problems. History is a major portion of the vehicle for learning to be accomplished by youth through the unit approach. Political understandings become significant as they are manifested in current emphases and problems. The child should learn that society develops through our organized institutions.

A change of emphasis in science teaching gives impetus to discovery and encourages use of the scientific process in developing scientific understandings. Through this approach the child is led to understand how man's culture is related to his environment. He learns how he can participate in planning and developing his own environment, utilizing a wide variety of resources. Science content should encompass the needs and interests of children in a world which is increasingly more complex and technical.

Man's tendencies toward the aesthetic — the beautiful and creative — are vital in the development of all basic skills of communication and understanding. Emphasis should be placed upon means whereby the individual can enjoy those things which he can use and share through creative construction, developing perceptions of qualitative, sensed differences. Avenues for expressing the aesthetic include physical fitness, moral and spiritual values, music, and art.

The child should learn the importance of developing his body to its maximal potential and protecting it from the hazards of society. Provision should be made for each child to engage in a program of physical activities in keeping with individual growth and development. School environment, facilities, and policies should provide for the health needs of each child.

The school should share in the responsibility for teaching children about religion and in developing a sense of values in keeping with the moral standards, religion, and democracy which are our heritage. Two important means for fulfilling this responsibiilty are teachers who are models for character development and opportunities for children to engage in reflective thinking in regard to moral values.

Music, as a universal medium of communication, should be taught in a manner that affords children opportunities to express feelings of joy, devotion, sorrow, and patriotism. Means provided should include, singing, dancing, playing an instrument, listening, and composing. Emphasis should be placed upon the pleasure and appreciation which come from participation in a music experience.

Individual creativity is vital to development of expression through art. A basic point of view to be kept in mind by the teacher is that art is self-expression. The art program should provide for learning activities, self-directed activities, and integrated activities. As in other areas of the curriculum, consideration should be given to maturity in utilizing the media most appropriate for the individual in each situation.

The teacher should be aware of the vast volume of subject matter and learning experiences available to each classroom situation. He should be equally aware that it is not possible to provide a curriculum in which the child can learn all he needs to know as an adult citizen. During the time available in the elementary school the amount of data that can be imparted to children is meager. It thus is imperative that major emphasis be placed upon guiding them in learning skills which can be used in gaining new information. It is in this light that confidence is put on teaching which utilizes appropriate content for extending basic skills.

QUESTIONS FOR DISCUSSION

1. Schools are encouraged to define their educational objectives. To what extent should these objectives determine curriculum content and skills?
2. What influence should curriculum guides, courses of study, and textbooks have in determining skills and content to be mastered by students?
3. What are the respective roles of the teacher and students in selecting content?
4. Explain the point of view which holds that use of appropriate content develops and extends basic skills. What are the advantages of this curriculum approach?
5. How can the following groups of skills and understandings be developed through appropriate content?

   a. Communication skills
   b. Socialization skills
   c. Environmental understandings
   e. Aesthetic understandings

TOPICS FOR RESEARCH

1. Examine several curriculum guides and courses of study to observe different approaches to organization of content and skills. Compare them with the approach set forth in this chapter.
2. Examine textbooks for children in the various content areas. Relate the skills and understandings suggested in this chapter to the content of the respective areas in the children's textbooks.
3. Choose some specific skills and select appropriate content for extending these skills with children.
4. Specify the place of drill in extending basic skills.
5. Observe the teaching of a skill area in several classroom situations to note different teaching approaches.
6. Describe a situation in which children bring local realia, such as a turtle or a rabbit, into the classroom. Show how you would utilize this for teaching skills needed by these children.

BIBLIOGRAPHY

BANKS, J. HOUSTON. *Learning and Teaching Arithmetic.* Second edition. Boston: Allyn and Bacon, Inc., 1964.

BECK, ROBERT H., WALTER W. COOK, AND NOLAN C. KEARNEY. *Curriculum in the Modern Elementary School.* Second edition. Englewood Cliffs, N. J.: Prentice-Hall, Inc., 1960.

BLOUGH, GLENN O. AND JULIUS SCHWARTZ *Elementary School Science and How to Teach It.* Third edition. New York: Holt, Rinehart and Winston, 1964.

BERGETHON, BJORNAR AND EUNICE BOARDMAN. *Musical Growth in the Elementary School.* New York: Holt, Rinehart and Winston, Inc., 1963.

DECHANT, EMERALD V. *Improving The Teaching of Reading.* Englewood Cliffs; Prentice-Hall, Inc., 1964.

FLEMING, ROBERT S. (ed.) *Curriculum for Today's Boys and Girls.* Columbus: Charles E. Merrill Books, Inc., 1963.

FLOURNOY, FRANCES. *Elementary School Mathematics.* Washington: Center for Applied Research in Education, Inc., 1964.

GREENE, HARRY A. AND WALTER T. PETTY. *Developing Language Skills in the Elementary Schools.* Boston: Allyn and Bacon, Inc., 1963.

HARRIS, ALBERT J. *Effective Teaching of Reading.* New York: David McKay Company, Inc., 1962.

HOWARD, CHARLES F. AND ENOCH DUMAS. *Basic Procedures in Teaching Arithmetic.* Boston: D. C. Heath and Company, 1963.

JAROLIMEK, JOHN. *Social Studies in Elementary Education.* Second edition. New York: The Macmillan Company, 1963.

KAMBLY, PAUL E. AND JOHN E. SUTTLE. *Teaching Elementary School Science, Methods and Materials.* New York: The Ronald Press Company, 1963.

LEE, J. MURRAY AND DORIS MAY LEE. *The Child and His Curriculum.* Third edition. New York: Appleton-Century-Crofts, Inc., 1960.

LOGAN, LILLIAN N. AND VIRGIL G. LOGAN. *Teaching the Elementary School Child.* Boston: Houghton-Mifflin Company, 1961.

MANNING, DUANE, *The Qualitative Elementary School.* New York: Harper and Row, Publishers, 1963.

McFEE, JUNE KING. *Preparation for Art.* San Francisco: Wadsworth Publishing Company, Inc., 1961.

MICHAELIS, JOHN U. *Social Studies for Children in a Democracy.* Third edition. Englewood Cliffs: Prentice-Hall, Inc., 1963.

MYERS, LOUISE RIFER. *Teaching Children Music in the Elementary School.* Englewood Cliffs: Prentice-Hall, Inc., 1961.

SHANE, HAROLD G., MARY E. REDDIN, AND MARGARET C. GILLESPIE. *Beginning Language Arts Instruction With Children.* Columbus: Charles E. Merrill Books, Inc., 1961.

SHUSTER, ALBERT H. AND MILTON E. PLOGHOFT. *The Emerging Elementary Curriculum.* Columbus: Charles E. Merrill Books, Inc., 1963.

SHIPP, DONALD E. AND SAM ADAMS. *Developing Arithmetic Concepts and Skills.* Englewood Cliffs: Prentice-Hall, Inc., 1964.

SOWARDS, G. WESLEY AND MARY-MARGARET SCOBEY. *The Changing Curriculum and the Elementary Teacher*. San Francisco: Wadsworth Publishing Company, Inc., 1961.

STRICKLAND, RUTH G. *The Language Arts*. Second edition. Boston: D. C. Heath and Company, 1957.

TIEGS, ERNEST W. AND FAY ADAMS. *Teaching the Social Studies*. Boston: Ginn and Company, 1959.

WOLFE, DON M. *Language Arts and Life Patterns, Grades 2 through 8*. New York: The Odyssey Press, Inc., 1961.

Wise utilization of instructional media, such as television, enriches student educational experiences.

Chapter 11

Utilizing
Instructional Media

The amount of knowledge recorded by man in the last decade equals the sum total of all that had been recorded up to that time. It is predicted that in less than ten years it will double again. It is easy to recognize that the student of today who will be the community leader of tomorrow cannot now acquire all the information that will be required of him as an adult citizen. With the strong competition the school faces for the time and interest of the child, the mere imparting of a body of facts on a given subject to a class has little appeal for the majority of the students. With all of society's children seated in the classrooms side-by-side, and with many of them viewing this as a sentence imposed upon them for twelve years — ages six to eighteen — it is little wonder that the teacher frequently finds himself frustrated. Educators must recognize that extra hours and harder work alone cannot meet the changing demands of the times. Brown, Lewis, and Harcleroad clearly set forth the responsibility before the educator of today when they state that:

> True learning has certainly not occurred unless the act of communication has succeeded in making a permanent and meaningful addition to the student's own communication skills. Classroom communication, therefore, involves far more than the unilateral presentation by the teacher of new words or new facts or new ideas; it requires inter-communication between students and teachers, a mutual sharing of experiences, a continual feedback process of reciprocal response adjustments.[1]

[1] James W. Brown, Richard B. Lewis, and Fred F. Harcleroad (A-V *Instruction Materials and Methods* (New York: McGraw-Hill Book Company, 1959), pp. 8-9.

Effective teaching should provide learning experiences appropriate to the needs and interests of children in a manner which makes sense to them. Fortunately, together with our accumulation of knowledge have come a better understanding of the learning process and a wider variety of instructional media for the educator to build up the instructional program.

PERCEPTION — THE FOUNDATION FOR LEARNING

History and archaeology reveal that men have sought for centuries to improve the learning process for children by devising instructional aids. Stone tracing tablets designed to help Roman children learn to form their letters have been unearthed after having been entombed for centuries in Pompeii. Flash cards have been traced back as far as the fourteenth century. Many ideas regarding instructional materials were provided in a handbook by Jean Baptiste de la Salle, a Catholic educator writing in the late seventeenth century.[2]

The professionalization of teaching materials, however, is a development of the present generation and is a direct outcome of new insights and concepts regarding learning. The educator of today has found that more effective learning takes place where it seems worthwhile to the learner and that learning experiences are improved through the involvement of more than one of the senses. Modern learning theories also hold that the learner interprets problems in the light of his own background of experiences, and that he communicates in a like manner. If two persons are to communicate, they must be able to perceive similarly. They thus will be able to translate in a similar manner the words, sounds, and motions each has experienced.

Widely differing kinds of sensory experiences depend upon the sense organs and the nervous system. They are the basis of our knowledge of the world about us. Without them, there would be no awareness of anything.[3] It is this awareness which provokes images or impressions and provides for the experiences that become a part of the individual and enable his learning through sensory perception. It is important for us to realize words are merely symbols that stand for an object, activity or feeling; there must be a means of establishing an association. Wittich and Schuller remind us that:

> Our perceptor sensory mechanisms are our continuing contacts with our world of things and events. The eye, the ear, the nerve endings which respond to pressure, to heat and cold, and to odor and taste are the means through which almost all learning is accomplished. They are the means

---

[2]Harold G. Shane, *The American Elementary School* (New York: Harper Brothers, 1953), pp. 233-234.

[3]Howard L. Kingsley, *The Nature and Conditions of Learning* (New York: Prentice-Hall, Inc., 1947), p. 262.

of perception. . . The normal learner, insofar as the functions of his perceptor mechanisms are concerned, gains understanding in terms of multiple impressions recorded through eye, ear, touch, etc. These functions do not occur in isolation but rather through a blended pattern from any or all of the perceptor mechanisms that are stimulated by external occurrences.

Effective perception is thus a blending of sensations which then gives rise to thoughtful shuffling, arranging, and selection of a pattern. This pattern may be thought of as an understanding of an event or object.[4]

As understanding is attained through exercising the sensory mechanisms, thinking is taking place. The thinking of the learner is dependent upon the variety, number, and breadth of perceptions he has had. It therefore can be expected that his thinking will be effective in keeping with the extensiveness of his experiences. During any experience the child may be confronted with a problem or have a curiosity aroused. If this problem area is within his scope and if he is encouraged to pursue the issue, this may be the motivating point for some intensive study resulting in the development of permanent impressions. If on the other hand he is blocked by materials too difficult, a schedule too strict, or lack of encouragement and motivation, this may become just another discouraging experience and he will lose an opportunity to use the talents and abilities which are his to enjoy.[5]

When the child's experiences are marked by accomplishment, he may be stimulated to explore other areas and build positive attitudes. Where he repeatedly meets defeat and discouragement, insecurity and lack of self confidence may result.

The problem of understanding mounts more as the child approaches content that is less related to his experience. The student who has spent his life on the Mississippi Delta or the plains of the midwest has little idea of a mountain. The child who sees the milkman put bottles of milk at the front door and has never seen a cow possibly thinks of it as some mechanical gadget. Images in the mind of the individual form the backlog of knowledge which he can call upon for communication. This has been described by Woodruff as follows:

> The human mind is the depository for all of our experiences. It has a way of storing experiences something like a motion picture record. This stored record makes possible the recollection of past experience almost as if it were happening again. The record is a composite of meaning or under-

[4]Walter Arno Wittich and Charles Francis Schuller, *Audiovisual Materials: Their Nature and Use* (third edition; New York: Harper & Brothers, 1962), p. 30. Copyright © 1953, 1957 by Harper & Brothers. Copyright © 1962 by Walter Arno Wittich and Charles Francis Schuller. Reprinted by Permission of Harper & Row Publishers, Inc.
[5]*Ibid.,* p. 31.

standing, feeling, and the value to them. This combination of meaning, value, and symbols is called a concept.[6]

Woodruff further explains that there is a common central characteristic, a bit of meaning of the word concept, which is at least partially organized into a meaningful idea that is understandable in various ways by different people. All ideas belong to the brain where they originate and are retained. A concept is not a concrete entity but a construct made by the brain as the person seeks to understand and cope with something. It cannot be passed from one person to another literally even though teachers often try. All the teacher can do in expressing his own concept of something is to talk about it. These words cannot give the other person a clear picture. Audio-visual aids may help in developing a concept but each person has to make his own. The individual must understand, feel, symbolize an idea to build a concept.[7]

There is a wide span of experiences which serves as the foundation for learning. Children have varying degrees of ability to communicate in terms of these, but the stages of their understanding develop as their experiences increase and as they visualize and have some acquaintance with a concrete object or situation. The ultimate in the educational process is to help the child feel and verbalize his experiences in an intelligent manner.

The first step is to help him see that man has adopted symbols that represent certain objects, activities, or feelings. For example, *C O W* means a four-legged animal that gives milk. The child must recognize that the word does not look like a cow and is not a cow, but that it is an acceptable symbol in our society for an animal of this description. He then must learn to associate the word with the picture and object. After acquiring a number of words in a similar manner, the child should recognize that sometimes he can learn new words in context with the old ones. Then he learns that a word with more than one meaning must be identified from the context and the association of the word with certain actions. This is where audio-visual aids are effective. Many times the real object or experience cannot be provided to teach the words but a picture, model or other aids can be used to give understanding.[8]

The educator's challenge is to take advantage of the eager curiosity and enthusiasm children have when they come to school before it is misdirected or becomes latent. The question is, "What are schools doing now or failing to do in teaching and in the use of instructional materials that accounts for

---

[6]Asaheld D. Woodruff, *Basic Concepts of Teaching* (San Francisco: Chandler Publishing Company, 1961), p. 64.

[7]*Ibid.*, pp. 64-66.

[8]Paul R. Wendt, *Audio-Visual Instruction* (Washington: National Education Association, 1957), pp. 3-4.

a decrease in student eagerness and curiosity?" Is it that the child does not have proper perception of the activities in which he finds himself? It seems evident that the schools "change signals" on the children. Almost without warning, they are asked to learn in ways that are very different from those by which they were learning before they came to school. Teachers are using language as the chief medium of instruction, with little opportunity for the child to make any association between the abstract and the concrete, or that which is real to him. Generally, children are expected to learn what they are told at a specified time. If they cannot repeat or verbalize as required by the teacher, it is frequently erroneously assumed that they are unintelligent and uninformed. The school must begin to recognize that children have learned at their own rates and pretty much independently of any set group before starting school. Too often children's lack of ability to comprehend and respond in an acceptable manner is due to the failure of the school to provide perceptive experiences rather than the inability of the child to perceive.

MOVING FROM CONCRETE TO ABSTRACT

The instructional program of the school takes place in an environment which directly influences the educative experiences of the child. These experiences too often give little consideration to the fact that learning proceeds from the concrete to the abstract. Thus the child moves into a sea of words to sink or swim from kindergarten through college. Fortunately for the child, during the last quarter of a century educators have begun to realize that instructional materials can bridge the gap between the world of the preschool child and his school experiences. It is now being recognized that a storehouse of meanings can be built up for the child through direct and simulated experiences under guidance of a skillful teacher. From infancy the child has been building his own system of verbal and nonverbal concepts related to the experiences he has had. By the time he reaches school his dependence on concrete or nonverbal clues is less necessary. The need for some concrete experiences in new areas continues, however, as long as a person learns.

By the time a child enters school he is beginning to verbalize without reference to actual experience. He is drawing upon that which has already become a part of his everyday expression as he communicates with his family and friends. Such communications usually are centered around purposes pertaining to things necessary for enjoyment of living. When he enters his school experiences, however, he is faced with an environment that is foreign and with a routine which is too often very uncomfortable. This is further complicated by teachers' expectations that he commit to memory and recite series of words which may have little meaning to him. It is at this point that the child must know the why of certain activities; what he is supposed to be experiencing; and how this new knowledge is expected to apply to what he already knows and wants to do in the immediate future.[9] Pressey remonstrates that:

> Other things being equal, material will be remembered in proportion as it is meaningful . . . Learning will last in proportion as it is made significant to the learner. That a great deal of subject matter is so rapidly forgotten is thus a tart comment on its value to the pupil.[10]

The why, the what, and the how become more and more the problem of the teacher as he seeks to coordinate the experiences of children toward sequential developmental learning. Instructional media are the instruments in the hands of the teacher which can be used for clarifying these important problems. The term "instructional media" refers to all types of materials used in teaching including books, chalk, paper, crayons, machines, various kinds of audio-visual materials, and techniques for bringing about a learning experience. It is these materials and devices which bridge the gap from the concrete to the abstract in a manner that enable the child to see relationships, move at his own academic pace, and establish reason for learning.

The well-known "Cone of Experience" as devised by Dale provides a rather descriptive picture of the varying levels of experience as children move from the direct or concrete to the abstract in a manner that causes them to see relationships. The "Cone" as modified by Sowards and Scobey in Figure 38 shows clearly how the learner moves from active to passive participation as the experience changes from concrete to abstract.

One must readily recognize that there is considerable overlapping and possibilities for interchange of activities at the various levels of abstraction as he views the learning situations with any individual and more especially within any group of learners. The basic point of view to keep in mind is that learning is a process of experiencing, and that a child learns best when the learning tasks are adjusted to his level of maturity and readiness. The direct, purposeful experience represents the foundation of all learning; however, every person does not have to start at this point. Each person builds upon his background of related experiences to ascertain his particular level of maturity, be it arithmetic, reading, voting, planning, diagramming, multi-

---

[9]Edgar Dale, *Audio-Visual Methods in Teaching* (revised edition; New York: Dryden Press, 1954), p. 23.

[10]Sidney L. Pressey, *Psychology and the New Education* (New York: Harper and Brothers, 1944), p. 407.

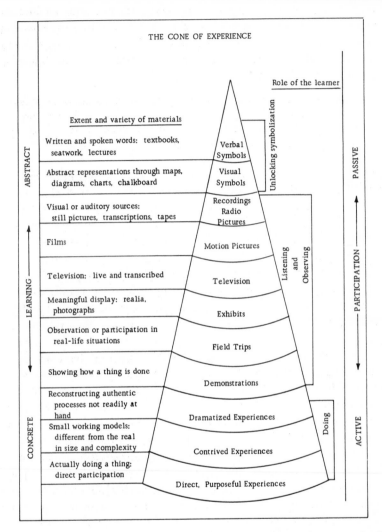

THE CONE OF EXPERIENCE

Figure 38. The Cone of Experience. G. W. Sowards and M. M. Scobey, *The Changing Curriculum and the Elementary Teacher,* (Belmont, Cal.: Wadsworth Publishing Co., 1961), p. 445. As adapted from Edgar Dale, *Audio-Visual Methods in Teaching* (revised edition; New York: The Dryden Press, 1956) p. 43, copyright © 1954, Holt, Rinehart & Winston, Inc. Used by permission of the publishers.

plying, or otherwise. It is the task of the teacher, however, to help the child recognize his level of maturity or achievement in each learning skill and content area and to select the appropriate instructional media for the next step in his goals for learning. Selection and provision of suitable instructional media become major functions of the effective teacher.

FACTORS AFFECTING INSTRUCTIONAL MEDIA

Provision, selection, and utilization of instructional media vary among schools and even within classrooms. The reasons for this variance are found in the wealth of a given community and its size and composition; the willingness of the administrative personnel to exercise their leadership in procuring materials; the resourcefulness of the teachers, and the philosophy of the school.

Regardless of the availability of instructional materials and various media, the major responsibility for providing an appropriate selection lies with the individual classroom teacher. It is up to him to acquaint himself with what is available and to plan in advance so that the media can be selected, provided for, and utilized.

PROVISION FOR MEDIA

Sources for obtaining instructional media and assistance in using them ordinarily at the disposal of the teacher include the local school library, materials center, and the teachers and principal in the school. The school system may provide a professional library, instructional materials center, and a coordinator of instructional media, who serves all schools in the administrative unit. In practically every case there will be a person at the systemwide administrative level responsible for working with teachers in the improvement of instruction who will recognize that the provision of appropriate instructional media is a major function in effective teaching. This person may be known as the curriculum director, the general supervisor, the assistant superintendent, the special area supervisor, or the resource teacher. Regardless of the title, the principal and teachers will receive valuable assistance from this person if they will use him.

Another source for instructional media at the disposal of the teacher is the community itself with its service personnel and agencies. Publishing company representatives and consultants and free and inexpensive material prepared by industrial concerns are available upon request. Institutions of higher education provide extensive consultative services and professional materials. Professional journals, publications, and conferences are designed to assist the teacher in selecting and providing the newest and most appropriate instructional media.

Soon after employment in any situation, the teacher should begin to explore the resources and instructional materials available, and ascertain the policies and procedures for procuring them. He should also collect and maintain a file of instructional materials for himself. This collection should begin as soon as a person decides to make teaching his career and should be continually revised by adding new materials and discarding those out-of-date. Such a collection will contain flat prints, periodicals, pamphlets, brochures, sketches of bulletin board ideas, notes on selected readings, and catalogs of films, recordings, and other instructional materials. These materials can be filed in manila folders and organized under headings of the various content areas with subheadings such as "Science-Magnets" or "Arithmetic-Fractions." Samples of children's work at different age levels may also prove helpful. The teacher's files should include resource teaching units prepared during his preparation for teaching and added to as new units are developed and carried out each year in the classroom.

Teachers usually find it desirable to share their collection of professional materials with others. Some schools provide a central materials center where instructional materials can be pooled, thus providing an extensive layout which can be cooperatively catalogued and made easily available to all. An example of this is the College Avenue School in Athens, Georgia. The practice of sharing instructional materials was begun a number of years ago when all teachers brought their personal files to a room adjoining the principal's office. Special committees were set up for sorting, preparing, cataloguing, and filing with each teacher contributing in some manner and alternating on committees. Some in-service education time has been given to this project yearly, and the materials center has continued to grow in quantity and use by both the teachers and children as units of work are developed in the various classrooms. This practice has provided for a wide variety of instructional materials with an extensive range of topics.

The teacher can also avail himself of helpful instructional media as he works closely with the community so that the local resources are easily identified. The community resources will include public libraries, civic organizations and their leaders, industrial personnel and their resources, and community service personnel such as postmen, storekeepers, policemen, firemen, sanitary engineers, recreational leaders, and welfare leaders.

The teacher should read the local papers, attend civic functions, and keep in contact with people. Through knowledge and acquaintance with these sources the teacher is in a position to guide children's exploration of their community outside the school and able to contact people who may contribute as resource persons.[11]

[11]George A. Beauchamp, *Basic Dimensions of Elementary Method* (Boston: Allyn and Bacon, Inc., 1959), pp. 155-157.

The teacher should not be expected to provide the major bulk of instructional materials. In fact, what the teacher supplies should merely supplement that furnished by the local school and school system. All basic instructional equipment and materials should be provided through the regular school channels. Generally parents want their children to have adequate and appropriate instructional materials. When they are properly informed of the needs of the school and the use of certain materials, they usually are willing to supplement instructional materials, especially the expendable type, by contributing a small amount for each child. An example of how one county school system in North Carolina developed and operated a plan involving parental support in providing instructional materials has been recorded by Wootton as follows:

> The Board of Education of Alamance County initiated a policy designed to furnish the schools of the county system with an adequate supply of teaching materials, both for elementary schools and secondary. The plan provided that the Board of Education make a basal appropriation of one dollar per pupil enrolled in the schools of Alamance County. The board then agreed to match each dollar raised in any local school and to add this to the budget of the local school.
>
> The following is an example of how this plan worked with a school of 500 students called "A" in this report:
>
> The board set up $1 per pupil as a basal appropriation for the school. This provided $500. ....$ 500
>
> The local school "A' collected $1 per pupil. This provided $500.   500
>
> The local school P.T.A. raised $300 for this budget   300
>
> The county matched the amount paid by students — $500 and the amount provided by the P.T.A. — $300. The matching fund from the county was then $800.   800
>
> These four sources then provided the total instructional materials for the local school for a given year. ....$2,100[12]

By providing adequate funds for instructional materials in this manner, teachers in Alamance County were challenged to use the materials in an effective program. In-service education for teachers became an ongoing phase of the work of the teacher. Through this means teachers learned new instructional techniques, about new materials and how to use them. As a result, over-all instructional services in the system were gradually improved.[13]

---

[12]Lutian R. Wootton, *A Study of the Instructional Services of the Alamance County, North Carolina Schools,* 1933-1955 (unpublished Doctoral dissertation, The University of Virginia, Charlottesville, 1957), pp. 121-123.
    [13]*Ibid.,* p. 473.

It is imperative that provision be made for adequate instructional materials if teaching is to be effective. Too many storage rooms are filled with unused instructional materials. It is of utmost importance that materials be selected carefully, in keeping with the objectives of the program and in cooperation with the users.

SELECTION OF MEDIA

The selection of instructional materials involves deciding what is to be done and determining what is needed to fulfill the purposes of the learner as well as of the teacher. When the purposes have been made clear, participants in the teaching-learning process have some basis for deciding which activities are most worthwhile and which materials are necessary. Instructional materials become a means whereby the learner can come in contact with ideas, values, and concepts. Selecting the appropriate media is essential to fulfilling the learning process adequately and appropriately.

Proper selection of materials must be based on careful evaluation prior to use. It is folly to gamble on the use of a film, a book, or a tape recording that has not been selected for the specific purpose. Reliability, accuracy, validity of content, and compliance with technical standards can be determined by educators in places of leadership. Through curriculum directors and other resource persons, approved lists of materials can be made available to the classroom teacher at a great saving of time. The selection of a particular item for a specific purpose is the responsibility of the teacher in charge of the learners. The teacher should examine the specific media to determine if:

1. The material selected is in keeping with the purposes sought.
2. The materials selected aid learning toward the desired goal.
3. The material selected is appropriate to the specific learning situation.
4. It provides genuine, real, and valid learning.
5. It is appropriate to the individual differences of the learner.
6. It makes possible either overt or covert participation on the part of the learner.
7. The material promotes cooperative learning, improves human relationships, helps children recognize and accept both individual and group research, and develops problem solving skills.[14]

Catalogues and handbooks describing instructional materials, especially films, filmstrips, tapes, and recordings, should be made available to the teacher. The teacher should build up his own file of evaluation of materials

[14]G. Wesley Sowards and Mary-Margaret Scobey, *The Changing Curriculum and the Elementary Teacher* (Belmont, Cal.: Wadsworth Publishing Company, 1961), pp. 450-451.

which facilitates the use of appropriate media. Every school should be provided with a room that has equipment set up for quick examination of materials such as films, filmstrips, tapes, and recordings.

The educator must keep in mind that provision for and selection of instructional media is an ongoing continuous process and should be provided for in the schedule of the teacher. More than this, provision should be made for the production of new materials by the pupils and teachers as a part of the ongoing learning process.

UTILIZATION OF MEDIA

It is the responsibility of the school administration to make materials easily accessible and to encourage the appropriate use of them. He should remember that a variety of instructional media can be used to provide meaningful experiences for children and to motivate them to engage in worthwhile activity, and to substitute simulated instructional experiences where direct, contactual experiences are not feasible. Time should be provided in his schedule for helping teachers to become acquainted with materials and media and a system provided whereby materials will be easily accessible.

Improved technology is rapidly providing more instructional media; these are tempting to teachers to use because they are new. The educator must realize, however, that the new media have no built-in sense of direction or value system. Their appropriate use is dependent upon the wisdom of the teacher. Miller and Goldberg state that it is obvious computers can group children quickly and efficiently, yet there is little research to support most grouping procedures used. Research, they report, has shown that sequential information such as grammar lessons can be taught effectively through self-instructional devices and programmed material. Research has also shown, however, that if the purpose of teaching grammar is to help the student become a better writer programmed material is a waste of time.[15]

Miller and Goldberg further point out that the importance of examining teaching purposes and then selecting appropriate tools must not be minimized. Because of the expense and skill required to prepare certain materials, it must be recognized that when the school and teacher commit themselves to a given program the material available must be accepted even though it does not meet the learners' needs and might be contrary to the philosophy and method of the teacher. As an example, the commitment to a certain program such as a series of television programs, a set of films or a book club obligates the school to the philosophy behind the project.

---

[15]William C. Miller and Albert L. Goldberg, "Technology-Progress." *Educational Leadership*. Volume XX, Number 7 (April, 1963), pp. 432-433.

It thus is vitally necessary to analyze purposes and then to answer the question as to whether the new tools can help accomplish the chosen objectives of the school and particular group more efficiently and effectively than other approaches.[16]

The teaching effectiveness of films is greatly increased when they are used under the guidance of a teacher. Wendt has reported that the value of a teaching film is enhanced as much as 100 per cent, as measured by achievement results, if the class is prepared for the film showing, with discussion immediately after the viewing and a second showing in conclusion. It has also been found that film is most effective when used to fill an expressed need.[17] It is logical that other instructional media such as maps and globes, recordings, teaching machines, field trips, debates, and dramatization may enhance learning in a similar manner when carefully selected, appropriately used, and efficiently evaluated.

Some general rules which are helpful to teachers in the use of instructional materials have been suggested by Beauchamp:

1. It is generally accepted that direct, contactual types of experience are preferred over vicarious experience for learning on the part of elementary school children.
2. Some instructional materials substitute for direct experiences.
3. Many instructional materials have motivational values.
4. Instructional materials can be used for demonstrating purposes.
5. Children should use instructional materials to explore ideas and insights.
6. Teachers should screen instructional materials before using them with children.
7. Instructional materials are a means of program enrichment.
8. The effectiveness of the use of instructional materials should be evaluated.[18]

The foregoing list may be considered as a guide rather than as a blueprint to follow and is certainly not intended to be all-inclusive. The good judgment of the teacher, working with children in a manner which frees them for experimentation and evaluation of outcomes, is the best guide to the effective use of instructional media.

INSTRUCTIONAL MEDIA OVERVIEW

Just as the architect calls upon the building supplier, the plumber, the electrician, the carpenter, the mason, the landscape artist and many others in designing and constructing a building, so the educator calls upon a wide

---

[16]*Ibid.*
[17]Wendt, *op. cit.*, p. 16.
[18]Beauchamp, *op. cit.*, pp. 163-167.

variety of resources in selecting and providing instructional media for an appropriate curriculum. The architect has an over-all knoweldge of the work of each of these resources and knows how and when to call on them for the completion of the job in the most effective manner and according to the predetermined blueprint. The teacher must also have an overview of a wide variety of instructional media and the know-how to bring the appropriate ones into the classroom. Among the media desirable for the teacher are textbooks and teacher's manuals; workbooks and practice materials; chalkboard, bulletin board and flannel board; maps and globes; flat prints, graphs, and charts; realia, exhibits and displays; field trips and excursions; films, filmstrips, film slides and recordings; radio and television, and teaching machines. The teacher should be prepared to use art and construction materials and methods, panels, forums, and debates, and dramatization — including interpretation, role playing and creative expression, and newspaper and bulletin production. He should also be informed as to the availability of and the techniques necessary for using personal, social, industrial, and natural resources.

TEXTBOOKS, TEACHER'S MANUALS, AND PRACTICE MATERIALS

Textbooks are used because they have been designed to present subject matter in a sequential manner in graded series generally accepted by educators. There is, and will be for a long time to come, a need for this type of book to provide information in terms of curriculum content units, even though some designers of programmed materials have predicted that textbooks as such would soon become obsolete. This does not mean that the textbook should be the only means of presenting content to the learner. Cross and Cypher have reminded us that words alone are frequently inadequate because they do not evoke any recall of past experiences. The reader may not have the maturity or the background to provide a basis for word comprehension. This is the point at which the picture symbol and vicarious experiences become very important as a medium for communicating information and help compensate for this lack of experiential background.[19]

Ohlsen advises that there seem to be three distinct and divergent ways the textbook fits into the teaching scheme. The first way is that the textbook is actually a complete teaching-learning situation in print. It is not in any sense merely another book but is a carefully, deliberately designed book intended for specific school use. The second point holds that the text-

---

[19]A. J. Foy Cross and Irene F. Cypher, *Audio-Visual Education* (New York: Thomas Y. Crowell Company, 1961), pp. 244-245.

book is more or less a general outline for a course of study, rather than a complete teaching-learning instrument in print. This point ascribes a far more important and decisive role to the teacher. In the third place, Ohlsen maintains that the textbook is simply a cyclopedic book containing authoritative information in certain branches of knowledge. It is identical with any other book of a factual or specialized nature suitable for pupils of varying abilities, and should be used as a library reference to help fulfill some purpose of the learner.[20]

The teacher who believes the textbook to be a complete teaching-learning instrument in print often holds the book in his hands as he conducts a recitation on the pages assigned for home study the preceding night. Sometimes the students are required to answer the questions at the end of a given section and write them in a notebook. In some cases no variation is allowed between what the book says and what the students say. In this case the writer of the book dominates the minds of the students.[21]

When the textbook is more or less a general outline for a course, it serves as a guide and a starting point for study and gives something specific that both the teacher and students can use as a place of departure. This way of utilizing the textbook allows for study of other sources to broaden and enrich the topic. It also provides for bringing different materials into the teaching-learning situation to meet individual needs. Books other than the adopted text are called supplementary books and are used for extending and reinforcing learning. In this situation, the teacher plays a more determinate role by acting as the guide and arbitrator in selection of the materials and resources. The textbook is helpful in providing an overview of the course, but the teacher must be prepared to select from a large number of teaching techniques to enhance the meaning of the course for the learner.[22]

Those who recognize the textbook simply as a cyclopedic book place it with many books which are selected by the learner or the teacher for a particular purpose at a given time. This position implies that there is a curriculum design or course of study other than the textbook which is prepared by the local school, the school system or state department of education. Units of work, persistent life situations, or problems of living are the sources of content selection, with the teacher acting as the major guide and determiner of the learning environment. Consideration of the pupils and their involvement in basic choices concerning their own learning influence

---

[20]Merle M. Ohlsen, *Modern Methods in Elementary Education* (New York: Henry Holt and Company, 1959), pp. 149-153.
[21]*Ibid.*
[22]*Ibid.*

strongly what is to be learned. These considerations also influence how learning is to take place and the books and other materials to be used. Following this point of view toward learning, the textbook is completely different from that in either of the first two views described. This procedure advocates using selected bits of subject matter from textbooks while ignoring the methodology around which they were built.[23]

Assuming that either point of view one or two is used, it is essential to effective teaching that an adequate supply of different level books on a wide variety of topics is provided. It is imperative the teacher know the achievement level of his pupils in the various subjects in order that books can be supplied. Skill texts should be provided for the child mainly at the work-study level, which is one-half to one year below his score on a standardized test. Skill texts refer mainly to reading, arithmetic and spelling. Social studies and science texts should also be selected at the work-study level. Much supplementary material in these areas should be provided at the independent level, however, which is one to two years below his grade placement equivalent on standardized tests.

Most book publishers provide a teacher's manual to serve as a guide to the use of each specific book designed as a skill text. Many of these guides are bound with the text and are called a teacher's edition. The teacher always should consult these guides in planning and carrying out a program in a skill subject. Each guidebook presents techniques and a philosophy of teaching for presenting the skill or subject. The teacher must be aware of the philosophy of the guidebook and prepare his lesson plans using only that material which is applicable to pupils in a given situation.

The teacher should also realize that skill texts are prepared to teach a set of skills according to some sequential developmental plan. Maximum results can be gained from a set of skill texts and particularly from a reading series only when the books' content is used according to the purpose for which it was developed. Most often the guidebook also includes plans for use of workbooks, companion books, drill books, or other such designated materials. These, too, have their particular function in building a set of related developmental skills. Again, it is the responsibility of the teacher to select those particular exercises and supplementary activities needed by the learner to further understanding and or give practice in the skill to assure mastery. A basic principle to remember in the use of drill exercises is that for the most effective learning understanding precedes drill.

The teacher can find almost any kind of preplanned and do-it-yourself course exercises which promise to save time and make life easy for him and

---

[23]*Ibid.*

his pupils. All of these have their place and many can be used to supplement the basic program. Others give assistance in some remedial cases. The teacher must keep in mind the total program of the child as well as of the school. However, excessive amounts of commercial drill exercises and remedial gymnastics may do more to block the interest of the child than they do to accelerate the mastery of a skill with which he is having difficulty.

Workbooks or drill books may enhance the learning situation when a variety of workbooks on different levels is available and used to further a specific skill. Teachers have found workbooks helpful in meeting individual needs when they belong to the school and are bought in sets of five, ten, or fifteen. With this plan, answers to questions are written on separate answer sheets rather than in the workbook. Only exercises that have particular meaning for certain groups at a certain time are worked by the students. The exercise forms are left clear for the next group to use. Schools with limited funds find that through this plan an extensive supply of appropriate practice books can be provided by using the funds each child would spend yearly to buy one drill book. This plan relieves the teacher and the parents from feeling that each child must complete *his* exercise book whether or not he needs the practice.

Some school systems provide many books other than the basic textbooks and regular library books to supplement learning experiences. The books usually are called supplementary books. The elementary school accreditation plan of the State of North Carolina, as an example, requires that each grade in a school have a minimum of 80 supplementary books plus 20 books for each additional section of the grade and that the books be in sets of five, ten, or fifteen with each of seven content areas provided for in the collection.[24]

The example of the plan followed by Alamance County School System in North Carolina for handling supplementary books is descriptive of the place of these books in a school and shows something of how they are used:

> Schools in Alamance County have made generous provision for the use of supplementary books. Most schools have more supplementary books of various types than the minimum required by the State Department of Public Instruction for accreditation. The policy of adding some new books each year is generally followed.
>
> Each school makes available to all teachers a mimeographed list of all supplementary books belonging to the school. This list of books supplies information as to the grade level, type of book, title, number of copies, series, publisher, and the copyright date. This is brought up to date as new

---

[24]*Handbook for Elementary and Secondary Schools* (Raleigh: North Carolina State Department of Education, 1955), p. 20.

books are added, and is revised annually to show which books remain on the State Approved List of Supplementary Books.

All supplementary books listed on the five latest lists provided by the Division of Textbooks are acceptable in meeting the minimum number of required books for State accreditation. Books on these lists should be used for specific purposes in the classroom and not taken home by children. Supplementary books not on these current lists and on a grade level below that in which the child is enrolled should be supplied by the teacher to children needing special help in reading and taken home by the child for help with reading at home.

Supplementary books are provided for the use of the school as a whole rather than for individual grades. Where space permits, they are kept in a central storage room which makes them more readily acceptable to all teachers at any time. When books are not currently in use in a classroom they should be returned to the storage room or otherwise made available for other teachers to use. In the use of supplementary books for the improvement and enrichment of the reading program, it is recommended that they be used in directed reading activities rather than merely as library books.[25]

PERIODICALS, NEWSPAPERS, AND FREE MATERIALS

Every classroom should be well supplied with or have access to periodicals, newspapers, and free materials. Some periodicals appropriate for the individual classroom are desirable on the basis of group membership; however, most periodicals should come to the school library. Periodicals such as the *Weekly Reader* and *Junior Scholastic* which come to the entire membership of each classroom can be used to encourage students to keep in contact with the world about them and to stimulate additional reading. The individual classroom should also subscribe to at least one daily newspaper which can be used to keep the class abreast of current events and provide a vehicle which relates the tools of learning to the ongoing educational process. A supply of back numbers of magazines can be used by the students to good advantage.

Much free material is prepared by commercial concerns for advertisement. When carefully evaluated by the teacher or some reliable source such as Educators Progress Service, some of this material provides a rich resource for the classroom.

CHALK, BULLETIN, AND FLANNEL BOARDS

With the exception of the textbook, chalkboards have been utilized as a teaching medium longer than any other instructional device. According to

---

[25]*Teacher's Handbook* (Graham: Alamance County Public Schools, 1956-57), p. 8.

Dale, educational historians have found that the use of wall boards for writing dates back at least 400 years.[26] They have become so commonplace that they are found today in every classroom; however, the space given them in the classroom has lessened somewhat in recent years. Traditionally, chalkboards covered all available classroom wall space. The average classroom today contains one chalkboard approximately four by twelve feet. Wider use of individual writing paper and teacher use of larger sheets of chart paper have lessened the need for chalkboard space.

The use of mimeographed materials and workbooks has also minimized the need for chalkboard writing. The latest gadget which competes with the chalkboard is the overhead projector through which the teacher or student can flash before the room on a screen work in progress or specifically prepared materials. The chalkboard still maintains a deserved place in the room in that it is the most accessible means of communicating in writing to the whole class, and because the writing can easily be erased. The chalkboard continues to be useful for the student or groups of students to work arithmetic problems and demonstrate a graphic image of a verbal impression.

The chalkboard must be kept ready for use if it is to be effective. The following suggestions from Dale are worthy of consideration:

1. Keep the chalkboard clean.
2. Make letters and drawings on the board large enough to be seen from all parts of the room.
3. Do not cover up the material on the chalkboard by standing in front of it.
4. If the drawing is complex, put it on the board before your class starts.
5. Do not put unnecessary and time consuming accuracy into a drawing when accuracy is not called for.
6. Forms that are regularly used, such as lines in a first grade room, can be painted or scored on the board.
7. Occasionally a dramatic visual presentation can be made by preparing the entire chalkboard in advance and covering it with strips of paper which will be removed, one by one, as the demonstration proceeds.
8. Do not put too much material on the chalkboard at one time unless your specific purposes make this necessary. Remember that the board is a display, a showcase; clutter must be avoided.[27]

When the wall space used by chalkboard was lessened, room was made on the classroom walls for the bulletin board, which is sometimes called

---

[26]Dale, *op. cit.*, p. 310.
[27]Edgar Dale, *Audio-Visual Methods In Teaching*, (revised edition; New York: Dryden Press, 1954) pp. 312-314. Copyright © 1954, Holt, Rinehart and Winston, Inc., Used by permission of the publishers.

a tackboard. Today the bulletin board has become a teaching tool comparable to the chalkboard. It can be used by the teacher to motivate interest in a particular topic by arranging a display that will attract student attention and stimulate them to raise questions. Materials prepared by former students occasionally can be shown to help the present group have a basis for comparison of their work. Most of the time the bulletin board should display children's work or their collections of material on a given topic. At all times the teacher and class should recognize that the bulletin board is to serve them and that what is placed there may further their learning experiences. The teacher is often concerned that all children's work cannot be displayed at one time. By selecting children's work for display according to themes, predominant color schemes, and other designations decided upon by the teacher and class, a series of displays can be used. One or two days' showing of each grouping followed by another in sequence can give every child an opportunity to display his creation. The teacher should give attention to variety in display as well as other factors pertinent to the effective use of bulletin boards.

Each bulletin board display should be prepared for a specific purpose. Whether it is to exhibit children's art, introduce a unit of study, recognize a special day or occasion or serve as a series of ongoing displays relating to the development of a special study, the purpose should be obvious to the observer. Specific information is essential to the effective bulletin board arrangement. One display does not necessarily provide extensive data but what it presents should be authentic, worthy of consideration, and easily discernible by the viewer.

A caption well-placed and appropriate to the display may make a difference in the effectiveness of the idea to be presented. This does not need to be gaudy but should be easy to read from a distance and fit into the decor of the arrangement. The collection of material on a bulletin board should show unity, that is, the total display on any one board or section of a board should be related. Each part and item of the display should contribute toward presenting a central idea or total picture. Visual unity of the subject may be gained by repeating colors, shapes, sizes, and textures. Material such as string, wire, and ribbon used as connectors may also enhance visual unity. Other means of showing unity in a display are uniformity in lettering and symbols or grouping of small items.

Illustrations provide the major medium of any good display. An ever-increasing supply of flat prints, maps, charts, graphs, book jackets, and such materials filed by the teacher provides a ready source for depicting the appropriate display. These materials help create topic meaning by stimulating the viewer to capture the significance of the display and encouraging him to broaden his own understanding of the subject.

Color is an effective element in a display. Its most important function is providing contrast which attracts the viewer and gives him a pleasing experience. Choice of congenial colors and use of one dominant color provide attractiveness and distinctiveness. The color of the background of the bulletin board can be varied through the use of colored felt, burlap, or crepe paper.

Simplicity and clarity are essential to the effective display. Taken literally, the foregoing criteria might tend to make the use of the bulletin board complicated and forbidding to many. These criteria, however, are intended to provide for more effective displays rather than to make each display a major work of art requiring unnecessary effort and time.

Space used well to set forth the main features of a display is more important than extensive data and materials in one arrangement. Any item worthy of display deserves sufficient pins, thumbtacks, or adhesive to hold all its corners firmly in place.

Regardless of its worth, each display soon fulfills its purpose and loses its effectiveness. Frequently a display will serve its purpose within two or three days. During the study of a unit, however, the basic elements of a bulletin board display may be left in place while certain portions of it are changed as the need arises. This progression in use of a display is often very effective and lends itself to less change of the total bulletin board.

The bulletin board can serve as a graphic step-by-step development of a social studies, science, health, or arithmetic unit. Materials removed from the bulletin board periodically can build a pictorial review of a unit of work as they are fastened together under one cover. The possibilities of such culminating activities as this give much encouragement to children. Usually all they need for full use of the bulletin board is a little motivation, guidance, permissiveness, and recognition on the part of the teacher.

The flannel board, also known as the felt board, flannel graph, or visual board, is another medium which assists in making communication more graphic to students. The flannel board is a board covered with a fuzzy material, usually flannel or felt. It may be permanently mounted on the wall but is more adaptable when portable and set up at a slightly tilted angle. Its size varies from four by six feet to eighteen by twenty-four inches. Both sides of the board can be prepared for use, with each being a different color to provide varied background for different displays. The board may be hung from the top of the chalkboard by screw eyes and hooks or placed on an easel for use, then removed when not needed.

Many different lightweight materials may be attached to the flannel board surface. Letters and objects to be used can be prepared for mounting by applying a backing of flannel, felt or sandpaper. Construction paper cutouts can be roughened by rubbing sandpaper over the back surface so that the object will adhere to the flannel board surface. The interlocking fibers of the two materials cause the objects to stay in place.

Advantages which can be gained from the use of the felt or flannel board as expressed by Dale are:

1. Items to be displayed can be prepared in advance, filed and used over again and again. You can build up a collection of such material as you do a picture collection.
2. The items can be moved about and used one at a time or together with other items. This advantage offers educational possibilities that are not found with other illustrative materials.
3. Because a story, chart, or other presentation is built up as the demonstration proceeds, no element can distract the viewers before its function has been introduced.
4. The felt board enables the teacher to design learning materials uniquely suited to the needs of a given situation.
5. Children can learn creatively with this medium. They can experimentally reconstruct concepts visually; they can create and improvise as they work out a story or an idea.[28]

MAPS, GLOBES, CHARTS, AND GRAPHS

In our world of changing conditions, transient people, and rapid transportation, it becomes increasingly necessary that the student master specific knowledge and concepts of the earth's surface, space, time, geographic, and climatic elements. It is also expedient that man acquire the ability to interpret symbols and follow directions. Media used extensively in communicating these concepts and knowledge are maps, globes, charts, and graphs. In recent years, the automobile has made the road map standard equipment for the traveler and the airplane has tied the continents together so that world travel is becoming commonplace. Space ships are now opening the way for interplanetary travel. Travel experiences of individual members of almost any class can provide the motivation for learning necessary skills in the use of maps, globes, charts, and graphs.

The principle that understanding is more effective when learning starts at the level of the student in any area should be applied in the use of graphics also. Maps and globes are visual representations of specific land and water masses of the earth or some portion of it or of the earth itself.

---

[28]Dale, *op. cit.*, p. 153.

Teachers must realize that the use of these visuals involves some complex skills, and that beginning in the primary grades they must gradually develop in their students an understanding of the nature and function of maps, globes, graphs, and charts.

In keeping with social studies topics related to the community Kinder has pointed out that mapping of the local community appears to be a logical place to begin study of maps. Primary children might well start by drawing a floor plan of their schoolroom, indicating doors, windows, cabinets, and the teacher's desk. This might lead to an outline of the schoolyard and eventually the community, possibly with a rough sketch of the streets traveled by the children enroute to school. The route taken on a class field trip or the territory covered by a particular postman could easily lead to using a scale for drawing. Pictures from magazines or one of any member of the class can be used to develop the concept of size of visuals and its relation to actual objects. This should lead to the understanding that a map is a modified picture. Through exercises such as these, children develop ideas of direction, relationship, and shape.[29]

The teacher, however, must be careful in treating the map as a picture of the earth for this is only a half-truth. Kinder has pointed out that:

> A map is more complex than a picture: it is a conventionalized graph built upon a mathematical base involving a knowledge of many symbols and data. Maps are not made in accordance with the whims of cartographers: they are systematically drawn acording to well-established formulas. Maps have been called the shorthand of geography. They tell their stories by means of symbols, such as colors, shading, lines, circles, stars, and squares. Reading a map, then, is like reading a printed page: it is a process of associating ideas with symbols.[30]

It should be stressed that in order to show place relationships and localize events and facts, the map and globe should be used together. Cross and Cypher have cautioned us that, "If we were to derive all our concepts of the world from a flat map alone, we would never be able to understand the problems facing the aerial navigator, who flies above the earth, as compared with those facing the ship navigator, who is hampered and restricted by land masses."[31]

Charts and graphs help to make statistical data more real. Herein lies the value of treating maps and charts in relation to maps and globes. Since charts and graphs "make use of pictures and symbols to illustrate statistics,

---

[29]James S. Kinder, *Audio-Visual Materials and Techniques* (second edition; New York: American Book Company, 1959), pp. 418-419.
[30]*Ibid.*, p. 135.
[31]Cross and Cypher, *op. cit.*, p. 135.

they have often been called international statistical language. Even though titles and descriptions are printed in one language, the symbols, by international agreement, are above language barriers and thus easily understood everywhere."[32]

Graphs and charts may be classified with maps and globes because they are pictorial materials in that they are guides to depicting time or place and numerical and factual relationships. A graph is usually an exacting pictorial presentation or analysis of some statistical or mathematical computation. It may be considered as a pictorial guide or map to aid in showing relationships of facts and figures. A graph presents a condensed understandable form of statistics which might otherwise be ignored or misunderstood by the reader.

As the child learns to understand something of the value of the symbolism of maps, globes, charts, and graphs he feels more inclined to seek to master the skills which are necessary for utilization of these media for learning. The skills needed for reading and interpreting maps and globes are:

1. Orient the map and note directions.
2. Recognize the scale of a map and compute distances.
3. Locate places on maps and globes by means of grid systems.
4. Recognize and express relative locations.
5. Read symbols and look through maps to see the realities for which the symbols stand.
6. Correlate patterns that appear on maps and make inferences.[33]

Selection of the appropriate map, globe, chart or graph in keeping with the use of specific skills and abilities is essential to effective teaching. Dependence upon a single map or globe may limit the learning of children. There are three principal types of maps: (1) physical maps which show terrain, (2) political maps designed to depict governmental areas, and (3) special service maps.

There are also three basic types of globes: (1) political, (2) physical-political, and (3) slated outline. Political globes depict man-made divisions of the earth. The physical-political show basic features of the terrain and include some political or man-made divisions. The slated outline is an outline globe which includes major physical and political features. It is made of material on which desired c .ta can be inserted with chalk and erased easily. Charts and graphs are as varied as the data and ideas of the indi-

---

[32]Ibid.
[33]Helen M. Carpenter (ed.), *Skills in Social Studies* (Twenty-fourth yearbook; Washington: National Council for the Social Studies, NEA, 1953), pp. 146-147.

vidual. The following listing of types of maps, globes, charts, and graphs by Cross and Cypher is indicative of the wide selection of materials available to meet a particular need:

1. Maps: physical, political, physical-political, road, picture, military campaign, temperature, weather, soil and vegetation astronomical exploration, city planning, language, literary, sand table, outline, relief, airplane.
2. Globes: terrestrial, celestial, political, physical, relief.
3. Charts: genealogical, table, flow, chronological, financial.
4. Graphs: line, bar, area (curve or circle), pictorial.[34]

FLAT PRINTS, SLIDES, FILMSTRIPS, AND RECORDINGS

Flat prints, slides, filmstrips and recordings provide a rich resource which can be filed for easy access to the teacher to provide for enrichment in the instructional program. A collection of pictures may be as extensive as the teacher wishes. A rich collection can be built of clippings from old magazines with no expense other than the effort and time required for being observant and filing the clippings where they are accessible.

Slides can be purchased to cover a wide variety of topics. The two-by-two slide can be photographed with a 35 mm. camera. These slides can be shown with most filmstrip projectors or with less expensive slide projectors. This is the most popular do-it-yourself means of providing a rich collection of graphic material including pictures of geographical and historical settings, activities within the school, and visuals depicting local resources.

The filmstrip is a related sequence of still pictures on a strip of 35 mm. film which is easily used by the teacher or student in a classroom. Filmstrips can be obtained in color or black and white. Recordings are provided for some filmstrips to narrate the script; however, most filmstrips project the script together with the picture. Probably the most desirable feature of this media is that it can be operated at any speed desired and can easily be moved back to a preceding frame or forward at the will of the viewer. It also is light, easily handled and takes little storage space.

The sequential order of the frames on a single strip is an advantage over the film slide. Since the filmstrip is prepared to develop a particular purpose it should be selected to develop a specific learning experience.

Because of the relative inexpensiveness of this medium, a filmstrip can be obtained on almost every conceivable subject. Many local school systems find it desirable to provide their own ever-increasing library of filmstrips which are readily accessible to the classrooms. Filmstrips and slides are

---

[34]Cross and Cypher, *op. cit.*, p. 135.

effective means of communicating factual information and certain specific skills at different grade levels. They are being used increasingly by individuals and small groups for independent study within the classroom. Research findings cited by Brown, Lewis, and Harcleroad support the impression, long held by many teachers, that filmstrips are an effective teaching device, particularly when used in combination with other types of learning experiences such as field trips, sound films, and recordings.[35]

Recordings of programs, readings, drama, and music can be made on plastic disks or magnetic tape. Teachers find recordings easy to use because of their timing flexibility and the wide range of materials increasingly available. Disk recordings are particularly valuable in bringing to the classroom authentic voices of historical persons such as the Roosevelts, Hitler, Caruso, Edison, and Churchill. They re-create the tenseness and importance of historical events through recorded series like CBS' "You Are There" in which the audience "witness" the signing of the Magna Carta and the death of Julius Caesar.

Tape recordings are increasingly available, particularly in current programs, concerts, and educational conferences. The tape is very desirable for student use in the classroom in preparation for a program and in speech improvement. A good feature of the tape is the absence of the mechanical noise of the phonograph recording. In addition the tape can be played many times without any audible change in sound quality. The same tape also can be erased and used many times for recording different programs.

"Tapes for Teaching" services provided by a number of American universities and colleges are adding to the collection of tapes for use in the classroom. Such institutions as the universities of Minnesota, Michigan, Illinois, and Iowa review educational radio program series and tape the most significant for circulation. Carefully annotated descriptions of these tape recordings are available in catalogues issued by each university. A composite catalogue of the materials can be obtained from the Department of Audio-Visual Instruction of the National Education Association.[36]

Through the opaque projector, flat prints, excerpts from magazines and books, picture post cards, and other material of this nature can be utilized in talks and lectures. Songs can be flashed on a screen for group singing. Simple and complicated diagrams of machines and survey data can be presented on short notice. The opaque projector can also be used effectively for the enlargement of maps, pictures, charts, and diagrams by flashing the subject on the size paper desired and making a drawing from the image.

---

[35]Brown, Lewis, and Harcleroad, *op. cit.*, p. 139.
[36]*National Tape Recording Catalog* (Washington: Department of Audio-Visual Instruction, National Education Association, issued annually).

The overhead projector works much like the opaque projector but allows for more flexibility. Sketches and data can be projected as they are drawn on a transparent plate by the teacher while he talks. This gives the students an ongoing contact with the image and the verbal message. By using opaque material, overlays can be prepared to show a build-up of data and the relation of one object to another. As an example, overlay material showing the organs of the human body, their location in the body, and proximity to one another can be very effectively presented by this machine. The teacher can stand at the front of the room, facing the class, while working at the projector. The image reflected by the projector on a screen appears behind and a little above the teacher, in full view of the class.

RADIO, MOTION PICTURE, AND TELEVISION

Much effort has been expended in providing prepared radio, motion picture, and television programs for classroom instruction. Since the beginning of systematic use of radio in classrooms in 1919 through WHA, state-owned University of Wisconsin station, there has been a continuous effort in school systems across the nation to provide basic education and enrichment in instructional experiences through mass-media programs. When listening situations are carefully planned in advance, radio can capture the pupils' attention and stimulate imagination and the desire to seek further learning. Such fields as science, social science, art, music, and safety education can provide additional information or techniques for student and teacher enrichment.

Radio education for the classroom has been handicapped by static, differences in the curriculum of individual schools, inappropriate scheduling and the inability to "go back" or "skip ahead" to adjust to programs not directly related to current study and limitations of one-way contact. Tape recording of radio programs by the local school system for off schedule use helps with the scheduling problem. Room-to-room telephone contacts are used in a limited number of places. Even through radio is faced with difficulties, there is indication that it continues to contribute to the educational curriculum. Wittich and Schuller support this contention in stating that:

> Today millions of pupils in elementary and secondary schools receive basic as well as enrichment instructional experiences through educational radio. During the last decade, some educators thought that radio would be entirely submerged under the wave of motion-picture and television educational materials and broadcasts. This has not happened.[37]

---

[37]Wittich and Schuller, *op. cit.,* p. 271.

Radio programs for school use are available through public service broadcasting by commercial stations, school-owned and nonprofit stations and educational radio networks. "Standard School Broadcast" sponsored by Standard Oil Company of California, according to Brown, Lewis, and Harcleroad has been on the air since 1928. Examples of broadcasting from stations owned by school systems are Cleveland (WBOE), Chicago (WHEZ), and Atlanta (WABE). Some educational networks which broadcast programs for in-service listening include Empire State FM School of the Air in New York State, Wisconsin School of the Air, Minnesota School Broadcast Service, Indiana School of the Sky, and Ohio School of the Air.[38]

In order that the teacher can make the best use of radio programs in the classroom, advance information is necessary. Valuable prebroadcast program information can be obtained from such sources as the supervisory staff or materials center of the local school system, the state department of education, local commercial radio stations, U. S. Office of Education, and the National Association of Educational Broadcasters.

Children who watched, by means of television, Colonel John Glenn (February 20, 1962) become the first American astronaut to orbit the earth witnessed history in the making through a medium of communication which can bring the world into the classroom instantaneously. This is a communication medium and a teaching instrument without parallel when used with discretion.

Hagerstown, Maryland, with its closed circuit central programming television, provided basic research which has stimulated experimental work in educational television across the nation. Television is a new and constantly improving medium, and its advantages for education seem to be mounting. The fear that television might replace the classroom teacher has subsided. The television teacher has unique strength that stems from his ability to arrange highly complex, appropriate demonstrations which call for hours of planning and for learning materials usually not available to the classroom teacher. The strength that comes from face-to-face classroom teaching cannot, however, be overlooked. The real value comes from television teaching when the joint skills of the classroom teacher and the television teacher are joined to further student goals.

Two important contributions of classroom television which cannot be gained as effectively in any other manner are receiving current happenings at the time of origin and bringing to the classroom teacher techniques, materials, and content appropriate to the instructional program .The teacher

---

[38]Brown, Lewis, Harcleroad, *op. cit.,* pp. 198-203.

should be informed concerning the television lesson or current events and ready the students for the experience. Preparation should be through teacher-pupil planning, reading, and discussion. After the stage is set by the classroom teacher, the TV teacher enters the room by way of the screen. Following the viewing, as when any other resource is used, the classroom teacher should continue in a cooperative relation with the students to capitalize upon the experience and to plan follow-up activities designed to reinforce the learning from the viewing experience.

A major contribution to the education of children is out-of-school television viewing. The teacher must recognize that television has greatly broadened the experiences of today's children, bringing to the classroom a generation with different and much broader concepts of life than former students. The teacher needs to watch children's programs at least enough to understand their language and ideas. He must recognize that the programs seen by children out of school are put on by showmen who are trained to capture their audience and to entertain. This develops a great area of competition between the teacher and the outside world of the child. The wise teacher capitalizes upon these experiences of children. He relates the academic skills, particularly those of communication, to the content, attitudes, and concepts gained by children through commercial televiewing. By keeping up with current and projected television programs the teacher can also guide children in selection of programs more in line with educational objectives. If the teacher looks ahead and suggests certain programs, he can utilize these to full advantage in the classroom.

Like radio, television is faced with its problems. Poor reception and lack of proper viewing facilities are yet to be overcome. Differences in school curriculums, appropriate scheduling, inability to "go back" or" skip ahead," difficulty in adjusting to programs not directly related to current phases of study and limitations of one-way contact face educational television. Many school systems are providing closed circuit television for the schools under one organization. States are setting up stations and relays to cover the schools under their administration. Midwest Program on Airborne Television Instruction (MPATI) brings television to an estimated 5,000,000 pupils and 200,000 teachers in parts of six states. Some evaluation of these efforts to education through television is summarized by Wittich and Schuller in this manner:

> MPATI can provide high-level instruction in subjects not now offered in certain localities because of budget limitations or the lack of teachers or instructional facilities. As such, MPATI is upgrading educational opportunity; and as its program continues, it will open the way for other regional

— and ultimately, world-wide — planning and use of educational television.[39]

The fact that lessons for MPATI are prepared on video tape and transmitted to classrooms by video tape recorders carried on a plane traveling 20,000 feet in the air verifies the effectiveness and adaptability of video tape. The kinescope, telefilm, and video tape are all, in essence, little more than glorified motion pictures which have been used in the classrooms of our public schools for a quarter of a century. The employment of films in schools has been a slow but gradual and effective movement. Telefilms provide a new type of recording for classroom use, making possible complete television originated courses by means of 16 mm. sound projectors. These offerings in motion picture add to the great wealth of instructional resources in 16 mm. educational films already available.

Research has shown that utilizing teaching films in the classroom brings about more effective learning. In an experiment concerning the effectiveness of film reported by Witty, Fitzwater, and Gorman, it was found that at second-grade level 95 per cent of the children improved in reading, 95 per cent showed vocabulary improvement, 70 per cent expressed more and better ideas during class discussion, and 99 per cent wanted to continue the work with films.[40]

The value and effectiveness of classroom films when used in an appropriate manner are fittingly summarized by Wittich and Schuller as follows:

> During thirty years of research concerning its role and usefulness in classroom learning, the strength of the 16 mm. motion-picture film has been demonstrated. Language laboratories, educational television, and other techniques have appeared since 1950, but the importance of the 16 mm. sound motion-picture film continues.
>
> This medium offers many opportunities for the improvement of instruction. Through basic motion-picture techniques such as direct and changing-speed photography, photomicrography, and animation, great areas of desirable but heretofore inaccessible instructional experiences and visualized explanations can now be brought into any classroom . . .
>
> The classroom use of teaching films has many values. For example, pupil interest is heightened, more learning is accomplished, the retention of learned materials is more permanent, and interest in reading is increased.[41]

---

[39]Wittich and Schuller, *op. cit.*, p. 420.

[40]Paul A. Witty, James Fitzwater and Harriet Gorman, "An Experiment with Films, Film-Readers, and the Magnetic Sound Track Projector," *Elementary English*, Volume XXX, Number 4 (April, 1953), pp. 232-241.

[41]Wittich and Schuller, *op. cit.*, pp. 403-404.

The teaching film has a wide range of possibilities for improving the teaching-learning situation. Its limitations are mainly those of accessibility at the appropriate time and the selection and use of the film by the teacher.

TEACHING MACHINES AND PROGRAMMED LEARNING

The latest and probably most controversial instructional medium before the educator today is the teaching machine. The term when used literally has a wider connotation than that implied by the educational jargon of today since, various teaching machines have been in use for many years. In his description of the trends of the audio-visual wave, Finn lists five types of teaching machines. He says that he would:

> . . . class all teaching equipment designed for individual or near-individual operation as being in the category of teaching machines. At present, then, there are approximately five types, listed here on an ascending scale of sophistication: (a) individual reading pacers and similar devices; (b) individual viewing and listening equipment for existing slides, filmstrips, motion pictures, and recordings; (c) language laboratories of all types; (d) specifically programmed printed verbal materials such as Crowder's (1959, Homme and Evans), etc.; and (e) true teaching machines of the Skinner or Pressey type containing carefully worked out verbal or pictorial programs with various ingenious mechanical or electronic arrangements to test student reaction, inform him of his progress, errors, etc.[42]

The first two types listed by Finn are generally accepted and used by educators; however, the newest devices which present programmed material give rise to consternation and challenge. These auto-instructional materials can be classified basically according to two models: the linear program model and the branching program model. The linear program model is attributed to the supporters of psychologist B. F. Skinner. This group is classified as the "purists," who base their actions on the results of laboratory studies of learning. Models which are classified as branching programs are developed mainly by followers of technologist Norman Crowder, the inventor of the scrambled book.[43]

There is considerable argument over which is more important, steering or propelling, since the branching programmers are more concerned about the guidance of learning while the linear programmers give more attention

---

[42]James D. Finn, "Technology and the Instructional Process," *Teaching Machines and Programmed Learning*, (ed.) A. A. Lumsdame and Robert Glaser (Washington: Department of Audio-Visual Instruction, National Education Association, 1960), p. 389.

[43]Robert E. Stake, "The Teaching Machine: Tool of the Future or Passing Fancy?" *Phi Delta Kappen,* Volume XLIV, Number 6, (March, 1963) p. 247.

to the efficiency of learning. While each group has persuasive arguments for its own emphasis, Stake concludes that both camps seem to agree that:

> (1) teaching must be more effectively individualized, that (2) each student should be actively involved in the pursuit of learning, and that (3) knowledge of the appropriateness of each response should follow without delay. It is the logic of these conclusions rather than any research results that has made the rank and file psychologist a supporter of the teaching machine movement.[44]

The teaching machine program is developed on the basis that certain bodies of subject information are constant in nature. Subject areas which seem most appropriate for programming include spelling, arithmetic, rules of grammar, certain scientific knowledge, geographical information, and dates and places of historical significance.

Programmed material is designed so that the individual can progress at his own rate of speed and master a given body of data on his own. Programming is also expected to free the teacher from time consuming drill in order that he can give more time to developing the creative aspects of students and assisting them in personal, social, and vocational development. Through teaching machines or program books, a class can work with different materials at rates in keeping with the needs and progress of each individual.

Program gadgets — books or machines — provide the learner with a developmental sequence of judgments arranged in logical order. The material to be learned is presented to the learner one "frame" at the time. The student gives his response in the appropriate space and flips the page of a book or pulls the lever of a machine to expose the correct response. Direction is given to proceed according to the response recorded by the student. The interaction between the learner and the subject content is such that there is intense individual application designed to sustain activity in each student. The material is presented at a pace which the student can master step by step, from less to more difficult providing for repeat and reinforcement according to the correctness of responses.

Learning with an auto-instructional device changes the pace of the learner from that of responding only a few minutes at a time in a class to that of being directly and continuously involved for the entire time he is at work. He moves from step to step without delay, which causes fatigue more quickly than when working in a class situation.

An increasing number of types of programs are being made available to the teacher including linear or step-by-step, branching, and cross-media.

---

[44]*Ibid.*, pp. 248-249.

The step-by-step program is broken down into the most logical sequence of developmental steps the student can take as fast as he is able. Branching programs provide intervals larger than the step-by-step program but lead the student into supplementary steps as needed. Cross-media materials are more complex, utilizing slides, filmstrips, audio tapes, and sound motion-picture films.[45] Whatever the material, the teacher serves as a guide and coordinator for the students as they work in their individual ways at the stages of the programmed data. The most comprehensive source for determining what is available in programmed learning is *The Educational Media Index.*[46]

In reaction to the value and permanancy of teaching machines as they are known, Stake has stated that:

> Programed texts and teaching machines, as we know them, like the player piano and the stereopticon, are something of a passing fancy. The current equipment will be superceded, replaced by new and better and surely much different "passing fancies"; and eventually replaced by something more accommodated to the schools of today. The 1963 materials will be rejected, not because they will be found "of no value," but because our standards of value and utility change. Tomorrow we won't tolerate the inadequacies of today's techniques.[47]

COMMUNITY RESOURCES

Recognizing that man learns that which he actually sees, feels, and touches, it is important that the child have firsthand knowledge of that which is around him. This can be realized best when the elementary school is operated as a community or neighborhood school. The community-school concept places primary importance upon recognizing the school as a part of the human affairs which surround it, knowing the community, serving it, and using it as a source for learning. When the school operates under this point of view, field trips, resource persons, realia, exhibits, and displays become part of the ongoing process of learning for children.

This philosophy can be strengthened through a statement of policy by the local board of education similar to that of Madison, Wisconsin, as cited by Wittich and Schuller: "In order to provide the most effective teaching environment, field trips and excursions outside the classrooms and school buildings and grounds under the supervision of members of the school staff are considered by the Board of Education as an extension of the classroom

---

[45]Wittich and Schuller, *op. cit.*, pp. 465-473.
[46]*The Educational Media Index,* (New York: McGraw-Hill Book Company, published annually.)
[47]Stake, *op. cit.*, p. 247.

and an integral part of the educational program."[48] The first step of any school group obviously is to determine the policy of the administration in regard to out-of-school experiences.

After the teacher reviews the board of education policy on utilizing community resources, he should make a systematic search for resources which will improve the instructional program of his class. This survey should be carried out in relation to previous studies made of the community and the prior experiences of the various class groups. The school may have already set up a file of resources and designated the community resources most appropriate for the respective grade levels. Using the community as a resource, the teacher should assist the children in finding people, places, and things to bring to the classroom and determine places to which to take them. The wise teacher should consider the previous utilization of those materials and media in order to avoid needless repetition.

Irrespective of the type of community experience, the teacher should accept full responsibility for correlating the activities with classroom mastery of content and skills. A guide to assist the teacher in accomplishing this task has been suggested by Wittich and Schuller thusly:

1. Preliminary preparation.
2. Preliminary discussion of study objectives.
3. Observation.
4. Follow-up discussion and evaluation.
5. Follow-up projects growing out of community study.[49]

The teacher should visit the community resource in advance of a scheduled visit by students to consult with personnel and plan for observation of the appropriate realia, exhibits, and displays. He should determine and further the interest of children in the resource. He should then plan with the group and help develop procedures which will extend learning in the topic under study.

With the help of the students, the teacher must see that the proper persons are contacted and that the administration is advised of and approves this particular community experience. When transportation is involved appropriate permission from parents, arrangements for vehicles, and provision for other persons to accompany the class must be attended to. The teacher must see that the date, time, and place are clear and that those involved are fully informed as to the anticipated activities.

---

[48]Wittich and Schuller, *op. cit.*, p. 251; *Bulletin* 89, Madison Public Schools, Madison, Wisconsin.
[49]Wittich and Schuller, *op. cit.*, pp. 254-255.

Careful consideration should be given to seeing that a maximum number of suitable learning objectives are planned for each community experience. Definite responsibilities in regard to gathering data, such as taking notes, asking questions, and collecting any appropriate specimen, should be assigned. Where feasible, pictures should be taken to aid in recalling situations as the group summarizes and evaluates the experience.

Classroom discussion should be encouraged following an experience. The teacher should seek to relate it to furthering communication skills without marring the values to be gained from the social experience. Descriptive accounts, letters to friends describing the experience, news releases for the class or school newspaper, letters of appreciation, and graphic and pictorial records of the experience can give meaning and at the same time further the skills in reading, writing, speaking, and listening. A simple evaluative guide can be prepared to help individuals in writing their reactions to the experience. This will assist the teacher in providing follow-up activities with the group and in planning the use of resources in the future. Follow-up activities also serve as a means of stimulating the group to further related activities such as the construction of models, murals, and displays. In addition they may open the way for participation of individuals or the group in some kind of service or civic project. Careful evaluation and utilization of one community resource may build interest in and pave the way for the use of another.

The teacher should recognize that there are things to see, hear, and examine which can be brought into the classroom; trips to take to governmental agencies, industries, museums, conservation camps, and recreational centers; and research surveys available which may involve these agencies. Survey techniques may also be applied by small groups and individuals who should bring their findings and collections into the classroom to further student learning.

DRAMATIZATION

Reaction to the printed page and to life situations and individual experiences may take such forms as story telling, role playing, creative interpretation, choral speaking, forum, panel, debate, discussion, and play acting. Presently, vocalization is used primarily as a means for teaching in the classroom. Leavell has stated that, "Any teacher standing before the class lecturing more than twenty-five per cent of the time is out of bounds."[50] The teacher should have received his practice in talking before being thrust upon a captive audience of twenty-five to forty young people.

---

[50]Ullin W. Leavell, Class Lecture (Charlottesville: University of Virginia, July 15, 1956).

The child is the one who needs the practice. It is the teacher who can provide the opportunity for each child to find a medium through which he can express himself best.

Children enjoy story telling by the teacher who gives some feeling to the tale. They also enjoy telling stories themselves. Getting peer reaction through this medium helps them to grow and realize the difference between truth and fiction. Role playing provides an opportunity for the child to be in fiction what he often would like to be in reality. Through creative interpretation the teacher can determine what the child feels and gets from a story.

A child who fears his own voice may lose himself in verbalization as he engages in choral speaking with the class or a small group. The panel, forum, and debate provide opportunities for individuals to prepare themselves on a topic to be presented before an audience. Each child competes with another for an interpretation of a topic, is queried by the audience, or matches wits with a team of peers and in so doing tempers his fears of verbalization.

When held to a given topic and not dominated by the teacher in a question and answer fashion, class discussion allows for a give-and-take among peers and a testing of individual ideas and points of view. This medium provides for the youngster who otherwise would not accept a formal assignment for presentation.

Many students gain satisfaction from learning a script and playing the part of some real character. Others relish the zest that comes from extemporaneous acting of a part in a drama in which, after gaining an understanding of the plot, the students supply the script as the play moves along. Ward summarizes the purposes of play making as:

1. To provide for a controlled emotional outlet.
2. To provide each child with an avenue of self realization in one of the arts.
3. To encourage and guide the child's creative imagination.
4. To give children experience in thinking on their feet and expressing ideas freely.[51]

The major value of this type of learning experience lies in the fact that it allows the child to forget himself and concentrate on the subject at hand and to organize his thinking around a given topic. In so doing he must be mindful of others and conduct himself in a manner acceptable to them. He must try to put himself into the position of another and think and act

---

[51]Winifred L. Ward, *Playmaking with Children* (second edition; New York: Appleton-Century-Crofts, Inc., 1957), p. 8.

accordingly, giving attention to reasons for his actions, speech, and manners. Value gained from dramatization and discussion hits the heart of educational objectives very succinctly and has been expressed well by Cross and Cypher:

> We want students who are able to read between the lines of the printed page, who can discriminate between the picture sequences of a film or filmstrip. Dramatizations and discussions help in this respect, for they literally project the student into the situation — he is not accepting a message from the page of a book or the projection screen; he is part of an actual experience which has real-life meaning for him.[52]

Just as with all educational media, dramatization techniques must be used with discretion by the teacher and the class. Certainly all the foregoing media cannot be used with any one unit of work. However, when the problem-solving approach is utilized and students work in groups, more than one of these techniques can be employed at a given time. More than one group within a single classroom also may employ the same medium at the same time in separate parts of the room.

DEMONSTRATION, EXPERIMENTATION, AND OBSERVATION

Demonstration, experimentation, and observation are closely related in providing problem solving learning experiences in the classroom. A demonstration seeks to show others a process of doing. Experimentation implies that someone is engaged in the act of determining what will happen under given circumstances. Observation infers that a process or action is seen by someone. Demonstration, experimentation, and observation may all be involved in one situation. The teacher may seek to determine what happens when a given prescription is compounded. He may demonstrate to a class how he conducts an experiment. At the same time, students may learn to observe techniques of procedure as well as results of an experiment.

The teacher demonstrates constantly as he works with students. His performance sets a pattern, and the students imitate his actions in such things as speaking, writing, and problem solving. Demonstrations are used to focus attention on and dramatize important basic steps in the solution of a problem. Through demonstration the time for learning a new technique or concept may be reduced and fixations of wrong ideas may be avoided. Demonstrations of skills and techniques should be geared to the ability of the group observing.

Such activities as candlemaking, glass blowing, and metal etching may be demonstrated in the classroom by a person skilled in the particular art.

---

[52]Cross and Cypher, *op. cit.*, p. 235.

The child also learns to use the medium of demonstration to communicate with his peers and to contribute to the total classroom situation. Multiple media such as chalkboard, flannel board, filmstrip, recording, flatprint, model, and realia may be involved in a single demonstration.

The experiment calls for a more complex operation in that it involves combining ingredients or elements according to a plan or formula for the specific purpose of testing a hunch or hypothesis. Children should be taught from the beginning that experimentation is something one does to find out what takes place under certain conditions and that results of this procedure are natural results which are understandable and not trickery or magic. Experiments should be planned in cooperation with the children and related to furthering objectives of the class on the topic under study. Petersen and Hayden have pointed out that if experimentation by children is to proceed at its best, there must be an air of permissiveness in the classroom. Children must be free to propose experiments related to the study topic and to seek and obtain assistance in carrying out their proposals. They should learn that experiments that do not work also can be valuable learning experiences.[53]

Learning to observe is of utmost importance to the child, since more of them will make decisions and draw conclusions through observation than will ever carry out scientific experimentation. Small animals are of much interest to the young child and something he is willing to observe closely. White rabbits, hamsters, chickens, frogs, and turtles provide excellent opportunities for children's observation of changes in animal growth and habits. The aquarium and terrarium furnish much observational experience for children in the classroom. Collections of shells, rocks, leaves, and seed pods also give material for observation. A walk through the schoolyard and neighborhood periodically can help the child to recognize changes in nature. As the child matures, more complex observational experiences should be provided.

Many tend to think of demonstration and experimentation as confined to science. They are, however, equally effective in other areas of learning. Many of the craft industries have capitalized upon the desire of people to observe the skilled worker by encouraging the public to visit the craftsman at work. Nothing is more fascinating to the child or adult than to follow the automobile plant assembly line and observe the work as the single car parts start down the line and are put together one by one until a worker steps into the finished automobile, starts the motor and drives it away. To capture some of these likes and urges of people is to make school a

---

[53]Dorothy G. Petersen and Velma D. Hayden, *Teaching and Learning in the Elementary School* (New York: Appleton-Century-Crofts, Inc., 1961) pp. 290-294.

place where the child finds not only a place to express himself but a place to gain new skills that he can use.

RHYTHMIC EXPRESSION, CREATIVE ART, AND CONSTRUCTION

Emphasis upon release of talent rather than suppression of expression is the keynote to problem solving in the learner-centered school. With this point of view, rhythms, dance, construction, and painting become outlets for the child in expressing his feelings, urges, and desires. Through these media he learns to understand and interpret the customs, struggles, and patterns of living today as well as those of earlier periods within the different cultures.

The teacher must recognize the child's need to express himself in rhythmic movement and the possibilities of this expression for developing his creativity. Andrews points out that, "When a child is given an opportunity to use movement, it is as expressive for him as it was for primitive man. Through this medium the child can react to the world about him, use it as a means of communication, and express the thoughts and feelings which are deep down inside . . . Movement is the child's universal langauge."[54]

Creativity through rhythms requires a receptive atmosphere, time to create, space for movement, and teacher guidance. The earlier a child's rhythmic sense is developed, the better will be his preparation for appreciation and understanding of all the arts. There seems to be no particular sequence for developing rhythmic expression. This lies basically with the teacher and the children under his supervision. He studies the children and selects those experiences which seem to stimulate them. Rhythmic activities which usually appeal to elementary children include animal rhythms, mechanical rhythms and dance.[55]

Simple and natural rhythmic activities most often used by primary children include walking, skipping, running, hopping, jumping, and leaping. More advanced movements of galloping, marching, tiptoeing, trotting, stretching, bending, and the side step are also valuable modes of expression for the primary child. Children enjoy depicting animal movements as they listen to music, pretending they are the lumbering bear, the heavy treading elephant, or the waddling duck. Mechanical rhythms involve the child in movements of the pack mule as well as the streamliner. He also enjoys the action of the spinning top or the bouncing ball. Folk dances and

---

[54]Gladys Andrews, *Creative Rhythmic Movement for Children* (Englewood Cliffs: Prentice-Hall, Inc., 1954), p. 25.
[55]Lillian M. Logan and Virgil G. Logan, *Teaching the Elementary School Child* (Boston: Houghton Mifflin Company, 1961), pp. 542-549.

singing games take the child into another era as he participates in dances and songs native to a particular group of people. There is no limit to original rhythm and dance that can be expressed by the children as music frees and stimulates them to give their own uninhibited responses.[56]

Creativity through art and construction may include drawing, painting, modeling, sculpturing, constructing with paper and wood, and the use of other similar media. The same principles of creativity apply to art and construction as to other media. The major goal to work toward is increasing student self-direction and responsibility. Method is not to be imposed upon the student but opportunity should be provided him to see many alternatives for development. Children need to be stimulated by seeing, feeling, and becoming involved in real experiences. As they become involved and develop convictions, they will want to express them. When art media are available and there is free time, the uninhibited child is likely to turn to art for expression.

Art is a means of self-expression for every child, not for just a talented few. Thus the teacher must recognize the expression of the individual child rather than the product. He should keep in mind that art is creative and as such may enhance the mental, emotional and spiritual aspects of the child. Art has the power to contribute, awaken, extend, and develop the best within the child when he is given time and media for experimentation.[57]

Construction is closely related to dramatic play. In developing a unit on purpose and drive to learning. When properly motivated, children are usually eager to construct objects which they can use in individual and group experiences. The joy of constructing may be the means of motivating the child to read, discuss, and gain information pertinent to the success of a group project or for an individual class report. It must be kept in mind that the construction of an object contributes to a social learning and that the constructed object is not the end product. Values of most importance to be gained from construction are those that come when careful planning is involved, the object is authentic, a significant purpose has been accomplished, and the activity is used to stimulate further learning.

Construction is closely related to dramatic play. In developing a unit on transportation in the primary grades children need engines, tank cars, a depot, roundhouse, and turntable. Study of air transportation calls for hangars, planes, signal tower, wind sock, and gas trucks. As children develop in maturity, blocks, boxes, boards, and easily made items are replaced

---

[56]*Ibid.*

[57]J. Murray Lee and Doris May Lee, *The Child and His Curriculum* (third edition; New York: Appleton-Century-Crofts, Inc., 1960) p. 526.

by props with more detail and precision, even authentic replicas of trains, airplanes, automobiles and ships.

Construction activities afford many values which help children relate the academic to problems of living. When constructing for group needs, opportunities are provided for cooperative planning and evaluating, sharing of tools and materials, acceptance and discharge of responsibility, self-direction, and proper care of equipment. It is emotionally satisfying to the child to make things and to use them for purposes significant to the group.

Opportunities to improve problem solving ability are provided through construction as children decide how big to make a replica of Lincoln's cabin or where the control tower goes on the ariport layout. Such activities enable children to produce and use objects representative of those being studied. Meanings may be clarified, enriched, and deepened as they build the replica of the cabin or lay out the airport. Opportunities and motivation for development of language and number skills should be a definite objective of construction activities.[58]

The teacher can create an environment and provide the conditions leading to creativity of expression, but it is up to the child to utilize these in a productive manner. The child must choose the medium which seems most satisfactory in expressing himself. The teacher kindles the fire and stands by to give assistance and encouragement. When the teacher is adept in the use of many media and employs them wisely, he has set the wheels in motion toward helping the child find a means of expressing himself in an effective and satisfying manner.

EXPERIENCE CHARTS, BULLETINS, AND SCHOOL NEWSPAPERS

Since the major purpose of the school is to teach children to read, write, speak, and listen, it is obvious that they are going to be expressing themselves through writing. Too often the writing is copying material that is dull and boring to children, answering questions at the end of a chapter and filling in blanks or, at best, writing themes on topics selected by the teacher. The seventh grade youngster, who regularly wrote letters for his uncle reporting on sales of their hogs, lamented that he just could not get started on a theme assigned to him by his teacher on "What a Daffodil Thinks of Spring."

The first grade child who helps his class prepare the morning bulletin each day learns that writing and reading are associated with real life. He also learns that he can write something for others to read and that they

---

[58]John U. Michaelis, *Social Studies for Children in a Democracy* (second edition; Englewood Cliffs: Prentice-Hall, Inc., 1956), pp. 347-351.

enjoy reading what he has written. An experience such as a birthday party or a walk around the block, when recorded in their own words, may become real reading matter for the children. When these activities are transferred to a large sheet of paper by the teacher in the form of an exprience chart, the children may read the chart many times with much enjoyment. When this reading matter is mimeographed with other stories written by the class and put in a booklet for each child, this becomes a cherished possession which he proudly reads to those who will give him audience.

The child moves from group writing with the teacher as recorder to writing experiences in his own words and style. Sharing these written experiences with his neighbors is his beginning recognition that news is what happens to people and that books and papers are the records of these happenings. As early as the second grade, children can begin to prepare their own newspaper for distribution to their parents and friends as well as other classes in the school.

The school newspaper may also become a motivating factor for other classes within the school when the experiences of the various groups are reported and others are kept in contact with the highlights of each room. Too often school newspapers become collections of poems on fictitious topics. Some of this is desirable, but basically the school newspaper should report actual happenings, which depict something of the realistic approach to educational goals, of each room and the school as a whole.

SUMMARY

The vast amount of recorded data available to the learner should challenge the educator to find new and more efficient means of helping the student acquire the skills necessary for solving problems and keeping abreast of the rapidly changing society in which he lives. Learning experiences must be provided which are in keeping with the needs and interest of the learner. The most effective learning takes place when the learner recognizes value in the educational experience and when more than one of his senses is involved.

Learning involves perception. Perception is a composite of meaning, feeling, and symbols which relate to experience. Direct, purposeful experience provides basic learning but is not possible, practical, or feasible at all levels of learning. Man's effort to provide simulated experiences through the ages is now in an advanced state of technology. A tremendous array of materials and media with mammoth problems of selection, procurement, and utilization confronts the teacher. He must resolve these as he seeks to engage the child's time, interest, and energy in working toward acceptable educational goals.

The teacher should keep in mind the kinds of experiences by which the child learns at different levels as he moves from the concrete to the abstract. The role of the teacher is changing to serving as a coordinator of learning experiences rather than a dispenser of knowledge. The teacher should utilize available resources such as specialized professional personnel, libraries, materials centers, the community, technological devices, special service agencies, and industrial facilities and personnel. He should continually evaluate, collect, and file those materials most pertinent to his instructional needs. He should work with the school system in developing an ongoing program for making appropriate instructional materials and media known to teachers and available to all children.

The teacher should strive for a balance between cooperatively planned group and individual activities and select appropriate media for each endeavor. He should be acquainted with and able to use all kinds of printed matter, writing and display boards, visuals of various types, auto-instructional devices, dramatizations, creative activities, and techniques involving aural-oral and written expression. The new and old, the book and the machine, should find their appropriate places in the ongoing process of involving youngsters in real life experiences in and out of the classroom.

The school should continue in its effort to find better and more effective learning processes for children. It should seek to provide more information about the children and help the teacher with individualization of instruction. It should seek to free the teacher from unnecessary detail and provide time for more effective preparation. Each book, gadget, device, machine, and technique has possibilities for instruction. The emphasis placed upon each, the creativeness with which each is used, and the appropriateness of the selection will determine its teaching effectiveness.

QUESTIONS FOR DISCUSSION

1. Perception is considered the foundation of learning. What are the implications of this point of view for use of instructional media?
2. What does the term "moving from concrete to abstract" mean? Utilizing Dale's "Cone of Experience," give examples for application of this term in the classroom.
3. How can many of the usual problems encountered in the provision, selection, and utilization of instructional media be eliminated?
4. Identify a variety of instructional media which is desirable for use in the classroom. To what extent should the teacher be knowledgeable about and able to use these media?
5. The role of the teacher is changing to that of coordinator of instructional media. How can this be justified?

TOPICS FOR RESEARCH

1. Select appropriate instructional media which will provide a variety of experiences for a specific unit of work.
2. Learn to operate the instructional machines most likely to be found in the regular classroom, such as filmstrip projector, motion picture projector, tape recorder, and overhead projector.
3. Select a motion picture as an instructional aid for a particular topic. Plan a lesson which provides for the most effective use of this film.
4. Demonstrate to the class the use of two or three instructional media. Explain why these were chosen and how you expect to use them in enriching a learning situation with children.
5. Examine programmed text material to determine its value in providing for individual instruction.

BIBLIOGRAPHY

ANDREWS, GLADYS. *Creative Rhythmic Movement of Children.* Englewood Cliffs: Prentice-Hall, Inc., 1954.

BEAUCHAMP, GEORGE A. *Basic Dimensions of Elementary Method.* Boston: Allyn and Bacon, Inc., 1959.

BROWN, JAMES W., RICHARD B. LEWIS, AND FRED F. HARCLEROAD. *A-V Instruction: Materials and Methods.* New York: McGraw-Hill Book Company, 1959.

CARPENTER, HELEN M. (ed.). *Skills in Social Studies.* Washington: National Council for the Social Studies, NEA, 1953.

CROSS, A. J. FOY, AND IRENE F. CYPHER. *Audio-Visual Education.* New York: Thomas Y. Crowell Company, 1961.

DALE, EDGAR. *Audio-Visual Methods in Teaching.* Revised edition. New York: The Dryden Press, 1956.

Handbook for Elementary and Secondary Schools. Raleigh: North Carolina State Department of Education, 1955.

KINDER, JAMES S. *Audio-Visual Materials and Techniques.* Second edition. New York: American Book Company, 1959.

KINGSLEY, HOWARD L. *The Nature and Conditions of Learning.* New York: Prentice-Hall, Inc., 1947.

LEE, J. MURRAY AND DORRIS MAY LEE. *The Child and His Curriculum.* New York: Appleton-Century-Crofts, Inc., 1960.

LOGAN, LILLIAN M. AND VIRGIL G. LOGAN. *Teaching the Elementary School Child.* Boston: Houghton Mifflin Company, 1961.

MICHAELIS, JOHN U. *Social Studies for Children in a Democracy.* Third edition. Englewood Cliffs: Prentice-Hall, Inc., 1963.

MILLER, WILLIAM C. AND ALBERT L. GOLDBERG. "Technology-Progress," *Educational Leadership,* Volume XX, Number 7 (April, 1963), pp. 431-433.

National Tape Recording Catalog. Washington: Department of Audio-Visual Instruction, NEA, 1962.

OHLSEN, MERLE M. (ed.). *Modern Methods in Elementary Education*. New York: Henry Holt and Company, 1959.

PETERSON, DOROTHY G. AND VELMA D. HAYDEN. *Teaching and Learning in the Elementary School*. New York: Appleton-Century-Crofts, 1961.

PRESSEY, SIDNEY L. *Psychology and the New Education*. New York: Harper and Brothers Publishers, 1944.

SHANE, HAROLD G. (ed.) *The American Elementary School*. New York: Harper and Brothers Publishers, 1953.

SOWARDS, G. WESLEY AND MARY-MARGARET SCOBEY. *The Changing Curriculum and the Elementary Teacher*. Belmont, Cal.: Wadsworth Publishing Company, 1961.

STAKE, ROBERT E. "The Teaching Machine: Tool of the Future or Passing Fancy?" *Phi Delta Kappan*. Volume XLIV, Number 16 (March, 1963), pp. 247-249.

Teachers' Handbook. Graham, North Carolina: Alamance County Public Schools, 1956-1957.

WARD, WINIFRED L. *Playmaking with Children*. Second edition. New York: Appleton-Century-Crofts, Inc., 1957.

WENDT, PAUL R. "Audio-Visual Instruction." Bulletin 14 on *What Research Says to the Teacher*. Washington: Department of Classroom Teachers, American Educational Research Association of the NEA, 1957.

WITTY, PAUL, JAMES FITZWATER, AND HARRIET GORMAN. "An Experiment with Films, Film-Readers, and the Magnetic Sound Track Projector," *Elementary English*. Volume XXX, Number 4 (April, 1963), pp. 232-241.

WITTICH, WALTER ARNO, AND CHARLES R. SCHULLER. *Audiovisual Materials: Their Nature and Use*. New York: Harper and Brothers Publishers, 1962.

WOODRUFF, ASAHELD D. *Basic Concepts of Teaching*. Concise edition. San Francisco: Chandler Publishing Company, 1961.

WOOTTON, LUTIAN R. "A Study of the Instructional Services of the Alamance County, North Carolina, Schools, 1933-1955." Unpublished Doctor's dissertation, The University of Virginia, Charlottesville, 1957.

Teachers continue to improve professionally through in-service education.

Chapter 12

The Professional
Elementary School Teacher

The elementary school teacher serves a vital role in our American society. He is charged with the responsibility of directing student learning in order that the children can develop socially useful skills, attain necessary knowledge, and acquire wholesome attitudes that will enable them to become contributing members of our democratic society. This is a monumental undertaking, but the elementary teacher has performed this function in an exemplary manner in the past and will be called upon to provide the same service in the future.

THE TEACHER AS A PERSON

Much has been written and said about the personal attributes the individual elementary school teacher should possess. Items frequently mentioned are his preparation, traits, competencies, and ethics. The successful elementary teacher most certainly has thorough and appropriate preparation, acceptable traits, demonstrable competencies, and ethical behavior.

PREPARATION

The modern elementary teacher is the product of a broad liberal education. The first two years of his bachelor's program are composed of work in the areas of English, mathematics, speech, psychology, art, music, natural and physical science, social science, and philosophy. This study constitutes the general education segment of teacher preparation.

Approximately one-half of the upper-division or the junior and senior years study is given over to specialized content courses in which the teacher studies elementary school reading, science, arithmetic, social studies, and the like. A concentration can be acquired in any one of these areas by utilizing electives in course selection.

The other one-half of the upper-division study affords learnings in professional education courses. It is through this portion of preparation that the teacher learns how to utilize his general education and specialized content knowledge to the best advantage in the actual process of teaching children.

The elementary teacher acquires a perspective of the social world, physical world, and work of the world in his general education course study. Through studies in such courses as anthropology, history, psychology, economics, and philosophy, the future teacher acquires an understanding of the world's peoples and their institutions thereby gaining for himself a meaningful philosophy of life.[1]

The special content courses enable the teacher to learn the material he is to teach. These courses are a vital aspect of teacher preparation in that they provide him with a knowledge of the subject matter of the elementary school. Thorough preparation in specialized content courses will better enable the teacher to stand before his class with the assurance that he is capable of meeting his students' educational needs.

The professional education courses the elementary teacher studies provide him with a knowledge of children and promising teaching procedures. Professional courses offered in the upper-division program include child growth and development, educational psychology, children's literature, curriculum development, and student teaching.

The elementary teacher should recognize the fact that education is never terminal — it is continual. He therefore should plan to enroll in graduate work where he can study in greater depth in content, methodology, or theories of learning and earn an advanced degree or certificate. The in-service education program of his own school system should provide him with an avenue of professional growth and stimulation also. He should willingly participate in both the formal education program of the teacher education institutions and the in-service program of the school to become more proficient as a teacher.

TRAITS

The individual elementary teacher possesses certain traits which contribute to his teaching success or serve as deterrents to his effectiveness. He

[1]George C. Kyte, *The Elementary School Teacher at Work* (New York: The Dryden Press, 1957), p. 494.

should learn which of these are the most critical in order that he can make trait adjustments which will enhance his teaching prowess. Desirable traits may include open-mindedness, patience, good sense of humor, scholarliness, knowledge of subject matter, sympathetic attitude, tactfulness or good judgment, enthusiasm, personal appearance, fairness, impartiality, self-control, cooperativeness, leadership ability, multiple interests, good health, creativeness, industriousness, and forcefulness.[2]

These traits, which contribute toward effective teaching, should serve as a guide to the teacher who purposes to become the most effective professional person possible. They can be developed by the teacher. If he determines that he does not possess those mentioned, he should purpose to develop them. The teacher who does not possess them and makes a conscious effort to develop them will likely become a truly professional person. Such an attitude is characteristic of a "becoming" teacher.

COMPETENCIES

The professional elementary school teacher is expected to possess and display many competencies in the performance of his duties. He is primarily a director of learning and therefore needs appropriate competencies in this capacity. He should, however, have facility in other areas which are equally important and necessary. The following comprehensive teacher competency check list first outlined by a committee of California teachers headed by Kinney and later revised by Williams and others is recommended as a guide for becoming more effective in professional activities.

Roles of the Teacher in Promoting Pupil Growth

I. Director of Learning
Adapts principles of child growth and development to planning of learning activities.
Recognizes and deals with each pupil according to his needs.
Helps individuals acquire the skills of effective group membership.
Works closely with specialists, parents, and community agencies in the solution of physical and mental health problems.
Makes and uses pupil records in ascertaining needs, planning work and guiding the learning process.
Plans teaching-learning situations in accord with acceptable principles of learning.

---

[2]See Renato Mazzei, "Desirable Traits of Successful Teachers," *Teaching In America* (ed.) Anthony C. Riccio and Frederick R. Cyphert, (Columbus, Ohio: Charles E. Merrill Books, Inc., 1962), p. 367; Marie A. Mehl, Hubert H. Mills, and Harl R. Douglass, *Teaching in Elementary School* (New York: The Ronald Press Company, 1958), pp. 476-479.

Provides effective and continuing motivation.

Develops cooperatively with pupils objectives for large units of study, daily class work, and special activities.

Arranges for differentiated assignments to meet needs and abilities of individual pupils.

Uses a variety of instruments and techniques for keeping pupil informed of his progress.

Utilizes a variety of classroom activities.

Selects and uses a wide variety of instructional materials. Provides abundant and varied opportunities for individual and group expression in appropriate creative fields.

Helps pupil make application of his experience to many situations.

Demonstrates effective instructional procedures.

Provides a physical environment which facilitates learning.

Makes assignments skillfully.

Provides opportunities for wide participation.

Utilizes adequate evaluation procedures.

Carries on evaluation as an integral part of instruction.

Enlists cooperation of pupils and parents in developing programs of evaluation.

Uses a variety of devices and procedures.

Organizes and summarizes data for meaningful interpretation.

Reports to parents in terms of growth in knowledge, skills, attitudes and social behavior.

Uses evaluative evidence to improve teaching-learning experiences.

Leads the learner to assume an important role in the evaluation of his own growth and development.

Maintains an effective balance of freedom and security in the classroom.

Shows an honest liking and sincere regard for boys and girls.

Emphasizes responsible group living with standards of conduct comparatively determined.

Develops relations among pupils that are cooperative and natural.

Provides opportunities for pupils to develop qualities of leadership and of self-direction.

Plans management of classroom routine as a worthwhile learning experience for pupils.

II. Counselor and Guidance Worker

Utilizes effective procedures for collecting information about each pupil.

Makes effective use of informal procedures: anecdotal records, interviews, questionnaires, check lists.

Utilizes standard tests.

Is familiar with the more useful ones in his own field.

Selects those most appropriate for his purpose.

Is skillful in constructing and using informal tests and socio-metric devices.

Appraises the characteristics of the test.

Interprets test results.

Provides pupils and parents with adequate reports.

Bases grades [marks] and reports on cumulative records.

Uses diagnostic and remedial procedures effectively.

Identifies learning difficulties.

Knows common diagnostic and achievement tests in own and related fields.

Administers and interprets diagnostic and achievement tests.

Selects appropriate remedial materials for instruction in relation to pupil's level of achievement.

Reveals ability to work correctively with the pupil at the level of his abilities, achievements, and interests at the given time.

Prepares and uses accurate and adequate records.

Makes case studies.

Keeps cumulative records.

Helps the pupil to understand himself.

Establishes effective relationships with individual pupils.

Utilizes suitable counseling techniques.

Maintains effective relationship with the home.

Assists the pupil in self-evaluation.

Helps him to understand his own abilities and limitations.

Guides him in the analysis of his personal problems.

Assists him in defining realistic goals.

Directs him to sources of information on vocational opportunities and careers.

Works effectively with the specialized counseling services.

Recognizes serious problem cases.

Refers serious cases to the specialist, with adequate background information.

III. Mediator of the Culture

Draws on a scholarly background to enrich cultural growth of pupils.

Directs individuals and groups to appropriate significant life appli-cation of classroom learning.

Utilizes his field of subject matter and/or general education in the solution of social, economic, scientific, and ethical problems.

Reveals the wide significance of his own subject matter field.

Develops an understanding of the interrelationships among the great disciplines.

Designs classroom activities to develop pupil ability and motivation for:

Finding democratic solutions to current social problems.

Recognizing and identifying key problems.

Understanding their interrelationships and defining the issues.

Directs pupils in learning to use those materials from which they will continue to learn after leaving school.

Teaches pupils to locate information on current problems.

Utilizes effective activities to develop pupil skill in using such materials in analyzing current problems.

Develops pupil-attitudes and skills necessary for effective participation in a changing democratic society.

Uses democratic techniques and skills in teaching.

Provides for the use of democratic attitudes and skills by the pupils in the classrooms, through:

Teacher-pupil planning of problem units.

Development of effective discussion practices.

Guidance in effective committee and other group participation.

Helps his students acquire the values realized as ideals of democracy, such as:

Mutual respect.

Willingness and ability to cooperate in the solution of problems.

Willingness and ability to use intelligence in problem solving.

Goals and standards for effective living in our culture.

IV. Link with the Community

Utilizes available education resources of community in classroom procedures.

Invites parents and other adults to share hobbies, talents, and experiences with students.

Utilizes field trips to draw on community resources.

Interprets community to pupils through his own field and incidental activities.

Reveals to the public the significance of the school program through pupil activities in classroom, school, and community projects.

Initiates students into community responsibilities appropriate to their age level.

Secures cooperation of parents in school activities.

Knows when and how to obtain assistance for school or class affairs.

Conforms with policies of Parent-Teacher Associations and other cooperating groups relating to cooperation with the school.

Encourages parents to visit regular classes and special school events.

Conducts individual and group parent conferences with increasing skill.

Assists lay groups in understanding modern education.

Participates effectively with various socioeconomic groups.

Keeps parents and public informed of school activities through bulletins, class letters, and newspaper articles.

Initiates opportunities to discuss educational problems and accomplishments with friends, neighbors, and community acquaintances.

Accepts invitations to speak upon educational subjects.

Communicates effectively with the public as well as with members of the profession.

Participates in definition and solution of community problems relating to education.

Contributes to service in the community.

Participates as a member of the profession in school betterment programs, bond issues and legislative matters.

Draws upon reliable sources for information and assistance.

V. Member of the Staff

Contributes to the definition of the over-all aims of the school.

Works effectively with the public to define school aims.

Interprets the relationship of school program and activities to the desired aims.

Articulates his classroom objectives to those of the school.

Contributes to the development of a school program to achieve its objectives.

Participates effectively in all-school curriculum developments.

Utilizes effective procedures in curriculum building.

Demonstrates familiarity with current curricular projects and patterns.

Articulates his classroom program to the school curriculum.

Contributes to the effectiveness of over-all school activities.

Participates in planning and guidance of student activities.

Assumes appropriate administrative responsibility for operation of the school as a whole.

Cooperates effectively in the evaluation of the school program.

Can define school aims in terms suitable for evaluation.

Participates in collection of relevant evidence.

Interprets the evidence to indicate needed revisions in program and aims.

VI. A Member of the Profession

Demonstrates an appreciation of the social importance of the profession.

Renders appropriate service to society beyond that for which he has contracted.

Contributes to the honor and prestige of the profession by his personal conduct.

Actively seeks to upgrade professional standards through selective recruitment and retention programs.

Interprets to others the goals and practices of the profession.

Contributes to the development of professional standards.

Takes part in the development of a functional code of ethics.

Adheres to the accepted code of ethics.

Helps to enforce the code of ethics in upgrading standards of professional behavior.

Supports an adequate system of certification and accreditation.

Helps improve pre-service and in-service programs of preparation.

Contributes to the profession through its organizations.

Becomes a member of the organization.

Takes active part in the formulation of the organizational policies.

Supports the policy once formed until it is changed by the democratic process.

Seeks and supports legislative programs to improve the program of education as well as the economic and social status of the profession.

Takes a personal responsibility for his own professional growth.

Develops and tests more effective classroom procedures.

Keeps informed on current trends, tendencies, and practices in his field by use of professional literature.

Participates in conferences, workshops, etc., dealing with professional problems.

Enlarges his horizons through academic and nonacademic experiences.

Acts on a systematic philosophy, critically adopted and consistently applied.

Expresses a systematic philosophy of education held with deep personal conviction.

Identifies and clarifies the philosophical assumptions underlying various and conflicting policies for his work in the six roles of professional practice.

Utilizes explicitly his philosophical views in making consistent choices of educational policies and practices.[3]

ETHICS

Every elementary school teacher should subscribe to an acceptable code of ethics. It may be his own which he has derived through experience of professional endeavor. The local school district, the state department of education, or the National Education Association code may be adopted by the teacher. The important point is that he does adhere to a system of ethics which he accepts. The National Education Association's *Code of Ethics* is very comprehensive, succinctly stated, and presented here as a suggested creed for the teacher.

First Principle

The primary obligation of the teaching profession is to guide children, youth, and adults in the pursuit of knowledge and skills, to prepare them

---

[3]Lois Williams et al., *Six Areas of Teacher Competence* (Burlingame: California Teachers Association, 1964), pp. 18-26; See also Lucien Kinney et al., *The Measure of a Good Teacher* (San Francisco: California Teachers Association, 1952).

in the ways of democracy, and to help them to become happy, useful, self-supporting citizens. The ultimate strength of the nation lies in the social responsibility, economic competence, and moral strength of the individual American.

In fulfilling the obligations of this first principle the teacher will —
1. Deal justly and impartially with students regardless of their physical, mental, emotional, political, economic, social, racial, or religious characteristics.
2. Recognize the differences among students and seek to meet their individual needs.
3. Encourage students to formulate and work for high individual goals in the development of their physical, intellectual, creative, and spiritual endowments.
4. Aid students to develop an understanding and appreciation not only of the opportunities and benefits of American democracy but also of their obligations to it.
5. Respect the right of every student to have confidential information about himself withheld except when its release is to authorized agencies or is required by law.
6. Accept no remuneration for tutoring except in accordance with approved policies of the governing board.

Second Principle

The members of the teaching profession share with parents the task of shaping each student's purposes and acts toward socially acceptable ends. The effectiveness of many methods of teaching is dependent upon cooperative relationships with the home.

In fulfilling the obligations of this second principle the teacher will —
1. Respect the basic responsibility of parents for their children.
2. Seek to establish friendly and cooperative relationships with the home.
3. Help to increase the student's confidence in his own home and avoid disparaging remarks which might undermine that confidence.
4. Provide parents with information that will serve the best interests of their children, and be discreet with information received from parents.
5. Keep parents informed about the progress of their children as interpreted in terms of the purposes of the school.

Third Principle

The teaching profession occupies a position of public trust involving not only the individual teacher's personal conduct, but also the interaction of the school and the community. Education is most effective when these many relationships operate in a friendly, cooperative, and constructive manner.

In fulfilling the obligations of this third principle the teacher will —
1. Adhere to any reasonable pattern of behavior accepted by the community for professional persons.

2. Perform the duties of citizenship, and participate in community activities with due consideration for his obligations to his students, his family, and himself.
3. Discuss controversial issues from an objective point of view, thereby keeping his class free from partisan opinions.
4. Recognize that the public schools belong to the people of the community, encourage lay participation in shaping the purposes of the school, and strive to keep the public informed of the educational program which is being provided.
5. Respect the community in which he is employed and be loyal to the school system, community, state, and nation.
6. Work to improve education in the community and to strengthen the community's moral, spiritual, and intellectual life.

Fourth Principle

The members of the teaching profession have inescapable obligations with respect to employment. These obligations are nearly always shared employer-employee responsibilities based upon mutual respect and good faith.

In fulfilling the obligations of this fourth principle the teacher will —
1. Conduct professional business through the proper channels.
2. Refrain from discussing confidential and official information with unauthorized persons.
3. Apply for employment on the basis of competence only, and avoid asking for a specific position known to be filled by another teacher.
4. Seek employment in a professional manner, avoiding such practices as the indiscriminate distribution of applications.
5. Refuse to accept a position when the vacancy has been created through unprofessional activity or pending controversy over professional policy or the application of unjust personnel practices and procedures.
6. Adhere to the conditions of a contract until service thereunder has been performed, the contract has been terminated by mutual consent, or the contract has otherwise been legally terminated.
7. Give and expect due notice before a change of position is to be made.
8. Be fair in all recommendations that are given concerning the work of other teachers.
9. Accept no compensation from producers of instructional supplies when one's recommendations affect the local purchase or use of such teaching aids.
10. Engage in no gainful employment, outside of his contract, where the employment affects adversely his professional status or impairs his standing with students, associates, and the community.
11. Cooperate in the development of school policies and assume one's professional obligations thereby incurred.
12. Accept one's obligation to the employing board for maintaining a professional level of service.

Fifth Principle

The teaching profession is distinguished from many other occupations by the uniqueness and quality of the professional relationships among all teachers. Community support and respect are influenced by the standards of teachers and their attitudes toward teaching and other teachers.

In fulfilling the obligations of this fifth principle the teacher will —

1. Deal with other members of the profession in the same manner as he himself wishes to be treated.
2. Stand by other teachers who have acted on his behalf and at his request.
3. Speak constructively of other teachers, but report honestly to responsible persons in matters involving the welfare of students, the school system, and the profession.
4. Maintain active membership in professional organizations and, through participation, strive to attain the objectives that justify such organized groups.
5. Seek to make professional growth continuous by such procedures as study, research, travel, conferences, and attendance at professional meetings.
6. Make the teaching profession so attractive in ideals and practices that sincere and able young people will want to enter it.[4]

SELF-EVALUATION

The effective teacher is one who is continually in the process of learning or becoming. He should realize the benefits that come from accepting a challenge, experimenting, trying new approaches, and applying research in the various disciplines of the elementary curriculum. One of the most effective means of growth is self-evaluation.[5]

Areas in which the teacher should occasionally engage in self-introspection include his efforts to continue his education, his planned professional reading program, his participation in civic, professional, or political groups and the like. Brown's self-evaluation rating scale which follows will enable the teacher to evaluate himself in his professional growth fairly and impartially.

1. Do I seek to achieve personal growth and development by means of some plan whereby I can enlarge my horizons as well as fill gaps in my knowledge and experience?

---

[4]See *NEA Handbook* (Washington, D. C., NEA, 1961) pp. 326-328. Reproduced by permission of the National Education Association.

[5]"The Process of Becoming," *Perceiving, Behaving, Becoming: A New Focus For Education,* 1962 Yearbook (Washington, D. C.: Association for Supervision and Curriculum Development, 1962), p. 236.

2. Do I subscribe to (or have access to) and regularly read at least the following:

   a. Some reliable news medium such as *Time, Newsweek,* or the Sunday New York *Times.*
   b. Some "quality" magazine dealing with current thought and opinion such as *Harper's, The Atlantic Monthly, The American Scholar.*
   c. Some magazine devoted at least in part to book reviews and literary criticism such as *The Saturday Review of Literature,* the New York *Times Book Review,* or the New York Herald *Tribune Book Review.*
   d. A first-rate professional journal?

3. Do I during the year (apart from school assignments) read at least two dozen serious books in the fields of biography, history, current affairs, social problems or literature (including a fair number of classics read or re-read)?

4. Do I make some serious effort to increase my understanding and appreciation of art, literature, and music through the use of pictures, lectures, concerts, records, plays, books, and selective radio listening?

5. Do I follow some consistent plan for building a personal library and do I already own and regularly use

   a. a good dictionary
   b. a good atlas
   c. a good one-volume encyclopedia
   d. a Bible
   e. at least three other reference books such as Bartlett's *Quotations, A Dictionary of Dates,* Fowler's *English Usage?*

6. Do I have some consistent plan for professional reading and for professional growth and development?

7. Do I have an interest in, and an awareness of, the world of nature so that I can identify and enjoy birds, flowers, trees, and stars?

8. Do I have some enriching and relaxing hobby or interest such as weaving, wood or leather working, cabinet making, book binding, or gardening?

9. Do I belong to and actively participate in at least three of the following organizations

   a. a professional society
   b. a religious body
   c. a civic group
   d. a political group
   e. a literary, art, or music group
   f. a scientific society
   g. a social action group?

10. Do I have some consistent and orderly plan for budgeting and handling my income so that I am able to

    a. meet my obligations promptly

    b. get the greatest possible benefit from my income

    c. make reasonable provision for the future?

11. Do I have some consistent and orderly plan for budgeting and handling my time so that I can

    a. meet my personal and professional obligations

    b. render some service to my fellow men

    c. have time for enriching leisure?

12. Do I fulfill my obligations as a citizen by

    a. voting regularly and as intelligently as possible

    b. civic participation (serving on boards or committees, aiding in Red Cross, Community Chest, and other drives, etc.)

    c. some regular volunteer service (time and money) to a religious or civic organization engaged in community betterment?

13. Do I take care of my health through proper habits of eating and sleeping, judicious use of exercise and rest, and regular physical examinations including eyes and teeth?

14. Am I particular in habits of personal cleanliness and grooming, and in the selection, care, and repair of my clothing?

15. Am I careful in my oral and written speech habits including enunciation, pronunciation, vocabulary, and sentence structure, and do I attempt to correct known deficiencies?

16. Do I practice the kind of good manners that come of a thoughtful awareness and consideration of others?

17. Am I honestly attempting to achieve those qualities of character I most genuinely admire such as integrity, fortitude, compassion, tolerance?

18. Do I make a persistent effort to rub off the rough edges of my personality and to become a friendly, likeable person who brings out the best in others?

19. Am I continuously enlarging the horizon of my knowledge, interest, and concern so as to become in the best sense of the word a citizen of the world?

20. Am I honestly trying to develop what Overstreet calls "The Mature Mind" so that I may grow up before I grow old?[6]

When this rating scale is applied to ascertain where his professionalism and strengths are found by the teacher, he should make provision for retention of them. When the scale points up areas wherein his professional growth needs improvement, he should plan to alleviate his deficiencies. The major idea the teacher should keep in mind is that education is a continuing process and never a terminal issue. As the teacher grows in service, he will do well to remember that his responsibilities reach outside of the class-

---

[6]Ina Corinne Brown, "Twenty Questions — A Personal Rating Scale," *Peabody Journal of Education*, XXVIII (September, 1950), pp. 89-91.

room to endeavors which encompass civic activities. Just as he becomes more proficient in his professional duties at school, so must be become more adept and dedicated in performing his civic obligations if he is to completely fulfill his role in society.

PROFESSIONAL RELATIONS WITH OTHERS ON THE JOB

The elementary teacher will have many contacts with pupils, school personnel, and the public in discharging the responsibilities of his office. He therefore needs to develop skills in human relations early in his teaching career in order to insure maximum effectiveness in this area as well as in classroom instruction. Skill in developing and maintaining good human relations is just as essential to the teacher as good teaching technique. If the teacher is weak on either count his effectiveness will be lessened.

PUPIL-TEACHER RELATIONSHIPS

The most vital human relationships the elementary teacher is confronted with are those between the pupils and himself. The success or failure of his teaching in large measure rises or falls upon this relationship. It therefore is imperative that the teacher establish rapport with the children early in the school year so that maximum achievement can be effected.

Rapport is more easily established in a laissez-faire setting in which the children feel that the over-all classroom atmosphere and working conditions are enjoyable and pleasing. The teacher can achieve this environment by encouraging children to participate constructively and creatively in child-centered activities. The following suggestions of Burr, Harding, and Jacobs are common sense methods whereby good human or interpersonal relations can be established between the teacher and his pupils.

1. Be friendly but not familiar. Your child-like behavior should be outgrown. Children prefer you to be a sympathetic, kindly adult.
2. Know not only the children's names but also much about their personal backgrounds which affect their relationships in the classroom.
3. Recognize sensitively children's individual differences. Build constructively upon these differences rather than expect every child to fit into an identical pattern.
4. Take into account the maturation levels of the group and proceed to get better acquainted and to establish rapport in the light of these observable growth gradients.
5. Be as consistent a personality in dealing with the children as is humanly feasible. Do not be too strict one day and too lax the next.
6. Face each day's work realistically and cheerfully with the children. Even when you do not feel cheerful, you must remember the negative effect upon children if you reflect your problems and anxieties.

7. Create an atmosphere in which every child is, first of all, free to be himself and free to let you see him be himself.
8. Plan with and in consideration for children in such democratic ways that your guidance is prized by the other members of the group.
9. Participate actively and naturally with children in what they enjoy doing in their work and their play.
10. Take time to listen to the children's questions, problems, joys, and dilemmas, and treat their confidences clinically and confidentially.
11. Demonstrate to the children that you believe in them and in their potentialities.
12. Encourage every child in the cultivation of self-confidence, self-expression, independence, and social effectiveness.[7]

TEACHER-TEACHER RELATIONSHIPS

Another factor which contributes greatly toward teaching success is good relationships with one's fellow teachers. Through sharing ideas and information, teachers can contribute to one another's professional growth and teaching effectiveness. One teacher's methods may not work for another, but the professional stimulation which may be obtained through free sharing is desirable in the elementary school.

The elementary teacher should endeavor to build good human relationships with his peer group whether he is begining or experienced in teaching. He should realize that there are deterrents to good teacher-teacher relationships which frequently cause dissension. Some of these deterrents have been enumerated by Harrison and Gowin as follows:

Holding pupils who rightfully belong under another's supervision (in shops, playgrounds, gymnasiums, music rooms)
Sympathizing with pupils who have been disciplined by another teacher
Commenting unfavorably about another teacher or his work
Grading too highly (so as to reflect unfavorably upon another teacher's evaluation)
Carrying tales of school out of school
Laxness in discipline (making discipline more difficult for others)
Cliquishness
Being a chronic griper[8]

ADMINISTRATOR AND SUPERVISOR RELATIONSHIPS

Just as it is imperative to maintain good relations with pupils and fellow teachers, so is it essential that the teacher create good human relationships

---

[7]James B. Burr, Lowry W. Harding, Leland B. Jacobs, *Student Teaching in the Elementary School* (second edition; New York: Appleton-Century-Crofts, Inc., Second Edition, 1958), pp. 201-202. © 1950,1958. Reprinted by permission of Appleton-Century-Crofts, Inc.
[8]Raymond H. Harrison and Lawrence E. Gowin, *The Elementary Teacher In Action* (San Francisco: Wadsworth Publishing Company, Inc., 1958), p. 90.

with administrators and supervisors. Teaching is a cooperative team effort between the individual teacher and the administrators and supervisors. The teacher is charged with the responsibility for the actual teaching. The primary responsibility of the administrator and supervisor is to help the teacher to teach most effectively.

Too often in the past, teachers have viewed their administrative leaders as "bosses" and their supervisory helpers as "inspectors." Today, however, most elementary teachers accept administrators and supervisors as co-workers whose responsibility is to assist them in the improvement of the instructional program. It is difficult indeed to find an autocratic administrator or supervisor involved in present day elementary education. Instead their function has evolved into the role of a democratic, professional leader.

Several factors have contributed toward this changed image of the administrator and supervisor. First, they usually have had many years of classroom teaching experience themselves and are consequently sensitive to the needs and views of the teachers. Second, they have acquired a great deal of formal education in order to be properly certified and qualified for the positions they hold. Third, they are skilled in creating and maintaining good human relationships since they were chosen for their positions not only on the basis of their experience and education but on their leadership ability.

The elementary teacher should recognize the advantages of creating good relationships with the administrators and supervisors. He should encourage their professional assistance in helping him provide enriched learning experiences for his students. The teacher can obtain a wealth of ideas, materials, and guidance from administrators and supervisors by willingly cooperating with them to accomplish the educational objectives of the school.

PARENT-TEACHER RELATIONSHIPS

Good parent-teacher relations are essential to teacher effectiveness in the classroom. If the parents do not respect and accept the teacher one cannot expect their children to do so. Conversely, if the parents hold the teacher in high regard and recognize him as a capable professional person, the children's actions will likely reflect this same attitude. Hence, the degree of the teacher's success in the classroom will be determined in large measure by the quality of the parent-teacher relationships he establishes. With so much depending on good relations, the teacher cannot afford to jeopardize his teaching effectiveness by neglecting them.

There are a number of things the elementary teacher can do to create good parent-teacher relationships. First, he needs to be frank but tactful with parents at all times. Second, he should demonstrate the fact that he is sympathetic to the individual uniqueness and needs of his pupils. Third, he should deal fairly and impartially with both parents and children, and fourth he should be open-minded. The teacher should listen attentively to parents and maintain an objective attitude about their views concerning their children and related circumstances in the teaching-learning situation. Finally, the teacher should be patient, kind, and understanding in working with parents, teachers, and others in the performance of his educational duties.

Good parent-teacher rapport is imperative for teaching success in the elementary school. Teachers must not assume that the parents automatically owe them their respect, admiration, and cooperation; they must earn it. In so doing, they will create the type and quality of rapport essential to their classroom effectiveness.

NONCERTIFIED PERSONNEL RELATIONSHIPS

The services the school provides for society are enhanced by its noncertificated employees. These include secretaries, receptionists, custodians, maids, cooks, and many more. They perform a vital function in the process of education. Teachers should accept them as colleagues in mutual cooperative efforts to provide the best learning situations possible for boys and girls. Teachers should not view the noncertificated personnel as second-class employees or citizens.

The individual teacher can easily establish rapport with the noncertificated personnel by respecting them as individuals and acknowledging the services they provide the school as being useful and necessary. Furthermore, good human relationships with them will be facilitated by recognizing the fact that they perform their work under the direction of the building principal. Since the teacher is answerable directly to the principal, he will be wise to refrain from trying to direct the work of the noncertificated personnel. When an important issue arises which affects the normal classroom situation and noncertificated personnel are involved, the teacher will do well to refer the matter to the principal for action.

The work of the noncertificated personnel is essential to the school as it strives to provide a better educational program for its students. Where good rapport exists between the certificated and noncertificated personnel, the program of instruction can move with greatest dispatch and efficiency. The certificated teachers should assume the lead in establishing and maintaining good relations with the noncertificated employees.

THE TASK AHEAD

Teaching is a complex, many faceted task. It is not enough for the teacher to have been adequately prepared for teaching, have acceptable personal traits, demonstrable competencies, ethical behavior, and skill in creating and maintaining good human relationships. These are only requisites for his major task: releasing student creativity through good teaching procedure to develop autonomous individuals.

We live in an age of continuous and rapid change. Science and technology are unlocking the mysteries of every area of living at an increasing rate of speed. One has only to examine the brevity of the Atomic Age which has been superseded by the Space Age to place the rapidity of change in our culture in proper perspective.

Historically, the public school has always measured up to the demands which society has placed upon it. As we enter the Space Age with new frontiers to conquer, our society will have more need than ever for imaginative and creative citizens. Once again the school will be called upon to meet this need.

The teacher in the Space Age school will be expected to educate each student so that he will become a self-regulating, autonomous individual. This will not be an easy task. In accomplishing it, the teacher will realize that uniform assignments, standards, and expectations for all students will not develop such a person. Present attempts at grouping children will not meet individual student needs when instruction is geared to the level of the group. If student imagination and creativity are to be released, the teacher must adjust the level of instruction to the individual within the group in order to meet his unique needs. The Space Age teacher will need to recognize the fact that programs with unchanging methodology characterized by the Socratic method of questioning and answering and textbook-centered teaching are actually deterrents to the development of imaginative, creative, and autonomous students.

The effective Space Age elementary school teacher will be one who can release student creativity. His teaching will be characterized by helping children learn "how" to think rather than telling them "what" to think. The characteristics of the classroom in which creative teaching and learning take place has been described in the 1962 Association for Supervision and Curriculum Development Yearbook as follows.

> Less teacher domination; more faith that children can find answers satisfying to them.
>
> Less teacher talk; more listening to children, allowing them to use the teacher and the group as a sounding board when ideas are explored.
>
> Less questioning for the right answer; more open-ended questions with room for difference and the exploration of many answers.
>
> Less destructive criticism; more teacher help which directs the child's attention back to his own feelings for clarification and understanding.

Less emphasis on failure; more acceptance of mistakes — more feeling on the part of the child that when he makes a mistake it is done, accepted and that's it. As one child said, "She doesn't rub salt in."

Children's work is appreciated, but praise is not used to put words in the mouths of children.

Goals are clearly defined; structure is understood and accepted by the group.

Within appropriate limits, children are given responsibility and freedom to work. "For once a teacher told us we could do it ourselves and really meant it."

Children are free to express what they feel and seem secure in their knowledge that the teacher likes them as they are.

Ideas are explored; there is an honest respect for solid information, an attitude of "let's find out."

There is a balance of common tasks and individual responsibility for specific tasks which are unique and not shared.

The teacher communicates clearly to children that learning is self-learning. Faith is demonstrated that all children want to become and pupils show satisfaction as they become aware of their growth.

Evaluation is a shared process and includes more than academic achievement.

Motivation for learning is high and seems inner-directed; pupil activity seems to say, "I've got a job I want to do."[9]

The task ahead for the professional elementary school teacher will be to gain a new perception of his role as an agent of change in our culture. Through teaching procedure which releases student imagination and creativity, the teacher fulfills his major task; this technique will enable the individual student to adjust to societal changes by gaining necessary knowledge, attitudes, and skills to insure his becoming an autonomous, self-regulating individual. This is the ultimate goal which the elementary teacher should continually strive to attain.

SUMMARY

There are many things which contribute to the success of the professional elementary school teacher. A good formal education is most important. Such a preparation gives the teacher a broad background of general education upon which he can draw for information in working with students. The professional education he attains also enables him to devise acceptable techniques whereby the factual information he has acquired in general and special content course study can be transmitted effectively to his students.

---

[9]"The Process of Becoming," *Perceiving, Behaving, Becoming: A New Focus For Education, op. cit.,* p. 237.

Another factor which contributes to successful teaching is the acquisition and development of acceptable teacher traits. Some of these are good judgment, self-control, considerateness, honesty, leadership, and scholarship. They are deemed important by fellow teachers, administrators, pupils, and parents. At least two other factors can be mentioned which contribute to successful teaching. They are the ability of the teacher to develop his competencies to maximum potential and his adherence to an acceptable code of ethics.

The professional elementary teacher must develop good human relations easily. People with whom he needs to establish rapport if he is to teach effectively include pupils, fellow teachers, parents, administrators, supervisors, and noncertificated personnel. Each of these groups is directly related to and concerned with the individual teacher, the teaching-learning situation, and student outcomes. All of these people contribute in one way or another to the instructional program. The teacher will do well to cooperate with them in a professional, ethical manner in order that his work can be achieved most expeditiously.

The role of the school is to develop each child to the maximum degree possible in order that he can become a responsible, contributing member of our democratic society. The professional elementary teacher should devote himself unreservedly to the accomplishment of this task. As a teacher, he can contribute nothing greater; society should ask nothing more.

QUESTIONS FOR DISCUSSION

1. The professional elementary school teacher is expected to possess desirable personal attributes. What are these attributes and how do they compare with those of nonschool professional people?
2. How and in what areas does the National Education Association *Code of Ethics* give guidance to the professional teacher?
3. Why is it important for the teacher to continuously engage in self-evaluation?
4. With whom must the teacher maintain good professional relations? What are his responsibilities to each of these persons?
5. What challenges does the task ahead propose for the elementary school teacher?

TOPICS FOR RESEARCH

1. Make a list of complaints you have heard about teachers. Propose ways the teacher should plan to avoid criticism on these points.
2. Select an effective teacher that you know. Study the behavior of this individual to determine why he is effective.

3. Study available professional journals. Determine the unique and specific contributions each makes to the elementary teacher.
4. Examine the objectives and activities of professional organizations open to elementary teachers. Enumerate the opportunities each seems to offer the teacher.
5. Study and enumerate the various opportunities available for in-service education of the teacher.
6. Observe in two or three different schools. Compare the professional activities observed with those you read about in professional literature.

BIBLIOGRAPHY

BROWN, INA CORINNE. "Twenty Questions — A Personal Rating Scale," *Peabody Journal of Education*. XXVIII, September, 1950, pp. 89-91.

BURR, JAMES B., LOWRY W. HARDING, AND LELAND B. JACOBS. *Student Teaching in the Elementary School*. Second edition. New York: Appleton-Century-Crofts, Inc., 1958.

HARRISON, RAYMOND H. AND LAWRENCE E. GOWIN. *The Elementary Teacher in Action*. San Francisco: Wadsworth Publishing Company, Inc., 1958.

KINNEY, LUCIEN, et al. *The Measure of a Good Teacher*. San Francisco: California Teachers Association, 1952.

KYTE, GEORGE C. *The Elementary School Teacher at Work*. New York: The Dryden Press, 1957.

MAZZEI, RENATO. "Desirable Traits of Successful Teachers," *Teaching In America*. (ed.) Anthony C. Riccio and Frederick R. Cyphert, Columbus, Ohio: Charles E. Merrill Books, Inc., 1962, p. 367.

MEHL, MARIE A., HUBERT H. MILLS, AND HARL R. DOUGLAS, *Teaching in Elementary School*. New York: The Ronald Press Company, 1958.

WILLIAMS, LOIS, et al. *Six Areas of Teacher Competence*. Burlingame: California Teachers Association, 1964.

NEA Handbook, Washington, D. C.: NEA, 1961, pp. 326-328.

"The Process of Becoming," *Perceiving, Behaving, Becoming — A New Focus For Education*. 1962 Yearbook, Washington, D.C.: Association for Supervision and Curriculum Development, 1962.

Index